William J. Do

Speech and Rhetoric in

j

fl

early imperial verse.
with warm regards,
Bui (March 1994)

Altertumswissenschaftliche Texte und Studien

Band 27

William J. Dominik

Speech and Rhetoric
in Statius' *Thebaid*

1994
Olms-Weidmann
Hildesheim · Zürich · New York

William J. Dominik

Speech and Rhetoric in Statius' *Thebaid*

1994
Olms-Weidmann
Hildesheim · Zürich · New York

© Georg Olms AG, Hildesheim 1994
Alle Rechte vorbehalten
Printed in Germany
Umschlagentwurf: Prof. Paul König, Hildesheim
Herstellung: Weihert-Druck GmbH, 64295 Darmstadt
Gedruckt auf säurefreiem Papier
ISSN 0175-8411
ISBN 3-487-09814-8

FOR TRISTAN AND CHANTELLE

TABLE OF CONTENTS

TABLE OF CONTENTS

TABLE OF CONTENTS

ix

ACKNOWLEDGEMENTS

This book is published with the aid of a subvention from the University of Natal Publications Committee. The University Inter-Faculty Research Review Committee awarded me a University Research Fund grant to provide assistance in its preparation. I express my thanks to the University for its financial support.

I should like to thank Anthony Boyle (University of Southern California) for his critical assistance, guidance and support in the writing of an earlier version of this book. Peter Davis (University of Tasmania) and John Sullivan (University of California, Santa Barbara) read this earlier version in its entirety and made many valuable comments. Special thanks are due to William Wehrle (College of William and Mary) for reading the final draft and to Adrian Ryan for his help in the preparation of the appendices and indices.

This book could not have been written without the patience, assistance and encouragement of Teresa Dominik. It is dedicated to our children.

University of Natal   W.J.D.
Durban, South Africa
November 1993

INTRODUCTION

The aim of this book is a critical analysis of the speeches in the *Thebaid* of Statius. Particular attention is given to the background and formulation of the speeches, to their rôle in the thematic and narrative design of the epic, and to other issues pertaining to their function in the epic. The purpose of the study ultimately is to increase the understanding of Statius' artistic practice.

The purpose of chapter 1 ('An Overview of the Speeches') is to introduce the reader to the speeches, including a taxonomy of speeches presenting the general principles governing their classification. Chapter 2 ('Narrative Strategy and the Rôle of the Speeches') is concerned mainly with the relationship between the speeches and the narrative of the epic. Issues raised and treated deal with the significance of the positioning of particular speeches in relation to the overall design of the poem, the relationship between individual speeches and the surrounding narrative, the manner in which the speeches afford the reader a conceptual framework against which to evaluate the narrative, the rôle of the speeches in advancing and embellishing the narrative, and the essential and unessential aspects of the speeches in the development of the narrative and the treatment of subject matter. The investigation also considers the rôle of the speeches in the creation of theme and mood. Relevant issues examined include the manner in which the speeches are used to establish atmosphere and mood; the effectiveness of the infusion of graphic detail (description) into the speeches and surrounding narrative in setting the mood, eliciting emotions and amplifying the epic circumstances; the specific emotions elicited within the speeches; the particular moods created by individual speeches; and the predominant atmosphere and mood of the speeches.

The formal analysis in chapter 3 ('Rhetorical-type Speeches') and chapter 4 ('Nonrhetorical-type Speeches') consists of a rhetorical and literary description of the various speech types; the former considers the literary and rhetorical tradition of the speech types, the influence of rhetorical principles and formulae upon the formulation of the speeches, the structural characteristics of the speeches, and the *topoi* and motifs of the speeches, while the latter investigates the literary tradition and origin of the nonrhetorical speech types in the epic, the circumstances in which the various types of nonrhetorical

1

speeches are delivered, and the typical mode of literary expression for each of the nonrhetorical speech types. Homeric and Vergilian speech types are regularly adduced for comparison. These chapters also consist of appropriate commentary on the speeches, chiefly the content and meaning of individual speeches that are of special significance in establishing theme, creating mood and defining character. This includes exploring the relationship between the individual speeches and their immediate thematic and dramatic contexts as well as considering the relationship of the speeches to the broader issues of the epic. Where discussion would involve undue repetition of the ideas expressed in my forthcoming *The Mythic Voice of Statius: Power and Politics in the Thebaid*, I have referred readers to this book for a full discussion of the speeches and their contexts (e.g., 1.197ff., 1.557ff., 5.49ff.).

Even a cursory analysis of the epic and occasional poetry of Statius reveals a deep indebtedness to the literary and rhetorical traditions that preceded him; this is the case with respect to the different generic forms and conventions of literature and rhetoric, especially the various speech types. An overview and examination of the major design features of the speeches, particularly the identification of certain types of recurring patterns and topical elements, forms a necessary ingredient of a systematic and unified inquiry into the function and rôle of the speeches in an epic. The thrust of the argument here is that there are groups of formal, technical or informal characteristics existing among speeches of the same type in epic and other genres that transcend time, place of composition and subject matter, and that these characteristics, when they define a particular work like the *Thebaid*, are of basic significance in talking about the epic.

An analysis of the permutations in the generic patterns of some of these speeches suggests that their composition is generally determined by the Roman view of rhetoric that largely mirrors Hellenistic rhetorical doctrine. While the typology or structural characteristics of these speeches are loosely based on the rhetorical prescriptions or formulae recorded by the ancient rhetoricians, some aspects of their composition are heavily dependent upon rhetorical principles and figures. The composition of other speeches relies more on the tradition and generic determination of epic speech composition. The former speeches are termed 'rhetorical' (in the restrictive sense) and are discussed in chapter 3 under that heading, while the latter are labelled 'nonrhetorical' and are treated in chapter 4. Admittedly this division is somewhat arbitrary, but the basis for the division is that the former are generally well documented in the rhetorical handbooks, while the latter do not appear in the manuals. One of the aims of these chapters is to identify the great variety of primary and secondary elements in Statius' technique of speech composition and to individuate the differences between the different speech types and various speeches of the same type. Although the conventional form of some of the rhetorical speeches presupposes to a certain extent characteristics of structure or pattern that give dramatic expression to the content of each speech, the large number of *topoi* ensures that virtually every speech represents a pattern or shape that develops in a manner consistent not only with the specific requirements of the immediate dramatic context but also the content and meaning of the epic as a whole.

The extent of the influence of rhetorical principles and formulae upon the conformation of Statius' speeches is difficult to determine with any real degree of precision under the best of circumstances, perhaps least of all when his treatment is virtually identical with the prescription of a rhetorician, as in the composition of Adrastus' formal hymn to Apollo (1.696-720). Yet the rhetorical training of Statius, manifest in the *Silvae*, is often suggested in the *Thebaid* in his treatment of the speeches along the lines suggested by the rhetoricians. It would have been impossible for Statius to escape the influence of his training—the *Silvae* bear graphic witness to this—yet it is equally difficult to differentiate between the formal and natural characteristics of his speeches. There is probably little question that in many instances Statius' use of rhetoric as a structural principle and his apparent attention to the manuals of the rhetoricians is best attributed to unconscious borrowing or even just plain commonsense.

With the exception of the speech of praise and noncombat exhortation, which are discussed in conjunction with their counterparts, the speech of blame and combat exhortation (*cohortatio*), respectively, the topical elements of the speech types discussed in chapter 3 generally accord with those mentioned in the rhetorical manuals;[1] therefore it is reasonable to identify those elements in the speeches of the *Thebaid* as 'rhetorical', even though they are often found in Vergilian or even Homeric speeches. It is at this point that the meaning of 'rhetorical' and 'generic' merge, in that both terms suggest the systematisation of rules, explicit or implicit, governing the composition of the speeches.

---

[1] Unfortunately there is no extant rhetorical treatment of the combat exhortation, or *cohortatio*, a type that is well attested in the works of the ancient historians.

The nonrhetorical speech types are examined in chapter 4 for their structure and *topoi*, which are discernible in some cases (especially in the two long narrative speeches of Adrastus and Hypsipyle) but not according to rhetorical principles. This is not to suggest, however, that speeches of the 'nonrhetorical' type are not themselves 'rhetorical' in the general sense of the word. Most are remarkable for their elevated and excited style, their arousal of pathos, and their striving after bold and novel effects, qualities that may justly be termed 'rhetorical'. Kenney describes this phenomenon well when he says:

> A poem may be composed in a manner that is perfectly just to call 'rhetorical' and yet exemplify not a single schema from the handbooks. It is a matter of degree and proportion in the systematic exploitation of linguistic and literary resources and of the relationship of ends to means.[2]

The same can be said clearly for many of the speeches dealt with here in which Statius creates an oratorical tone without recourse to the rules of the handbooks. There is no question that the conformation of these speeches is dependent principally upon the narrative circumstances.

Generic typing of speeches is valuable mainly in the preliminary stages of critical investigation, although this process is not without its inherent dangers such as the inevitable arbitrariness of the categories and the tendency to impose them upon the various speeches.[3] Although each classification is intended to cover all the speeches of that particular type, this is not to suggest that the form, *topoi* and style of these speeches are uniform but rather to point out certain properties that appear frequently among them.

The process of classifying speeches would certainly be excessive and misguided if it served no useful purpose beyond the obsessive act of classifying for its own sake. For the critic speech classification should not be an end in itself but a means to an end—a heightened appreciation of a particular work. A knowledge of generic typology can aid the critic in his/her understanding of particular speeches in an epic without necessarily impinging upon his/her critical sensibilities in evaluating the entire work; more importantly, perhaps, a generic awareness can aid in the considered

---

[2] Kenney (1966: 331).
[3] On the problem of speech genres, see Bakhtin (1986: 60-102).

exegesis of a speech in relation to its epic context and militate against the formulation of intemperate critical judgements.

Chapter 5 ('The Revelation of Character in the Speeches') examines the rôle of the various speakers and addressees in the composition of the epic, the way in which the speeches help to convey the emotions of the individual speakers, the manner in which the speeches help to define generally the personalities of the characters, the important psychological traits of the characters revealed in the speeches, the tendency in the speeches toward dynamic characterisation in which the personalities of certain figures develop, the static quality of the speeches of particular individuals whose personalities do not change, and the influence of supernatural powers upon various human figures in shaping their characters and motivating their actions. The investigation in chapter 6 ('Elements of Style in the Speeches') focuses on the rôle of the various elements of poetic and rhetorical style in producing special effects, enhancing the effectiveness of dramatic scenes, and underscoring the themes of particular speeches.

An 'Afterword' considers Statius' position as an epic poet and his use of rhetorical and poetic techniques. There is a brief examination of the evidence presented in chapters 1-6 in order to establish the extent of Statius' debt to rhetoric in the composition of the speeches in the *Thebaid*. The discussion centres on whether conscious rhetoric or emotional effect forms the essence of the speeches in the epic. A summary of the rôle that the speeches play in the epic concludes this section.

The statistical appendices are designed to furnish the reader with statistical information on the speeches in the works of Statius, particularly the *Thebaid*. Fourteen statistical appendices list and classify all of the speeches according to various criteria. Their purpose is not only to verify the assertions made in the text and notes of this study concerning the statistics of the speeches but also to provide statistical information for scholars working on Statius.

CHAPTER 1

AN OVERVIEW OF THE SPEECHES

Definition and Statistics

For the purposes of this study a speech is defined as the words actually spoken, imagined or recounted on one occasion without the intervention of another speaker.[1] On the basis of this brief definition there are 3,448 1/12 lines of speech in the *Thebaid*.[2] This figure is determined by counting part lines fractionally[3] rather than as whole lines as Lipscomb apparently does in arriving at his excessive figure of 3,582, for which he provides no hard statistical evidence.[4] There are 265 speeches, including eight inserted (i.e., reported) speeches.

Lipscomb counts 248 speeches, ignoring the inserted speeches, but once again does not support his figure.[5] In general it is difficult to ascertain the validity of Lipscomb's statistics when he makes so little effort to corroborate them. Other places of disagreement in the figures[6] are in the percentage of direct speech (his thirty-seven per cent versus my 35.4 per cent), the average length of speech (his 14.44 lines to my thirteen lines[7]), and the frequency of occurrence (his one speech per thirty-nine lines of text versus my one for every 36.8 lines[8]).

---

[1] Cf. Highet (1972: 15).

[2] For the breakdown by books, see stat. app. 1, table 1; for a conspectus of the speeches, see stat. app. 1, table 2.

[3] I have followed Highet's lead in counting lines of verse in metrical half feet and in not making a distinction between a trochaic word and a monosyllabic word of one-half foot. On this see Highet (1972: 18f.).

[4] Lipscomb (1909: 15). Lipscomb does not consider parenthetic expressions in his determination of length. Cf. Daniels (1905: 11), who gives the grossly inflated figure of 3753 lines of speech in the epic.

[5] Lipscomb (1909: 15).

[6] Lipscomb (1909: 15).

[7] There are 13.4 lines per speech, not counting inserted speeches.

[8] There is one speech for every 37.9 lines, not counting reported speeches.

6

Lipscomb considers the longest speech—Hypsipyle's narrative in book 5—to be 450 lines,[9] which is virtually the same as my figure of 449 5/6 lines.[10] The shortest speech in the epic, according to Lipscomb, is three words long (*cohibete gradum quicumque*, 10.393).[11] But he misses five short speeches of one word (one-sixth foot) at 4.811, 4.812, 9.350, 9.356 and 12.458.[12] Over two-thirds of the speeches in the *Thebaid* fall under the average of thirteen lines per speech.

Distribution of Speeches by Books

There are about twenty-two speeches per book on average. Some books fall below this figure, while others naturally rise well above it. The variation in the average length of speeches and the percentage of direct speech in the books forms an important element in the narrative technique of Statius.[13] As illustrated in chapter 2, Statius alternates books of intense action and less speech with books of more speech and less intense action to afford contrast or symmetry. Periods of intense action in the *Thebaid* are accompanied by shorter speeches of more frequent occurrence (but not necessarily more speakers), especially in the second half where the real fighting takes place between the Theban and Argive armies. Speech also intervenes little in book 6 where the incessant activity of the funeral games honouring Opheltes occurs. Where speech predominates there is little real action, as in book 5 where Hypsipyle narrates her tale of the Lemnian massacre.

---

[9] Lipscomb (1909: 12, 15). Cf. Butler (1909: 211), who gives a grossly inflated figure of 481 lines as the length of Hypsipyle's narrative.

[10] Lipscomb (1909: 9 n. 1), however, wrongly maintains that Hypsipyle's narrative is the longest speech in Roman epic, for Aeneas' narrative in books 2 and 3 of the *Aeneid* is much longer. Highet (1972: 11 n. 15) observes that Hypsipyle's narrative 'recalls the recital of Aeneas both in its introduction, "immania uulnera, rector, / integrare iubes" ≈ *Aen.* 2.3, and in its close, "me praedonum manus . . . / . . . uestras . . . transmittit in oras" ≈ *Aen.* 3.715. Therefore Statius himself considered Aeneas' narrative to be a speech.'

[11] Lipscomb (1909: 10, 15).

[12] Therefore Lipscomb (1909: 10) remarks erroneously that the shortest speech in Roman epic is in Claudian's *De Bello Getico* (*ipse uenit*, 461); cf. Highet (1972: 11 n. 15).

[13] On the rôle of the speeches in the narrative strategy, see ch. 2.

Taxonomy of Speeches

One of the aims of this study is to identify and examine certain types of recurring patterns, topical elements and stylistic devices in the speeches of the *Thebaid*. Although the system of speech categorisation presented here may seem complex, it is actually far less intricate than the general division into classes of various types of speeches such as prayers, hymns, encomia and ceremonial addresses proposed by the ancient rhetoricians and scholiasts. For instance, the third century rhetorician Menander divides his epideictic orations into encomia of deities and praise of mortal subjects; his praise of gods is further divided into nine classes of hymns.[14] In the various manuscripts of Horace there are twenty-four appellations employed in referring to the *Odes*.[15]

Some of the distinctions outlined in the chapters between the different speech types and between various speeches of the same general type are detailed and the descriptive names employed in this process of differentiation somewhat arbitrary; these characteristics are inherent in any system of classification to some extent. The divisions proposed below are not exclusive to epic; nor are all speeches in epic modelled upon the forms that appear in the *Thebaid*.

Every speech type consists of a set of primary constituents or elements that are common to the speeches of that particular class and distinguish it from other classes of speech. For instance, the principal constituents of the prayer are a human suppliant, a divine addressee, and the issuance of the actual entreaty. Across virtually every speech of this type these principal elements are uniform. In addition to these principal constituents there are a number of commonplace or secondary elements, frequently referred to as *loci communes* or *topoi*, that appear in the prayers.[16]

---

[14] These classes are kletic (Men. *Epid.* Sp. 3.333.4, 8-10), apopemptic (333.4, 10-12), scientific (333.5, 12-15), mythical (333.5, 15-18), genealogical (333.5f., 18-21), fictitious (333.6, 21-24), precatory (333.6, 24f.), deprecatory (333.6f., 25f.) and combinative (333.7). Cf. Burgess (1902: 174). Menander's treatise illustrates the ancient practice of delineating generic patterns and topical elements. On generic classification and *topoi*, see Cairns (1972: 70ff.).

[15] See Burgess (1902: 174 n. 2).

[16] Compare the discussion of Cairns (1972: 6) on primary and secondary elements of the various rhetorical and nonliterary genres he identifies.

One of these commonplaces is invocatory and consists of an invocation of a deity by his/her name, frequently by the use of the interjection *o!* showing deep emotion; this constituent is an outstanding feature of the prayer and characterises the prayer's sublime style. Another commonplace in deliberative invocations to the gods in poetry is votary and is distinguished by the speaker's promise to the addressee of suitable votary offerings or other rewards in return for assistance. Although these and other commonplaces are not exclusive to the speech types in which they appear, they assist in defining the different classes of speech along with the principal constituents, which are the primary determinants of the various speech types.

There are seventeen different speech types in the *Thebaid*. Six of these are rhetorical; the rest are nonrhetorical. Rhetorical types include forensic orations, deliberative speeches, prayers, speeches of mourning and consolation (laments, consolation, *epikedion*), speeches of encouragement (combat exhortations [*cohortationes*], noncombat exhortations) and praise and blame speeches (laudation, vaunts, vituperations). Nonrhetorical speech types include narrative speeches, descriptive speeches, soliloquies, apostrophes, challenges, taunts, threats, commands, oracular and prophetic speeches (interpretations of oracles and omens, prophecies, oracular pronouncements), questions and responsions (to deliberations, questions, challenge, threat, responsion).[17] There are also mixed forms or combinative types of speech, as in 1.285-292 where Jupiter replies to Juno during their forensic debate on the fate of Argos, then commands Mercury in the same speech (292-302). For convenience such mixed types are classified according to their preponderant principal and secondary elements and are discussed under the heading of the dominant classification.

Comparison Between Speech Classification Systems

The system of speech categorisation proposed here for the *Thebaid* merits a comparison with those put forward for the *Iliad* and *Odyssey* by Fingerle (1939) and for the *Aeneid* by Highet (1972). Fingerle classifies

---

[17] For a statistical analysis of the speech types in the *Thebaid*, see stat. app. 2, table 3; for a breakdown of each speech type by book and a comprehensive catalogue of the speeches by type, see stat. app. 2, tables 4 and 5, respectively.

most of the speeches in the *Iliad* and *Odyssey* into sixteen categories,[18] while Highet also has sixteen classifications along similar lines for the *Aeneid*.[19] My system of classification for the *Thebaid* includes seventeen categories, some of which neither Highet nor Fingerle employ in their classification systems; on the other hand, the system I propose for the *Thebaid* absorbs some of Highet's and Fingerle's categories into classes of similar nomenclature and purpose. Readers will note that the system of speech categorisation proposed for the *Thebaid* bears a strong resemblance to the one put forward by Highet, but this is fortuitous rather than intentional and is testimony to the general applicability of Highet's system to classical epic.[20]

Fingerle asserts that a typology is the key to analysing Homeric poetry.[21] The stated aim of his work is to formalise the speeches in the *Iliad* and *Odyssey* according to their typological characteristics.[22] He describes and classifies the speeches according to the number of speakers, their content and other criteria in the first half of his work,[23] while in the second half he explores what he considers to be the basic forms of rhetoric such as discussion, monologue, request, wish, exclamation, report, and narrative within the speeches.[24] Although Fingerle suggests that the typological approach can be used to support analytical points of view, such as confirming that the *Iliad* is older than the *Odyssey*,[25] his main contribution lies in the system of classification he proposes for the epics. He makes little real use of the data he collects, because he does not really show what is to be achieved by classifying the speeches and makes no real attempt to analyse them and discuss their function.

Highet is the first scholar since Fingerle to develop a comprehensive system of categorisation for the speeches in an epic. He argues that Vergil

---

[18] See the *Inhaltsverzeichnis* in Fingerle (1939: 2f.).

[19] Highet (1972: 291, esp. 305).

[20] Cf. Highet (1972: 347), who observes that Fingerle divides the speeches in the *Iliad* and the *Odyssey* 'into types along lines roughly the same as those used' in his analysis of the *Aeneid*'s speeches.

[21] Fingerle (1939: 1).

[22] Fingerle (1939: 1).

[23] Fingerle (1939: 8-304; cf. 2).

[24] Fingerle (1939: 305-459; cf. 2).

[25] Fingerle (1939: 3).

disguises the structure of his speeches in the *Aeneid* and does not arrange them according to the schemes of the rhetoricians; rather, the structure of a speech, according to Highet, is determined by its own inner logic, which he defines essentially as the rôle of the speech in the epic, the specific context of its delivery, and the personality of the speaker.[26] Highet draws a distinction between the speeches of the assembly hall and those that are strongly emotional.[27] The debates in the tenth and eleventh books are formal[28] while soliloquies, threats and entreaties are designated informal.[29] Highet is rightly cautious about imposing a conventional rhetorical structure on the speeches, but he sometimes fails to observe that the structure of a speech can be highly formalised yet fall outside the boundaries of conventional rhetoric. For example, he discusses Jupiter's carefully wrought prophetic speech in 1.257-96 under the heading 'Informal Speeches', as he does Dido's carefully arranged soliloquy in 4.590-629.

Perhaps Highet's most serious error in classifying is his belief that an emotional speech must be classified as informal. There is no reason why this should be so. According to Cicero, the three functions of the orator are to prove his case, gain the sympathy of his audience, and to incite their emotions to whatever level the case demands for its favourable reception (*De Orat.* 2.26.115). It was the persuasive force of such a speech that mattered most in the orator's attempt to gain control of his audience—public or private. The effective manipulation of the audience's emotions by whatever means required by the circumstances of the case was central to the success of the orator. Lack of structure is not a requisite for a highly emotional speech. Juno's reply to Venus' attack (10.63-95) is anything but calm and rational, yet it is certainly designed—architechtonically and emotively—to move Jupiter to the desired action.

Although Highet does use his data to analyse and illuminate various aspects of the speeches in relation to the narrative and the overall structure of the epic, like Fingerle, the principal achievement of his work is the classification system he proposes. The following table compares Highet's and Fingerle's speech classification systems with the one I propose for the *Thebaid*:

---

[26] Highet (1972: 97).

[27] Highet (1972: 48; cf. 97).

[28] Highet (1972: 48; cf. 55-72).

[29] Highet (1972: 48; cf. 97ff., esp. 114ff.).

SPEECH AND RHETORIC IN STATIUS' *THEBAID*

Comparison Between Speech Classification Systems

Thebaid (Dominik)	*Aeneid* (Highet)	*Iliad, Odyssey* (Fingerle)
Apostrophes	Apostrophes	
Challenges Threats Taunts	Taunts, Threats, Challenges	Schelt- und Drohreden Spottreden Kampfreden
Commands	Commands	Botenauftrag- und Botenbericht
Deliberative Speeches	Persuasions	
Descriptive Speeches[30] Narrative Speeches	Narratives, Explanations, Descriptions[30]	
Speeches of Encouragement (Combat Exhortations [*Cohortationes*], Noncombat Exhortations)	Encouragements (*Cohortationes*)	Feldherrnreden Kampfaufrufe
Forensic Orations	Diplomatic or Political Speeches Legalistic Speeches	Versammlungsreden (Agorareden und Bulereden)
Speeches of Mourning and Consolation (Laments, Consolation, *Epikedion*)		Totenklagen Klagereden Trost- und Ermunterungsreden
Oracular and Prophetic Speeches (Interpretations of Omens and Oracles, Oracular Pronounce- ments, Prophecies)	Oracles, Prophecies, Interpretations of Omens and Oracles	Traumreden
Praise and Blame Speeches (Laudation, Vaunts, Vituperations)	Vituperations	Lobreden Triumphreden
Prayers	Prayers	Bittreden[31]

---

[30] Highet (1972: 105) uses the term 'description' to mean a statement of 'facts unknown to the listener', while I use the expression to signify a verbal picture of a static or moving scene.

[31] Fingerle (1939: 195) also uses *Gebet* when the addressee is a god.

12

Thebaid	_Aeneid_ (Highet)	_Iliad, Odyssey_ (Fingerle)
Questions	Questions	
Responsions (to Deliberations, Questions, Challenge, Threat, Responsion)	Responses to Questions, Commands, and Various Types of Persuasion	[32]
Soliloquies	Soliloquies	
	Farewells Greetings	Begrüßungs- und Abschiedsreden
		Tis-Reden (Chorreden)

Speeches by Characters

There are eighty-one characters who speak in the _Thebaid_;[33] nineteen of these are divine, including demigods and spirits of the dead,[34] while the others are human speakers, either groups or individuals.[35] Supernatural figures deliver forty-six speeches,[36] while human characters make 219 speeches.

Naturally the number of speeches that the characters make affords an indication of their relative prominence in the epic. It has often been argued that the _Thebaid_ lacks a central character, which is true, but Tydeus and Adrastus together figure in one out of every 5.8 speeches made. They speak more frequently and more lines than any of the other central characters. Adrastus makes only two fewer speeches than Tydeus and speaks more lines than any other figure except Hypsipyle, who speaks almost five hundred lines in only four speeches. An interesting point is that Jupiter makes only seven

---

[32] Fingerle (1939: 6) sometimes uses _Gesprachsrede_ for colloquy.

[33] For the totals by books, see stat. app. 3, table 6; for a statistical compárison between speeches by central figures, see stat. app. 3, table 7.

[34] Except Amphiaraus' spirit. For a list of speeches of divine and semi-divine figures (including spirits other than Amphiaraus' spirit), see stat. app. 3, table 8.

[35] Including Amphiaraus (and his spirit). For a list of speeches by humans, see stat. app. 3, table 9.

[36] Including the recounted deliberation of Amphiaraus' spirit (10.206-16). Lipscomb (1909: 19) mentions the figure of forty-one but, as in other instances, provides no evidence to verify his assertion.

speeches averaging about twenty lines per speech.[37] No other divine figure makes more than five speeches.

There are six circumstances in which a character speaks who is disguised as another person.[38] Naturally only supernatural figures are capable of performing this feat.

Collective and Tandem Speeches

There are eight instances in the *Thebaid* where Statius makes use of the collective speech where individuals in a group speak the same words.[39] This type of speech is relatively rare in Roman epic.[40]

Lipscomb counts seven collective speeches in the *Thebaid*.[41] He omits the vituperative speech of the Lemnian crowd (5.491f.) and the cohortative exclamation of the Arcadian warriors (6.618), wrongly considers the anonymous Theban's vituperative speech of Polynices and Eteocles (1.173-96) to be collective because of the indefinite *aliquis* (1.171), and curiously describes the thought in 12.472f. as collective speech (of whom?).[42] However, he is correct in suggesting that the words spoken by two groups of Thebans in 10.584-87, 588 form two separate speeches.[43]

An unusual sequence of speeches occurs in 11.257-62 where two or more of Eteocles' companions speak in four successive turns without the intervention of narrative or stage directions; Lipscomb considers these four short speeches to be one speech made collectively by Eteocles' companions.[44]

---

[37] Lipscomb (1909: 19) contends that Jupiter speaks eight times but does not list his speeches.

[38] Compare the *Aeneid*, where this occurs seven times. See Highet (1972: 340) for a list. For a list of disguised characters' speeches in the *Thebaid*, see stat. app. 4, table 10.

[39] For a list see stat. app. 5, table 11.

[40] Lipscomb (1909: 44f.) contends there are only four collective speeches in the *Aeneid*, five in Valerius Flaccus, nine in Silius Italicus, nine in Lucan, and ten in Claudian.

[41] Lipscomb (1909: 45).

[42] Lipscomb (1909: 45).

[43] Lipscomb (1909: 45). These speeches could be interpreted less accurately as a single speech spoken by alternate groups of Thebans.

[44] Lipscomb (1909: 45).

14

There are a few instances in the epic where two individuals speak at the same time.[45] A variation of this occurs in 12.458f. where Argia and Antigone each make in turn without any intervening narrative two short comments in a sequence that can almost be considered as one speech.[46]

Gods, Humans and Objects of Address

Of human and divine figures in the *Thebaid*, Polynices and Eteocles are addressed more times than any other characters. Each are addressed on twenty separate occasions, while Tydeus (fourteen), Adrastus (thirteen), Jupiter (twelve) and Antigone (nine) follow far behind.[47] The Argive and Achaean warriors are addressed a surprising seventeen times and the Theban warriors on fifteen different occasions, although they speak together only three speeches. Tydeus and Adrastus speak or are addressed thirty-eight and thirty-five times, respectively, slightly more than Polynices (thirty-three) and Eteocles (thirty) and significantly more than Jupiter and Argia (nineteen). That these characters figure so prominently in speech situations stresses the significance of their rôles in the epic.

In Statius almost every speech is addressed to either a god, demigod or human figure. There are three occasions on which this is not strictly so,[48] and another three where a personified object or abstract is addressed.[49]

---

[45] For a list see stat. app. 5, table 12.

[46] On this sequence of brief speeches see, p. 302 n. 58.

[47] For the statistics on other major characters, see stat. app. 6, table 13.

[48] See stat. app. 6, table 14.

[49] See stat. app. 6, table 15.

Inserted Speeches

There are eight inserted speeches in the *Thebaid*.[50] This means that there are eight speeches that appear within other speeches.[51] These inserted speeches total eighty lines.[52] One-half of them occur in Hypsipyle's long narrative on the Lemnian massacre in book 5. There is even one occurrence in Hypsipyle's narrative where she cites verbatim Polyxo's reporting of Venus' command (5.136, 137f.).

In 10.355 Hopleus has Tydeus' mother utter a brief hypothetical question (*ubi funus?*) to Dymas upon the Arcadian's imagined return to his homeland, but I do not consider the hypothetical question to be an inserted speech because on no occasion prior to the conversation between Hopleus and Tydeus does the latter's mother actually voice this question.

Monologues and Speech Clusters

Heinze[53] and Lipscomb,[54] among others, have noted that two elements of the increasing tendency among the later Roman poets to restrict the amount of speech are the limitation of both the length of the speech cluster (dialogue, trialogue, or tetralogue) and the number of speakers in a particular scene.

There are 158 monologues in the *Thebaid*, five speeches of general interlocution, but only thirty-five clusters where two or more speakers engage in conversation.[55] There are twenty-eight dialogues, of which two consist of four speeches (3.502-47, 7.247-73) and one of six speeches

---

[50] See stat. app. 7, table 16 for a list. Lipscomb (1909: 15) counts nine, including Eteocles' words in 11.248f.; however, this prayer addressed to Jupiter is not an inserted speech.

[51] According to Lipscomb (1909: 15), there are four inserted speeches in Lucan, seven in Vergil, four in Valerius Flaccus, eleven in Silius Italicus, and only two in Claudian.

[52] Excluding the sole inserted speech within an inserted speech (5.136, 137f.).

[53] Heinze (1908: 397f.).

[54] Lipscomb (1909: 26-29).

[55] For the statistical analysis by book of monologues and clusters, see stat. app. 8, table 17; for a list of the monologues and clusters, see stat. app. 8, tables 18 and 19, respectively.

(4.753-85, 5.20-498).[56] There are six trialogues, one consisting of seven speeches (4.501-644) and another of eight speeches (1.438-695). Only one tetralogue occurs (5.656-89). On twelve occasions the first speaker in a cluster of speeches speaks again at least once in that same cluster[57] (1.214-92, 1.438-695, 2.393-467, 3.502-47, 3.607-69, 4.501-644, 4.753-85, 5.464-89, 7.247-373, 10.423-41, 11.669-754, 12.366-401[58]).

Speeches Commencing, Concluding or Interrupted in Midline by Narrative

Kvíčala,[59] Norden,[60] Elderkin,[61] Lipscomb[62] and Highet[63] are among those who have remarked on the Roman practice of frequently beginning and ending a speech in the middle of a verse in contrast with the Greek practice where the epic poets customarily begin a speech at the start of a line and conclude it at the end of a verse. Only once does Homer begin a speech within a line (*Il.* 23.855)[64] and only on a single occasion does he conclude a speech before the end of a verse (*Il.* 2.70). There are relatively

---

[56] Lipscomb (1909: 27) asserts that 'in no case in Statius is the dialogue carried to the extent of six speeches', but if we include Hypsipyle's address to Adrastus and the Argive warriors in her long narrative (5.49-498), there are six speeches in the dialogue between Hypsipyle and Adrastus.

[57] This figure does not include the brief speech made by Eteocles' companions to the monarch (11.257) or that of Antigone (or Argia) to the Theban soldiers (12.458), since the speakers do not address each other but rather a third person who does not reply in *oratio recta.*

[58] Lipscomb (1909: 27) lists only five occasions in which the first speaker replies (1.214ff., 1.557ff., 2.393ff., 3.607ff., 10.423ff.).

[59] Kvíčala (1881: 265ff.).

[60] Norden (1915: 135).

[61] Elderkin (1906: 7-10).

[62] Lipscomb (1909: 36-38).

[63] Highet (1974: 189ff.).

[64] But Leaf (1902: 469), cited by Elderkin (1906: 7), contends that the passage in which this speech occurs in spurious. Elderkin (1906: 7) maintains that only one of the forty-nine inserted speeches (*Il.* 6.479) commences within a verse.

few exceptions to the Homeric practice among later Greek epic poets such as Apollonius, Quintus Smyrnaeus and Nonnus.[65]

Ennius departs from this custom, as does Lucretius later.[66] Vergil is the first Roman epic poet to commence or conclude a speech freely within the verse. Kvíčala[67] and Lipscomb[68] provide statistical evidence to show that on roughly one occasion in every four Vergil begins a speech in midline and just as often concludes a speech at the close of a verse. Vergil's successors generally were even freer in their placement of speeches within the narrative.[69]

Statius commences a speech within the verse more frequently than the other later Roman epic poets; he also concludes a speech in midverse more often than anyone except Lucan. On fifty-two per cent of occasions Statius commences a speech at the opening of a hexametral line and fifty-five per cent of the time he concludes a speech at the end of a verse. Two-thirds of the time the opening or close of a speech occurs in midverse. On average only just over one out of every five speeches opens at the beginning of the metrical line, closes at the end of the line, and is uninterrupted by narrative or parenthetic expressions. These figures indicate that Statius was freer than any later Roman epic poet in his placement of speeches within the narrative.[70]

Norden suggests that Greek epic poets avoided shifting from narrative to speech in midverse on account of their heightened sensitivity to the natural rhythm within the verse.[71] Elderkin attributes the Greek practice to the feeling that the transition from narrative to speech is more natural when it occurs at the beginning of a line and proffers that the Roman ear objected

---

[65] Apollonius, in fact, always commences his speeches at the opening of a verse and ends them at the close of the line, as does Hesiod. Quintus begins four speeches in midverse (*Posthom.* 4.408f., 12.37f. [an inserted speech], 12.254-58, 12.602-04). Nonnus offers rather more exceptions to the rule (e.g., *Dion.* 15.417-19, 42.38f.); on this see Highet (1974: 189f.) and Elderkin (1906: 8).

[66] See Highet (1974: 190f.).

[67] Kvíčala (1881: 266ff.).

[68] Lipscomb (1909: 37).

[69] See the table of comparison by Lipscomb (1909: 37).

[70] For the figures on Statius, see stat. app. 9, tables 20 and 21; stat. app. 9, table 22 furnishes the statistical evidence for the totals shown in tables 20 and 21.

[71] Norden (1915: 136).

less to an abrupt transition from narrative to speech within the line.[72] Presumably this is to deny the later Roman epic poets, notably Statius, any real measure of artistic intention and control in the placement of speech within the narrative framework.[73]

Opening, Interposing and Closing Formulas to Speeches

The introductory and closing words to a speech in epic naturally constitute the frame of the speech and serve the practical function of defining its beginning and end for the auditor or reader. Homer never leaves the auditor in doubt where a speeches commences and ends, because his introductory and terminal phrases are fairly rigid and well defined.[74] This method is in direct contrast with the practice of later Roman poets such as Vergil and Statius, who are much less concerned with delineating clearly the transition from narrative to speech.

Statius introduces most of the speeches in the *Thebaid* with an introductory verb or verbal phrase, although on a number of occasions he intromits the formulaic word or phrase after the commencement of a speech; sometimes the introductory formula, including the *uerbum dicendi*, is omitted. When it is employed, there is a wide range of introductory formulas in his speeches. This is a notable departure from Homeric technique where the variation of the opening formula is restricted by rules that require that the speaker be introduced and his/her intention to speak announced.[75] Vergil varies his introductory phrases so that the auditor or

---

[72] Elderkin (1906: 9); cf. Highet (1974: 191f.).

[73] On the rôle and function of the speeches in the narrative strategy of the *Thebaid*, see ch. 2. Loesch (1927) traces the development of the Roman technique from the Greek and discusses the utility of the practice in conveying certain emotions of the characters in Roman epic.

[74] On this aspect see Fingerle (1939: 343, 373).

[75] On this see Fingerle (1939: 306). According to Fingerle, the typology of the introductory formula is easier to define than the closing formula. Fingerle (1939: 308) provides evidence to show that the most common introductory verb of speech, προσέφη, appears on 205 occasions (110 in the *Iliad*, ninety-five in the *Odyssey*), while ὣς φάτο is the most common closing formula (1939: 349), occurring 138 times (seventy-three in the *Iliad*, sixty-five in the *Odyssey*).

reader knows not only that the speech is forthcoming but also understands the manner of its delivery and the emotional condition of the person speaking.[76]

That Statius also varies widely his opening verb or phrase is evident from the fact that no single introductory formula occurs more than nine times in the *Thebaid*. This is in sharp contrast with Vergil who, according to Gjerløw, uses *fari* and its compounds sixty-six times as an opening formula for a speech in the *Aeneid*.[77] This shows that Statius varies his introductory phrase even more widely than Vergil did. The manifold nature of the introductory phrases to the speeches in the *Thebaid* conveys an air of epic informality and heightens dramatic suspense while at the same time permitting an exactitude in the description of a speaker's movements, emotions, the tone of his/her speech, the mood of the situation, and even the effect of the speech on his/her audience. The most common openers indicating speech are the neutral *incipit* (*-iunt*), *profatur*, *tunc* [*profatur*, etc.] and *refert*,[78] but the stronger verbs—*clamat, conclamat, exclamat, hortatur, increpat, increpitans, precatur* and *uociferans*—are particularly effective in establishing the tone of the speeches, defining the character of the speakers, and in enhancing the mood of the dramatic context of the speeches.[79]

Interpolated phrases of saying are rare in Greek epic.[80] They are much more common in Vergil and other later Roman poets,[81] where the effect, as with the variation of the introductory word or phrase, is to produce an air of naturalness in the epic narrative. The use of interpolated phrases in the *Thebaid* such as *ait* (thirty-one times), *inquit* (thirteen times) and *clamat* (six times) marks a less abrupt transition from narrative to speech because of the apparent casualness of their insertion.[82] This effect is similar

---

[76] See Highet (1974: 189ff.). For a more comprehensive discussion, see Loesch (1927: 16ff.).

[77] Gjerløw (1956: 56).

[78] See stat. app. 10, tables 23 and 24.

[79] Cf. Loesch (1927: 65ff., esp. 67).

[80] See Elderkin (1906: 10).

[81] With the notable exception of Lucan and Claudian. See Lipscomb (1907: 36).

[82] Cf. stat. app. 10, table 23.

to the one created by the interpolation of narrative of one-half line or less describing the emotional state or actions of a speaker or addressee.[83]

Phrases denoting the termination of speeches in the *Thebaid* vary more widely than interposing formulas but are more rigid in their formulation than introductory phrases.[84] The most common are *sic ait* (fourteen times), *dixerat* (thirteen times) and *dixit* (thirteen times).[85] The conclusion of a speech is always marked either by a phrase of speaking, the continuation of the narrative, or the introduction of another speech.

Statius' skill in establishing and varying the *color* of the speeches is evident from the wide range of formulaic phrases of speech introduction, interpolation and termination in the *Thebaid*. The colourless one-word formula *ait* appears thirty-nine times in 265 speeches, while its variant *sic ait* occurs only fifteen times. Together they constitute only about ten per cent of the formulaic phrases employed in the *Thebaid*. No other formulaic phrase appears more than thirteen times.

Potential Speeches in True and Virtual Oratio Obliqua

There are 265 occasions in the *Thebaid* where Statius chooses to express directly the thoughts and emotions of his characters, and these speeches constitute over one-third of the epic. But there are many dramatic situations in which Statius chooses to convey indirectly the words and thoughts of his characters. Sometimes he cites the very words in *oratio obliqua* that we might expect to hear in *oratio recta*. In 7.227-29 the Theban messenger reports the Argive advance on the city in true *oratio obliqua*. Elsewhere Statius merely reports the speech or reflexion, as in 2.370 where Tydeus volunteers for the embassy to Eteocles; this I have labelled as virtual *oratio obliqua*.

---

[83] See pp. 28ff. for a related discussion on the effect of the interpolation of narrative within speeches in the *Thebaid*. For examples of Statius' technique of interweaving narrative and parenthetic expressions of saying with speech, see the discussions on the various speech types and individual speeches in chs. 3 and 4.

[84] Unlike Homer; see p. 19 n. 75.

[85] For the statistics on the other closing formulas, see stat. app. 10, table 23; see stat. app. 10, table 24 for the specific occurrences of the most common closing formulas.

On average there are sixteen occasions in each book where Statius expresses the substance of what is spoken or reflected upon in true or virtual *oratio obliqua* rather than reporting the speakers' words in the form in which they are actually spoken. The most obvious instances of this total 193,[86] although there are many other opportunities in addition to those I have nominated as true or virtual *oratio obliqua* that offered the poet an occasion for speech, such as when the Hellenes shout their approval of Capaneus' bellicose words (3.669f.) and when the Eleusinian priestesses lament the imminence of the war (7.411).[87] Occasionally Statius takes advantage of the opportunity for *oratio recta* that the dramatic situation presents to him by shifting to direct speech after commencing the indirect reporting of the words of a particular speaker or group (1.316-20, 8.170-207, 11.462-71).[88]

Lipscomb remarks that the *Thebaid* 'contains only about 65 verses of speech-material',[89] which presumably would increase the amount of speech by less than two per cent if converted into direct speech, judging by his comments on other later Roman epics.[90] However, this method of calculation is misconceived. The average speech in the *Thebaid* is thirteen lines long. If Statius had decided to convert the 193 speeches in virtual or true *oratio obliqua* (as I have defined them) into *oratio recta*, we might then expect as many as 2500 additional lines of verse in direct speech. Assuming that Statius did not increase the length of the narrative, the amount of speech

---

[86] For a comprehensive list of potential speeches in true and virtual *oratio obliqua*, see stat. app. 11, table 25.

[87] Other opportunities for speech occur in the lamentation of mothers over their deceased (3.125f.), Ide's lament over the death of her son (3.139), the death of Opheltes (5.541f., 547f., 552f.), the lamentation in the Argive palace over Opheltes' death (6.28f., 41-43, 50, 130, 229, 515), Capaneus' amazement at the crowd's murmur (6.784f.), Amphiaraus' arrival in the underworld (8.17), the Theban women's apostrophe over the death of Atys (8.644), and Eteocles' assembling of Theban troops (10.35f.).

[88] Loesch (1927: 67).

[89] Lipscomb (1909: 21).

[90] For example, Lipscomb (1909: 47), asserts that if the '200 odd verses of indirect discourse [in Lucan's epic were] converted into the direct form, [this] would increase the amount of speech in the poem less than one and three-fourths per cent'. For the *Aeneid*, according to Lipscomb (1909: 20), the 'not over 140 verses' of *oratio obliqua*, 'if converted into oratio recta, would increase the amount of speech in the poem only about one and one-half per cent'; however, Highet (1972: 342f.) totals only just on eighty-five lines of such material and provides evidence to sustain his assertion, unlike Lipscomb. Both Lipscomb and Highet consider expressions that could be classified only as true *oratio obliqua*.

in the epic would then comprise roughly one-half of the epic. This is comparable to the figure of fifty per cent that Elderkin (following Schneidewin) proposes for the percentage of direct speech in the *Iliad* and *Odyssey*[91] and 46.75 per cent that Highet claims for the *Aeneid*.[92] These figures illustrate the tendency of Statius to restrict the amount of speech in comparison with Homeric and Vergilian practice. Some of my aforementioned comments are suppositional in regard to what Statius could or might have done, but serve to highlight the point that he selects with special care those occasions for direct speech that best serve the advancement of the plot and the artistic aims of his epic.[93]

---

[91] Elderkin 1906: 6 (following Schneidewin 1884: 130). He divides this figure into forty-four per cent for the *Iliad* and fifty-six per cent for the *Odyssey*; Mackie (1988: 219) gives the figures of forty-five per cent and fifty-six per cent, respectively. However, Fingerle (1939: 79) maintains that over fifty-five per cent of the Homeric epics are composed of direct speech, with almost one-half of the *Iliad* and two-thirds of the *Odyssey* consisting of actual speech material. The difference between their figures is remarkable, especially in the number of speech verses that Elderkin cites for the *Iliad* and *Odyssey* (13,869) compared with the number recorded by Fingerle (15,323). Whereas Fingerle provides a list of speeches so that his figures can be verified, Elderkin unfortunately does not. But Mackie (1988: 219) counts 13,887 lines of speech in Homeric epic (7,054 in the *Iliad*; 6,833 in the *Odyssey*), a figure similar to the total of Elderkin. The difference between these sets of figures can be attributed mainly to the fact that Fingerle considers (rightly) the long narrative of Odysseus (*Od.* 9.2-12.453) to be a speech, while Mackie (1988: 219 n. 2) and Elderkin (1906: 4 n. 1) do not, but the difference may be partly due to different methods of counting lines of speech (i.e., counting less than complete lines of speech as part or whole lines).

[92] Highet (1972: 302). The figure is thirty-seven per cent excluding the lengthy narrative speech of Aeneas (2.3-3.715); cf. Highet (1972: 302f.), Mackie (1988: 219).

[93] See ch. 2 on the rôle of the speeches in the narrative strategy.

CHAPTER 2

NARRATIVE STRATEGY AND
THE RÔLE OF THE SPEECHES

The careful integration of speech into the narrative of the *Thebaid* demonstrates the traditional importance of the speech form in the epic genre. The prominence that the speeches come to assume in the narrative of the *Thebaid* is a reflexion not only of the significant debt of Statius to Homer and Vergil but also partly a reflexion of the importance of oratory in Roman public life. Artistic intention and control is a notable feature of Statius' placement of speeches within the narrative framework of the *Thebaid*. The speeches play a critical rôle in the narrative technique of the poet and the structural arrangement and thematic design of the epic. So my concerns in this chapter essentially are: why is *this* speech included, why *here* in this scene and with what effect? Statius uses direct speech for a variety of specific literary ends, including (but not limited to) the establishment of a sense of dramatic immediacy, a programme of theme and mood, and the revelation of character and motivation. The use of *oratio recta* enables the poet to manipulate directly not only the reader's perception of dramatic circumstances and thematic issues but also the character of important figures without editorial comment or interpretation. The speeches help to clarify the ideas and themes in the narrative and to define the personalities of the speakers, for we form our judgements about these issues and figures partly on the basis of what various characters say.

It is worthwhile taking a brief look at the structural organisation of the *Thebaid* before considering more carefully the rôle and function of the speeches within the narrative framework.[1]

---

[1] Amazingly enough, some contemporary critics maintain that the *Thebaid* has no structure and no message to impart. For instance, Ogilvie (1980: 233f.) argues that the *Thebaid* 'lacks an overall structure', 'is too studied', and 'cannot be said to be *about* anything'. This chapter shows that the episodic nature of the *Thebaid* does not preclude a structural unity based on theme and tone. On the themes of the *Thebaid*, see chs. 1-3 of my *The Mythic Voice of Statius* (forthcoming).

24

Structure of the Narrative

The structure of the narrative has provoked considerable discussion and disagreement among critics.[2] Venini and Turolla note a broad division between the two halves of the *Thebaid* that is reminiscent of the structural organisation of the *Aeneid*.[3] The first six books of the *Thebaid* and *Aeneid* deal with events leading up to the outbreak of war, which occurs in the seventh book, and the battle narrative dominates the second half of both works. In the *Thebaid* this broad division into preparatory (i.e., comparatively peaceful) and war sections is reinforced by the tone and manner of the concluding scenes in the books: books 1, 2, 4, and 5 close with an ironic prayer (1.696-720, 2.715-42, 4.832-50) or consolatory address (3.712-20, 5.733-52); books 7-12 culminate in the violent deaths of one of the main characters (7.794-823, 8.716-66, 9.865-907, 10.913-39; cf. 12.752-81) or end on a note of sombreness and pathos (11.757-61, 12.782-89).

Admittedly this division between the two halves of the *Thebaid* is of the most general kind, but there are some noteworthy parallels between the broad structural organisation of this epic and the *Aeneid*.[4] There is a noticeable break between books 6 and 7 of the *Thebaid*, although it is not as definite as the one between the two halves of the *Aeneid*. In addition, the Theban war commences late in the seventh book of the *Thebaid* (608ff.) and only after the direct intervention of Tisiphone who causes the war to begin by inciting a pair of Theban tigers to chase and slay some Argive warriors (564-607), much as the Italian war begins at a similar point in the narrative of *Aeneid* 7 (511ff.) after the similar intervention of Allecto who causes the hunting hounds of Iulus to pursue a pet stag of the Latins (475-510). Finally, books in the second half of both poems (*Theb.* 7, 8, 9, 10, 12; *Aen.* 10, 11, 12) conclude with the deaths of important figures in the battle narrative.

---

[2] For a general discussion of the problem and the views of various critics, see Kytzler (1986: 2913-16).

[3] Venini (1961a: 64), Turolla (1956: 139).

[4] Cf. Frank (1965), whose discussion of the structural parallelisms between both halves of the *Thebaid* is exaggerated; see Venini (1968: 132ff.).

Kytzler (following Ribbeck) identifies four triads in the twelve books of the *Thebaid*.[5] The first triad (books 1-3) revolves around divine and human actions that lead to the undertaking of war; the second section (4-6) concerns the departure of the Argive army and their stay in Nemea; the third triad (7-9) deals with the outbreak of the conflict and the first two battles; and the final section (10-12) deals with the final stages of the great war and the violent Athenian restoration of moral order in Thebes. Although this structural theory has attracted widespread criticism (as well as support) from various critics, there is sufficient evidence to sustain the notion of four general divisions. There are clearly perceptible breaks of a chronological or directional nature between the triads: there is a considerable period of two years between the first and second triads (4.1f.; cf. 3.718-20); the remotivation and redirection of the narrative toward war early in the third triad presents a dramatic contrast with the comparatively relaxed atmosphere of the second triad; and although slightly less discernible, there is a brief pause in the violent narrative at the beginning of the fourth triad.

Burgess proposes most sensibly three broad 'movements' or divisions to the poem: the initial impetus of the narrative toward war (1.46-4.645), the delay in Nemea (4.646-6.946), and the reactuation of the narrative toward war (7.1ff.);[6] the poet signalises his intent of altering the direction or impetus of the narrative by inserting within each of these broad narrative divisions an invocation to the Muses (1.1-45, 7.628-31) or Apollo (4.649-51) for divine inspiration in relating the subsequent events of the movement. Vessey anticipates the structural divisions of Burgess by dividing the poem into four major sections, a division that differs from Burgess only in the identification of a fourth section (12.464-809).[7] Less satisfactory is the fourfold division of Schetter (1.45-3.721, 4.646-7.144, 7.628-11.761, 12.1-809), which excludes two significant sections of the text (episodes 8, 9: 4.1-645; epis. 14, scenes 7-16: 7.145-627).[8]

Despite the disagreement among critics over the precise structural divisions of the *Thebaid*, it cannot be disputed seriously on a more basic level that the narrative structure (or plot) of the work is divided into twelve

---

[5] Kytzler (1955: 56ff., 71ff., 170), Ribbeck (1892: 224ff.); cf. Watkiss (1966: 426ff.), (Burck 1979: 311-26, esp. 313-26); *contra* Schetter (1960: 64ff.), Vessey (1973: 317ff.).

[6] Burgess (1978: 291).

[7] Vessey (1973: 320ff.).

[8] Schetter (1960: 78f.).

books, each with its own internal structure and unity.[9] Significantly eight of these books (1, 2, 4, 7-11) open with a scene highlighting the causative and destructive rôle of the gods in the forward movement of the narrative; this structural organisation acquires a special importance in books 7-10 where the battle narrative in each book is framed by an opening scene stressing the harmful nature of supernatural intervention and a culminating scene describing the demise of one of the Seven, the death in each case serving as an illustration of the supreme manifestation of divine interference in human affairs. Thus the structure itself of each book becomes a reflexion of the supernatural cause-human effect relationship: divine intervention precipitates human death and suffering.

The twelve books in the *Thebaid* naturally are divided into a number of major structures (episodes) that comprise a number of smaller narrative units (constituent scenes or incidents); these smaller structural units consist of action that occurs among the same grouping of characters for a continuous period of time in the same or vicinal location and themselves often consist of one or more speeches.[10] Understanding the relationship between the speeches and the narrative is central to appreciating the significance of various thematic and dramatic tensions in the poem. Often an important causative speech at the beginning of a major episode marks a point of transition in the narrative and sets events in motion either by communicating a plan of action (e.g., epis. 14: 7.1-627; speech: 6-33) or furnishing the motivation for subsequent action (e.g., epis. 1: 1.46-311; speech: 56-87). Generally the speeches are instrumental not only in varying the pace of the poetic narrative but also in creating tone and emotional intensity, since they reveal the feelings of the characters and their attitudes to particular situations in which they are directly or indirectly involved. The tone of the speeches either complements or contrasts with the mood or atmosphere created in the setting and descriptions so that certain thematic and dramatic tensions are established and stressed.

---

[9] But *contra* Krumbholz (1955: 252), who asserts that a book in Statius has no easily definable boundary and is not marked as a clear unit.

[10] Scenes in epic can be variously classified according to their structural function, technique and setting: there are, *inter alia*, dramatic (development), narrative (expository), descriptive, climactic, relief, transitional (bridge), speech (monologue, dialogue), battle and messenger scenes.

Narrative Pace

The rate of revelation in the plot determines the pace of the poetic narrative; naturally the narrative pace quickens when events occur in rapid succession. There are a number of factors that lead to a reduction in the speed with which the plot unfolds. Speech is only one of the basic elements that retard the narrative pace. When the narrative is punctuated by speech (including soliloquy framed as a speech), digression, peripheral scene, description, tableau, or an apostrophe of the poet, the pace of the narrative slows; naturally the effect of the interruption in the flow of events is dependent on the length of the speech or other insertion into the narrative. The lengthy description of the funeral games in honour of Opheltes (6.249-946) has a drastic effect on the pace of the main narrative since the games are not directly concerned with the main flow of events in the epic. Nevertheless, interest in the poem as a whole is maintained through the incessant activity of the games, which is largely unimpeded by the extremely brief speeches of characters involved in the episode.

The majority of the episodes in the *Thebaid* are designed clearly to advance the plot and to create renewed interest in the narrative. The speeches assume an important rôle in the narrative strategy of the poem since one of their main functions is to motivate action. Their careful integration into the epic at various points of the narrative enables Statius to control the pace of the poetic narrative with great precision. When he feels that the story is beginning to career violently forward, he can insert a speech at an appropriate point in the narrative to slow the progression of events. If he senses that the narrative is losing momentum because of excessive speech, he can excise some of the speech verses or other material incorporated into the narrative and increase the rate of revelation by converting some of the speech to *oratio obliqua* and returning immediately to the simple description of events in the narrative. The *Thebaid* usually progresses from scene to scene with the most intense action occurring at the end of major episodes or constituent scenes. Narrative description or scenes of less intense action are most often used as the means of transition between one episode or scene and another.

There are about twenty-two speeches per book on average. Some books fall below this average, while others naturally rise above it. The variation in the average length of speeches and the percentage of direct speech in the books form an important element in the narrative technique of Statius. Statius alternates books of intense action and less speech with books of more speech and less intense action to afford contrast or symmetry. The following figure helps to illustrate his technique.

Pct. of *Oratio Recta* and Ave. Length of Speech per Book

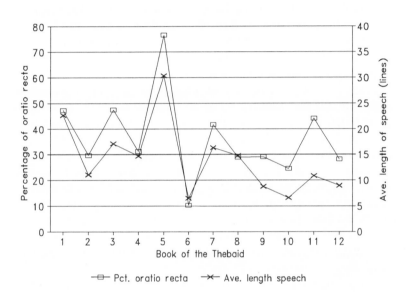

The resulting effect is similar to the one that Vergil produces in the *Aeneid* by varying the intensity of his narrative in the second, fourth and sixth books and also the seventh and ninth books by juxtaposing them with books of relative calm.

Statius also shifts the narrative pace frequently within books. As in the *Aeneid*, periods of intense action in the *Thebaid* generally are accompanied by shorter speeches of more frequent occurrence (but not necessarily more speakers[11]), especially in the second half (third and fourth triads) where the

---

[11] See p. 7.

29

narrative is dominated by an account of the fighting that takes place between the Theban and Argive armies. Here events unfold in rapid succession because the short speeches have only a slight effect in slowing the progression of the narrative pace. Speech intervenes little in book 6 (second triad) where the incessant activity of the funeral games honouring Opheltes occurs; this mirrors the practice of Vergil in his account of the funeral games in the fifth book of the *Aeneid*. Where speech predominates in the *Thebaid* there is generally little progression in the main narrative, as in book 5 (second triad) where Hypsipyle narrates her tale of the Lemnian massacre; similarly, the long narrative of Aeneas in the second and third books of the *Aeneid* impedes temporarily the advancement of the main plot.

The division of triads into major episodes and constituent scenes partly illustrates the close connexion between the narrative pace and the number of scene changes. As events unfold more rapidly, there is naturally a quickening of the narrative pace and an increase in the number of scenes within episodes or books. Apart from the important exceptions of the Coroebus and Hypsipyle digressions (1.557-672, 5.49-498) discussed immediately below and the occasional brief passages that slow the pace at which events unfold, the tempo of the narrative gathers momentum throughout the poem, as suggested in the increase in the number of scenes in successive triads (forty, forty-six, sixty-nine, seventy-six). Even when there is little advancement in the main plot, particularly in the second triad that consists mainly of an account of the delay of the Argives in Nemea, Statius generally appears intent upon accelerating progressively the tempo of the narrative.

Even though there are almost twice as many scenes in the third and fourth triads as there are in the first and second (145 versus eighty-six), a far greater percentage of those in the second half of the poem consist of direct speech (58.6 versus 51.2). Sixty per cent of the speeches in the *Thebaid* fall into the third and fourth triads, yet they constitute only 32.4 per cent of the text in these books (versus 38.5 per cent in the first and second triads) and average only 10.3 lines (versus 17.1 lines in the first half of the poem). Each triad in the *Thebaid* consists of less speech as a percentage of the text than the previous triad (41.8, 35.8, 32.8, 32) yet, with the exception of the second triad, contains more speeches (fifty-five, fifty-two, sixty-six, ninety-two). The average length of the speeches in each triad is a reflexion of the tempo of the narrative (16.6, 17.5, 12.4, 8.8).[12] Although the increased pace of the narrative is accompanied by less speech as a percentage of the text, the frequency of speech occurrence (speeches per lines of text) rises markedly since the number of speeches given increases;[13] therefore the drop in the average length of the speeches generally has the effect of increasing the tempo of the narrative and providing a renewed sense of dramatic vitality.

Nevertheless in some cases Statius incorporates speeches of moderate length into successive scenes and is still able to maintain the fairly rapid pace of the narrative. This suggests that it is not only the length of the speeches but also their content that are important matters to consider when examining the impact of a particular sequence of speeches upon the pace of the narrative. For the poet it was a matter of determining how many new revelations could be integrated effectively into a particular speech or series of speeches. For instance, in book 3 the action moves forward inexorably toward war in a quick succession of scenes consisting of one or more speeches of more than average length (17.6 lines per speech versus the overall average of thirteen lines). The poet is able to prevent the narrative pace from slowing too much by making sure that the longer speeches reveal a great deal both about the dramatic situation as well as the speakers and other characters involved in the scenes.

Statius devotes virtually entire scenes to passages of speech that bear little relation to the plot of the *Thebaid*. Naturally where speech predominates in the main narrative there is little or no progression in the narrative. Notable instances include the narrative speeches of Adrastus (1.557-672) and Hypsipyle (5.49-498). It can be argued that these lengthy speeches are tedious and that they retard unduly the action of the chronological narrative. There is some truth to this suggestion, since when Adrastus and Hypsipyle speak the flow of the chronological narrative comes to a grinding halt and attention is turned away from the major characters. The digressions can also be viewed as a means of filling out the size of the poem. But it must be remembered that the digressive speeches themselves consist of a new setting, new characters and much dramatic suspense that affords variety, enhances the texture of the poetic narrative, and helps to maintain interest in the poem as a whole.

---

[12] The percentage figures here take into account the recounted speeches.

[13] For the relevant statistical details on the speeches by book, see stat. app. 1, table 2.

Furthermore, the scenes consisting of the lengthy digressive speeches of Adrastus and Hypsipyle have a specific function to serve within the narrative framework. It is untrue to suggest, as many critics have, that these speech scenes are unconnected with the rest of the text.[14] Statius employs the speeches as narrative interludes complementing the thematic issues raised and the various moods created in the main narrative. Even though the speech scenes are quite clearly subordinate to the narrative into which they are inserted, they do not lessen the dramatic impact or thematic importance of the narrative since they are often full of emotional intensity and thematic significance themselves; rather, the digressive speeches afford a variation in the setting, content, characters and chronology of the main narrative and at the same time enhance the controlling themes of the poem through the reminiscence of events and ideas evoked in the main narrative.[15]

There are many dramatic situations in which the poet chooses to convey indirectly the words and thoughts of his characters. In 4.409-14 the indirect speech of Tiresias to Adrastus (true *oratio obliqua*) could easily be converted to *oratio recta*. In other places the mere fact of a speech or reflexion of a character is mentioned, as in 10.80-82 where the command of Jupiter to Iris is reported (virtual *oratio obliqua*). On average there are sixteen occasions in each book where the poet expresses the substance of what is spoken or imagined in true or virtual *oratio obliqua* rather than reporting the actual words of the speaker. The main disadvantages of employing indirect speech are that it is not as vivid as direct speech and does not reveal character nearly as effectively as the direct use of speech.

Facilitation of the narrative pace is the most obvious advantage gained from limiting the amount of direct speech; even the moderate use of indirect speech is beneficial for creating the impression of the rapid passage of time. The use of *oratio obliqua* permits Statius to pass quickly over potential speech situations. Its use also enables the poet to manipulate adeptly the arrival or departure of various characters. Two brief examples illustrate well

---

[14] Helm (1892: 172-74), Eissfeldt (1904: 385f., 423), Daniels (1905: 12), Legras (1905: 152), Butler (1909: 211f.), Dimsdale (1915: 460), Summers (1920: 31), Moore (1921: 171), Duff (1927: 383), Maher (1950: 119), Aricò (1960: 277), Venini (1961b: 376), MacKay (1965: 295), Mendell (1967: 124f.), Williams (1978: 198), Ogilvie (1980: 233).

[15] From this the reader can easily deduce that my use of the term 'digression' has no suggestion of pejoration. I use the term merely to refer to a section of the text that is superficially extraneous to the principal subject but in fact is essential to the unity of the work as a whole.

this narrative technique of the poet and the close interrelation of speech and action in the text. In 7.81 Mercury conveys Jupiter's message to Mars in virtual *oratio obliqua* (*ille refert consulta patris*) that had earlier been entrusted to him in *oratio recta* (7.6-33). Mars immediately sets out to fulfil Jupiter's command to incite the Greeks to war (*nec longa moratus*, 81). The effect of the rather abrupt transition from the impartation of Jupiter's order by Mercury to Mars' compliance without any intervening direct speech is to convey the impression of the swift passage of time and thereby quicken the pace of the narrative and heighten the sense of urgency about the situation at hand.

A similar effect is produced in 10.82f. when Iris acts immediately to relay the instruction of Juno to Iris. But the poet varies his technique by having Iris communicate Juno's message to Somnus in direct speech (10.126-31) that had been previously entrusted to the messenger goddess in virtual indirect speech[16] (*suamque / orbibus accingi solitis iubet Irin et omne / mandat opus*, 10.80-82). This technique prevents much needless repetition in the narrative and differs from earlier Greek epic where the custom was for the messenger to repeat the words of the original speaker.[17] Another effect of Statius' use of *oratio obliqua* is that it allows the reader to conjure visually for himself an image of the proceedings without the impediment of excessive speech, as in the depression of Polynices over his loss of kingship (1.314-20) and the Greek princes' urging of Adrastus (6.924-28).

An analysis of the speeches in the *Thebaid* suggests that the requirements of the speech situation frequently demand the abrupt break into or out of speech within the framework of the narrative. Statius' manipulation of the starting and closing points in a speech does much to convey the urgency of a situation and the emotions inherent in a particular epic context. His occasional insertion of brief narrative or parenthetic expression of one-half line or less within speeches effects an air of epic informality and sometimes provides a much-needed breathing space in a lengthy speech, but the interpolation of a longer narrative passage within speeches produces additional artistic and dramatic effects, such as showing the immediate effect of the speech upon the audience (e.g., 3.77-83, 9.165f.), stressing the intensity of the speaker's emotions and thereby eliciting a specific, desired

---

[16] On virtual and true *oratio obliqua*, see above, pp. 21f.

[17] On this see Endt (1903: 293-307), Elderkin (1906: 30-32) and Heinze (1908).

emotional response from the audience (e.g., 7.359-62; esp. speeches of lament, e.g., 6.173, 9.73f., 12.93), indicating a subtle shift in dramatic emphasis (e.g., 6.177-79, 11.627-30), or revealing the accompanying movements of the speaker (e.g., 12.92f.).[18]

Statius does not always delineate clearly the transition from narrative to speech in the *Thebaid*. This occasional lack of a clear definition in the boundaries of a speech extends to the transition from speech to narrative and from one speech to another by the same or another individual. For instance, it is unclear in 3.546 whether *quid furtim inlacrimas?* is spoken by Amphiaraus or Melampus,[19] while the comments made by Eteocles' companions in 11.257-62 can be interpreted either as a collective speech or four separate addresses by two or more individuals of the monarch's retinue.[20]   Admittedly the omission of an introductory formula clearly identifying the speakers' names creates confusion for the audience, but serves the valuable effect of maintaining the dramatic tension of the scene, whereas intervening narrative in the form of an introductory formula would lessen the dramatic effectiveness by lessening the general tone of the narrative.

Framing and Juxtaposing Techniques

Statius uses the techniques of juxtaposition and framing to add thematic and tonal dimensions to the narrative. Both techniques come to serve as a comprehensive commentary on several scenes between the lines of the text. While the juxtaposing technique frequently directs attention to central themes concerning the harmful effects of supernatural activity upon human stability and order, the framing technique sometimes focuses attention on a particular speech in a series of speeches in order to underscore these themes.

The opening episode (1.46-311) illustrates the use of juxtaposing technique to enhance the understanding of the epic. The poet juxtaposes the middle two scenes (sc. 3: 123-64; sc. 4: 164-96) showing the harmful effects of divine intervention in human affairs with passages highlighting this disastrous interference of the higher powers (sc. 1: 46-87; sc. 2: 88-122; sc.

---

[18]   See the relevant discussions in chs. 3 and 4 on the speeches surrounding the lines of narrative cited here.

[19]   See p. 281 n. 10.

[20]   Cf. pp. 14, 291 n. 21.

5: 197-311). This technique is effective in suggesting the destructive nature of the divine cause-human effect relationship that defines the rest of the poem.

The framing technique articulates the speech sequence in the fifth scene (197-311), thereby underscoring this important idea of the supernatural imposition of death and suffering upon humanity. It is significant that Statius chooses to place Juno's reply (242-82) to the forensic oration of Jupiter at the focal, most telling point of the entire scene on Olympus (sc. 5: 197-311).[21] The goddess points out the injustice of Jupiter's plan to punish the innocent Argive citizenry for the crimes of their ancestors and raises other possibilities for the punishment of Thebes that could easily exclude Argos, but Jupiter dismisses these lightly.

The speech of Juno (242-82) is framed by the opening speech of Jupiter (214-47) and his dismissive reply to the goddess' objections (285-302) in which he issues a command to Mercury that advances the narrative beyond the initial intervention of Tisiphone (123ff.). Juno's reply at the crux of the Olympian scene in the central, emphatic position is critical in interpreting her arguments and those of Jupiter, since it serves to focus attention on her comments about the injustice of the cosmocrator's plan to eradicate the Argive race. The framing technique affords the reader a conceptual framework against which to evaluate the speech of Jupiter and is critical in revealing his true motives and exposing the speciosity of his argument on the necessity for divine retribution of human sin.

Rôle of Individual Speeches in the Narrative

One of the purposes of this chapter is to examine the way in which Statius interweaves speech and narrative passages in order to produce certain specific thematic and mood-enhancing effects. In order to facilitate this investigation the narrative has been divided into twenty-four major episodes and 231 constituent scenes. The evaluation will consist of general comments on the structure of the narrative along with an examination of the rôle and

---

[21] Schubert (1984: 74) proposes a pentapartite division to this Olympian scene (1.197-311): (1) 197-213: Einberufung des Götterkonzils, (2) 214-47: erste Jupiterrede, (3) 248-82: Überleitung und Junorede, (4) 283-302: Überleitung und zweite Jupiterrede, (5) 303-11: Entsendung Merkurs.

function of the various speeches in the narrative design, with particular emphasis on the technique employed by Statius in inserting speeches into these major and minor structural units of the poem. Some of the later episodes and scenes receive far less treatment than previous sections,[22] mainly in order to avoid repeating points excessively that are made earlier in the chapter. The discussion on each book is preceded by a brief dramatic synopsis.

Prologue and First Movement (1.1-4.645)

The prologue and first movement deal with events that constitute the initial movement toward war (1.1-4.645). Books 1-3 describe the proceedings leading up to the undertaking of war at the commencement of the fourth book when the Argives assemble their forces for the march to Thebes. The major episodes in the first three books revolve around the supernatural causation of the war (1.46-311), the reception of Polynices and Tydeus in Argos (312-720), the intervention of Laius' shade (2.1-133), the royal marriages of Tydeus and Polynices (2.134-305), the mission of Tydeus to Thebes (306-743), the aftermath of the ambush in Thebes (3.1-217), and the aftermath of the ambush in Argos (218-721). These episodes contain just over one-fifth of the speeches in the poem. Many of them revolve around a series of set speeches; often one of these speeches is the focal point not only of the speech sequence or constituent scene but also of the entire episode.

BOOK ONE: DRAMATIC SYNOPSIS
Prologue (1.1-45)
Episode 1. Supernatural Causation of the War (1.46-311)
  1. 46-87: Curse of Oedipus
  2. 88-122: Flight of Tisiphone to Thebes
  3. 123-64: Attack of Tisiphone upon Eteocles and Polynices; agreement between the brothers
  4. 164-96: Reaction of the Thebans to the brothers' pact of alternate rule
  5. 197-311: Divine council on Olympus
Episode 2. Reception of Polynices and Tydeus in Argos (1.312-720)

---

[22] Especially those in the last triad, where the numerous speeches of brief length serve primarily to create a strong dramatic effect.

NARRATIVE STRATEGY AND THE RÔLE OF THE SPEECHES

1. 312-89: Exile of Polynices; his journey to Argos
2. 390-400: Adrastus' reflexions on the meaning of the Apollonic oracle
3. 401-07: Departure of Tydeus from Calydon and arrival at Argos
4. 408-30: Quarrel between Tydeus and Polynices
5. 431-81: Peacemaking intervention of Adrastus
6. 482-510: Entrance of Adrastus and the heroes to the Argive palace
7. 510-720 [incorporating the Coroebus digression, 557-672]): Royal banquet of Adrastus

The major function of the opening book is to draw immediate attention to the rôle of the supernatural powers in contriving to effect widespread human destruction and suffering. The purpose of the prologue (1.1-45) is consistent with this purpose. This introductory section allows Statius to provide essential background information relevant to his theme of *fraternas acies*; the description of the immense suffering that the gods have inflicted upon Thebes in the past and the suffering that her citizens are yet to endure immediately establishes an atmosphere of despair and hopelessness by pointing forward to the inevitability of tragic events.

After this introductory section Statius turns to the figure of Oedipus to commence the actual narrative of the poem (epis. 1, sc. 1: 1.46-87). The poet stresses that Oedipus is under the influence of the Furies (51f.) when he utters his curse against Eteocles and Polynices (56-87). This is the first motivating speech of the poem, since the prayer of Oedipus furnishes a cause that leads directly to the intervention of Tisiphone, who descends on the brothers at Thebes and inspires them to come to their fated pact of alternate rule (epis. 1, sc. 2: 88-122; sc. 3: 123-164, esp. 138f.). Thus the initial two scenes (and the opening lines of the third) of the opening episode emphasise the causative agency of the supernatural in precipitating the conflict that is to embroil Thebes and Argos in a bloody and fatal conflict. Confusion aroused in the minds of the populace over this policy (epis. 1, sc. 4: 164-96) is exemplified in the noncausative speech of the anonymous Theban (173-96), which shows the harmful effect of the goddess' intervention upon an innocent populace that is compelled to endure the vagaries of uncertain rule. The first speech of the poem (56-87) sets events in motion while the second speech reflects the unfortunate situation of the persons most affected by these events (173-96).

The fifth constituent scene of the opening episode takes place on Olympus at a divine assembly convened by the omnipotent Jupiter (1.197-311). Statius employs the framing technique here with great thematic effect.[23] The dissimulative speech of Jupiter (214-47) in which he outlines his plan for the destruction of Thebes and Argos dominates the scene. On a basic narrative level the speech functions to summarise events that have taken place in Thebes and Argos prior to the point at which the action of the main narrative commences. More importantly, the forensic speech of Jupiter functions dramatically as the supreme causative speech of the entire epic since it is the prime motivating factor behind the rest of the action in the poem and furnishes the motives for the numerous destructive actions of other malevolent deities, notably Mars and the Furies. The rôle of this speech in the thematic design resembles the function of Jupiter's opening speech in the *Aeneid* (1.257-96), which sets up the rôle of Rome as the founder and guardian of world stability and order. But the cosmocrator's opening speech in the *Thebaid* not only establishes the rôle of Jupiter as the prime mover of events on earth by revealing his annihilative intentions against Thebes and Argos but also demonstrates that the present-day inhabitants of these cities are to become the innocent victims of a supernaturally engineered plan of human destruction.

The next major grouping of speeches occurs in scene five of the second major episode (431-81) when Adrastus comes upon a feuding Tydeus and Polynices at the entrance to the Argive palace (435ff.). The verbal exchange between the trio dramatises the serious interaction of differing personalities and of ideas that are germane to the meaning of the epic. Not only do the speeches create a dramatic effect and help to define the personalities of the speakers, but they also motivate the reconciling action of Adrastus at this point of the narrative. On a thematic level they draw attention to the ability of humankind to solve its problems peaceably when the gods refrain from harmful intervention (cf. 478-81). Their characterising, causative and thematic functions demonstrate a purpose that goes far beyond that of merely adorning the narrative with dialogue or of varying the dramatic intensity of the scene.

The final two constituent scenes of the opening book describe the entrance of Adrastus and the heroes to the Argive palace (epis. 2, sc. 6: 482-510) and the royal banquet that is prepared for Tydeus and Eteocles

---

[23] As noted above, pp. 34f.

(epis. 2, sc. 7: 510-720). The prayers of Adrastus to Night (498-510) and Apollo (696-720) frame his narration of the Coroebus tale (557-672), near the end of which is placed an inserted prayer to Apollo, this time by Coroebus (643-61). While the narrative speech of Adrastus and inserted prayer of Coroebus draw attention to the extreme cruelty and hostility of Apollo to mankind, Adrastus' deferential prayer to gain the favour of Apollo is extremely ironic in view of the eventual destruction of Argos and stresses the hopelessness of the human condition in the face of overwhelming supernatural hostility. Thus the speeches in these scenes serve a characterising and thematic rather than causative function. They portray the piousness of the Argive regent while drawing attention to his tragic ignorance of divine malevolence and indifference.

BOOK TWO: DRAMATIC SYNOPSIS
Episode 3. Intervention of Laius' Shade (2.1-133)
  1. 1-88: Flight of Mercury and Laius' shade
  2. 89-133: Attack of Laius' shade upon Eteocles
Episode 4. Royal Marriages of Tydeus and Polynices (2.134-305)
  1. 134-200: Betrothal of Tydeus and Polynices to Adrastus' daughters.
  2. 201-13: Fama spreads the news of the royal weddings
  3. 214-305 (incorporating the tale of the fated necklace, 269-305): Royal weddings of the brothers
Episode 5. Mission of Tydeus to Thebes (2.306-743)
  1. 306-62: Brooding of Polynices over his loss of rule
  2. 363-74: Decision to send the embassy to Eteocles
  3. 375-88: Journey of Tydeus to Thebes
  4. 389-481: Tydeus' audience with Eteocles
  5. 482-95: Preparations for the nocturnal attack upon Tydeus
  6. 496-526: Setting of the ambush by the band of fifty warriors
  7. 527-723: Theban ambush of Tydeus; his massacre of the ambushers; intervention of Minerva

Both of the opening episodes in the first two books (epis. 1: 1.1-311; epis. 3: 2.1-133) emphasise the causative rôle of the supernatural powers in the movement toward war. Like the first major episode of the poem (1.1-311), the opening episode of the second book includes a description of a former Theban king that emphasises his personality by introducing him prior to his speech (2.1-133). The causative speech of Oedipus is situated toward the end of the first constituent scene in book 1 (46-87) and attention is then focused on the effect of the speech upon Tisiphone (88-122) and the consequences of the curse for the sons of Oedipus (123-64) and the innocent citizens of Thebes (164-96). On the other hand, the motivating speech of Laius is placed toward the end of the opening episode in the second book and only the immediate effect of the speech upon Eteocles is described (2.102-19). This speech of Laius is preceded by a lengthy description of the supernatural figure and his motive of revenge (encouraged by Jupiter [2.1f.; cf. 1.292-301]), which creates an overwhelming sense of foreboding. The placement of his speech toward the end of the third major episode suggests that the primary emphasis in the episode is on the act of influencing rather than being influenced; the effect of the description and speech is to place responsibility squarely on the shoulders of the supernatural powers for the subsequent hostility of Eteocles toward his brother (cf. 2.120-33). This episode is representative of those in the poem where a lengthy description or informative passage pertinent to the theme or atmosphere precedes a speech yet remains subordinate to the actual speech situation.

The next major episode in the second book (epis. 4: 134-305) describes the joyous preparations and wedding of Tydeus and Polynices to the daughters of Adrastus amid dire portents. Adrastus' speech in which he offers his daughters to Tydeus and Polynices (152-72) and their speeches of acceptance (176-88, 189-97) motivate the action for the rest of the episode in which the marriage actually occurs. The juxtaposition of the story of the fated necklace stressing the harm that afflicts the wearer or her family (269-305) further conveys the feeling of the inevitable ruination of Argos.

Statius then turns our attention at the beginning of the third major episode of book 2 (epis. 5, sc. 1: 306-62) to Polynices who is shown brooding over his failure to assume power in Thebes. The speech of Argia highlights her anxiety over the desire of her husband to return to Thebes (334-52). Polynices' expression of hope that Jupiter will defend his rightful claim to the Theban throne (356-62) and the realisation of the reader that this cannot be so draws attention to the injustice of the divine plan to destroy the Theban and Argive races. The dialogue is essentially noncausative since it does not possess any immediate causative function; however, the speech of Argia is important in furnishing the motivation for her later plea to Adrastus to undertake war on behalf of her husband's cause (3.687-710) and the response of Polynices foreshadows the war that he initiates in order to gain power in Thebes. Because of the noncausative dialogue, Statius must introduce a scene with an action or speech that pushes the action forward;

this is achieved with a decision to send an embassy to Eteocles (epis. 5, sc. 2: 363-74), a determination that leads directly into the next scene describing the journey of Tydeus to Thebes (sc. 3: 375-88).

The focal point of the embassy scene that follows (epis. 5, sc. 4: 389-481) is the speech of Eteocles in which he refuses to hand over the Theban crown to his brother (415-51). His speech is framed by two speeches of Tydeus: his exhortation to Eteocles to step down from the throne (393-409) and threatening prediction of a bloody war (452-67). The speeches of Tydeus are themselves framed by descriptions of his arrival at (375-88) and departure from the Theban palace (469-81). This framing technique not only balances the various elements of the scene but also focuses attention on a significant causative speech, since Eteocles' refusal to abdicate is the immediate cause of the great war and stresses the theme of monarchy as institutionalised tyranny.

The final three constituent scenes of the second book (epis. 5, sc. 5: 482-95; sc. 6: 496-526; sc. 7: 527-743) show Eteocles planning and carrying out the ambush of Tydeus on his return to Argos. Tydeus is the dominant figure in the ambush scene (527-743); he is the speaker or addressee in all ten speeches of the episode except one (620-23). The scene is punctuated with a series of very brief speeches between Tydeus and his adversaries (535, 547-49, 641, 649-54, 655-59, 661-68) that defines his aggressive personality and helps to relieve the monotony of the lengthy narrative describing the massacre. When the Calydonian slays all but one of his opponents, Minerva tells him to refrain from further slaughter and to retire from the field (686-90).

After Tydeus commands Maeon to return and tell Eteocles to prepare for war (697-703), he prays to Minerva for continued favour and promises her further offerings after he returns from the war (715-42). The aforesaid speeches of Minerva (686-90) and Tydeus are clearly causative: the directive of the goddess compels Tydeus to refrain from further bloodshed, while the command of Tydeus (697-703) motivates Maeon to return to Thebes and bear a war message to Eteocles. Tydeus' concluding prayer to Minerva at the end of book 2 (715-42), like the one of Adrastus at the close of the opening book (1.696-720), is replete with dramatic irony; the Calydonian hero cannot know that his hope of returning alive from the war will not be fulfilled.

BOOK THREE: DRAMATIC SYNOPSIS
Episode 6. Aftermath of the Ambush in Thebes (3.1-217)
    1. 1-57: Return of Maeon to Thebes

In book 3 the relatively quick progression of minor incidents has the effect of quickening the narrative pace so that the movement toward war becomes pronounced, particularly at the close of the second scene of the seventh episode when Mercury hastens to Argos with instructions from Jove to incite the people to war (316ff.). The linear juxtaposition of human and divine scenes defines the narrative structure of this book. Just as the first and second books open with unflattering descriptions of past Theban monarchs, book 3 commences with an unfavourable portrayal of the reigning monarch.

The first scene of the book (epis. 6, sc. 1: 3.1-57) commences with Eteocles soliloquising anxiously over the fate of the ambush party sent against Tydeus (6f., 9-18); the soliloquy is noncausative since it merely records the thoughts of the monarch. Maeon's defiant vituperation of Eteocles (59-77, 83-87) is the focus of the second scene; his speech interrupts the normal flow of the narrative toward war yet is causative in the sense that it provokes Eteocles to forbid burial of the slain hero's corpse (96-98). The search of the Theban women for the corpses of their slain husbands and sons (epis. 6, sc. 3: 114-32) follows immediately upon Creon's refusal to allow the body of Maeon to be inhumed (paralleling the later action of Creon in denying burial to the Argives in 11.662f.; cf. 11.680f., 12.94-102). After describing the search and unrestrained lamentation of the women (3.114-32), the poet turns the attention of the reader to the figure of

Ide (epis. 6, sc. 4: 133-68). Her verbal lament is designed to particularise the general sense of loss and sorrow that pervades the dramatic situation and thereby reinforces the despairing tone of the narrative. The bitter consolatory speech of Aletes concludes the episode (epis. 6, sc. 5: 169-217; speech: 179-213) and like the vituperation of the anonymous Theban in book 1 (173-96) draws attention to the undeserved suffering of the Theban race.

The setting for the first two scenes of the next episode shifts to Olympus and the heavens (epis. 7, sc. 1: 3.218-59; sc. 2: 260-323). As in the earlier Olympian (epis. 1, sc. 5: 1.197-311) and embassy scenes (epis. 5, sc. 2: 2.389-481) of similar length, Statius employs the framing technique with brilliant effect. The plea of Venus (3.260-91) drawing attention to the unmerited suffering of Thebes is framed by the speeches of Jupiter (227-59) and Mars (291-323) stressing (despite their attempts to dissimulate their real motives) their destructive propensities. In focusing the attention of the reader on the speech of Venus, Statius stresses the suffering endured by the Theban people as the result of harmful divine intervention. The speech of Jupiter is significant not only since it illustrates his inborn cruelty but especially because (in terms of its narrative function) it serves to remind the reader that the Olympian is firmly in control of events in Thebes and Argos (cf. esp. 235-38). Specifically his speech motivates the action of Mars in inspiring the Argives to a furious war lust (cf. esp. 3.420-24, 575-93).

The second scene of the episode reverts to the aftermath of the Theban ambush of Tydeus (epis. 7, sc. 2: 3.324-44; sc. 3: 345-406). The consequences in Thebes have already been described (epis. 6: 1-217); now the narrative turns to describe the effects upon the Argives (esp. 365-406). Speeches of Tydeus (348-65) and Polynices (367-81) inflame the citizens with a desperate yearning for war, but Adrastus intervenes and is able to assuage the anger of his subjects (388-93). The verbal exchange between the three figures recalls the earlier dialogue between the trio when Adrastus intercedes to prevent the shedding of blood between his future sons-in-law (1.438-73). Mediative speeches of Adrastus at these critical junctures of the narrative are designed to show that humankind can successfully mediate its disputes provided that it is left alone by the supernatural powers. The artful juxtaposition or near-apposition of scenes featuring the intermediative speeches of Adrastus (1.408-30, 3.345-406) with scenes illustrating the harmful intervention of Jupiter and Mars in human affairs (1.197-311, 3.218-59, 3.260-323, 3.407-39) serves not only to stress the inability of humanity to control its own destiny in the face of pervasive and overwhelming supernatural hostility but also to highlight the causative rôle of the gods in the inexorable movement of the narrative toward war.

The subject of the next series of scenes revolves around the taking of auspices by the prophets Amphiaraus and Melampus (epis. 7, sc. 5: 407-39; sc. 6: 440-55; sc. 7: 456-59; sc. 8: 460-575; sc. 9: 575-97). In this sequence the poet uses the framing and juxtaposing techniques with great effect. Narrative scenes setting forth the causative agency of Mars in instigating war (420-39, 575-97) frame the descriptions of Adrastus and the prophets who are distressed at the prospect of imminent warfare and whose attempts to prevent the outbreak of hostilities are rendered futile by the intervention of the war-god (440-55, 566-75). The centrepiece of the entire episode is the augury (460-575), which consists of a series of framed speeches: the speeches of Amphiaraus (471-96, 546-57) frame those of Melampus (502-15, 546), which in turn enclose the important descriptive speech of Amphiaraus foretelling the tragic deaths of the Seven (516-45). The poet therefore makes this speech of Amphiaraus highlighting the inevitability of human death and destruction the focal point of the speech sequence as well as the entire augural scene. Furthermore, the linear juxtaposition of narrative passages in the episode expressing the opposition of Adrastus and the prophets to war with those describing the motivating interventions of Mars again draws attention to the complete powerlessness of humanity before the gods.

The heated exchange between Capaneus and Amphiaraus dominates the penultimate scene of book 3 (epis. 7, sc. 10: 598-677). Again the framing technique informs the structure of the scene and is identical to the technique used in the scene on Olympus in book 1 (197-311). In the Olympian scene the pacificatory speech of Juno (1.250-82) is framed by the hostile speeches of Jupiter (214-47, 285-302), which in turn are flanked by narrative passages, one describing the Olympian setting (197-213) and another reporting the response of the addressee Mars to the command of Jupiter to incite the Argives to war (303-11).

Similarly narrative passages introduce and conclude the scene in Argos, one setting forth the dramatic context (3.598-607) and the other describing the effect of Capaneus' violent rhetoric upon the Argive citizenry (669-77); these passages flank the war-fevered speeches of Capaneus (607-18, 648-69), which in turn frame the focal speech of Amphiaraus whose warning against undertaking war goes unheeded (620-47). In both the aforesaid divine and human scenes (1.197-311, 3.598-677) the central speeches promoting peace are immured by those promoting violence and destruction; this framing technique reinforces the inexorable movement of the narrative toward war and underscores the futility of attempting to obstruct the forces of inhumanity. The concluding scene of the third book (epis. 7, sc. 11: 678-721) features the speeches of the pitiful figures of Argia and Adrastus (687-721) who reconcile themselves to the inevitability of war, thereby demonstrating that the gods can draw even the most noble characters of the human race into a war against their will.

The movement of the narrative toward war slows perceptibly in books 4-6 in comparison with the first three books of the *Thebaid*. This is apparent especially in the distribution of constituent scenes that constitute these books: whereas the first three books (1-3) contain forty scenes (seven episodes) that move the main narrative inexorably toward war, the next three (4-6) consist of only fifteen scenes (episodes 8, 9) that advance the main narrative. The action in books 4-6 revolves mainly around the departure of the Argive troops for Thebes and their long stay in Nemea. The major episodes in this second triad deal with the assembling and departure of the Argive army (4.1-344), the reaction of the Thebans to the approach of the Argive army (345-645), the drought in Nemea (646-843), the death of Opheltes (5.1-946), the obsequies of Opheltes (6.1-248), and the funeral games for Opheltes (249-946).

These episodes constituting the second triad contain less than one-fifth of the speeches in the poem; the succession of mainly brief speeches in the constituent scenes helps to advance the action in the narrative and creates a dramatic effect. The inclusion of four major episodes at Nemea in books 4-6 allows Statius to achieve three important objectives: the dramatic slowing down of the main narrative so that the great war is postponed until the second half of the poem (much as Vergil defers the outbreak of war in the *Aeneid* through his account of events in books 4-6), the creation of a narrative interlude between events portraying the inexorable movement toward war (books 1-3) and those describing the actual hostilities (books 7-11), and the incorporation of traditional epic features such as the catalogue of troops (4.32-344) and the funeral games (6.1-24, 249-946).

BOOK FOUR: DRAMATIC SYNOPSIS
Episode 8. Assembling and Departure of the Argive Army (4.1-344)
  1. 1-12: Bellona's incitation of the Argives to a frenzied desire for war
  2. 13-31: Departure of the Argive warriors

3. 32-73: Cataloguing of Adrastus' troops
4. 74-92: Polynices' mustering of his squadrons
5. 93-115: Tydeus and his forces
6. 116-44: Hippomedon and his soldiers
7. 145-64: Tirynthian troops
8. 165-86: Capaneus and his squadrons
9. 187-213: Eriphyle's acquisition of the fated necklace
10. 214-46: Amphiaraus in the midst of his troops
11. 247-308: Parthenopaeus and his Arcadian forces
12. 309-44: Plea of Atalanta to Parthenopaeus

Episode 9. Reaction of Thebans to Approach of Argive Army (4.345-645)
1. 345-405: Fear and desperation in Thebes
2. 406-14: Eteocles' consultation with Tiresias
3. 414-645: Necromantic rites of Tiresias and Manto

Events in the first three books lead to the decision by the Argives to undertake war. The beginning of the fourth book shows the Argives assembling their forces for the march to Thebes (epis. 8: 1-344). At this point the main narrative slows perceptibly and there is little advancement in the plot. The scene commences with a description of the goddess Bellona rousing the Argive warriors to arms and incorporates a lengthy catalogue of warriors who under the influence of Mars (cf. 35f.) flock from every part of Greece to fight under the Argive banner (32-344). This assembling of the troops is one of three major episodes in the book and contains only two speeches. Inserted roughly at the midpoint of the catalogue is the soliloquy of Argia showing how the fatal necklace comes into the hands of Eriphyle (200-10). This soliloquy obviously helps to define the character of a pious and devoted wife but also has causative, prognosticative and thematic functions: the denial of ownership by Argia opens the way for Eriphyle to claim the necklace (211f.; cf. 190-95), forebodes the death of Amphiaraus (190-94), and stresses the primary rôle of the gods in promoting human death and destruction (189-91; cf. 213). The poet emphasises the human cost of the impending conflict when he concludes the scene with the speech of Atalanta to Parthenopaeus in which she makes a desperate but vain attempt to dissuade her son from going to war (318-40).

The opening lines of the second episode in the book (epis. 9, sc. 1: 4.345-405) describe the temerity of the Thebans who as yet are untainted by the violence of Mars and his agents of destruction (345-68); this passage is juxtaposed with a brief episode describing the divine intervention of Fama, the fear she arouses in Thebes (369-77), and the prophetic prayer of a Bacchanalian queen portending imminent disaster for Thebes (383-404, esp. 397-404). This speech provides a pathetic climax to the scene and furnishes an air of foreboding that overhangs the subsequent necromantic rites. The following scenes of the episode (epis. 9, sc. 2: 406-14; sc. 3: 414-645) feature the necromantic rites in Thebes. After the preparatory rites (414-18) and a description of the site (419-42), the necromancy of Tiresias that follows (443-645) is dominated by the speeches of the priest and his assistant Manto (473-624), which infuse the narrative with much picturesque detail. The third scene culminates in the confusing prophecy of Laius' shade that forewarns of war but otherwise leaves the priest and priestess uncertain about its precise meaning (626-44). Like so many other climactic speeches in the poem, the prophetic speech not only advances the plot by pointing forward to future events but also stresses the complicity of the supernatural powers in the disaster that is about to befall Thebes and Argos: the gods (633), especially the Fates (636, 638), the Furies (633, 636, 643), and the war-god (638f.) are all conspiring to drive these cities to destruction.

Second Movement (4.646-6.946)

The second movement deals with the delay of the Argive army in Nemea and the events that take place during its stay (4.646-6.946).

BOOK FOUR: DRAMATIC SYNOPSIS (cont.)
Episode 10. Drought in Nemea (4.646-843)
1. 646-79: *Invocation*; resolution of Bacchus to delay the Argives
2. 680-98: Intervention of Bacchus and the water nymphs
3. 699-785: Effect of the drought upon the landscape and the Argives; the meeting with Hypsipyle
4. 786-803: Hypsipyle's abandonment of Opheltes
5. 804-850: Rescue of the troops by Hypsipyle

The introductory scenes in the first episode of the movement (epis. 10, sc. 1: 4.646-79; sc. 2: 680-98) concern the decision of Bacchus to delay the Argives so as to postpone the destruction of his native city. Naturally the focus of the scenes is the speeches of Bacchus: the soliloquy reveals his determination to slow the advance of the Argives toward Thebes (669-78), while his instructions to the nymphs to desiccate the earth (684-96) motivates the action of the nymphs in carrying out his command (697-715), with the

SPEECH AND RHETORIC IN STATIUS' *THEBAID*

exception of the nymph of Langia who ignores it (723-29, esp. 723f., 726f.).
But the real significance of the speeches lies in their thematic purpose: the
references to the connivance of the gods (672-77, 689f.), demigods (cf.
684-89) and other universal forces (691f.) in effecting the partial destruction
of humanity centres attention on the cruelty of these higher powers.

A description of the effects of the disastrous drought upon the Argives
(730-45) and the discovery of Hypsipyle (746-52) precedes the prayer of
Adrastus to the former Lemnian queen (753-71), whom the regent mistakes
for a goddess (epis. 10, sc. 3: 699-785). The favourable response of
Hypsipyle to Adrastus' plea for water (776-85) is juxtaposed with a brief
mention of her desertion of the innocent Opheltes (epis. 10, sc. 4: 786-803)
that draws attention to both the imminence of his tragic death (786) and the
rôle of the supernatural in bringing it to pass (787). Adrastus' pious words
(753-71) recall his ironic prayer to Apollo (1.696-720), especially his hope
that Jupiter will allow his army to return safely to Argos (4.768f.). The
drought episode (epis. 10: 4.646-850) and book climaxes with the ironic
expression of a similar hope in the prayer of an anonymous Argive chieftain
(832-50, esp. 846-50).

Books 4-6 are carefully designed to reinforce the controlling themes of
the work: three of the first four books (1, 2, 3) commence with scenes
describing the agency of the gods and the rôle of past and present monarchs
(the earthly counterparts of the gods) in causing maximum human destruction
and suffering. The fact that three of the first four books (1, 2, 4) also end
with prayers that go unfulfilled by the gods draws attention not only to the
indifference of the higher powers toward mankind but also to the very limited
nature of human power and knowledge.

BOOK FIVE: DRAMATIC SYNOPSIS
Episode 11. Death of Opheltes (5.1-946)
1. 1-16: Reassembling of the Argive troops
2. 17-498: Narrative of Hypsipyle
3. 499-540: Death of the infant Opheltes
4. 541-54: Search of Hypsipyle for her charge
5. 554-87: Slaying of the serpent
6. 588-637: Lament of Hypsipyle
7. 638-90: Reaction of Lycurgus to news of Opheltes' death
8. 690-709: Adrastus' pacification of the Nemeans
9. 710-30: Reunion of Hypsipyle with her sons
10. 731-53: Oracular pronouncement of Amphiaraus

48

Book 5 centres on the tragic death of the infant Opheltes (episode 11: 1-946). The opening scene shows the Argive army slaking their thirst and reforming their lines for the march to Thebes (1-16). Statius prepares the way for the long narrative of Hypsipyle (49-498) by incorporating a brief exchange of speeches between her and Adrastus (20-47) in which she is encouraged to reveal her identity (20-27) and relate her tale of suffering (43-47). The pronounced effect of a long narrative speech (in this case, one that features five of the eight inserted speeches in the poem) in terms of interrupting the flow of the main narrative has already been noted[24], but it would be remiss not to point out that the insertion of a lengthy digression at this juncture of the narrative is a stroke of poetic genius. Bacchus has already revealed his determination to delay the Argives on their journey to Thebes (4.677ff.) and the drought is the means by which he resolves to achieve this end (684ff.).

Statius was astute enough to realise that the mere description of the drought (4.697-722, esp. 697-715) and its effect upon the Argives (730-45) would do little to convey a real impression of the time that the Argives were delayed in Nemea. So he extends his account of events in Nemea into the fifth book of the poem in order to help convey the psychological impression of a long delay. But the real *tour de force* is achieved by his insertion of a digression (5.49-498) that so arrests the flow of the chronological narrative that the impression of a long delay in the progress of the Argive army toward Thebes is further strengthened. Although this turning away or suspension of the action from the main narrative appears to result in an apparent loss of dramatic cohesion, interest in the epic as a whole is still maintained through the vivid description of events by Hypsipyle, the relevance of the themes in her narrative to the central thematics of the poem, the similarity in mood and atmosphere between the digression and the narrative, and not least because the former Lemnian queen features prominently in both the main narrative and her account of events on Lemnos. The Hypsipyle digression can stand on its own—hence the term *episodic* that is often used to describe the narrative structure of the *Thebaid*—but it still functions as an integral part of the overall thematic design of the epic.

The main narrative that resumes following the narrative speech of Hypsipyle focuses on the death of Opheltes (epis. 11, sc. 3: 5.499-540). A description of the innocent Opheltes (502-04) and the accursed serpent of

---

[24] See above, pp. 28ff.

Jupiter (505-33) is followed by an account of the infant's death (534-40) and the response of Hypsipyle and the Argives (541ff.). The causative (and characterising) speech of Capaneus in which he vows to slay the serpent (565-70) is followed immediately by a description of this deed and the threatened retaliatory action of Jupiter (570-87); this scene (epis. 11, sc. 5: 554-87) anticipates the fatal confrontation between Capaneus and Jupiter in the antepenultimate book (epis. 21, sc. 3: 883-920; sc. 4: 921-39).

The reaction of the Nemeans to the death of Opheltes is the subject of the second half of book 5 (epis. 11, scenes 6-10: 588-753). This lament section serves as a pathetic climax to the scene depicting the violent death of Opheltes; the consequences of harmful divine intervention are stressed in the lament of Hypsipyle, which serves as a fitting verbal manifest for the grief felt by the Nemeans (608-35). The subsequent heated verbal exchange between Lycurgus and Tydeus (656-89) and the conciliatory speeches of Adrastus (669-71, 701-03) motivate the action in the narrative and create a dramatic effect. Important speeches at the close of the episode are the prophecy of Lycurgus (681-89) and the oracular speech of Amphiaraus (733-52), which draw attention to the destructive rôle of the higher powers (688f., 735-40).

The speech of Amphiaraus (5.733-52) is especially significant. In addition to focusing attention on the destructive purpose of the gods, the speech provides a pathetic climax to the entire scene since it ends on a consolatory note that does little to deflect concentration away from the pathetic aspects of Opheltes' death; in this sense the speech mirrors the ironic or despondent tone of other speeches in the poem, especially prayers and laments, that often conclude scenes of hope or death. Furthermore, Amphiaraus' speech motivates two subsequent events (one remote, the other immediate) of the narrative: it provides narrative impetus toward the distant goal of a great war that will prove ruinous for the Argive people (735-40) and feeds directly into the events of book 6 by stressing the necessity of paying honours to the infant Opheltes (esp. 741-43). And perhaps most importantly (from the viewpoint of narrative technique), the speech establishes that an account of the obsequies and funeral games in honour of Opheltes will be used by Statius in the sixth book as a means of helping to convey the impression of a prolonged stay on the part of the Argive army in Nemea (cf. 741-45) and consequently to increase the sense of interruption in the progress of the narrative toward war. These effects are the same as those achieved by the poet when he inserts the lengthy narrative of Hypsipyle

(49-498) into the second scene (17-498) of the delaying episode featuring the death of Opheltes (epis. 11: 5.1-946).

BOOK SIX: DRAMATIC SYNOPSIS
Episode 12. Obsequies of Opheltes (6.1-248)
1. 1-24: Gathering of the Argive princes
2. 25-44: Mourning of Lycurgus and Eurydice
3. 45-52: Consolation of Adrastus
4. 54-83: Construction of the funeral pyre of Opheltes
5. 84-117: Building of the funeral pyre of the serpent
6. 118-248: Funeral of Opheltes
Episode 13. Funeral Games for Opheltes (6.249-946)
1. 249-95: Gathering of the crowd
2. 296-354: Assembling of the competitors for the chariot race
3. 355-88: Mourning of Apollo on Parnassus
4. 389-549: Chariot race: Amphiaraus and Polynices; intervention of Apollo
5. 550-645: Foot-race: victory of Parthenopaeus
6. 646-730: Discus event: Hippomedon and Phlegyas
7. 731-825: Boxing match: Capaneus and Alcidimas
8. 826-910: Wrestling match: Tydeus and Agylleus
9. 911-23: Sword fight: Agreus and Polynices
10. 924-46: Archery contest: Adrastus; dire omen of ricocheting arrow

The only direct speeches in the twelfth episode (6.1-248) are those of Opheltes' parents, Eurydice and Lycurgus; they hold the supernatural powers directly responsible for the death of their son and their suffering. The lament of Eurydice (138-73, 174-76, 180-83) and brief prayer of Lycurgus (197-201) are violent in tone and reflect the animosity of the royal couple against the gods and their unfulfilled expectations for their son. Their sentiments bear testimony both to the malevolence of the higher powers and the tragic futility of war.

The Nemean games (epis. 13: 249-946) are held in honour of Opheltes (now the newly deified Archemorus) who has become the first victim of the war (cf. 5.647). The games comprise seven events: the chariot-race (389-549), foot-race (550-645), discus (646-730), cestus (731-825), wrestling (826-910), sword fighting (911-23) and archery contests (924-46). These scenes consist mainly of a description of the contests punctuated by twelve brief speeches (comprising less than seven per cent of the narrative) of the

51

participants and observers. The succession of short speeches in the games helps to motivate the action in the narrative and creates a dramatic effect. From a prognosticative and mood-enhancing standpoint the most important speech is the command of Adrastus (914-19); in addition to pointing forward to the great war that will dominate the action of the next five books, the command creates an air of the inevitability of war, an impression that is confirmed immediately at the start of book 7. The insertion of a brief scene featuring Apollo (epis. 13, sc. 3: 355-58) just prior to the commencement of the first event in the games is calculated generally to enhance the feeling of ultimate supernatural control over the games; specifically the scene anticipates the intervention of Apollo in the chariot-race (490-530) and foretells the death of Amphiaraus in the next book (7.818-23). It centres on the soliloquy of Apollo, which emphasises the power of Jupiter and the Fates (376) and presages the death of the Argive priest (381-83).

Third Movement and Epilogue (7.1-12.819)

The third movement deals with the major incidents of the great war as well as events leading up to and following from this conflict (7.1-12.809). The careful organisation of the first three books in the second half of the *Thebaid* recalls the structure of the first three of four books in the first half of the poem (1, 2, 4), which commence with scenes emphasising the control of various supernatural figures over events in Thebes and Argos and conclude with ironic prayers for divine favour. Books 7-9 begin with similar episodes stressing divine control over the direction of the narrative and conclude with descriptions of disastrous events that are attributable directly or indirectly to the harmful machinations of the higher powers. The revived plan of Jupiter in book 7 (epis. 14, sc. 1: 6-33) sets the stage for the outbreak of fighting and leads to the earthquake and disappearance of Amphiaraus (epis. 15, sc. 4: 771-823); similarly the destructive intentions of Pluto in the next book (8.34-79) give rise to the hideous anthropophagy of Tydeus (epis. 16, sc. 15: 751-66). The tragic death of the young and naïve Parthenopaeus at the close the ninth book provides an appropriately pathetic climax to the second and most intense engagement of the great war, focusing as it does on the supreme emblematic victim of a war planned by the malevolent Jupiter and fomented by his *agent provocateur* Mars (cf. 9.831-74).

52

Major episodes in books 7-9 revolve around the final stage of preparations for the great war (7.1-627) and the *aristeiai* and deaths of Amphiaraus (7.628-8.341), Tydeus (8.342-9.194), Hippomedon (9.86-569) and Parthenopaeus (570-907). The pace of the narrative increases noticeably in book 7: there are more scenes in the seventh book (twenty) than in any previous book (except the fourth) and far more changes of scene in the third triad (sixty-nine) than in each of the first two triads (forty, forty-six). These periods of intense action in the third triad are accompanied by shorter speeches of more frequent occurrence (averaging 12.4 lines versus 17.1 lines in books 1-6), especially in the battle narrative (7.621ff.). The short dramatic speeches that interrupt at various points have a minimal impact on the pace of the battle narrative because of their brevity.

BOOK SEVEN: DRAMATIC SYNOPSIS
Episode 14. The Final Stage of Preparations for the Great War (7.1-627)
1. 1-33: Remotivation of the war by Jupiter
2. 34-63: Flight of Mercury to Thrace
3. 64-84: Arrival of Mercury in Thrace; his impartation of Jupiter's command to Mercury
4. 84-89: Assuagement of Jupiter's wrath
5. 90-104: Completion of the funeral rites in Argos
6. 105-44: Mars' instigation of the Argives to a furious war-lust
7. 145-226: Meeting between Jupiter and Bacchus on Olympus
8. 227-39: Incitation of Theban allies to war by Mars
9. 240-373: Phorbas' identification of Theban troops to Antigone
10. 374-97: Martial oration of Eteocles to the Theban and allied armies
11. 398-451: Advance of the Argive army upon Thebes
12. 452-69: The fearful situation in Thebes
13. 470-85: Journey of Jocasta to the Argive camp
14. 485-563: Appeal of Jocasta to Eteocles; retort of Tydeus
15. 564-607: Disastrous intervention of Tisiphone
16. 608-77: Flight of Jocasta from the Argive camp; the outbreak of war
Episode 15. The *Aristeia* and Death of Amphiaraus (7.628-8.341)
1. 628-48: *Invocation*; general fighting
2. 649-87: Death of Eunaeus
3. 688-770: *Aristeia* of Amphiaraus
4. 771-823: Earthquake and disappearance of Amphiaraus

Like four of the five constituent scenes (1-3, 5) in the first episode of the poem and the opening two scenes in the seventh episode (3.218-59, 260-323), the initial four scenes in the seventh book (epis. 14: 1-33, 34-63, 64-84, 84-89) emphasise the causative rôle of the gods, especially Jupiter, in the movement toward war. In all these scenes the supreme ruler is portrayed as the major force promoting human death and destruction and as the prime motivator of the war between Thebes and Argos. The focus of the first scene in book 7 is a Jovian command directed to Mars in which the supreme deity threatens to dispossess the war-god of his destructive powers if he does not lay waste to these two cities (6-33, esp. 22-33). The function of this speech is identical to the rôle played by the speeches of Jupiter in the two previous Olympian scenes of the poem (1.214-47, 285-302; 3.229-52) in that it furnishes the motivation for subsequent events and reestablishes the momentum of the narrative toward war; this is especially important after the lull of the previous books. Jupiter's menacing tone is especially striking after the relatively nonthreatening atmosphere of the sixth book, which can be attributed primarily to the absence of the gods (excluding 6.355-89, 491-512).

At this point of the narrative the scene shifts briefly back to Argos (epis. 14, sc. 5: 7.90-104) where the funeral rites are being concluded with an ironic prayer by Adrastus for victory addressed to the newly-deified Archemorus, whose own death foreshadows the defeat of the Argives in the coming war (93-103). The speech gains added significance through its insertion between two divine sections (epis. 14, scenes 1-4: 1-89; sc. 6: 105-44) stressing supernatural malevolence and control over events in Argos and Thebes. This ironic human prayer is followed by a scene on Olympus (epis. 14, sc. 7: 145-226) consisting of a verbal exchange between Bacchus (155-92) and Jupiter (195-221) that demonstrates that the plan for the destruction of Thebes is unjust and entirely the creation of a vindictive ruler.

The juxtaposition of this Olympian scene stressing the primary causative rôle of Jupiter (sc. 7: 7.145-226) with scenes showing his *agent provocateur* Mars inciting the Argives (sc. 6: 105-44) and the Theban allies (sc. 8: 227-39) to war against each other further stresses the primary rôle of the supernatural powers in the instigation of human destruction. These divine scenes featuring Mars are framed in turn by a brief speech scene in Argos portraying the inefficacy of human prayer (sc. 5: 90-104) and another in Thebes (sc. 9: 240-373) portraying the despondency of Antigone (esp. 247-49) and Phorbas (esp. 363-67) as the Thebans assemble for war. Thus

NARRATIVE STRATEGY AND THE RÔLE OF THE SPEECHES

the framing of the divine scenes drawing attention to the destructive intentions of the gods with passages emphasising the pitiful human situation in Argos and Thebes creates a foreboding atmosphere pointing toward imminent disaster. Antigone's deliberative speeches (247-52, 291-93) prompt Phorbas, her faithful manservant, to identify the troops of Thebes and her allies from a Theban watch-tower (254-89; 294-358, 363-73); this exchange of speeches dominates the teichoskopic scene, which appears designed to present the Theban heroes in a manner different from the earlier catalogue of the Argives that takes the form of simple narrative (4.32-344). Their speeches serve a prognosticative as well as mood-enhancing function, since the poet blends elements into their speeches, particularly those of Phorbas, that point forward to the disastrous events of the war and the reappearance of various warriors in the battle scenes. The scene culminates with a combat exhortation of Eteocles that is designed to justify his cause to his troops and encourage them to fight bravely in the forthcoming war (375-90); however, his attempt to distort and misrepresent the circumstances leading up to the outbreak of hostilities is evidence that the Thebans will fight an unjust and dishonourable war on behalf of a scheming and unscrupulous tyrant.

The *teichoskopia* at Thebes is the first episode in a series of scenes whose focus shifts between Thebes and the approaching Argive troops. Scenes depicting the apprehension of Antigone and Phorbas (epis. 14, sc. 9: 7.240-373) and martial fervour of Eteocles (sc. 10: 374-97) are followed immediately by a scene depicting a hostile Argive army on the march toward Thebes (epis. 14, sc. 11: 398-451); the troops are filled with so great a lust for war that they scarcely pause to rest or eat along the way (398-402) and they ignore the portents of imminent disaster (402-23). This brief scene is juxtaposed with another describing the fear and panic in Thebes over the approach of the enemy (epis. 14, sc. 12: 452-69). Thus the poet contrasts effectively the confidence and war fervour of the Argives with the anxiety and dread of the Thebans and thereby points toward the success of the Argives in the initial stage of the opening battle.

The stage is set for war, but the poet inserts a scene describing the last-ditch attempt of Jocasta to prevent its occurrence (epis. 14, sc. 14: 7.485-563). Adrastus has tried on previous occasions to prevent or at least delay the outbreak of war (e.g., 3.388-93; cf. 440-52, 712-20) and now Jocasta makes a similar but vain attempt. Her appeal for peace (497-527) moves the Argives, but this is counterbalanced by the combined effect of the hostile words of Tydeus (539-59) advocating war and the intervention of the

55

Fury (559-63). In the next scene (sc. 15: 564-627) Tisiphone sets a pair of Theban tigers upon the Argives with the result that the Arcadian warrior Aconteus slays them and is killed in turn by the Bacchic priest Phegeus (564-607); this disastrous intervention by a hostile deity leads directly to the outbreak of hostilities between the two armies (sc. 16: 608-627) and emphasises the causative and destructive rôle of the supernatural powers in events leading up to the war.

At this point of the narrative Statius prefaces his account of the war by invoking the Muses another time and asking them to recount the battles of the war that has just commenced (7.628-31), much as Vergil inserts a new invocation to his muse and an appeal for guidance in *Aeneid* 7.37-45 before beginning his account of the Italian war that constitutes the second half of the *Aeneid*. This brief invocation of the Muses in the *Thebaid* is followed by an account of the first two battles of the great war; this recital of events constitutes the rest of the third triad of the poem (7.632-9.907) and features four major scenes revolving around the *aristeiai* of Amphiaraus (7.628-8.341), Tydeus (8.342-9.85), Hippomedon (9.86-569) and Parthenopaeus (9.570-907).

Although there is little feeling of a dramatic progression taking place in the scenes featuring the *aristeiai* of these heroes, these units of action are structured carefully for dramatic effect.[25] The constituent elements common to these large narrative blocks encompassing the *aristeiai* of these heroes are a preliminary description of the general fighting (7.632-48, 8.342-547, 9.196-314, [cf.] 9.540-69), the death of a young and inexperienced warrior (7.649-83, 8.554-606, 9.315-50, 9.865-907), a lament scene highlighting the tragic consequences of the war for the surviving relatives of the victims (7.683-87, 8.607-54 [esp. 636-54], 9.315-445, 9.570-636), the initial appearance of the hero in battle (7.690ff., 8.548ff, 9.196ff., 9.683ff.), a bestial, fluviatile or celestial simile highlighting his destructive propensity (7.709-11, 8.460-65, 9.220-22, 9.739-43), a description of the devastation the hero wreaks upon the battlefield (7.711-22, 8.475-78, 9.289-314, 9.744-75), one or more intervallic passages focusing on the bloodshed caused by other combatants and/or highlighting the tragic consequences of the war for the surviving relatives of the victims (7.723-43, 8.480-518, 8.607-54 [esp.

---

[25] Cf. Krumbholz (1955: 254), Burgess (1978: 328).

636-54],[26] 9.225-83, 9.570-636, 9.670-82), a harmful or revengeful divine intervention (7.736ff., 8.757ff., 9.148ff., 9.712ff.), a description of the effect upon the hero of the divine intervention (7.744-49, 8.760-62, 9.165-76, 9.736-75), the reemergence of the hero and more carnage (7.744-70, 8.659-701, 9.289-314[27]), and a supernatural intervention or appearance just prior to or at the death of the hero (7.771-89, 8.758-66, 9.446-532, 9.831-44).[28]

After the new invocation to the Muses the account of the fighting in the first battle is continued (epis. 15, sc. 1: 7.628-48). The description of the confrontation between Eunaeus and Capaneus (sc. 2: 649-87) stresses the disparity between the combatants and includes brief combat speeches drawing attention to the harmful intervention of Bacchus (663-68; cf. 662f.) and highlighting the futility of the unwarlike efforts of the young Bacchic priest against an experienced and powerful opponent (esp. 677-79). Amphiaraus' *aristeia* (sc. 3: 688-770) and disappearance during the supernaturally contrived earthquake (sc. 4: 771-823) follow next. The focus of the latter scene is on the brief colloquy between Amphiaraus and Apollo, which stresses the inevitability of events divinely ordained (772-88). The seventh book is the first of four consecutive books (7-10) that culminate in the death of one of the Seven (Amphiaraus, Tydeus, Parthenopaeus, Capaneus).

BOOK EIGHT: DRAMATIC SYNOPSIS
Episode 15 (cont.). The *Aristeia* and Death of Amphiaraus (7.628-8.341)
5. 1-20: Descent of Amphiaraus into the lower world
6. 21-83: Reaction of Pluto to intrusion of Amphiaraus; the destructive plan of the underworld deity
7. 84-126: Plea of Amphiaraus to Pluto
8. 127-33: Fear of the Argives over the earthquake

---

[26] Schetter (1960: 105ff.) observes that this scene (Ismene's farewell to the dying Atys) and other unwarlike episodes in books 7-11 are inserted in the battle in order to avoid the tediousness of continuous battle scenes. Of course such a touching vignette as the Atys episode also serves the purpose of stressing the immense suffering endured by the relatives of war's victims.

[27] Parthenopaeus does not have a chance to reappear since the youthful warrior is slain on his initial appearance by Dryas (9.586ff.).

[28] Cf. Holland (1976: 143-45), Fenik (1968: 9-11, 22-23, 192), Burgess (1978: 317). Holland argues that the martial conduct of the major heroes in the *Thebaid* conforms to the typical pattern of the *aristeia* in the *Iliad*.

9. 134-52: Report of Amphiaraus' disappearance to Adrastus
10. 152-61: Flight of Argive troops from the battlefield
11. 162-217: Grief of the Argives over the death of Amphiaraus
12. 218-39: Joyous reaction of Thebans to the demise of the Argive priest
13. 240-58: Reaction of Oedipus to news of Opheltes' death
14. 259-70: Despondency of Adrastus
15. 271-93: Selection of Thiodamas as the new priest of Apollo
16. 294-341: Prayer of Thiodamas to the Earth

Episode 16. The *Aristeia* and Death of Tydeus (8.342-9.195)

1. 342-62: Rearousal of the Thebans to battle by Tisiphone and Bellona
2. 363-72: Dispiritedness of the Argive troops
3. 373-94: Mars' incitation of the armies
4. 395-455: General combat
5. 456-65: Victims of Tydeus
6. 466-96: Slayings of Haemon
7. 497-518: Meeting of Hercules with Minerva
6. 519-35: Desertion of Haemon by Hercules; withdrawal of the Theban warrior from his duel with Tydeus
9. 536-53: Death of Prothous
10. 554-606: Duel between Tydeus and the youthful Atys; the death of the young warrior
11. 607-54: Lament of Argia and Ismene
12. 655-714: *Aristeia* of Tydeus
13. 715-44: Mortal wounding of Tydeus by Melannipus
14. 745-50: Retrieval of Melannipus' corpse by Capaneus
15. 751-66: Anthropophagy of Tydeus; flight of Minerva from the scene

As book 7 opens with a restatement of the destructive intentions of Jupiter (6-33) and culminates in the disastrous earthquake (794-823), so the eighth book commences with underworld scenes (epis. 15, sc. 5: 1-20; sc. 6: 21-83; sc. 7: 84-126) revolving around a new plan of human destruction by the infernal ruler Pluto (34-79) and concludes with the first direct consequence of that plan in the anthropophagy of Tydeus (epis. 16, sc. 15: 751-66). Pluto's command is the supreme motivating speech of the last five books, providing the prime causative factor behind each of four hideous deeds in the narrative: the fratricide of Eteocles and Polynices (69-71; cf. 11.387ff.), the anthropophagy of Tydeus (71f.; cf. 8.751), the decree of Creon outlawing the burial of the Argive corpses (72-74; cf. 11.661-64), and

Capaneus' challenge of Jupiter (76f.; cf. 10.381ff.). The third scene consists of the deferential prayer of the priest Amphiaraus to Pluto (90-122), which differs markedly in tone from the command of the infernal deity (34-79) in the preceding scene (sc. 6: 21-83) and provides a smoother narrative shift to subsequent scenes portraying the fear and grief of the Argives (scenes 8-11, esp. 8: 127-33; 162-217).

The culmination of the Argive lament (epis. 15, sc. 11: 8.162-217) is the *epikedion* of the troops (174-207), which serves as a verbal manifest of their deep sorrow and sense of loss over the disappearance of their beloved priest. This scene in the Argive camp is set against two other scenes in Thebes describing the unrestrained delight of the Thebans (sc. 12: 218-39) and the reaction of Oedipus (sc. 13: 240-58) upon hearing the news of the death of Amphiaraus. The focus then shifts back immediately to the Argive camp to show a dispirited Adrastus (sc. 14: 259-70). This contrast of scenes depicting the intense grief and anxiety of the Argives with the description of the joyful mood in Thebes intensifies the sense of loss and suffering that pervades the narrative. The culmination of the scenes in Argos (scenes 14-16: 259-341) is the prayer of the new augur Thiodamas to Tellus (303-38), which draws attention to the tragic misconception of humankind that its misfortune results mainly from offenses committed against the gods (esp. 318).

There is a lull in the battle narrative (epis. 15, scenes 5-16: 8.1-341) after the disappearance of Amphiaraus, so the poet shows the supernatural powers arousing the armies to a furious war lust (sc. 1: 342-62, esp. 344-49; sc. 3: 373-94, esp. 383-85); this divine incitation of the armies to battle serves as yet another reminder of the causative rôle of the gods in the perpetration of human violence and destruction. The centrepiece of the entire episode (8.342-9.85) is the lament scene featuring Antigone and Ismene who mourn the fate of Thebes and the tragic death of the youthful Atys (sc. 11: 607-54 [note the focal speech of Ismene, 622-35]), the classic victim of a cruel war. The juxtaposition of battle scenes (sc. 1: 342-62; scenes 3-10: 373-606; scenes 12-15: 655-766) with brief scenes depicting the dejection of the Argives (sc. 2: 363-72) and the lament of Ismene and Antigone (sc. 11: 607-54) serves to emphasise the human cost of the supernaturally inspired war. Brief battle speeches, mainly those of Tydeus, intervene in the *psychomachia* scenes; they function not only to infuse the narrative with dramatic vitality but also to define the personality of Tydeus.

SPEECH AND RHETORIC IN STATIUS' *THEBAID*

BOOK NINE: DRAMATIC SYNOPSIS

Episode 16 (cont.). The *Aristeia* and Death of Tydeus (8.342-9.195)
16. 1-31: Reaction of the Thebans to the anthropophagy of Tydeus
17. 32-85: Lament of Polynices over Tydeus' corpse

Episode 17. The *Aristeia* and Death of Hippomedon (9.86-569)
1. 86-143: Fight over Tydeus' corpse
2. 144-76: Intervention of Tisiphone
3. 177-95: Capturing of Tydeus' body by Thebans
4. 196-314: General fighting in the river
5. 314-50: Death of Crenaeus
6. 351-403: Search of Ismenis for Crenaeus; her lament over the
   death of her young son
7. 404-45: Reaction of Ismenos to the death of Crenaeus
8. 446-509: Violent struggle between Ismenos and Hippomedon
9. 509-21: Intercession of Juno in behalf of Hippomedon
10. 522-39: Death of Hippomedon
11. 540-69: Slaying of Hypseus by Capaneus

Episode 18. The *Aristeia* and Death of Parthenopaeus (9.570-907)
1. 570-636: The mournful appeal of Atalanta to Diana on behalf of
   Parthenopaeus
2. 637-69: Meeting of Diana with Apollo
3. 670-82: General fighting
4. 683-711: Parthenopaeus on the field of battle
5. 712-35: Intervention of Diana in behalf of Parthenopaeus
6. 736-820: *Aristeia* of Parthenopaeus; intervention of Diana
7. 821-40: Intervention of Mars; withdrawal of Diana from the
   battlefield
8. 841-76: Mortal wounding of Parthenopaeus by Dryas
9. 877-907: Death of Parthenopaeus

As with the preceding episode featuring Amphiaraus (epis. 15:
7.628-8.341), the description of Tydeus' *aristeia* overlaps two books (epis.
16: 8.342-9.85), which helps to reinforce the impression of continuous
psychomachia in the narrative. The first two scenes in the ninth book
describe the reaction of the Thebans to the anthropophagy of Tydeus (epis.
16, sc. 16: 1-31) and the lament of Polynices over the death of Tydeus (sc.
17: 32-85). The opening scene centres on the hostile speech of Eteocles
(12-24) while the lament section focuses on the lament of Polynices over the
corpse of Tydeus (49-72), the victim not only of Polynices' desire to ascend
the throne (cf. 52-60) but also of supernatural hostility toward humanity

60

(71f.). Significantly the entire episode is framed by scenes depicting the supernatural reactuation of war (sc. 1: 8.342-62) and the human suffering that results from this divine interference in human affairs (sc. 17: 9.32-85). The *aristeia* and death of Hippomedon follow next (epis. 17: 9.86-569). As with the previous episode revolving around the *aristeia* and death of Tydeus (8.342-9.85), the lament scene (sc. 6: 9.351-403) is the focal point of the entire episode. Featuring the lament of Ismenis (376-98), it is framed by scenes depicting the fighting between Hippomedon and the Argive troops (scenes 1-5: 86-350) and the fatal clash between Ismenos and the brute warrior (scenes 7, 8). As with the other *aristeiai*, the episode culminates in the death of the hero (sc. 10: 522-39). The battle narrative is punctuated mainly by brief battle speeches and prayers for divine assistance, which instil the episode with dramatic feeling.

Although the passages describing the *aristeia* and death of Parthenopaeus (epis. 18: 9.570-907) comprise most of the elements common to the other episodes featuring the *aristeiai* and deaths of the Seven, the ordering of the constituent elements of the Parthenopaeus episode differs from the usual arrangement. Most often the *aristeia* episodes centre on the lament of a surviving relative of a youthful victim whose death is described in the main battle narrative immediately preceding the scene of mourning; usually the death of the main hero or a lament over his passing forms the climax of the episode. In the Parthenopaeus episode there is no lament over one of the youthful victims of his *aristeia*, since the young hero himself is the victim of martial violence. Unlike the other episodes, the scene of mourning in the Parthenopaeus section is placed at the beginning (sc. 1: 570-636) and the death of the young hero at the end (sc. 9: 877-907). The opening lament (570-636) and divine scenes (sc. 2: 637-69), especially the mournful prayer of Atalanta (608-35) and prophetic speech of Apollo (650-62), create a sense of foreboding over the entire episode and stress the inevitability of Parthenopaeus' death, which is the pathetic climax of the entire episode (877-907); this death scene culminates in the pathetic speech of the youth, which arouses sympathy for the youthful victims of war and their loved ones (885-900, 901-07).

The chief episodes in the fourth triad deal with the nocturnal massacre of the Thebans (10.1-474), the *Opfertod* of Menoeceus (10.475-826), the death of Capaneus (10.827-11.56), the duel between Polynices and Eteocles (11.57-647), the aftermath of the fraternal combat (11.648-12.463), and the Athenian overthrow of Creon (12.464-809). Despite having over one-third of the speeches in the poem (ninety-two), the narrative in the fourth triad is vigorous and swift-moving. This is partly because speech constitutes only thirty-two per cent of the text (versus 36.5 per cent in books 1-9) and more especially because the average length of each speech is only 8.8 lines (versus 15.3 lines in books 1-9); in addition, about one-third of the scene changes in the poem occur in the fourth triad (seventy-six).

BOOK TEN: DRAMATIC SYNOPSIS

Episode 19. The Nocturnal Massacre of the Thebans (10.1-474)

1. 1-48: Theban encirclement of the Argive camp
2. 49-69: Appeal of the Argive women to Juno
3. 70-83: Resolution of Juno to aid the Argive women
4. 84-136: Description of the cave of Sleep; relaying of Juno's command to Sleep by Iris
5. 137-55: Sending of a deep sleep upon the Thebans by Somnus
6. 156-75: *Furor* of Thiodamas
7. 176-261: Despondency of Adrastus; Thiodamas' incitation of the Argives; catalogue of attackers
8. 262-346: Massacre of the dormant Theban troops
9. 347-83: Journey of Hopleus and Dymas to Thebes
10. 384-448: Meeting of Amphion and the Thebans with Hopleus and Dymas; the deaths of the Argive pair
11. 449-52: Triumphant reaction of Amphion
12. 453-65: Return of Thiodamas and the ambushers to the Argive camp
13. 466-74: Discovery of Theban corpses by Amphion; flight of his Theban band to Thebes

Episode 20. The *Opfertod* of Menoeceus (10.580-826)

1. 475-530: Argive attack upon Thebes
2. 531-88: Defence of Thebes; fear and panic in the city
3. 589-627: Capnomancy of Tiresias; demand of snake of Mars for a victim; sorrowful response of Creon
4. 628-85: Intervention of Virtus; the determination of Menoeceus to sacrifice himself
5. 686-737: Meeting of Menoeceus with Creon
6. 738-55: *Aristeia* of Capaneus
7. 756-82: Sacrifice of Menoeceus
8. 783-826: Recovery and veneration of the corpse of Menoeceus; the lament of Creon and Eurydice

Episode 21. The Death of Capaneus (10.827-11.56)

1. 827-52: *Invocation*; Capaneus' ascent of the Theban walls

2. 853-82: Arrival of Capaneus at the summit; his devastation of the towers
3. 883-920: Reaction on Olympus to Capaneus; his challenge of the gods
4. 921-939: Destruction of Capaneus by Jupiter

The opening scene of the tenth book (epis. 19, sc. 1: 1-48) furnishes a brief respite from the dramatic tension of the battle narrative. The passage not only makes thematic reference to the supreme rôle of Jupiter in the instigation of martial violence and bloodshed (1-4, esp. 2f.) but also provides a structural link between the events of the second battle (5-14) and those of the nocturnal massacre (15-48). This brief scene focuses on the causative speech of Eteocles in which he rouses his troops to battle against the Argive foe (10.21-35).

Four brief scenes follow (10.49-69, 70-83, 84-136, 137-55). Since they revolve around the successful appeal of the Argive women to Juno, their causal connexion is manifest, but the technique employed demonstrates the crucial rôle of the speeches in the variation of the narrative pace. The second scene (49-69) culminates in the appeal of the Argive women to Juno (67-69) and the action in the fifth scene (137-55) stems directly from the indirect command of Juno to Somnus relayed by Iris (126-31), but an obvious opportunity for direct speech is not taken up in the third scene (cf. 79-83) where the poet merely reports the speech of Juno to Iris. This brief divine scene is one of many dramatic instances in the poem in which the omission of speech has the marked effect of increasing the tempo of the narrative.

In the next two scenes (sc. 7: 10.176-261; sc. 8: 262-346) the exhortative speeches of Thiodamas (188-218, 269-71) and Adrastus (236-44, 266-68) convey the motivation for the Argive massacre of the warriors in the Theban camp. The second section of the episode (scenes 9-13: 347-474) describes the failure of the heroic mission of Hopleus and Dymas, who attempt unsuccessfully to recover the corpses of Parthenopaeus and Tydeus. The juxtaposition of this section highlighting the futility of human devotion and piety (cf. 384) with another portraying the success of the divinely sanctioned nocturnal massacre epitomises the hopelessness of the human condition as portrayed in the epic. However, just as the joy of the Argives over the success of the nocturnal raid is short-lived and they suffer a reversal of fortune when they are routed after the death of Capaneus, so the delight of Amphion and his troops quickly turns to horror when they spot the corpses of their compatriots.

Statius enlarges on this deliberate contrast between human devotion and impiety in the next two episodes. On a general level the heroic and selfless Menoeceus (epis. 20: 10.475-826) is set against the bold and impudent Capaneus (epis. 21: 10.827-11.56), yet each suffers death directly as the result of a harmful divine intervention. While Virtus inspires Menoeceus to seek death openly in order to save Thebes (10.628-85, esp. 661-77; cf. 628-30, 657), an act that proves futile in the end (cf. 12.696), Capaneus' challenge of Jupiter is directly attributable to the destructive plan of Pluto (10.831ff.; cf. 8.76f.). Both episodes commence with speeches of Capaneus (482-86, 845-47) that assist in defining his shamelessly bold personality. The placing of the mini-*aristeia* of the raging Capaneus (epis. 20, sc. 6: 738-55)[29] against the heroic sacrifice of Menoeceus (sc. 7: 756-82) highlights the contrast between the two figures and reinforces the sense of injustice suggested by the similarity in the violent manner of their supernaturally inspired deaths. The Menoeceus episode culminates in the lament scene featuring Eurydice (sc. 8: 783-826). This scene is only one of a number of scenes in the epic that are framed around speeches of mourning and consolation spoken over the youthful victims of violence.

BOOK ELEVEN: DRAMATIC SYNOPSIS
Episode 21 (cont.). The Death of Capaneus (10.475-11.56)
  5. 1-8: Reaction on Olympus to death of Capaneus
  6. 9-20: Corpse of Capaneus; reaction of Thebans to his death
  7. 21-38: Rout of the Argive troops
  8. 39-56: Defence of the Argive camp
Episode 22. The Duel Between Polynices and Eteocles (11.57-647)
  1. 57-68: Summoning of Megaera by Tisiphone
  2. 69-74: Flight of Megaera to Tisiphone
  3. 75-118: Obtainment of Megaera's aid by Tisiphone in inciting the brothers

---

[29] The *topoi* constituting the entire mini-*aristeia* of Capaneus include the appearance of Capaneus (10.738ff.), the fluviatile simile emphasising his destructive tendencies (864-69), the description of the devastation he causes in the fray (738-55), intervening passages of the bloodshed perpetrated by another warrior (Menoeceus) and the mourning that follows his demise (756-826), the reappearance of Capaneus and concomitant destruction (837-82), and the intervention of a higher power (Jupiter) just prior to the hero's death (913ff.). On the typical pattern of the Statian *aristeia*, see pp. 56f.

4. 119-35: Decree of Jupiter to the Olympians not to watch the duel
5. 136-39: Flight of Tisiphone to Polynices
6. 140-204: Intervention of Tisiphone; determination of Polynices to fight Eteocles; plea of Adrastus
7. 205-314: Decision of Eteocles to accept Polynices' challenge
8. 315-23: Reaction of Jocasta to news of the impending duel
9. 324-53: Entreaty of Jocasta to Eteocles
10. 354-87: Attempt of Antigone to dissuade Polynices from meeting Eteocles in single combat
11. 387-423: Intervention of Tisiphone; meeting of the brothers on the battlefield
12. 424-46: Peacemaking attempt of Adrastus
13. 447-56: Intervention of Fortuna
14. 457-73: Reaction of Pietas to the fraternal combat
15. 474-96: Intervention of Pietas; her repulse by Tisiphone
16. 497-579: Culmination of the duel between the brothers
17. 580-633: Lament of Oedipus over the death of his sons
18. 634-47: Suicide of Jocasta

Episode 23. The Aftermath of the Fraternal Combat (11.648-12.463)
1. 648-64: Accession and burial decree of Creon; the plea of Antigone
2. 665-756: Exile of Oedipus by Creon
3. 757-61: Abandonment of the Argive camp

The action in the eleventh book centres on the duel between Polynices and Eteocles (epis. 22: 11.57-647). Tisiphone's deliberation, in which the Fury seeks the aid of her sister Megaera (76-112), draws attention not only to her considerable influence over previous events in the war (81-91) but also to her instigation of the subsequent fraternal combat in the face of predictable human opposition (97-105, 109-11) and remorse (105-08). The juxtaposition or near-apposition of scenes describing the disastrous interventions of the Furies with scenes depicting the unsuccessful attempts of various human and benevolent divine figures to forestall the fratricide—the speeches of Jocasta (329-53), Antigone (363-82), and Adrastus (429-35; cf. 196f.) are especially important—bears testimony to the inability of humanity to control its own destiny against overwhelming supernatural hostility. As with the Menoeceus and other sections focusing upon the disastrous consequences of war for the surviving relatives or friends of the victims (e.g., 10.475-826, 3.169-217, 9.32-85), the episode culminates on a note of pathos with a description of the grieving parents, in this case the lament of Oedipus (sc. 17: 580-633) and suicide of Jocasta (sc. 18: 634-47).

The subsequent episode concerns the aftermath of the fratricide (epis. 23: 11.648-12.463) and commences with Creon forbidding the burial of the Argive dead (sc. 1: 648-64; cf. 12.93-103) and banishing Oedipus from Thebes (sc. 2: 665-756). Creon's refusal to permit the inhumation of the Argive corpses leads directly to the plea of the Argive women to Theseus (12.546-86) and the subsequent fall of the Theban monarch (752-81).

BOOK TWELVE: DRAMATIC SYNOPSIS

Episode 23 (cont.). The Aftermath of the Fraternal Combat (11.648-12.463)

4. 1-59: Search and mourning of the Thebans for their dead
5. 60-104: Funeral rites of Menoeceus
6. 105-40: Band of Argive women on their way to bury the dead
7. 141-204: Meeting of Ornytus with the band of Theban women; despondency of the women; plan of Argia
8. 204-67: Journey of Argia to the Theban battlefield
9. 267-90: Search of Argia for the corpse of Polynices
10. 291-311: Intercession of Juno in behalf of Argia
11. 312-48: Discovery of Polynices' corpse by Argia; her lament over his corpse
12. 349-61: Flight of Antigone from Thebes to the battlefield
13. 362-408: Meeting of Antigone with Argia on the Theban battlefield; lament of the two women
14. 409-12: Bearing of the corpse of Polynices to the river Ismenos
15. 413-46: Cleansing of Polynices' body; splitting of the funeral pyre of the brothers
16. 447-63: Earthquake; seizure of the women by the Theban guards; their return to Thebes

Episode 24. The Athenian Overthrow of Creon (12.464-809)

1. 464-80: Approach of the Argive women at Athens
2. 481-518: Arrival of the women at the Altar of Clementia
3. 519-610: Return of Theseus to Athens; supplication of him by the Argive women; reaction of Theseus
4. 611-38: Mustering of the Athenian troops
5. 639-55: Martial oration of Theseus; departure of the Athenian army
6. 656-76: March of the Athenian army to Thebes
7. 677-97: Rejection of the Athenian embassy by Eteocles
8. 698-708: War preparations of the Thebans

9. 709-29: Arrival of Theseus at Thebes; meeting of the Athenian and Theban armies on the battlefield
10. 730-51: *Aristeia* of Theseus; general fighting
11. 752-81: Single combat between Theseus and Creon; death of the Theban monarch
12. 782-96: Meeting of the armies in friendship; joyous reaction of the women
13. 797-809: Mourning of the Argive women over their dead
Epilogue (12.810-19)

Just as the beginning of the sixth book is dominated by the obsequies of Archemorus (epis. 12: 6.1-248), so the twelfth book commences with the Theban lament of the dead (epis. 23, sc. 4: 1-59) and the funeral rites of Menoeceus (sc. 5: 60-104). Significantly this final book is framed by scenes of general mourning over the victims of two different wars (epis. 23, sc. 4: 1-59; epis. 24, sc. 13: 797-809). Even though the brief armed conflict between Athens and Thebes is admittedly more 'just' than the great war waged between Argos and Thebes, the consequences of martial violence are the same for the survivors on both sides of these wars who are compelled to suffer the deaths of their loved ones.

Altogether the twelfth book contains three scenes of general lamentation and three scenes of mourning for particular figures highlighting the tragic senselessness and human cost of war. All but one of them occur in the penultimate episode (23), which focuses on the plight and sorrow of the Theban and Argive women; the bereavement of both groups is merged in the dual lament of Antigone and Argia (sc. 13: 362-408), who together make fifteen of the twenty-two speeches made by human figures in the episode. The scenes of general lamentation depict the sorrow of the Thebans (epis. 23, sc. 4: 1-59) and the grief of the Argives (epis. 23, sc. 6: 12.105-40; epis. 24, sc. 13: 797-809) over their dead, while the scenes of mourning for individuals centre on the lament of Creon during the funeral rites of Menoeceus (epis. 23, sc. 2: 60-104; speech: 72-92, 94-102), the lament of Argia over the corpse of Polynices (sc. 11: 312-48; speech: 322-48), and the various speeches of Argia and Antigone over the same figure (sc. 13: 362-408; speeches: 366f., 374-80, 382-85, 392-404, 406-08).

The aforementioned Theban and Argive scenes of general mourning are followed by scenes focusing on the grief and bereavement of particular figures over specific victims. While the scenes of general mourning consist entirely of narrative description, those portraying the grief and suffering of

67

mourners over individual victims focus on lament speeches that particularise the sense of loss and sorrow that pervades the dramatic context in the preceding scenes of general mourning. In addition to invigorating the narrative and heightening the dramatic effect of the episode, the lament speeches enhance the atmosphere of grief and loss and also the credibility of the dramatic situation generally.

This chapter has examined aspects of the structural organisation and narrative design of the *Thebaid*, primarily in relation to the rôle, function and placement of the speeches. On the most basic level the speeches are important for the variety they afford to the scenes and the welcome relief they bring from descriptive narrative. Far more vital is the rôle that the speeches play in the narrative strategy, since they serve not only to establish and vary the pace at which events unfold but also to provide motivation for subsequent action (causative function) and to treat the causes of previous events (noncausative function); the speeches also serve the related function of providing a means of facilitating the transition from one scene to the next. The causative function of the speeches is especially significant, since their motivation of the action pushes the narrative forward and points forward to future events in the epic; the noncausative speeches emphasise and explore issues already presented in the narrative. The succession of short speeches that forms the basis for many of the dramatic scenes advances the action and creates a strong dramatic effect.

One of the most crucial functions of the speeches is the revelation of character. The characterising function of the speeches is treated in chapter 5, but the brief comments on the subject in this chapter reveal that the speeches help to define the personalities of the characters generally and to furnish psychological characterisations of the speakers in specific dramatic situations. Another important function of the speeches considered briefly in this chapter is the presentation of information extraneous or peripheral to the main plot; these speeches deal with events that have occurred prior to the action of the scene in which they are placed or at the same time as the main action but in another setting.

Not only are the speeches of vital importance in terms of their effect on the development of the poetic narrative, the psychological characterisation of leading individuals and presentation of peripheral information, but they also assume a critical rôle in the thematic design of the epic, namely the presentation and treatment of thematic elements. Understanding the interactive relationship and ongoing dialectic between speech and narrative is crucial to appreciating the thematic and dramatic tensions raised by conflicting issues. The narrative affords a conceptual apparatus against which to evaluate the speeches, which examine, emphasise, and clarify the thematic issues raised in the main narrative, thereby reinforcing the thematic link between the speech passages and narrative substance of the poem. In addition, the speeches are also important for their rôle in establishing tone and mood, varying the level of emotional intensity in the narrative, and amplifying the epic circumstances through the infusion of graphic detail. Ultimately the speeches function as vehicles of expression of Statius' own thoughts and feelings on the position of humankind in relation to fellow humanity and the supernatural powers.

CHAPTER 3

RHETORICAL-TYPE SPEECHES

Forensic Orations

Forensic[1] speeches before an assembly are common in Homeric epic but comparatively rare in Roman epic.[2] There are only two speeches in Statian epic that can be considered properly to be forensic.[3] Both are delivered before a council of the gods (*Theb.* 1.197-311). The *concilium deorum* is a conventional literary theme that epic poets employ for a variety of purposes. The important speeches of Jupiter (1.214-47) and Juno (250-82) are spoken in a setting that is closely modelled on other epic *concilia* such as those of Ovid and Vergil.[4]

---

[1] Also commonly referred to as 'dicanic', 'judicial', 'legalistic' or 'political' speeches.

[2] Fingerle (1939: 295ff.) lists sixty-five *Versammlungsreden* (assembly speeches) in the *Iliad* and thirty-six in the *Odyssey*, which include *Agorarden* (speeches delivered at an assembly of the people) and *Bulereden* (speeches delivered at a council of chiefs or elders). Highet (1972: 380f.) cites ten forensic speeches (which he calls 'political and legalistic') in the *Aeneid* but curiously includes those not actually spoken before an assembly, council or court, such as the private speeches of Anna to Dido (4.31-53), Aeneas to Dido (4.333-61) and Latinus to Turnus (12.19-45).

[3] Forensic oratory is concerned specifically with the art of speaking in the courtroom, but refers generally to any type of speech-making in which an individual denounces or attempts to justify, explain or even rationalise the past actions of others. The theme of such a speech usually evolves around the ideas of justice and rightness. The term *forensic* is also used in the contemporary sense of a debate before an assembly concerned with the deliberation and evolution of policy on a matter of vital public importance. It is true that the speeches of Jupiter (1.214-47) and Juno (1.250-82) are not spoken in the courtroom; however, they are certainly forensic because the speakers condemn and rationalise the behaviour of the Theban and Argive races in a setting analogous to a political debate.

[4] See ch. 1 of my *The Mythic Voice of Statius* (forthcoming).

70

Arrangement

Rhetoricians and poets in the early Empire would have been well versed in the composition of a forensic speech and its attendant divisions. Forensic oratory formed the foundation of rhetorical theory, particularly in regard to structure, since it was a highly schematised speech type that almost invariably demanded the same elements. The rhetorician would sometimes develop his argument along the traditional lines of division for such a speech in his treatment of the *controuersia*, a judicial exercise requiring a similar strategy to that employed by the advocate before a court or an assembly; in both situations the task of the speaker essentially was to condemn or defend the proposition or actions of another person or group.

Quintilian divides the forensic speech into five parts. He names these as the *prooemium* (*exordium*), the opening of the speech; *narratio*, the statement of facts; *probatio*, the argument itself (includes the *propositio*, the main proposal); *refutatio*, the refutation of an opposing argument; and *peroratio* [*conclusio*], the concluding statement. Cicero divides the speech into four parts (*principium* [*prooemium*], *narratio*, *confirmatio*, *peroratio*), in his *Partitiones Oratoriae* (1.4, 2.33-51), following the lead of Aristotle (*Rhet.* 3.13-19). But earlier in the *De Inuentione* he had followed the example of the *Rhetorica ad Herennium* in dividing the speech into six parts, separating *partitio* (the organisation of the main points to be treated in the argument) from *narratio* and *reprehensio* (*refutatio*) from *confirmatio* (*probatio*). This pattern became the traditional arrangement of the speech, at least in the Republic. But Quintilian treats the *propositio* as a component part of the *probatio*, because the speaker obviously has to propose what he intends to prove in his case (*Inst.* 3.9.1f.). Quintilian tells us that during his time most authorities favoured the fivefold division he proposes (3.9.1).

The sole purpose of the *prooemium* is to make the audience well disposed, attentive and willing to receive instruction. This can be achieved directly or by suggestion (*Inst.* 4.1.5; e.g., *Theb.* 1.214-18, 250f.). The *narratio* sets forth the facts of the situation in as favourable a light as possible in order to lay the groundwork for the *propositio* that follows (cf. *Inst.* 4.2.20ff.; e.g., *Theb.* 1.219-23, 251-58). They should be stated in a concise, lucid and credible manner (*Inst.* 4.2.31f.).

The *probatio* is technically the most important part of the forensic speech (e.g., *Theb.* 1.224ff.). In this section the speaker sets forth his/her claim or *propositio* (e.g., *Theb.* 1.224-26, 241-43, 243-45, 259, 270-72) and presents the evidence and reasons for accepting or adopting it. The argument will usually consider the ideas of justice and injustice (e.g., *Theb.* 227ff., 260-62, 266-70, 273-80)—but can also consider other matters of expediency, honour and necessity (of which there are various subdivisions), although Quintilian rejects the last (*Inst.* 3.8.22ff.).[5] *Refutatio*, the rebuttal of an opponent's argument (e.g., *Theb.* 1.250-82), is acknowledged by Quintilian as being more difficult than *probatio*, but the methods of argumentation employed are the same (*Inst.* 5.13.1f.).

In the *peroratio* the speaker should be as brief as possible, taking no longer than is necessary to encapsulate the main points of the argument (e.g., *Theb.* 1.280-82). The purpose of this practice is to refresh the mind of the judge with the pertinent facts of the case without giving the appearance of presenting a second speech (*Inst.* 6.1ff.). The second function of the peroration is to appeal to the judge by amplifying his feelings (6.1.9). These appeals should be brief (6.1.27). The appeal to emotions can be of use in other parts of the speech but should be employed more briefly (6.1.51). The amplification of human emotions in literary speeches was a general feature of literature during the postclassical period. This characteristic was an offshoot of the natural impulse of the rhetoricians and poets to devote their attention to and elaborate on a particular idea.

Naturally the speaker before a court or assembly did not always develop his arguments along the traditional lines of division for a forensic speech. Nor did Statius, whose arrangement of ideas in his literary speeches often owes rather less to the traditional rules of rhetoric than to the impetus of the speeches and his desire to create a bold stylistic effect.

The Debate Between Juno and Jupiter (1.214-302)

JUPITER (1.214-47), JUNO (1.250-82)

The narrative preceding the first speech of Jupiter depicts him as the supreme ruler of the universe who inspires awe and fear in the lesser gods (1.197-213, esp. 212f.; cf. 248); the subsequent speech confirms this initial impression by betraying the unremitting hostility of this omnipotent tyrant

---

[5] Technically, the issue of justice (*iustum*) is only one aspect of the general consideration of honour (*honestum*).

toward humanity and his intention of effecting the partial destruction of the human race (214-47, esp. 241-43, 245f.; cf. 291f.). The thesis of the first speech is that the inherent criminality of humankind is deserving of divine retribution. Jupiter catalogues a list of past crimes perpetrated by various human figures but which in fact were either committed by them unknowingly, instigated largely by the gods, or which have already been avenged (1.227-47; cf. 3.180-205, 4.553-78 for the similar catalogues of Aletes and Manto, respectively). Notwithstanding any possible degree of guilt that should be attributed to some of these individuals, there still remains the burning question of why the innocent descendants of these figures should be made to suffer for the crimes of others. What seems apparent is that the concept of divine 'justice' does not take into account the degree of human accountability in the perpetration of a criminal act, only the fact that an offence has occurred and retribution is required. Thus human beings are often made to suffer for the crimes of the gods.

Jupiter has no adequate defence to the important argument of Juno concerning the injustice of punishing innocent citizens for the crimes of their ancestors (1.266-70). Her rebuttal containing references to the harmful intervention of Jupiter in human affairs draws attention to his purely destructive aspect (251-58). The feeble reply of the cosmocrator (285ff.) to the objections raised by Juno to his plan bears testimony to the unconcern of the supreme deity for natural justice; the concluding words of his reply (*certo reliqua ordine ducam*, 302)—and significantly of the entire scene—place responsibility for the events that ensue squarely on the shoulders of the omnipotent deity.[6]

Deliberative Speeches

Deliberative[7] speeches are spoken frequently in Homeric and Vergilian epic. The situation is no different in Statian epic; over one-fifth of the

---

[6] For a full treatment of this scene, see ch. 1 of my *The Mythic Voice of Statius* (forthcoming).

[7] The term 'deliberative' is used in the sense of a person attempting to persuade someone else to perform some action or to agree with his/her point of view on a particular matter. Deliberative oratory is also referred to commonly by the terms 'persuasory', 'hortatory', 'advisory' and 'symbouleutic'.

speeches in the *Thebaid* can be classified purely as deliberative. However, if other types of speeches that are persuasive in intention are included, such as forensic orations, prayers, combat and noncombat exhortations, then it can be safely said that well over one-third of the speeches fall into this category. The average length of the deliberative speeches is 12.7 lines; they range in length from just one-sixth of a line (12.458) to forty-one lines (12.546-86).

The purpose of a deliberative speech quite obviously is to effect persuasion. Ultimately the effectiveness of a deliberation should be judged on whether it is successful or not in persuading the listener. Quite naturally the most effective deliberation in the *Thebaid* is the one in which the speaker is able to arouse the sympathy of the addressee and convince him of the merits of his/her argument. Almost two-thirds of the deliberative speeches are at least partly successful in achieving their aims.[8] The speaker of a deliberation does not always adhere strictly to the truth in narrating the facts of the situation, as shown in the speech of Laius' shade to Eteocles (2.102-19).[9] Even though Laius' shade feels compelled to employ every possible deception available to him—verbal and supranormal—Eteocles is convinced as to his sincerity.

Statius is obviously aware that the most important aspect of the deliberation is its effect upon the listener. The rhetorical elements of style play a most important rôle in this regard, since when they are carefully deployed, they exert a most powerful effect by intensifying and clarifying the thoughts and feelings of the speaker so they can be conveyed more readily (cf. Cic. *De Or.* 3.215-17). Rhetorical questions and exclamations are frequently employed for this purpose and serve the added purpose of helping to distinguish the deliberation from the surrounding narrative.

It is not always possible to distinguish clearly between the different divisions of speeches in the poem; this in part can be attributed to the desire of Statius to convey an air of naturalness in the speeches of his characters. In this regard he mirrors the actual practice of the ancient orator. Ultimately

---

[8] Thirty-six of the fifty-six deliberative speeches wholly or partly (appear to) secure their real objectives: 2/2 of prophets and attendants (4.610-24, 12.406-08), 12/17 of human women (3.687-710, 5.104-29, 132-42, 5.245-47, 7.247-52, 7.483-85, 11.708-39, 12.196-204, 12.458, 12.458, 12.459, 12.459, 12.546-86), 7/11 of supernatural figures (2.102-19, 9.511-19, 9.825-30, 10.206-11, 10.662-71, 11.76-112, 12.299-308), and 15/26 of monarchs, princes and warriors (1.468-73, 2.152-72, 3.367-81, 5.43-47, 7.539-59, 8.138-50, 8.735-44, 9.211-17, 9.815-19, 10.330-35, 10.351-59, 11.242-45, 11.269-96, 11.594f., 12.149-66).

[9] See pp. 80f.

74

the speeches are not controlled by rhetorical principles but control them; as such the speeches function as an integral part of the poetic narrative and are governed by many nonrhetorical conditions.

Arrangement

The basic five parts of a forensic speech discussed by Quintilian (*Inst.* 3.9.1)—*prooemium, narratio, probatio* (including the *propositio*), *refutatio* and *peroratio*—were easily adapted by orators and poets to suit the requirements of the deliberative speech. As in the forensic speech, each section of the deliberation has a specific function. Some of the sections in the deliberative speech differ slightly in purpose, approach and emphasis from the sections that comprise the forensic oration. Specifically, the *prooemium* is intended to make the addressee attentive and receptive to the rest of the deliberation; the *narratio* is the presentation of the facts of the situation in such a way that the subsequent request (*propositio*) is likely to gain the sympathy of the listener; the *probatio* (*tractatio*) is the setting forth of the reasons—based usually on matters of expediency and honour—for acceding to the request; the *refutatio* is the rejection of the opponent's argument; and the *peroratio* consists of a brief summary of the main points and an emotional appeal in which the speaker attempts to play on the feelings of the addressee.

In the sense that the aims of forensic and deliberative speeches are identical—namely, to convince the audience of the merits of the case and to win them over—there is little to distinguish between these two types of oratory. Although the parts of the forensic speech can be readily applied to the composition of deliberative speeches, the special requirements of the deliberation demand some adjustment in the structural arrangement of the speech. The structure required for deliberative oratory is considerably freer than that needed for the forensic oration, in which the semblance of a pentapartite scheme is almost always apparent. Often the arrangement of the speech is unsystematic, lacks one or more parts, or the divisions between the sections are difficult to define because the sections appear to run together.

Sometimes the speakers in the *Thebaid* dispense with a *prooemium* when they are not interested in placating their addressees (e.g., 2.393ff.) or when it is apparent that their interlocutors are well disposed toward them from the start (cf. Quint. *Inst.* 3.8.6). The speakers in Statian epic frequently do not include a *narratio*, especially when the facts of the situation are understood by all parties to the issue (cf. Quint. *Inst.* 3.8.10). This parallels the actual practice of many declaimers in their treatment of the *suasoria*, a deliberative exercise in which the facts of the case are well set out in advance and whose treatment generally corresponds to that of the deliberative speech.

The request (or *propositio*) of the speaker in Statian epic is almost always stated in a lucid manner, often with the verbs in the imperative—as it frequently is by the declaimer in his treatment of the *suasoria*. Often the proposal consists of two, three or more parts inserted at appropriate points in the speech, as in the deliberation of Polynices (11.155-92). The *probatio* (or *tractatio*) of a deliberative speech in Statian epic is generally less elaborate and less concerned with ideas of justice and rightness—and therefore is more concerned with matters of possibility and expedience—than are the proofs in the forensic speeches of Jupiter (1.214-47) and Juno (1.250-82). Although the *refutatio* seldom figures in a speech of the deliberative type, sometimes there is an anticipation of one or more possible objections to the argument based on one of the general or minor themes for argument, as in Evadne's plea to Theseus (12.546-86, esp. 573).

The *peroratio* is a common but by no means necessary, constituent of the deliberation. Sometimes the speaker merely breaks off after stating his/her *propositio* and does not even bother to give the reasons for approving it. On those occasions where the speaker also dispenses with the *prooemium* and *narratio*, the deliberation is scaled down to the bare minimum, consisting only of the request or proposal, as in Oedipus' speech to Antigone (11.594f.).

Four deliberations are analysed below for their structure. Naturally the speakers often deviate from the traditional lines of division for such speeches. Even though it is not easy—nor perhaps even desirable—to distinguish between the parts of some deliberative speeches, they are nevertheless discernible in some cases. The deliberations owe their arrangement primarily to the natural impetus of the speeches themselves and the dramatic requirements of the narrative contexts in which they appear. In the final analysis the rules governing their arrangement are dispensable because of their elasticity. Notwithstanding the difficulties inherent in attempting a structural analysis of these speeches, some effort will be made below to demonstrate the relevance—or lack of applicability—of the traditional division to their composition. In so doing there is no suggestion on my part that Statius *consciously* arranged his deliberations according to this division. The great danger in such an exercise is to risk the possibility of imposing a structural framework upon the speeches of this type in a way never intended by the poet.

The structures of four deliberative speeches (Tiresias, 4.610-24; Tisiphone, 11.76-112; Polynices, 11.155-92; Evadne, 12.546-86) are analysed in order to illustrate the relevance of the traditional arrangement to the composition of deliberative speeches in the poem.

TIRESIAS (4.610-24)

Prooemium (610-14)

Renowned ruler of Thebes, there has been no day favourable to Thebes since your passing. O you who have avenged sufficiently your bloody death, O shade, whose offspring have fully expiated their crimes, O wretched one, whom do you flee?

Narratio (614-19)

That man Oedipus whom you complain about is a living corpse and feels joined to death; he is covered with dirt and blood and is destitute of vision. Believe me, it is a lot worse than death! There is no reason to avoid your innocent grandson.

Probatio (619-24)

> *propositio* (619-21): Look here and sate yourself with sacrificial blood; then reveal the future and the victims of the war, whether you are hostile or pity the lot of your family.
>> *iucundum* (622-24): Then I will allow you to cross the forbidden Lethe in a vessel of your choice and I will place you back gently in the sacred region.

TISIPHONE (11.76-112)

Prooemium (76-79)

I alone, sister, have borne the weight of Pluto's commands and the frenzied labours thrust upon me in the face of a hostile world, while you reside unthreatened in Elysium.

Narratio (80-94)

The rewards for my recent efforts are ample: bloodstained battlefields, blood-filled waters, the countless souls that swarm Lethe's bank—triumphs for which Mars takes the credit. It was I who inspired Tydeus and Capaneus to their deeds of lawlessness. Now I am exhausted by my labours.

Probatio (95-108)

> *propositio* (95f.): You are rested and still maintain your rage: let us combine our strength.

> *magnum, gloriosum* (97-100): It is no mere battle that we prepare, but fraternal strife. Although Fides and Pietas will resist, they will be defeated and the brothers will engage in hand-to-hand combat. A glorious deed!

propositio (100f.): Let us fit ourselves with hatred and armed discord.

> *facile* (101-08): You need to choose only whom you will provoke: both are tractable and susceptible to our influences, even though the mob is of two minds; Jocasta and Antigone may attempt to hinder our purpose; and Oedipus already regrets his curse.

Peroratio (108-112)

I do not wish to infect Thebes with madness without your aid. Incite Polynices to the crime; do not let Adrastus or the Argives delay you. Depart now and return to the mutual fray!

POLYNICES (11.155-92)

Prooemium (155f.)

I, who am the last survivor of my comrades and the Argolic nation, O father, have resolved belatedly. . . .

Narratio (157-67)

I should have fought Polynices in single combat before so much Achaean blood was shed. But since the moment for such austere bravery has passed, I should pay what I deserve. You hide your wounds and revere your son-in-law's affliction and shame. I came to your city when you were ruling in peace and justice. Some other city should have been my host—I who was exiled from my country and throne.

Probatio (167-86, 188-92)

> *propositio* (167-73): Exact your punishment. Do not attempt to dissuade me from challenging my brother; I will remain unmoved by all entreaties.

>> *iustum, debitum* (173-82): I have brought ruin and suffering to Argos. Many have perished on my account; I lacked the courage of some. Due requital for my wrongs must be made.

> *propositio* (183-86): Let the Argives, whose families and homes I have destroyed, see me fight my brother and pray for his victory.

78

propositio (188, 190-92): Beloved father, give my body due rights of burial; return my ashes to Argos; join Argia in marriage to someone more worthy than me.

mansuetum (188f.): I am not entirely to blame for what has happened: the gods and the Fates share the guilt with me.

Peroratio (187)[10]

Farewell, my wife, and farewell, Mycenae!

EVADNE (12.546-86)

Prooemium (546-48)

Warlike son of Aegeus, for whom Fortune affords the opportunity of reknown through our ruin. We are not strangers by race; nor are we guilty of a horrible crime.

Narratio (548-69)

Our home was not Argos; our husbands were princes. There was no need for them to chasten Thebes. We do not complain that our husbands were cut down: that is the law and fortune of war. Our husbands were not monsters: they were men like you. Creon forbids their burial, yet Nature, the gods, Jupiter and Athens do nothing. The seventh day has come since their deaths; already the birds and beasts detest the repulsive nourishment and the field exudes foul vapours. Little remains but bare bones and decayed matter.

Probatio (569-73, 579-82)

propositio (569f.): Hasten, venerable son of Cecrops!

decorum, *fas* (570-73): Such vengeance suits you, before others suffer and are denied the due rights of burial; Creon's fury has no bounds.

propositio (579f.): Consider this triumph to be worthy of you and perform this one labour.

fas (580-82): Earth, heaven and the underworld demand this deed.

Refutatio (573-79)[11]

I admit that we made war, but our hatred and anger has subsided. You also have warred, for we have heard of your extraordinary deeds.

---

[10] The expression of farewell is entirely appropriate for a concluding sentiment. It appears that Polynices has suitably concluded his speech in 11.187, but then he proceeds to make one final request almost as an afterthought.

[11] Statius places the brief anticipatory *refutatio* between the two *propositiones* of the *probatio*.

Peroratio (583-86)
May your battles never lack Minerva's assistance; may Hercules never envy your exploits; may your mother Aethra always behold you triumphant in your chariot; may Athens remain invincible and never make a prayer such as this one of mine.

Supernatural Deliberations

Except in the case of a supreme divinity like Jupiter, who can issue his decrees without any fear of retribution, the gods in the *Thebaid* entreat their fellow deities respectfully when seeking favours from them. Although a plea for aid addressed to a divine colleague is often made in a respectful and rational manner and consists of one or more pledges—even when addressed to an inferior deity—the ultimate success of the appeal often hinges more on the ability of the speaker to arouse sympathy than on the logic of the argument; this assumes, of course, that such an appeal does not oppose the will of Jupiter and his plan for the destruction of Thebes and Argos. To this end the traditional artifices of rhetoric are especially important. There is seldom any need for divinities to employ persuasive techniques in dealing with their human counterparts; when this occurs, the circumstances are indeed exceptional.

There are four supernatural deliberations of considerable significance; they are spoken by the shade of Laius (2.102-19), Venus (3.269-91), Bacchus (7.155-92) and Tisiphone (11.76-112).

SHADE OF LAIUS (2.102-19)

The speech of this supernatural being follows closely upon his arrival in Thebes (2.65ff.).[12] The ghost commences his speech by admonishing the monarch for his idleness and lack of concern for the actions of Polynices (2.102-04):

non somni tibi tempus, iners qui nocte sub alta,
germani secure iaces, ingentia dudum
acta uocant rerumque graues, ignaue, paratus.

---

[12] For a full discussion of this scene, see ch. 1 of my *The Mythic Voice of Statius* (forthcoming).

Laius' shade proceeds to tell Eteocles that his brother, encouraged by his Argive union and bond with Tydeus, is confidently plotting against him to seize the Theban throne (102-14). Laius' reproach of Eteocles actually demonstrates the monarch's innocence, since his repose and lack of concern over the activities of Polynices show clearly that he has not yet contemplated seriously the possibility of retaining the throne.

In addition, the accusation levelled by Laius against Polynices concerning the exiled prince's alleged intention to recover the throne by violent means is a gross distortion of the truth, for up to this point in the text there has been no substantive demonstration of Polynices' desire to ascend the throne—overwhelming as this is (cf. 1.314-23)—by a path other than the one negotiated amicably with Eteocles (cf. 1.138ff.). Even the exile's decision to journey to Argos, the result of which is his acquisition of the means to gain the Theban throne by force if desired, is depicted as an action motivated by forces outside his control (1.324-28). There has been no firm resolve on the part of Polynices—in spite of 1.314ff.—or the Argives to commence war with Thebes in order to gain the throne for the exiled prince; nor has there been any real indication prior to the harmful intervention of the gods that such a step may be necessary.

Laius is not content with these deceptions, but misrepresents Jupiter's purpose in asserting that the god has sent him to Eteocles out of pity to forewarn the monarch of Polynices' evil intentions (2.115f.). He conveys the supreme ruler's direction to Eteocles to retain the throne (116-19):

> habe Thebas, caecumque cupidine regni,
> ausurumque eadem, germanum expelle, nec ultra
> fraternos inhiantem obitus sine fidere coeptis
> fraudibus aut Cadmo dominas inferre Mycenas.

When Eteocles awakens he is full of horror and hatred for his brother and desires to wage war with his brother. His transformation is complete, as the subsequent simile stresses; Eteocles is likened to a tigress carrying off a man to feed her cubs (128-32). The effectiveness of Laius' persuasive speech is unquestionable.

VENUS (3.269-91)

After Jupiter dispatches Mars to incite the Argives to war against Thebes (3.229-39), Venus confronts the war god on his way to earth

(262ff.). The goddess commences her deliberation with a respectful invocation (*prooemium*) and a string of rhetorical questions (*narratio*) stressing the injustice of his intended action (269-74):

> bella etiam in Thebas, socer o pulcherrime, bella
> ipse paras ferroque tuos abolere nepotes?
> nec genus Harmoniae nec te conubia caelo
> festa nec hae quicquam lacrimae, furibundae, morantur?
> criminis haec merces? hoc fama pudorque relictus,
> hoc mihi Lemniacae de te meruere catenae?

Her protestations are designed to show Mars that she has a claim on his benevolence, especially the reference to the embarrassing incident when Vulcan ensnared her and Mars while they were in bed together.

The first proposal of Venus is ironically stated (*perge libens*, 275). She asserts that the injured pride of Vulcan would not stop him from performing any service on her behalf—or even for Mars, yet her simple prayer to the war god meets with deaf ears (275-82). The goddess complains about the marriage of their daughter Harmonia to Cadmus on account of the misfortunes that have plagued the Theban race and her since then, especially her daughter's metamorphosis into a serpent (282-91). She can see no justification for the affliction of Thebes (*nunc gentem immeritam*, 292). In spite of the self-interest that Venus betrays (*indigna parumne pertulimus*, 288f.), there is little question that Statius intends to elicit the sympathy of the audience for her on account of the numerous allusions in the text to Jupiter's unjust punishment of the Thebans, the great majority of whom are innocent of any wrong-doing. Here the reference to the metamorphosis of the innocent Harmonia into a serpent by the gods is evidence of the poet's belief that human suffering is not divine retribution for lawlessness; rather, it suggests that the innocent suffer no less than the guilty.

BACCHUS (7.155-92)

The inclusion in the narrative of a deliberative speech by Bacchus addressed to Jupiter is designed to demonstrate the injustice of Jupiter's scheme to punish Thebes. As in Venus' entreaty of Mars (3.269), Bacchus' invocation of Jupiter is respectful (*diuum sator optime*, 7.155). He attributes Jupiter's plan to destroy Thebes directly to Juno (156), a charge the divine ruler naturally denies (195f.). Bacchus excuses Jupiter for the violent death

82

of Semele—another example of harmful divine intervention—acknowledging that it was probably unintentional on his part, but observes that now he is purposely making plans to lay waste to Thebes (158-60).

Bacchus' speech confirms the impression that the plan for the destruction of Thebes is unjust and entirely the creation of a vindictive divine ruler. But Bacchus himself does not impress. He feigns powerlessness in war owing to his feminine attributes; therefore the Thebans are unwarlike and will be hopelessly outmatched on the battlefield (168-74). Judging by his previous actions (e.g., 1.11, 4.383-89, 7.211-14, 7.564-67), his claim of weakness is clearly unfounded and is intended primarily to elicit sympathy from the cosmocrator for his favourite city.

Bacchus describes the command of Jupiter for the annihilation of the Thebans as more cruel than their actual fate (176f.). He portrays the threatened destruction of Thebes as being directly the cause of Jupiter's unnecessary intervention in her affairs (155, 159f.) and the selection of a hostile Argos as her foe as evidence of the supreme deity's cruelty (175f.). He attempts to arouse the further sympathy of Jupiter by appealing for a new residence, but betrays an element of selfish concern by arguing that other divinities have been allowed to rule freely over various territories (182-88). Bacchus anticipates rightly that his claim on Jupiter's benevolence will not be received favourably, so he makes a final appeal for the welfare of Thebes based on his father's links with Thebes (189-92).

TISIPHONE (11.76-112)

As it becomes apparent in the penultimate book that the long-awaited duel between Eteocles and Polynices is fast approaching, the furies Tisiphone and Megaera are shown discussing the fate of the brothers (76ff.). Tisiphone asserts that she is accountable for the bloodshed and the deaths that have occurred in the war between Argos and Thebes—lines 56f. in the narrative preceding her speech substantiate her claim—even though Mars and Enyo maintain they are responsible for the devastation that has taken place (76-84). The Fury is especially proud of two bloody acts she has incited at the behest of Pluto (11.85ff.; cf. 8.69ff.). She has driven Tydeus to his horrible act of anthropophagy (11.85-88; cf. 8.71f., 751ff.) and provoked Capaneus to challenge Jupiter (11.88-91; cf. 8.76f., 10.831ff.). There remain two more deeds to provoke: the duel between Eteocles and Polynices (11.387ff.; cf. 8.69-71) and the refusal of Creon to permit the burial of the Argive corpses

(11.661-64; cf. 8.72-74). Tisiphone seeks the aid of her sister in effectuating the duel between the brothers. The strong impression conveyed by her speech is of the inevitability of the fraternal confrontation (cf. 11.79). The various attempts to prevent the fratricide by Fides, Pietas, Antigone and others will prove futile (cf. 98-108).

Deliberations of Monarchs, Princes and Warriors

Adrastus is the only monarch to make a deliberative speech in the *Thebaid*. Princes and warriors on both sides of the war make numerous deliberative speeches, the majority of them in the last third of the epic where most of the fighting takes place; the deliberations of Tydeus (2.393-409), Polynices (3.367-81, 11.155-92), and Creon (11.269-91) are among the most significant.

TYDEUS (2.393-404)

Tydeus arrives at the Theban court in the second book to persuade Eteocles to abide by his compact with Polynices and step down from the throne (389ff.). The envoy rudely dispenses with the customary ingratiatory references and launches a scathing attack upon Eteocles, accusing the monarch of having violated the compact of alternate rule with Polynices in retaining the throne and telling him that it is his turn to endure a year of harshness in exile (393ff.). Tydeus intentionally misrepresents the circumstances for his own purposes in suggesting that Polynices has endured harsh poverty while Eteocles has enjoyed the riches of Theban royalty (402ff.); in fact the situation is precisely the opposite, since Argos is far better off than Thebes in material wealth (cf. 1.144ff., 1.517ff., 2.432ff.). He further accuses Eteocles of having mocked Polynices during his brother's year of indigence and warns him of the consequences if he does not vacate the throne (406-09).

Not only is Tydeus unmindful of Eteocles' position in failing to address the monarch in a respectful manner, but also the hostile and threatening tone of his speech as well as his distortions are certain to alienate the monarch. However, there is of course nothing to suggest in the narrative that Eteocles would have been more conciliatory if Tydeus had been more ingratiating in his approach (cf. 387f.). Indeed a mild response from Eteocles to the admonitory speech of Tydeus would have been out of keeping with the usual behaviour of the monarch just as much as a diplomatic approach from Tydeus would have been out of character (cf. 391f.).

POLYNICES (3.367-81, 11.155-92)

After Tydeus returns from his ill-fated mission to Thebes, he tells of Eteocles' perfidy and exhorts the Argives to war (3.348-65). Polynices plays upon the alarm of the Argive councillors and skilfully manipulates the situation to his advantage. Every word of his artfully deceptive speech is cleverly contrived to win maximum support for his cause (367-81).

The exile commences his speech by claiming that he is despised by the gods for his guilty life (367f.). This is certainly true in a way that neither he nor the councillors can appreciate at the moment, but the meaning is all to apparent to the reader, who is only too aware of the gods' general hostility to the Theban royal line. The exile feigns anger over his brother's treatment of Tydeus and professes his shame in endangering the Aetolian's life by allowing him to go to Thebes to present his claim to the throne (368-70). Polynices realises that his brother would have killed him if he had returned to Thebes instead of Tydeus. In a brilliant *tour de force*, he actually expresses regret over having spared Eteocles the opportunity of slaying him, claiming that his brother's perpetration of fratricide would demand the worst possible punishment from the supernatural powers (371). Judging by the numerous instances of divine cruelty in the epic, the belief of Polynices in divine retribution is misfounded, since Eteocles' fratricide would merely serve as a convenient pretext for further supernatural violence against mankind.

Polynices offers to return to Thebes to meet his fate, arguing that the involvement of Thebes in his fate was never his intention (372-74, 378). He maintains that he understands how miserable it is to be torn from one's family and country and would not wish upon Argos the same sorrowful plight that has afflicted him (373-77). Polynices is not entirely honest, of course, since he has been graced with considerable good fortune through his marriage to Argia and is now a respected member of the Argive royal family. However, his purpose is to portray his predicament in the worst possible light in order to arouse the maximum sympathy of the councillors (cf. 381f.). His efforts in this direction are entirely successful, for the Argive men are moved to indignation and sympathy for his plight (382-86).

Polynices' deceptive speech contrasts markedly with his later words of genuine remorse for the devastation and suffering he has brought to Argos in the penultimate book (11.155-92). The exile resolves to fight Eteocles in single combat. His speech consists primarily of propositions to this effect and a plea for burial to Adrastus.[13] The most compelling sentiment of Polynices' speech to the Argives is his partial disclaimer of guilt in the unhappy fate of Argos (188f.):

> nec enim omnis culpa malorum
> me penes, et superi mecum Parcaeque nocentes

Polynices is aware that the gods and the Fates have conspired to implicate him in the doom of Argos. His unwillingness to accept the entire blame for the troubles that have plagued Argos since his arrival by rationalising his actions and placing them in a better light is not to be seen merely as an attempt to soothe his troubled conscience and gain the sympathy of Adrastus. The machinations of Jupiter and other divinities are all to apparent in the demise of Polynices and the ills that beset Argos.

CREON (11.269-96)

Creon is shown denouncing Eteocles in a memorable scene when the monarch shows indecision in responding to Polynices' challenge to meet in single combat (11.262ff.); his purpose is to provoke Eteocles into accepting the challenge of his brother. Creon is startled and angered by the possibility that Eteocles might not accept the challenge and commences his speech by pouring vitriol upon the monarch (269-72):

> ibis . . . neque te ulterius fratremque ducemque,
> pessime, funeribus patriae lacrimisque potentem,
> Eumenidum bellique reum, patiemur inulti.
> sat tua non aequis luimus periuria diuis.

Creon holds Eteocles directly responsible for the suffering that Thebes has endured and enumerates the ills that have visited the city under his rule. He likens the influence of Eteocles upon the city to a plague sent from heaven that has reduced the city to nothing yet still casts its shadow over its

---

[13] See pp. 78f. for the structure of this speech.

barrenness (273-75). This image is especially effective in conveying the desolation caused by the fraternal enmity of the brothers and in arousing sympathy for the victims of the war. The reference to the Theban corpses that have not received their due rights of burial (*hos ignis egentes / fert humus*, 276f.) is especially significant in view of the royal decree Creon issues upon his ascension to the throne prohibiting the burial of the Argive corpses (cf. 11.661-64, 12.94-103). Among the princes and warriors he cites who have suffered misfortune or death as a consequence of Eteocles' rule is his own son Menoeceus, whom he describes expressly as a victim of the throne (11.283f.).

In suggesting that Tiresias should conceive another oracle to bring about the death of his other son Haemon (11.288-92), Creon repeats an earlier belief that the oracle demanding Menoeceus' death was devised by Eteocles as a ruse to rid himself of a potential rival to the throne (cf. 10.699-703). Although there is no evidence in the text to substantiate his claim that Eteocles was involved in the manipulation of Apollo's oracle, the effect of such a charge serves to implicate the monarch more fully in the suffering of Thebes. Creon concludes his venomous attack on Eteocles by bringing the immediacy of Polynices' challenge back to his attention and asserting that even the monarch's mother and sister detest him (11.294-96).

Feminine Deliberations

The deliberations of women are among the longest speeches in the *Thebaid*. The deliberative speech of Evadne (12.546-86) is the most important.

EVADNE (12.546-86)

The sole speech of Evadne, wife of Capaneus, is the longest—and the last—persuasion in the poem. On behalf of the Argive women she speaks carefully and persuasively in her attempt to obtain the assistance of the Athenian king Theseus in burying their dead husbands, as a structural analysis of her speech reveals.[14] The structure and constituents of Evadne's plea to Theseus correspond substantially to the prescription for the *presbeutikos logos* recorded by the rhetorician Menander (*Epid.* Sp.

---

[14] For the structure see pp. 79f.

3.423.6-424.2). There is mention of Theseus and his achievements (*Theb.* 12.546, 575-79, 581f.; cf. Men. *Epid.* Sp. 3.423.7-14), the former standing of Argos (*Theb.* 12.549, 555-57); cf. Men. *Epid.* Sp. 3.423.14-19), a vivid description of the city's current misfortune (*Theb.* 12.552, esp. 558-69; cf. Men. *Epid.* Sp. 3.423.19-25), and a strong emotional appeal for assistance (*Theb.* 12.569f., 579-86; cf. Men. *Epid.* Sp. 3.423.25-32). The correspondences demonstrate that Statius was greatly influenced by the tradition of the *presbeutikos logos*, which was later preserved by Menander in his rhetorical treatise.

It is ironic that Evadne should base her appeal to Theseus for aid on the righteousness of her cause, for her husband is the most blasphemous figure in the war and the antithesis of a man such as Adrastus, who is portrayed generally as a representation of justice and rightness. The claim of Evadne that the husbands of the Argive women were neither Cyclopes nor Centaurs who had been felled in battle is technically true; however, the close relationship between the actions of the men—especially those of Tydeus and her husband Capaneus—and the monsters, who represent the baser forces of nature, is patently obvious. Notwithstanding any measure of guilt that is attributable to the Argive heroes for their various actions during the war, the claim of Evadne upon the services of Theseus is just, since Creon's violation of natural law demands correction and retribution.

Prayers

There are thirty prayers to the gods, demigods or deified spirits in the *Thebaid*.[15] They can be divided according to their structural and topical elements into two groups: demonstrative and deliberative. The first group of prayers consists of structural and topical elements that invite comparison

---

[15] Appel (1909: 51) lists thirty-five prayers in the *Thebaid*. The prayers in the *Thebaid* he neglects to mention are those of Adrastus (1.498-510), Hippomedon (9.506-10), Eteocles (11.210-25, 248f.) and Argia (12.256-67). The speech of Menoeceus in 10.680f. is not a prayer, as Appel asserts; rather, it is a responsion to a persuasion from a figure whom Menoeceus at first thinks is Manto, then realises is in fact Virtus disguised as the prophetess. Appel also mentions the prayers of the poet to Apollo, the Muses or other divinities in his list (4.32ff., 4.69ff., 6.296ff., 7.628, 9.315ff., 10.628ff., 10.827ff., 11.576ff.). I cannot accept Appel's citation of 1.22ff. as a prayer of the poet; perhaps he means 1.15ff. There are almost the same number of prayers (twenty-nine) in the *Aeneid* as in the *Thebaid*.

with the guidelines on hymnal composition recorded by later rhetoricians such as Menander and pseudo-Dionysius. This is hardly surprising, since the ancient rhetoricians regarded poetry as a branch of rhetoric and cited examples of rhetorical figures and of various generic classes from poetry and rhetoric of prayers composed loosely according to the fivefold division of the deliberative speech set out by Quintilian (*Inst.* 3.1.9ff.). Many of the topical elements that constitute the speeches in both groups resemble the components of Homeric and Vergilian prayers.

The importance of the prayers in the *Thebaid* is evident in their frequency and form. The profound solicitude of the suppliants over their relationship with the gods is inherent in the ritualism of the formal prayers. There are frequent references to the gods associated with the tendency for spoken prayers to accompany important actions. The suppliants customarily express a desire to earn the benevolence of the gods; their prayers usually involve appeals to sympathy, natural justice, expediency, honour or practical reason. In the majority of cases their pleas are sufficiently skilful to earn the favour of the gods, in spite of the pervasive hostility of the supernatural powers toward humankind.[16]

Although the prayers are diversified, particularly in their content, and their literary phraseology does not reflect the actual wording of genuine religious prayers, their formulation mirrors some of the exacting qualities that appear in Roman public and private invocations. The meticulous invocation of the deities and the formulation of the prayers to include every possibility betray the general anxiety of suppliants. The aspect of particularisation and the catalogue of divine appellations are further evidence of this solicitude. There is inherent in the composition of many of the prayers the notion that they may go unheeded unless the deities are invoked in keeping with the conventional practice. It is noteworthy that human suppliants never engage in dialogue with divinities in the *Thebaid*.

---

[16] A prayer fulfilled is one that earns a favourable response from the gods for the suppliant or the individual or group on whose behalf the invocation is made, even though sometimes the prayer may not be fulfilled in precisely the terms that the suppliant has requested, or is only partially or presumably fulfilled. Based on this definition, seventeen prayers are fulfilled in the *Thebaid*: 1.56-87 (Oedipus), 1.643-61 (Coroebus), 1.682-720 (Adrastus), 3.471-96 (Amphiaraus), 4.473-87, 4.501-18 (Tiresias), 4.753-71 (Adrastus), 6.197-201 (Lycurgus), 6.633-37 (Parthenopaeus), 7.779-88, 8.90-122 (Amphiaraus), 8.588-91 (Tydeus), 9.548-50 (Capaneus), 10.67-69 (Argolic mothers), 10.365-70 (Dymas), 12.256-67 (Argia), 12.771-73 (Theseus).

Statius could hardly be expected to conform strictly to the prescriptions for hymnal composition and the divisions of the deliberative speech recorded by the rhetoricians. The composition of the prayers in the epic depends primarily on the dramatic exigencies of the specific context for which they are composed. Statius does not always hold himself to the academic formula of the *diuisio* in his composition of deliberative prayers, either because of his tendency to strive for a bold and novel effect or because the circumstances of the prayer necessitate a deviation from the usual arrangement.

The prayers that reveal a debt to display rhetoric and poetry, such as the Sminthiac hymn and devotional rite, tend to be more formalised and less personal than private prayers. In public and private prayers the suppliants take care to ensure that the relevant divinities are invoked; sometimes the suppliants invoke unspecified deities whose benevolence they may have earned for their devotion. After the invocation is made, the residences of the deities are frequently listed and their functions designated. The recounting of deeds and the formal request is intended to foster a general benevolence on the part of the divinities invoked. In the majority of cases the approach to the god is reverential and the petition prudent; the argument is usually skilful, if occasionally plausible, specious or tragically ironic.

Demonstrative and deliberative prayers are spoken by gods, kings, ex-monarchs, warriors, priestesses and other women. Most of the deliberative type are protreptic, but there are a couple of apotreptic prayers. These deliberative prayers contain various components—sacrificial, votary, comminatory, prophetic and vituperative. The prayers and their contexts contribute significantly to the themes of the epic.

Demonstrative Prayers

A few prayers bear the topical and structural characteristics of the hymnal formulae composed by later rhetoricians such as Menander and pseudo-Dionysius. There is no doubt that these rhetoricians were influenced in their composition of the hymnal prescriptions by the cultural and social milieu of the Second Sophistic and the specific occasions of presentation. Nevertheless, the treatises of Menander and pseudo-Dionysius preserve the learning of earlier ages, for they cite the rules for hymn composition based on their studies of a number of poets and rhetoricians throughout classical antiquity; therefore an investigation of their relation to the prayers in the *Thebaid* is a worthwhile exercise. Modern scholars have examined the *Silvae* in order to determine their relation to the prescriptions of the handbooks,[17] but have neglected to consider the influence that the rhetorical treatises may have exerted on Statius in his composition of the speeches in the *Thebaid*. Since the *Thebaid* was frequently recited as a show piece, it is hardly surprising that some of the prayers reveal a debt to the influence of display rhetoric and poetry.

The Sminthiac Hymn

ADRASTUS (1.682-720)

Adrastus' formal hymn to Apollo in book 1 reveals a significant debt to display oratory. The context is Polynices' confession of his Theban ancestry to Adrastus (1.676ff.). The regent replies with compassion to Polynices' confession (682ff.) and naïvely alleges Polynices can escape punishment for the crimes of his ancestors (*nec culpa nepotibus obstat*, 690). Adrastus fails to recognise that humankind is enmeshed in forces that he/she can neither extricate himself from nor control. His deferential prayer to Apollo, whom he refers to as *seruator parentum* (694), is particularly ironic in view of the accompanying festivities and his kingdom's eventual plight, since Apollo is only too aware of what the future holds for the Argives.

Because of the identification and conflation of the Roman divinities with foreign deities, the major gods in the Roman pantheon were associated with a host of domestic and foreign localities. This phenomenon is illustrated in the opening lines of Adrastus' hymn—note the anaphora of *seu* (1.696f., 699, 701; cf. 705, 709, 717-719) and polyptoton of *te* (696, 698), figures characteristic of the formal hymn[18]—when the regent lists a number of Apollo's favourite abodes (696-702; emphasis added):

> Phoebe parens, *seu te* Lyciae Pataraea niuosis
> exercent dumeta iugis, *seu* rore pudico
> castaliae flauos amor est *tibi* mergere crines,
> *seu* Troiam Thymbraeus habes, ubi fama uolentem
> ingratis Phrygios umeris subiisse molares,
> *seu* iuuat Aegaeum feriens Latonius umbra
> Cynthus et adsiduam pelago non quaerere Delon.

---

[17] Leo (1892-93), Lohrisch (1905), Newmyer (1979: 10-44).

[18] Cf. Norden (1913: 177ff.).

This cataloguing and multiplication of geographical places is consistent with rhetorical practice (cf. Men. *Epid.* 3.334.27-335.20). Additionally, there is a psychological motive behind Adrastus' catalogue of Apollo's possible whereabouts. The regent presumes his hymn will not be heard by Apollo if it is addressed to a vacant abode of the god. Adrastus' catalogue of the god's residences appears to be an attempt to guard against this possibility.

Adrastus pleads in humble fashion to Apollo for divine favour. The structural and topical elements of Adrastus' formal hymn invite comparison with the prescriptions for honorific appeals to the gods described by the rhetoricians, including contemporaries of Statius such as Quintilian (*Inst.* 3.7, 12, 16) and (possibly) Aelius Theon (*Progymn.* Sp. 2.110). It would be inapt for the poet in epic to develop a speech to the extent of a complete Sminthiac oration, but the inclusion of certain topical elements in Adrastus' brief appeal to Apollo suggests that its composition is influenced by the prescriptions of the rhetoricians. Adrastus' plea conforms generally to the standard arrangement laid down by Menander in his rhetorical treatise.

Menander observes that the Sminthiac oration should commence with two *prooemia* and discusses the manner of commencing the oration and addressing Apollo (*Epid.* Sp. 3.437.6-438.29). In his oration Adrastus addresses Apollo by an appropriate epithet (*Phoebus parens, Theb.* 1.696), but dispenses with the *prooemium*. Menander next suggests that the orator should mention the origin of Apollo, present a brief encomium of the country, and proclaim the god as an ally (*Epid.* Sp. 3.438.29-440.20). After Adrastus addresses Apollo, the regent refers briefly to the myths concerning Apollo's birthplaces, mentioning Lycia (*Theb.* 1.696), Delos (702), and Cynthus (702), the abode of his mother Leto. Adrastus refers to Apollo's 'celestial parents' (*aetherii parentes*, 704), an oblique reference to Jupiter and Leto, which reinforces the earlier patronymic *Letoiden* (695). Menander notes that the encomiast should acknowledge Apollo's rôle as a helper of men (*Epid.* Sp. 3.440.20-24); however, Adrastus does not need to assert that Apollo is an ally at this point in the oration, since the regent did that earlier just prior to the hymn when he referred to the god as 'the saviour of the [Argive] fathers' (*seruator parentum, Theb.* 1.694).

According to Menander, the speaker should then cite Apollo's powers of archery (*Epid.* Sp. 3.441.3-442.8), prophecy (442.9-23), music (442.24-443.12) and medicine (443.13-444.2). This Adrastus does in the characteristically brief manner required of epic, omitting only a reference to medicine (*Theb.* 1.703-12). Menander observes that the rhetor should include mythological details to provide relevance to his appeal (*Epid.* Sp. 3.443.2-444.2). Adrastus refers deferentially to the god's victory over the giant Tityos (*Theb.* 1.709f.), the fate of Niobe (711), and his avengement of Phlegyas' burning of his temple at Delphi (713-15). The monarch's delineation of these powers and deeds is conventionalised (703-15; italics mine):

> tela *tibi* longeque feros lentandus in hostes
> arcus et aetherii dono cessere parentis
> aeternum florere genas; *tu* doctus iniquas
> Parcarum praenosse manus fatumque quod ultra est
> et summo placitura Ioui, quis letifer annus,
> bella quibus populis, quae mutent sceptra cometae;
> *tu* Phryga summittis citharae, *tu* matris honori
> terrigenam Tityon Stygiis extendis harenis;
> *te* uiridis Python Thebanaque mater ouantem
> horruit in pharetris, ultrix *tibi* torua Megaera
> ieiunum Phlegyan subter caua saxa iacentem
> aeterno premit accubitu dapibusque profanis
> instimulat, sed mixta famem fastidia uincunt.

The repetition and near repetition of the formal *tu* and its variant forms at or close to the beginning of clauses or lines again shows the importance of anaphora and polyptoton as characterising elements of the formal hymn.

Menander mentions that the orator should then go on to speak of the foundation of the city and its festivals (*Epid.* Sp. 3.444.2-26), then proceed to a description of Apollo's temple and statue (445.1-24); Statius omits these subjects in Adrastus' hymn, perhaps on account of the epic exigency for brevity. Adrastus concludes his oration thus (*Theb.* 1.716-20; my emphasis of anaphora):

> adsis o memor hospitii, Iunoniaque arua
> dexter ames, *seu* te roseum Titana uocari
> gentis Achaemeniae ritu, *seu* praestat Osirim
> frugiferum, *seu* Persei sub rupibus antri
> indignata sequi torquentem cornua Mithram.

This final appeal to Apollo, in which Adrastus employs various invocatory names of the god in identifying him with other sun-deities, mirrors the Menandrean prescription for the epilogue (*Epid.* Sp. 3.445.25-446.13).

An analysis of this demonstrative prayer appears to suggest that the poet composed the hymn section (*Theb.* 1.696-720) primarily in a conventional manner that precedes the content and meaning of the work as a whole. In fact Legras is so impressed by the similarity in form and *topoi* between Statius' version of the hymn and the rhetorical prescriptions that he fails to perceive the considerable thematic significance of the (general and specific) references in Adrastus' prayer.[19] Although the general references in Adrastus' prayer are commonplace in the Sminthiac hymn, their inclusion owes as much to the specific organic requirements of the poem as to the topical requisites of the oration. The careful manipulation of *topoi* germane to the theme without appearing to violate the conventional form of the hymn bears testimony to Statius' considerable skill as a poet.

One of these references, *mutent sceptra* (708), serves specifically to recall the abrogation of the agreement between Eteocles and Polynices. Other allusions relate more generally to the narrative and serve a general function in relation to the theme. The references to the violent accomplishments of Apollo (709-15) demonstrate the god's awesome destructive power and vindictive cruelty, thereby reinforcing the overall impression of Apolline and supernatural malevolence that pervades the epic. Vessey correctly interprets the significance of the phrase *mutent sceptra* (708), whose implications are obvious enough. It is more difficult to see the specific prognosticative function of some of the other references in Adrastus' prayer, but Vessey plausibly argues that the Giant Tityos (709f.) and Lapith Phlegyas (713-15) are symbols of the anarchy that predominates during the war between Argos and Thebes; his suggestion that the allusion to Niobe (711f.) whose sons were struck down by Apollo foreshadows the fate of Jocasta's sons in book 11 is particularly astute.[20] Furthermore, the mythological figures Adrastus cites suffer an especially harsh fate at the hands of Apollo, just as the god's punishment of Argos in the Coroebus story, which Adrastus has just related to Tydeus and Polynices (557-672), is without question wantonly cruel. Thus the references serve a triple function: they recall the divine ill will toward Argos in the past, anticipate the continued hostility of the gods toward the city in the future, and point up the irony inherent in Adrastus' present thanksgiving to Apollo.

---

[19] Legras (1905: 289).
[20] Vessey (1973: 135).

The significance of Titan (717), Osiris (718) and Mithras (720) at the close of the prayer has been the subject of much confused critical (and theological) discussion. Adrastus' syncretistic references to Apollo are commonplace in classical literature (e.g., Callim. *Ap.* 69-71 and Stat. *Theb.* 1.717-20) and receive a full treatment from Menander (*Epid. Sp.* 3.445.25ff.).[21] A knowledge of the rhetorical prescription for the conclusion of the Sminthiac oration suggests that the inclusion of the appellations is essentially conventional. The scholiast Lactantius Placidius acknowledges Statius' prescriptive use of the invocatory titles Titan (*Theb.* 1.717), Osiris (718) and Mithras (720) of Apollo in the composition of Adrastus' hymn (*In Stat. Theb.* 1.717-20). Adrastus' invocation of Apollo at the end of his prayer by his various titles and the expression *seu te uocari praestat* (717f.) illustrates the conventional practice in classical antiquity of making certain a god is invoked by the appropriate title. The suppliant traditionally catalogues a full range of alternative appellations a god might employ, then further covers himself by an inclusory phrase covering any unheard of invocatory titles. The practice presumably is designed to ensure the god cannot ignore the invocation. Adrastus' mention of these titles in the traditional manner is entirely consistent with our expectations of the regent, for his worshipful speech plays a critical rôle in the poet's depiction of Adrastus as a pious and god-fearing monarch; but he is no Stoic *sapiens*, since the syncretistic references to Apollo in his manifestation as the sun-god are impossible to account for within the Stoic framework. In fact Adrastus is anything but a Stoic sage: he is pious and therefore uses the appropriate (i.e., conventional) references for the Sminthiac hymn, but his own ignorance is revealed through his singular lack of appreciation of Apollo's destructive rôle in the affairs of Argos and his misplaced trust in this deity.[22] This revelation of character is obviously the most important function of his prayer.

The naming of Titan by Adrastus as a title for Apollo is conventional, as the use of the appellation for the god is commonplace in post-classical poetry (e.g., Ovid *Met.* 2.118, Sen. *Phaedr.* 678); however, this conventional synonymity *per se* does not preclude textual significance, since the

---

[21] Cf. Norden (1913: 165).

[22] Furthermore, Adrastus is not immune to the madness that afflicts his fellow citizens in the war with Thebes. He ignores omens that portend disaster for his city (cf. 3.456-58, 499-451, 619-47) and enthusiastically promotes the nocturnal slaughter of the dormant Thebans in their camp (10.227-44, esp. 236-44; 266-68).

appellation *Titana* is especially appropriate in the overall context. In early literature the Titan is presented as a plenipotentiary of chaos and as an agent of destruction (cf. Hes. *Theog.* 207-10, esp. 617ff., 820ff.), and here its primitive and feral qualities mirror those associated with the destructive rôle of Apollo in the epic. Apollo's cruelty is revealed in many incidents related by Adrastus in the tale of Coroebus (*Theb.* 1.557-672). Two notable examples of the god's destructiveness in the main narrative are his near-slaying of Polynices in the chariot race during the funeral games (6.491ff.) and his murderous rôle on the battlefield prior to Amphiaraus' descent to the underworld (7.440ff.). Significantly, Vessey does not offer an explanation for Adrastus' naming of Titan as a title for Apollo, presumably because he is unable to explain its inclusion in (favourable) terms similar to those of Osiris and Mithras.

Osiris, the sun-god (cf. Plut. *De Is. et Os.* 52), was naturally associated with Apollo, represented in the *Thebaid* most unfavourably. Vessey, however, attributes the identification of Apollo with Osiris, whom he sees as 'figure of beneficent law and cosmic order', to Theseus' rôle in book 12; he further suggests that Adrastus' reference to the Egyptian god specifically prognosticates the Athenian monarch's arrival in Thebes.[23] In Adrastus' hymn Osiris is depicted as a geoponic deity (*Osirim frugiferum*, *Theb.* 1.718f.) and Mithras is portrayed as a bull-slayer (*Persei sub rupibus antri / indignata sequi torquentem cornua Mithram*, 719f.). Although Osiris is represented by Statius as a patron god of georgic endeavour, there is nothing in the text to suggest that the poet is specifically associating his function with Theseus' rôle in the last book of the epic; nor is there anything at this point or anywhere else to suggest that the descriptive epithet *frugifer* (719) expressly foreshadows the reference to the Eleusinian mysteries in 12.501f., as Vessey asserts.[24] Even if Statius were associating Osiris with Theseus, the identification (as with Mithras and Theseus) would serve only to stress the hostility of the divine powers to humanity and the violence of Theseus' campaign against Thebes.[25] The depiction of Osiris as a geoponic deity appears to reflect the more favourable aspect of Apollo's ambivalent nature and his benefic potentiality; therefore the reference is ironic, since it

---

[23] Vessey (1973: 135f.).

[24] Vessey (1973: 136, 310 n. 1).

[25] On the ambiguous portrayal of Theseus and his 'war' against Thebes, see Dominik (1990: 87-92) and chs. 1 and 3 of my *The Mythic Voice of Statius* (forthcoming).

not only highlights specifically the ignorance of Adrastus in assuming that the pious and innocent will be more favourably treated by the gods than the wicked and guilty but also underscores generally the limited capacity of humankind to understand its position vis-à-vis the higher powers in the *Thebaid*.

Vessey uses Vermaseren's explanation (that the tauroctony in Roman Mithraism symbolises the predominance of life over death and disorder)[26] to argue that the reference to the tauroctony in Adrastus' hymn anticipates Theseus' liberation of Thebes from the evils of Creon. Vessey draws a connexion between the representations on Theseus' shield (*Theb.* 12.665-67) referring to Theseus' emancipation of Athens through his slaying of the Minotaur and the Athenian king's defeat of the tyrannical Creon. He asserts that the repetition of three words—*antri* (668), *torquentem* (669) and *cornua* (671)—that appear earlier in the closing lines of Adrastus' hymn (1.719f.) is partial justification for his view of a thematic link between the actions of Mithras and Theseus. However, Hinnells[27] refutes Cumont's[28] interpretation of the tauroctony (especially Mithras' rôle as the creator) upon which Vermaseren's view (and therefore Vessey's interpretation of 1.719f.) appears to be based and argues that it does not even remotely represent the triumph of life over death, order over disorder, or good over evil. In fact the tauroctonous scene in the *Thebaid* represents very much the opposite. The image of Mithras, traditionally identified with the sun (and therefore with Apollo), dragging a bull to be sacrificed represents the malevolent gods (especially Apollo) dragging Polynices and Eteocles to destruction, as the pair are compared frequently with bulls (e.g., 1.131ff., 4.397ff.; cf. 3.323ff., 11.251ff.). The bull functions as one of the most important metaphors in the *Thebaid*,[29] and the strategic placement of *Mithram* at the close of the first book's final line (720) underscores its metaphorical (and thematic) significance.

An interpretation of Adrastus' hymn to Apollo can be assisted by examining the *topoi* of the Sminthiac hymn as prescribed by Menander, especially with particular reference to *genos*, *praxeis* and *epilogos*. Adrastus' formal hymn is much briefer than what the schema presented by Menander

---

[26] Vermaseren (1963: 68-70).
[27] Hinnells (1975: 290-312).
[28] Cumont (1956: 132-37, esp. 137).
[29] Cf. Dominik (1990: 89f.) and ch. 2 of my *The Mythic Voice of Statius* (forthcoming).

allows for in the epic context. Statius is influenced by the tradition of Sminthiac composition in the formulation of Adrastus' speech, but the regent's speech is not patterned strictly after the Menandrean prescription. Adrastus' brief epic speech betrays the topical influence of the Sminthiac tradition because it contains some of the topical elements of the Sminthiac hymn. Even though the structure of Adrastus' formal hymn is generally faithful to the tradition, the references in this traditional hymn are linked closely with other passages in the epic and emphasise certain thematic and dramatic aspects of particular importance to the poet.

The Informal Hymn

AN ARGIVE CHIEFTAIN (4.832-50)

Although Adrastus' hymn to Apollo is the only formal hymn in the *Thebaid*, there is another prayer whose tone and content mirror those of the traditional hymn. The effects of the desiccation of the earth by the nymphs on Bacchus' command in book 4 leads to the one informal hymn in the epic. Hypsipyle rescues the Argives from an ignominious end by leading them to Langia's stream (804). When the Argives reach the banks of the nymph's river, all semblance of order is lost among the troops in the mad rush to quench their thirst (816ff.). An Argive chieftain spontaneously pours forth words of gratitude to the river for the gift (832-50); his prayer displays some of the qualities of the traditional hymn. Like Adrastus' hymn in book 1 (696-720), the chieftain's prayer concludes the book in which it is spoken. Although the hymn lacks the formal qualities that characterise Adrastus' prayer to Apollo, the hymnal elements are apparent.

The structure of the chieftain's prayer is bipartite: there is a brief address to Nemea (832-37) and a longer one to the nymph Langia's river (837-50). In the first part there is the customary invocation and praise of the glade (*siluarum, Nemea, longe regina uirentum, / lecta Iouis sedes*, 832), the acknowledgement of her considerable power (833-35), and a brief request for her to refrain from her obstructive action (836f.). The second section of the hymn consists of a solemn invocation to Langia's river (*tuque o cunctis insuete domari / solibus, aeternae largitor corniger undae*, 837f.), a minor request (*laetus eas*, 839), ingratiating references to her autogenous waters (839-43) and superiority to other celebrated rivers such as the Ladon and

98

Xanthus (844-46), and the promise of her celebration and honour after the war if the principal request is met (846-50):

> tu pace mihi, tu nube sub ipsa
> armorum festasque super celebrabere mensas
> (a Ioue primus honos), bellis modo laetus ouantes
> accipias fessisque libens iterum hospita pandas
> flumina defensasque uelis agnoscere turmas.

Like Adrastus' prayer for Apollo's blessing at the end of book 1, the chieftain's request that the Argives return in triumph to her waters after the war is made in vain. The chieftain's speech is also dramatically ironic, since he cannot know that his wish is to be unrealised.

The Proseuktic Hymn

Another prayer type that Menander discusses is the *proseuktikon*. The proseuktic prayer is commonly employed by the poets, philosophers and rhetoricians in classical antiquity. Menander (*Epid.* Sp. 3.342.21-343.4) notes that the *proseuktikon* appears in virtually every type of hymn where a god is invoked, but cites uncombined examples from Homer's *Iliad* (10.278f.) and Plato's *Phaedrus* (279B-C). According to Menander, the proseuktic prayer must be just, simple and succinct; these requirements are met not by providing information to the gods but requesting something that is obvious to them (*Epid.* Sp. 3.343.5-10). This type of prayer is rhetorical in function, for Menander observes that orators employ the *proseuktikon* in passages like πρῶτον μὲν ὦ ἄνδρες Ἀθηναῖοι, τοῖς θεοῖς εὔχομαι and καλῶ δὲ τὸν Ἀπόλλω τὸν Πύθιον (343.11-16). Menander's arrangement of the proseuktic prayer suggests that his rhetorical formula is consistent with the conventional literary and rhetorical practice in classical antiquity.

There are four proseuktic prayers in the *Thebaid* (4.473-87, 9.548-50, 10.67-69, 12.771-73), of which two are briefly treated below.

ARGOLIC MOTHERS (10.67-69)

The most legitimate example of the proseuktic prayer is the Argive matrons' supplication of Juno to demolish Thebes (10.67-69):

aspice sacrilegas Cadmeae paelicis arces,
siderei regina poli, tumulumque rebellem
disice et in Thebas aliud (potes) excute fulmen.

The maidens' invocation is salutary to their purpose, their request brief, their message succinct. There is no evidence produced or lengthy appeal made in the attempt to persuade Juno. The elements conform to the rhetorical prescription laid down by Menander in his treatise. The maidens' reference to Semele in the first line is intended to provoke Juno into granting their request.

CAPANEUS (9.548-50)

Capaneus' invocation to his right arm is the most remarkable proseuktic prayer (9.548-50; my emphasis):

ades o mihi, dextera, tantum
tu praesens bellis et ineuitabile numen,
te uoco, *te* solam superum contemptor adoro.

The polyptoton of *tu* and anaphora of *te*, figures that are often used to create a solemn effect in the formal prayer (e.g., 1.705, 709), stress Capaneus' self-conceit. The spectacle bears a close resemblance to two scenes in the *Aeneid*. In book 10 Mezentius prays to his right hand and his spear (773-76), while in the final book the maddened Turnus invokes his spear to slay Aeneas (12.95-100).

Deliberative Prayers

The second group of prayers in the *Thebaid* is deliberative; these prayers are protreptic or apotreptic in intent. Statius would have been well versed in the composition of the deliberative speech and its attendant divisions. Quintilian, a contemporary of Statius, divides the customary deliberative oration into five parts. As these have been treated fully elsewhere in this study, a quick review of the customary division will suffice here. The *prooemium* informs and ingratiates the addressee. The *narratio* sets forth the events that may persuade the addressee to be more receptive to the main proposal (*propositio*) that follows (cf. *Inst.* 4.2.20ff.). Quintilian treats the *propositio*, the main proposal, the organisation of the points for discussion, as part of the *probatio*. After the presentation and proof of the argument comes the *refutatio*, the rebuttal of the opponent's argument, then the *peroratio*, which serves either to restate in summary fashion the general thesis of the argument or to inspire the audience to a more favourable disposition toward it.

The purpose of the deliberative prayer is essentially twofold: to persuade the god that the petition is sensible and that the desired action is within the deity's power to effect. The suppliant's goal is to win the deity over to his/her point of view in such a way that the resultant divine action will benefit the speaker or other designated person. No suppliant in the *Thebaid* presumes a favourable result to his/her request. There is the awareness that the fulfilment of the prayer depends on divine benevolence and may not be granted; the human suppliant seldom adopts a demanding or imperious tone in his/her speech.[30] Dramatic irony frequently occurs when the speaker is ignorant of the true meaning of his/her words or the fateful outcome of his/her prayer.

The majority of prayers in the *Thebaid* are deliberative in intent. Given the constraints of epic composition, the deliberative rhetoric employed by the speaker naturally is not in the form of a full-fledged deliberative oration, but it does display the general rules of the art that imperial rhetoricians followed. The speaker's initial duty in the deliberative prayer is to gain the attention of the deity; consequently, in Statian epic deliberative prayers usually include a brief introductory invocation designed to make the divinity well disposed, attentive and receptive. Occasionally the speaker omits the *narratio*, either because the divine addressee is omniscient (cf. Quint. *Inst.* 3.8.10) or because of the necessity of confining the speech to a reasonable length. In most prayers the *probatio*, particularly the *propositio*, figures prominently.

In Statian epic the *propositio* is usually specific in nature; sometimes, particularly in a more formal oration such as Adrastus' hymn to Apollo in the first book (696-720), the request is designed to foster a general goodwill on the part of the deity invoked. Usually the reasons for considering the proposal and the argument favourably involve expediency, honour and necessity (cf. *Inst.* 3.8.22ff.). Prayers often consist of a claim that the speaker has on the god's benevolence. This claim usually involves a

---

[30] An exception to this general rule is Tiresias' comminatory prayer to the infernal goddesses (4.501-18).

demonstration of the suppliant's loyalty to the deity rather than his/her moral virtue and consists of a series of protatic, or conditional, clauses (*Theb.* 1.60-72, 4.504-11, 6.635-37). The *refutatio* seldom figures in the structure of the prayer, ostensibly because the suppliant is preoccupied with his/her own attempt at persuasion and because of the dramatic exigency of restricting the length of the appeal. The *peroratio* is naturally an essential part of the prayer because of the speaker's desire to inspire the god to a more favourable disposition toward his/her argument. In the *peroratio* the suppliant customarily makes a final appeal to the god by amplifying his/her feelings. This appeal to and amplification of emotions is a general feature of the prayer in the *Thebaid* and is no doubt a consequence of the psychological necessity for the speaker to move the gods to the desired action by whatever means required. Although the parts of the prayer assume an important rôle in the deliberative prayers, the suppliant does not always adhere to the customary arrangement. Often the omission of a part such as the *narratio* or the abbreviation of the prayer is necessary in order to arouse the god's emotions more effectively; sometimes the omission or abbreviation owes more to the dramatic exigencies of the epic context. The specific circumstances of the deliberative prayer always assume a greater importance than the rhetorician's guidelines.

The Protreptic Prayer

OEDIPUS (1.56-87)

The importance of the arrangement of the parts in the deliberative prayers is apparent in the first speech of the *Thebaid*. After Statius' invocation of Domitian in book 1, Oedipus invokes the underworld gods in a deliberative fashion (56ff.). He begins by addressing collectively the infernal deities in an awed and respectful manner in an attempt to ingratiate himself with the gods and conciliate them (56-58); he then specifically entreats the Styx and Tisiphone (59). The regent's special mention of gods whose assistance is viewed as essential for the fulfilment of his prayer and the collective address of other deities is intended to ensure that all possible means of divine assistance is canvassed.

Oedipus then proceeds with the *narratio*, in this case a summary of events in his life. He reminds the infernal gods in a series of protatic

statements that his wishes are worthy of fulfilment on account of their fatal
design and madding purpose (60-72; italics mine):

> *si* bene quid merui, *si* me de matre cadentem
> fouisti gremio et traiectum uulnere plantas
> firmasti, *si* stagna peti Cirrhaea bicorni
> interfusa iugo, possem cum degere falso
> contentus Polybo, trifidaeque in Phocidos arto
> longaeuum implicui regem secuique trementis
> ore senis, dum quaero patrem, *si* Sphingos iniquae
> callidus ambages te praemonstrante resolui,
> *si* dulces furias et lamentabile matris
> conubium gauisus ini noctemque nefandam
> saepe tuli natosque tibi, scis ipsa, paraui,
> mox auidus poenae digitis caedentibus ultro
> incubui miseraque oculos in matre reliqui.

It is apparent from this passage that Oedipus is confident that Tisiphone will
grant his perverse prayer on account of the previous assistance she has given
him and her obvious approval of the previous actions he has performed under
her control.

The conditional constituent characteristic of the deliberative
prayer—note the repetition of the conjunction *si* in the passage above—is a
noteworthy feature of Oedipus' speech. In the *probatio*, Oedipus bases his
argument upon issues of *iustum* and *pium*. The former regent appeals to
traditional values of filial piety in reminding Tisiphone that his sons callously
abandoned him after his abdication and greedily seized his crown (74-78); he
complains bitterly that Jupiter does not exact vengeance for this filial neglect
(79-80). Oedipus' *propositio* is a request for Tisiphone to work her
vengeance on his sons (80ff.). The former king concludes with another
appeal and brief *propositio* designed to inspire the goddess toward a more
favourable disposition toward his perverted prayer (85-87):

> da, Tartarei regina barathri,
> quod cupiam uidisse negas, nec tarda sequetur
> mens iuuenum; modo digna ueni, mea pignora nosces.

This final appeal is based primarily on the question of *facile* (85-87). It is
significant especially for the awareness that Eteocles and Polynices ultimately
will not be able to escape the influence of the curse or the hostility of the

Furies (86f.; cf. 123ff.). The fulfilment of his *peruersa uota* ensures the deaths of his sons and the destruction of Thebes. Like their descendants, the inhabitants of Thebes will be caught up in forces over which they have no control. It is significant that Statius depicts the former monarch as being under the influence of the Furies when he utters the curse against his sons (51f.). Oedipus' own prayer to Tisiphone shows that he is the victim of an inherited regenerative curse that has plagued the Theban house since its origination (227ff.).

HIPPOMEDON (9.506-10)

Some deliberative prayers consist of a barrage of rhetorical questions. Rhetorical questions predominate in deliberative speeches with a vituperative component; the profusion of rhetorical questions is intended to convey the impression of a spontaneous outburst of passion such as hatred, anger, contempt, indignation or despair (cf. Quint. *Inst.* 9.2.9f.). The struggle between Hippomedon and Ismenos furnishes the context for one of the deliberative prayers in the *Thebaid* that consist almost entirely of rhetorical questions (9.506-10). The struggle is predictably violent, but Hippomedon proves no match for the river god. In a scene reminiscent of Achilleus' struggle with the river Skamandros in *Iliad* 21.233ff., Ismenos and the Theban warriors combine to overwhelm Hippomedon. Achilleus' struggle with Skamandros in the *Iliad* is acrimonious and violent; the savage nature of the confrontation between Hippomedon and Ismenos in the *Thebaid* mirrors the tone and atmosphere of the *Iliadic* scene.

Hippomedon's speech betrays his alarm over his inglorious fate and is intended to elicit sympathy from Mars. The hero does not intend that the war-god reply to his prayer; his purpose is not to obtain answers to his indignant questions, for the manner in which he phrases his rhetorical questions makes a reply from Mars difficult. The purpose of his interrogatory prayer is to emphasise the injustice of his plight. Hippomedon's speech strongly resembles Achilleus' invocation to Zeus at *Iliad* 21.272. Both Achilleus and Hippomedon protest against the humiliation of being drowned, claiming they deserve a noble death in battle at the hands of worthy foes. The intervention of Juno and Jupiter occurs too late to save Hippomedon (*Theb.* 9.510ff.). Hippomedon's immense physical strength allows him to tower over his human opponents but in the end proves to be of little consequence. The manifestation of Hippomedon's superhuman physical strength draws him directly, although undesignedly, into a fatal conflict with a supernatural being.

THIODAMAS (8.303-38)

Thiodamas, priestly successor of Amphiaraus, supplicates Tellus in an attempt to mitigate the goddess' anger (8.303-38), for Amphiaraus' demise is attributed to her displeasure (294); his speech is one of three prayers of the deliberative variety in the epic.[31] The sombre atmosphere established by the invocation (303) permeates Thiodamas' speech and is reinforced by the deliberative manner of his plea to Tellus. The seriousness of the occasion demands that Thiodamas first conditions Tellus with an elaborate *prooemium* consisting of a few ingratiating flourishes in order to placate the earth goddess in her perceived anger. Thiodamas attributes to Tellus creative and providential powers and the central position in the universe (303-16). The priest virtually dispenses with the *narratio*, since ostensibly he believes that the omniscient Tellus knows the circumstances surrounding Amphiaraus' disappearance; he proceeds almost immediately to his argument. The race does not deserve the goddess' wrath for migrating to the Peloponnesus, since all men have the birth right to settle anywhere (320-22); the priest then proceeds with the first *propositio* to this effect (323-28). After another brief salutation of respect for the goddess' universal powers (329-32), Thiodamas beseeches Tellus in a final *propositio* to divulge the secrets of her worship so he can practice her divinatory rites (332-36). The *peroratio*, a brief laudatory statement about the power of the Earth (337f.), is designed to inspire Tellus to a more favourable reception of his supplication. The dramatic irony of the passage resides in the contrast between the Argives' perception of events surrounding Amphiaraus' death and the reader's knowledge of the situation that Thiodamas' supplication is futile and that events will unfold in their destined order. The reader knows that the Argives suffer under the misapprehension that Tellus' anger caused Amphiaraus' death.

---

[31] The others are spoken by Amphiaraus (3.471-96, 7.779-88).

The Sacrificial Component

Some of the deliberative prayers in the epic possess *topoi* in common with Homeric and Vergilian epic. One of the commonplace secondary elements involves the sacrifice of animals while the speaker is praying. This element of human worship doubtless stems from the custom in classical antiquity of formal prayers being accompanied by animal sacrifice (cf. Pliny *Nat. Hist.* 28.3.10f.). A literary example of this practice occurs in the final book of the *Aeneid* when Aeneas and Latinus sacrifice the offspring of a boar and a sheep while swearing oaths (12.169ff.). In *Thebaid* 4 a complex necromantic ritual involving the sacrifice of oxen and sheep precedes Tiresias' proseuktic invocation to the infernal deities to raise the dead (4.443ff.).

ETEOCLES (11.210-25, 248F.)

Eteocles' prayers to Jupiter for assistance in his forthcoming duel with Polynices is accompanied by the sacrifice of bulls (11.210-25, 248f.). The formula of the first prayer is consistent with the usual practice. Eteocles invokes Jupiter in recognition of his power (*ductor*, 205), recounts the reasons for the enmity of Argos and Juno (211-16), makes his request in anticipation of Jupiter's aid (217-21), and offers flocks, incense and a votive bull (222f.). The king further claims that Bacchus and Hercules will provide Jupiter worthy recompense for his divine favour (223-25). Immediately after delivering this prayer the scene becomes direful: the flame leaps against Eteocles' face and seizes the regent's diadem (226f.); the votive bull scatters the shrine with blood and runs rampant through the assembly, bearing the altar upon his horns (228-30). A similar scene occurs in *Aeneid* 4 when Dido resolves on death; the waters turn black and the wine transforms to blood (453-55). In the *Thebaid* Eteocles, manipulated by the Furies (11.208f.), is oblivious to the significance of the adverse omens. He issues in a brazen fashion another prayer, which contains a reference to Capaneus, *superum contemptor* (248f.):

> nunc tempus erat, sator optime diuum!
> quid meruit Capaneus?

As are many prayers in the epic, Eteocles' words are full of dramatic irony, since they actually anticipate his fate and that of his brother in the ensuing duel.

The Rite of Deuotio

MENOECEUS (10.762-73)

The offering of human life instead of animals to the gods is an interesting feature of Menoeceus' sacrifice (*Theb.* 10.756ff.). The devotion and piety of Menoeceus manifests itself in the form of an *Opfertod* not long after the deaths of Hopleus and Dymas. Virtus, disguised as Manto the prophetess, informs Menoeceus of his fate and exhorts him to accept his death (662-71). The youth willingly accepts his destiny and departs for Thebes despite the protestations of his parents (680ff.).

Menoeceus prays to the battle gods and Apollo just prior to his attempt to save Thebes by offering himself up to the gods (10.762-73). The structure and topical elements of Menoeceus' speech closely resemble those of the elder Decius' speech. There is the standard invocation of the gods:

Theb. 10.762f.:	armorum superi, tuque o qui funere tanto indulges mihi, Phoebe, mori . . .
Liv. 8.9.6:	Iane Jupiter Mars pater Quirine Bellona est potestas nostrorum hostiumque Dique . . .

a request for victory in the ensuing conflict:

Theb. 10.763f.:	. . . date gaudia Thebis. quae pepigi et toto quae sanguine prodigus emi.
Liv. 8.9.7:	. . . uos precor ueneror ueniam peto oroque uti populo Romano Quiritium uim uictoriam prosperetis . . .

and a plea for the annihilation of the enemy:

Theb. 10.765-68:	ferte retro bellum captaeque impingite Lernae reliquias turpes, confixaque terga fouentes Inachus indecores pater auersetur alumnos.
Liv. 8.9.7f.:	hostesque populi Romani Quiritium terrore formidine morteque adficiatis.

107

Menoeceus further prays that his Theban compatriots be restored to their *templa, arua, domus, conubia* and *nati* by his act of self-sacrifice (*Theb.* 10.768f.). In a series of protatic statements he argues his loyalty to the gods (769-71; emphasis mine):

> *si* uos placita hostia iuui,
> *si* non attonitis uatis consulta recepi
> auribus et Thebis nondum credentibus hausi.

This demonstration of devotion is intended to add further weight to his claim on the goodwill of the gods on Thebe's behalf. Menoeceus concludes with a dual proposal: he asks the gods to ensure the safety of Thebes and to reconcile his father to his earlier deception (772f.; cf. 721ff.).

The circumstances surrounding the apotropaic *Opfertodesfälle* of Menoecus (*Theb.* 10.756ff.) and Decius Mus (Liv. 8.9ff.) are remarkably similar. Schetter and Vessey note the similarities,[32] but they fail to recognise the full significance of Statius' adaption of this Livian scene. Statius certainly intends that his audience associate the *deuotio* of Menoeceus with the heroic and patriotic action of Decius Mus, thereby enhancing the significance of the scene. Menoeceus and Decius Mus are among the highest ranking and most valuable citizens of their communities. The preservation and welfare of their states are dependent upon their voluntary self-sacrifices. Their altruistic and noble actions render them heroic *sacri*.

The significant feature of Menoeceus' *deuotio* is that he takes his vow of self-sacrifice and immediately discharges his duty before the gods fulfil their part of the covenant. Like Decius Mus (Liv. 8.9ff.), he plunges into the enemy ranks to meet a noble death. His heroic and altruistic action stands in dramatic contrast to Capaneus' spiteful challenge of the gods later in the same book (*Theb.* 10.899ff.) and the selfish and individualistic actions of Eteocles and Polynices throughout the whole of the poem. In religious terms Menoeceus' *Opfertod* represents the supreme act of devotion, while in a patriotic sense his unselfish action is the highest example of *pietas*.

But there are some notable differences between the scenes of *deuotio* presented in Livy and Statius. Decius and Menoeceus sacrifice themselves willingly in order to save their cities, but the Theban is depicted as being inspired by Virtus to perform his heroic *Opfertod* (10.661ff., esp. 672-77;

---

[32] Schetter (1960: 13), Vessey (1973: 121f.).

cf. 628, 657). Whereas the self-sacrifice of the elder Decius ensures Rome's victory, the suicide of Menoeceus proves fruitless, since it does not save Thebes from defeat. Thus Menoeceus becomes an innocent victim of a supposedly benevolent goddess who deceives the youth into sacrificing himself without real cause.

COROEBUS (1.643-61)

The atmosphere of the primitive rite of *deuotio* is suggested in the tale of Coroebus, which Adrastus relates in 1.557-662. Coroebus rids Argos of a hideous monster sent by Apollo that sets upon and devours Argive children (597ff.). In vengeance the god subsequently sends a plague upon the citizens, which he will not remove until the slayer of the monster is sacrificed (627ff.). Coroebus journeys to Delphi and offers himself up to Apollo (641ff.). The recounted prayer of Coroebus to Apollo (643-61) appears just prior to Adrastus' own hymn to the god (696-720). After a brief *prooemium* in which Coroebus claims that *pietas* and *conscia uirtus* compel him to approach Apollo's shrine (643f.), the urgency of Argos' plight prompts him in the *narratio* to identify himself quickly and accept responsibility for slaying the monster (645-48).

Coroebus argues in the *probatio* that inhabitants of Argos are undeserving of Apollo's enmity (648-51); he alone assumes culpability for the death of the monster (651, 657). The youth's invocation of Apollo as *inique* (648) and *diuum optime* (651) is sarcastic as well as ironic, as suggested by his criticism of the ill will that the god shows toward the innocent inhabitants of Argos (648-57). Coroebus concludes his prayer with two *propositiones*, the first entreating Apollo to dispatch him quickly with his bow and quiver (658f.), the second asking for the pestilence to be lifted from Argos (660f.). Apollo ostensibly recognises the justice of the youth's appeal, spares him and dispels the deadly plague suspended over Argos (661-66).

On the human level, Crotopus is probably the only figure deserving of harsh retribution, since he is directly accountable for his daughter's execution. The people of Argos are made to suffer not only for the crime of Crotopus in executing Psamathe (cf. 584f.) but also for the cruelty (cf. 575) and neglect (597) of Apollo. This is unquestionably unjust, as Coroebus points out (648-57). There is no cogent reason why the entire Argive community should suffer for the crimes of Crotopus, despite the importance of his position. The actual punishments dispensed by Apollo far exceed the bounds of natural justice.

None of the events would have taken place if it had not been for Apollo's cruel rape of Crotopus' daughter in the first instance. His disastrous intervention in the life of Psamathe precipitates her execution, the death of their child and the numerous deaths of innocent citizens. The monster and pestilence that Apollo sends upon Argos are manifestations of the god's displeasure and symbolic of his own guilt. Admittedly Apollo is not *directly* responsible for the death of Psamathe and their child, but these incidents stem from his lust for her and subsequent neglect of his human family.

Coroebus' altruistic action in offering himself as a *piaculum* for his offence against Apollo mirrors the primitive ritual of *deuotio*. Coroebus prostrates himself before a vindictive deity in a heroic attempt to save his city from unjust divine retribution. In one sense, Coroebus' willingness to offer himself to Apollo can be viewed as an attempt to free the Argive community of responsibility for its collective guilt through its association with him. In another sense, his devotion can be seen as an attempt to atone for the crime of Apollo. In any event, Apollo's subsequent sparing of Coroebus and his people surprises. Perhaps the willingness of Coroebus to endure the punishment that is rightly Apollo's impresses the deity. A god cannot really exact retribution from one who accepts death willingly, especially when the individual is guilty only of protecting his community from divinely instigated ravages.

The magnanimity of Coroebus stands in marked contrast with the behaviour of Tydeus and Polynices, to whom Adrastus relates the tale of the youth's attempted *Opfertod*. Tydeus and Polynices refuse to give way not only to each other (1.408-27) but also their brothers (cf. 1.402f., 11.496-573), thus precipitating needless bloodshed and suffering. In the case of Polynices, supernatural powers act to ensure that the exile is given no chance to save his city. The gods' control of the situation in the main narrative is so effective that there is no possibility of Polynices even attempting to emulate the deed of Coroebus. Human fortune varies according to the whims of the supernatural powers.

The Votary Component

The votary element is a common feature in deliberative invocations to the gods in the *Thebaid* (1.498-510, 2.715-42, 4.753-71, 7.93-103, 7.730-35, 10.337-45, 11.504-08). This type of deliberative prayer is distinguished by the speaker's offering or promise to the addressee of suitable votary gifts in return for divine assistance. The usual *topoi* of this speech type are the address to the god (*prooemium*), the request (*propositio*), and the offering or promise of reward (*utile*). The speaker's promise of votary offerings in return for assistance rendered by the god forms a quasi-legal compact between the two parties; the votary offering becomes the payment for divine fulfilment of the suppliant's prayer. This promise of mortal recompense for divine service is an essential feature of the deliberative prayer with a votary component and distinguishes it from the proseuktic invocation, whose function is solely to request. The tone of the votary prayer is pious and marked by a sense of obligation on the part of the suppliant; the sacrifice or reward offered to the god is one that has been selected carefully to ensure that it gratifies the god. The occasion of the votary offering usually involves danger or misfortune.

ADRASTUS (1.498-510, 4.753-71, 7.93-103)

Adrastus' apostrophe to Nox conforms to the conventional arrangement of the deliberative prayer with a votary constituent. His plea is deeply emotional in expression, a characteristic of the votary prayer. The king respectfully invokes Nox with a protracted reference to his primary rôle in the natural order (1.498-501), beseeches the personified god to reveal the future (502-04), and offers black bulls as a sacrifice to encourage a favourable response (504-508). Dramatic irony, which features so prominently in deliberative prayers, is apparent in Adrastus' interpretation of previous events concerning the arrival of Tydeus and Polynices and anticipated good fortune (*deprendi, Fortuna, deos*, 510), since the regent is blind to the gods' deception in their pronouncements (*prisca fides tripodum*, 509).

After Bacchus delays the Argive army in Nemea by denying them a water source (4.684ff.), the troops come upon the goddess-like figure of Hypsipyle, who despite her dishevelled appearance is mistaken by Adrastus for Diana (746-71). Adrastus invokes her in a most reverent and ingratiating manner (753f.)

> diua potens nemorum (nam te uultusque pudorque
> mortali de stirpe negant) . . .

Adrastus acquaints her briefly with the reasons for their journey through Nemea (760-62) and importunes her to lead his army to water (755ff.). The extent of his desperation and distress is shown when he beseeches the goddess-like figure four times in his prayer to assist them in finding water (755f., 759f., 763, 766f.). Adrastus pledges to reward her amply from the plunder of Thebes in return for her aid if Jupiter allows them to return safely to Argos (768f.); he further promises to make numerous sacrifices to her and erect a magnificent altar in her honour (770f.).

The pious character of the Argive regent is further stressed in a votary prayer in book 7. As Adrastus pours wine upon the ground and propitiates Archemorus at the close of the obsequies for the newly proclaimed divinity, he briefly invokes the god (*parue*, 93), then entreats him to agree to a triennial festival in his honour that will be more esteemed than those of Jupiter, Apollo and Poseidon (93-97). This ingratiating proposal and the brief *narratio* describing both the elevation of Archemorus to divine status and the Argive mobilisation (98-101) are designed to make the new deity more receptive to the main proposal that follows. The regent vows a temple and widespread fame to the deity if he confers victory upon the Argive army in the war against Thebes (100-03).

The votary prayers of Adrastus are characterised by dramatic irony. Just as the king is ignorant of the disastrous consequences of Tydeus and Polynices' arrival in Argos in his prayer to Nox (1.498-510) and is blind to the fact that his plea to Apollo for divine favour will go unheeded (1.682-720), so he is unaware that his army will not return triumphantly to Argos (cf. 4.768f.). Adrastus' appeal to Archemorus for success in the war against Thebes is similarly ironic (7.93-103), since the reader knows that the new deity cannot grant a request in defiance of Jupiter and other supernatural powers.

THIODAMAS (10.337-45)

The Argive army's destruction of the Theban camp in book 10 furnishes the context for the prophet Thiodamas' deliberative invocation of

Apollo (262ff.). His prayer is preceded by advice from Actor to set a limit to the Argive's success by withdrawing from the camp (330-35). Thiodamas' speech shows the extent of the prophet's moral degeneration since the occasion of his reverential and eulogistic prayer of the deliberative variety to Tellus in the eighth book (303-38). Whereas the prophet's invocation of Tellus is tinged with deference and piety, his prayer to Apollo is cast in terms of sacrilege and blasphemy.

Thiodamas' first request is for prophetic inspiration (341). He acknowledges the crudity of dedicating the mutilated bodies of the dead Thebans to Apollo (342), but is still brazen enough to make a second request for a return to his home after the war (343), promising infinite votary gifts as a reward for Apollo's favour (344f.):

> templa, Lycie, dabis, tot ditia dona sacratis
> postibus et totidem uoti memor exige tauros.

The prophet's prayer demonstrates that the humility of the speaker toward his divine benefactor in a prayer does not necessarily preclude an air of fearlessness on the part of the human suppliant.

The Comminatory Component

TIRESIAS (4.501-18)

An element of threat rarely appears in the deliberative prayer in epic. Tiresias makes the only deliberative prayer with a comminatory element in the *Thebaid* (4.501-18) when he and Manto exercise necromancy to find out the result of the ensuing conflict between Thebes and Argos (406-651). After Tiresias' proseuktic invocation to Pluto to allow the pious shades to return to the light in a different group from the crime-ridden spirits fails to stir the dead (473ff.), the priest makes a second prayer to the underworld goddesses (501-518). Tiresias is impatient for a reply to his first invocation and dispenses with the customary ingratiating flourishes in addressing the goddesses (501-03). The priest at once reminds the goddesses of his claim on their infernal powers. In a lengthy rhetorical question he angrily rebukes the goddesses for their indifference to him; he suggests they do not treat him as seriously as they do witches who practice sorcery (504-11):

    an, rabido iubeat si Thessala cantu,
ibitis? et, Scythicis quotiens medicata uenenis
Colchis aget, trepido pallebunt Tartara motu?
nostri cura minor, si non attollere bustis
corpora nec plenas antiquis ossibus urnas
egerere et mixtos caelique Erebique sub unum
funestare deos libet aut exanguia ferro
ora sequi atque aegras functorum carpere fibras?

The substantives *Thessala* (504) and *Colchis* (506) are patent allusions to
Erichtho and Medea, both of whom practise the black arts. Because Tiresias
does not allow his supplication to degenerate into sorcery or magic, he
expects the prayer to manipulate the infernal deities to grant his request
automatically.

Tiresias warns the goddesses not to treat him lightly and evade their
responsibilities to him on account of his frail aspect and his refusal to
practise sorcery; the priest declares that he possesses a hidden power and
threatens them with its use (512ff.). Tiresias claims that his power is so
great that he can disturb the chthonian goddess Hecate (514f.). Yet he fears
Apollo (*Thymbraee*, 515) and *triplicis mundi summum* (516). Tiresias'
collective and particular address of deities is similar to Oedipus' invocation
of the underworld gods in the opening speech of the epic (1.56-59). The
priest's inclusory address of the underworld goddesses and his particular
mention of the prophetic god and the supreme being exhausts all possible
recourse to divine aid.

Tiresias' comminatory plea reflects the agitated mental state of a pious
but frustrated priest who momentarily feels neglected by the gods on whom
he has a special claim; however, the exertion of his authority demonstrates
that the relationship between a suppliant and the deity invoked in Statian epic
does not necessarily reduce the former to a vernile status. Tiresias' entreaty
is of special significance because it is the furthest that any suppliant comes
to censuring the gods in a prayer in the *Thebaid*. In his earlier supplication
(10.473-87) Tiresias approaches Pluto and the infernal deities with a simple
feeling of dependence and a simple request; the same priest only a moment
later accuses the gods of spiteful neglect.

The trinal aspect of the omnipotent power *triplicis mundi summum*
refers to the deity's influence over the celestial, terrestrial and chthonic
spheres of the cosmos. Out of his respect for this deity Tiresias breaks off
from his speech (10.518); the rhetorical aposiopesis effects an easy transition

from the priest's speech to Manto's description that immediately follows (519ff.). Tiresias' reference to a supreme deity is reminiscent of Erichtho's invocation in *Pharsalia* 6.743 to a similar power, which the scholiast *ad* 744 identifies with the Demiurgus and the imposition of order over chaos. The mysterious and benevolent power in the *Thebaid* is acknowledged by Tiresias as the supreme being opposing the forces of evil, represented in the figures of Medea, Erichtho and Hecate.

The Prophetic Component

BACCHIC PRIESTESS (4.383-404)

Deliberative prayers seldom contain a prophetic element. The assembling of the Argive forces before the gates of Thebes furnishes the context for the sole deliberative prayer with a prophetic element in the *Thebaid* (4.383-404). As desperation and panic reign in Thebes, the frenzied Bacchic priestess rushes through Thebes and fills the anxious city with frantic cries (378ff.). The Bacchic queen addresses Bacchus with a lengthy reference to his Oriental conquests, which attest to the violent and destructive nature of the god (383-89). The queen observes that the Thebans have abandoned worship of Bacchus to take part in an unholy war that will result in widespread destruction (390-92). She beseeches Bacchus to remove her to the far wilds beyond Caucasus rather than she should have to relate the tale of internecine warfare (393-97). The priestess finally relents under the pressure and employs a taurine metaphor to describe the war's outcome to the Thebans (397-400):

> similes uideo concurrere tauros
> idem ambobus honos unusque ab origine sanguis;
> ardua conlatis obnixi cornua miscent
> frontibus alternaque truces moriuntur in ira.

The death struggle between the bulls metaphorises the internecine conflict between the two brothers and highlights the purely animal and emotive aspects of the struggle. Because the brothers are equal in honour and origin (398), the manifestation of their anger and desire to punish each other presages their mutual destruction. The Bacchic queen reproves Eteocles directly for his precipitation of the war, warns him to abdicate the throne to

Polynices, and prognosticates his death and the surrender of Thebes to another power (401-04).

The Vituperative Component

The vituperative component is the essential aspect of the display oration of *uituperatio*; the vituperative component is included here for discussion because of its incorporation into the deliberative prayer. There are two prayers in the *Thebaid* that are implicitly deliberative and contain vituperative elements (6.197-201, 8.588-91), of which the second is briefly discussed.

TYDEUS (8.588-91)

The brief prayer of Tydeus to Minerva is vituperative in tone and explicative in intent. The context of the prayer is the death of the youthful Atys during Tydeus' *aristeia*. Displaying a casual indifference to the unwarlike Atys, Tydeus casually flings his spear at him, yet the shaft plunges deep into the youth's groin (8.583-86). Tydeus expresses a disdain for plundering the corpse of a weak opponent (588-91):

> neque enim has Marti aut tibi, bellica Pallas,
> exuuias figemus . . . procul arceat ipsum
> ferre pudor; uix, si bellum comitata relictis
> Deipyle thalamis, illi inludenda tulissem.

Although Tydeus does not specifically request something of Minerva, there is implicit in his vituperative explanation a request for the goddess' understanding of his refusal to plunder Atys' corpse and dedicate the youth's spoils to her.

Tydeus' prayer emphasises what is made clear in the narrative. Atys is betrothed to Ismene, but the war precludes their marriage, so the youth takes up arms against the Argives (554-62). The youthful ignorance of the dangers of war is epitomised in Atys' view of war as a mere spectacle (562-64) and his boyish fascination with military trappings (564-69). He gains a false sense of confidence on the battlefield by challenging, defeating and plundering a feeble squadron (569-72). Atys foolishly challenges Tydeus, misjudging his prowess (577-80). The experienced Tydeus, however, lacks no such awareness in sizing up Atys. The untimely death of the youth is a complete waste of a human life, for it achieves nothing.

116

Tydeus gains nothing from his easy victory, since his slaying of Atys brings him no glory.

The Apotreptic Prayer

The apotreptic prayer is the converse of the protreptic prayer: rather than supplicating a god to do something on his behalf, the speaker attempts to persuade a deity *not* to perform some impending action. From the psychological perspective of the speaker the apotreptic prayer is entirely negative: the purpose of such a prayer is not to *seek* divine favour but to *avoid* misfortune. There are two apotreptic prayers in the *Thebaid* (6.633-37, 8.90-122).

PARTHENOPAEUS (6.633-37)

The short apotreptic prayer of Parthenopaeus during the funeral games (6.633-37) illustrates Statius' technique of interweaving prayer and narrative in such a way as to create dramatic irony. The youthful Parthenopaeus is portrayed as a physical specimen of considerable beauty (571-73). During the foot race his rival Idas grabs the free-flowing yellow hair of Parthenopaeus as the youth is triumphantly crossing the finish line and robs him of victory (615-17). Parthenopaeus had previously dedicated his hair to Diana and pledged it to his country's altars upon his return to his homeland after the war (607-10).

The Arcadians immediately jump to defend the honour of the distraught prince (618-20). Adrastus, however, decrees that the race should be run again (627-30). Parthenopaeus invokes Diana and argues that his earlier disgrace was the result of his vow to honour the goddess with his golden tresses (633f.). The prince's observation about the dedication of his locks to Diana is consistent with the preceding narrative and lays particular stress on what has already been made clear in the narrative (607-10). Partheno-paeus, intimating that he is deserving of the goddess' assistance, implores her not to presage for him an inauspicious fate through defeat or to bring shame to his country (635-37; emphasis mine; note the conditional clauses characteristic of the deliberative prayer):

si bene quid genetrix, si quid uenatibus ipse
promerui, ne, quaeso, sinas hoc omine Thebas
ire nec Arcadiae tantum meruisse pudorem.

117

The dramatic credibility established by the link between the pileous references in Parthenopaeus' speech and the surrounding narrative underscores the dramatic irony inherent in the contrast between the youth's tragic ignorance about his fate and the reader's awareness of his plight. The interests of the youth are involved in a way he cannot discern in the present circumstances; as a result he unwittingly foreshadows his own death.

AMPHIARAUS (8.90-122)

An apotreptic prayer is spoken when Amphiaraus implores Pluto for mercy (8.90-122). The immediacy of the threat against the deceased priest demands that the *propositio* and *probatio* be pushed forward to the beginning of his speech. After a brief invocatory *prooemium* attesting to Pluto's significant rôle in the transmigration of souls (91-93), Amphiaraus beseeches the underworld god to refrain from inflicting his threatened punishment and to temper his anger (93f.). Amphiaraus declares that he has not descended into Hades for *Herculeos raptus* (95) or *Venerem inlicitam* (96), veiled references to Hercules' seizure of Cerberus (cf. 55f.) and Pirithous' attempted abduction of Proserpina (cf. 53f.). The latter reference suggests cleverly and subtly that Pluto can scarcely punish Amphiaraus for his unintended descent into the nether regions without committing a grave injustice when the infernal deity has unlawfully abducted Proserpina from the upper world (cf. 61-64, 98). Furthermore, as Amphiaraus himself maintains, he is ignorant of any crime (101-03); Eriphyle deceived him and he joined the Argive cause knowing his fateful end (104-07). Amphiaraus' plea forms the foundation of an effective *probatio* in which he aims to convince Pluto that he is a priest of strong moral character and was betrayed by a loved one.

Amphiaraus follows with a *narratio* explaining the circumstances of his arrival in the underworld and designed to stir emotion in the god's stern heart over his loss of family and friends in Thebes (107ff.). Amphiaraus reminds Pluto that he is incapable of venturing off with his steeds and is content with his lot in Hades, skilfully pointing out that he has no desire to practise his prophetic art since he knows that his skill is worthless to a god who commands the Fates (116-19; cf. 99f.). Amphiaraus' *peroratio* is an iteration of his earlier plea for mercy and an ethical appeal that Pluto deflect his wrath justly to his deceitful wife (119-22). Despite the distressed state of the priest, he is still able to keep his wits about him. The priest's dexterous argument and appeal to Jupiter's sympathy proves an effective combination when he convinces Pluto even against the god's will (123).

Speeches of Mourning and Consolation

The *consolatio* and *epikedion* were popular rhetorical and literary genres in the first century CE. The consolatory poems in the *Silvae* (2.1, 2.4, 2.5, 2.6, 3.3, 5.1, 5.3, 5.5) illustrate that Statius was thoroughly familiar with these genres. The *Silvae* bear many of the topical and structural characteristics of funeral speeches whose rules are cited by Cicero (*De Inv.* 1.55.106-56.109), Menander *rhetor* (Sp. 3.413.5-414.30, 418.5-442.4, 434.10-437.4) and pseudo-Dionysius (*Gen. Dem.* Rad. 277.6-283.19) in their rhetorical treatises. The four main divisions of the consolatory poems in the *Silvae* are the introduction (*prooemium*), praise of the deceased (*laudatio*), the lament for the dead (*lamentatio*), and the consolation offered to the mourner (*consolatio*). In the *Thebaid* the last two sections comprise the distinctive speech types of the lament and consolation; in addition, the *laudatio* forms a significant component of a third speech type traditionally known as the *epikedion* or *epitaphios*. These three categories of speeches accord roughly with Menander's three types of funeral orations: *monodia* (*Epid.* Sp. 3.434.10-437.4), *paramuthetikos* (413.5-414.30), *epitaphios* (418.4-422.4). Lament is the major feature of his discussion on the *monodia*; consolation is the primary concern of the *paramuthetikos*; and encomiastic elements predominate the *epitaphios*.

The various speeches of mourning and consolation draw attention to the suffering of humankind brought about by the loss of loved ones in war. Most of the lament speeches are delivered by mothers over their young sons who have become the victims of martial violence instigated by the higher powers. These verbal expressions of the grief experienced by the relatives of the slain particularise the atmosphere of loss and sorrow and the general feeling of frustration and helplessness that pervade the warring communities over the senseless waste of human life.

Laments

Speeches of lament in the *Thebaid* are notable for their spontaneous expression and unbridled emotion. The intensity and personal nature of the laments makes this type of speech one of the most compelling from a psychological standpoint in the epic. The speech reveals the misery of the speaker, who often apostrophises an unresponsive subject while kneeling and weeping over him. While the death of a mother's son provides the dramatic context for the majority of lamentable speeches, there are also laments delivered by a nurse over her charge, a wife over her husband, a father over his son, and a warrior over the loss of a comrade-in-arms. The majority of laments are spoken by women; it is significant that no woman is the subject of a lament. The majority of laments are spoken over the young innocent victims of war.

While the lament in Statian epic is frequently anticipated by the mourner's desperate search for the corpse of her loved one, it is accompanied typically by the wailing and physical self-infliction of the mourner, the touching of the victim's corpse and the cleansing of its wounds, and either the expression of blood from the hair and clothing of the victim or the immersion of the mourners' hair and garment in the blood of the deceased. The displays of grief by mourners over the loss of loved ones in the *Thebaid* correspond to the signs of grief shown by the bereaved in the *Silvae*.[33] The external signs of grief exhibited by mourners in both works are similar: there is loud lamentation and groaning (e.g., *Theb.* 3.44f., 3.114-39, 5.607, 6.33f., 6.41-43, 6.137, 9.375, 10.815f., 11.608, 12.386f.; *Silv.* 2.1.23, 2.6.82, 3.3.7, 3.3.180, 5.1.19, 5.3.262, 5.5.12, 5.5.21f.); physical self-abuse, such as tearing of the hair, scratching of the face, striking of the breast, and rending of the clothes (e.g., *Theb.* 3.135f., 6.133-37, 9.353f., 9.817f., 11.609; *Silv.* 2.1.22, 2.1.169-75, 2.6.82-84, 3.3.8, 3.3.176f., 3.3.180, 5.1.20f., 5.5.12); fainting (e.g., *Theb.* 3.128, 9.47f., 12.318f., 12.385-88; *Silv.* 2.1.170-72, 3.3.177); expression of resentment against the gods (e.g., *Theb.* 3.41, 5.610f., 6.143f., 9.71f.; *Silv.* 5.1.20-22); and the need for friends or slaves to restrain the mourner (e.g., *Theb.* 6.203, 9.77, 10.816f.; *Silv.* 2.1.25, 5.1.200, 5.3.262). These similarities illustrate the

---

[33] Cf. Manning (1978: 256-58).

close topical relationship between the epic and occasional poetry of Statius in his description of a mourner's grief. The importance of the lament in advancing and embellishing the narrative and defining personalities is evident in the special prominence it achieves in the *Thebaid*. This speech type forms the foundation for some of the most powerful dramatic scenes. The typical Statian lament is just long enough to be a compelling portrayal of sorrow without unbalancing the narrative. The incorporation of a formal lament (*monodia*) along the lines of the Menandrean prescription (*Epid.* Sp. 3.434.10-437.4) would be uneconomic and would compromise the effectiveness of the narrative. Nevertheless, the qualities of the informal lament in the epic genre have much in common with those described by Menander for the rhetorical *monodia*, whose purpose is to lament and express pity (434.18f.). This is unsurprising, given the rhetorical and exclamatory tone of the epic lament. Menander suggests the close relationship between heroic and rhetorical laments when he declares that Homer founded the rhetorical genre *monodia* and cites the monodic speeches of Andromache, Priam and Hekabe as poetic *exempla* (434.11-15).

As with any speech type, it is difficult to determine whether similarities in style and *topoi* between the epic lament and the formal lament elaborated upon by rhetoricians are fortuitous or intentional; this is certainly the case in Statian epic, where the formulation of the lament is contingent primarily upon the dramatic and narrative context in which it is interposed. Notwithstanding the typological complexities inherent in the task of defining a style that typifies the epic lament, the elements of style and *loci communes* that constitute the lament in the *Thebaid* suggest the strong influence of rhetorical training.

The outstanding stylistic features of the lament in Statian epic are short syntactic units of expression, parenthetic statements, rhetorical questions, apostrophes and exclamations. The lament is always accompanied by a show of spontaneous grief, usually indicated by such exclamatory expressions as *o!*, *en!*, *io!*, *heu!* and *ei mihi!* Virtually every lament commences and finishes with an exclamation, apostrophe or rhetorical question; these figures reveal the emotional distress of the mourner and help to arouse pity and sympathy. The informal style of the lament gives an air of unpremeditation to the utterance, thereby enhancing the credibility of the mourner's grief and the sense of loss.

The *topoi* of the Statian lament are variable, which further helps to create the effect of spontaneity. Many of the *loci communes* are discussed in considerable detail by Menander in his treatment of the *monodia*: the unfulfilled hopes for and expectations of the deceased, particularly if he is young (e.g., *Theb.* 3.160-64, 12.72-75; cf. Men. *Epid.* Sp. 3.431.34-435.4, 435.31-436.2, 436.21-24); the injustice of fortune and the gods (e.g., *Theb.* 10.795-801; cf. Men. *Epid.* Sp. 3.435.9-14); the contrast between past and present circumstances of the mourner and victim and the future hopes for the latter (e.g., *Theb.* 5.611-19, 6.138-42; cf. Men. *Epid.* Sp. 3.435.16-436.10); the use of apostrophe, frequently at the outset (e.g., *Theb.* 3.151f., 5.608-10, 9.49-52, 11.605-07; cf. Men. *Epid.* Sp. 3.435.30f.), and the amplification of pathos (e.g., 5.611-19; cf. Men. *Epid.* Sp. 3.436.2); and the contrast in the deceased's countenance with his former appearance (e.g., *Theb.* 3.154-56, 5.613-15, 9.381-84, 12.322-24; cf. Men. *Epid.* Sp. 3.436.15-21).

Other commonplaces of the lament include a gradual acknowledgement or unwilling acceptance of the victim's death (e.g., *Theb.* 12.344-48); the impotence and inconsolable grief of the speaker, shown by exclamations of affliction (e.g., 12.328, 340); reference to the wounds of the deceased (e.g., 3.153f., 9.69f., 10.813f., 11.624, 12.340); praise and subtle condemnation of the victim (e.g., 3.151f.); strong vituperation directed against the agent or cause of the victim's death, including self-reproach (e.g., 6.147-58, 10.811-14, 9.60, 12.341f.); the transference of blame from one individual or group, usually divine, to another or other figures, usually human (e.g., 5.620-27, 6.143-73 [esp. 143f., 147f., 150ff.], 9.60-72, 10.795-803, 10.811-814, 11.605-23 [esp. 617-23], 12.333-37, 12.340-43); the expression of the mourner's desire to bring harm to oneself (e.g., 11.611-15, 630f.); the mourner's wish for death as a punishment or release from emotional pain (e.g., 5.629-35); moral judgements on the plight of the victim (e.g., 6.138-42); an attitude of self-centredness and self-indulgence (e.g., 3.154-56); the desire for vengeance (e.g., 6.167-73, 12.342f.); and the wish that the mourner had never been born or given birth (e.g., 3.157-60). The large number of *topoi* suggests that the composition of the lament is determined primarily by the demands of the dramatic context.

The importance of the epic tradition is apparent in one type of unrealised wish in the lament concerning the birth of the mourner and her offspring: the mourner wishes either that she had not been born, or had not given birth, or both. An example of this type occurs in the *Iliad* when Andromache expresses the wish that she had never been born (22.480f.).

The strong influence of the rhetorical tradition in the composition of the *Thebaid* can be seen in the poet's frequent insertion of an animal or mythological simile into the narrative immediately preceding or following a lamentable speech in order to illustrate the grief of the mourner (cf. Men. *Epid.* 3.436.26-437.1). Not only does the simile embellish the narrative, but it also serves as a significant comment upon the dramatic situation and heightens the sense of pathos in the scene.

The primary function of the lament in the *Thebaid* is dramatic. This speech type forms the foundation for some of the most absorbing scenes in the epic in which various mourners spontaneously express their grief over the bodies of the deceased. The lament serves as a verbal manifest of an individual's passionate response to the loss of a kindred spirit. The violent emotional reaction of the speaker heightens the pathos of the scene and invigorates the narrative. Short sentences and the extensive use of figures further promote the atmosphere of grief and loss. The elaborate stylistic qualities of the lament serve the added purpose of adorning the narrative, but their principal function is to enhance the credibility of the dramatic situation.

The Feminine Lament

The lamentation of a mother over the impending or actual death of her son—the sorrowing mother image—is a characteristic feature of the narrative in heroic epic. Notable instances in the *Iliad* are the laments of Thetis (18.52-64) and Briseis (19.287-300) over Patroklos and those of Hekabe (22.431-36, 24.201-16, 22.748-59), Andromache (22.477-514, 24.725-45) and Helen (24.762-65) over the death of Hektor. The plaint of Euryalus' mother in the *Aeneid* (9.481-97) displays many of the *topoi* and stylistic devices characteristic of the informal epic lament, including the reproach of the victim, the desire for a pitiless death, and the frequent use of rhetorical questions and exclamations. There are five feminine laments of considerable importance in the *Thebaid* (3.151-68; 5.608-35; 6.138-73, 174-76, 180-83; 10.793-814; 12.322-48).

IDE (3.151-68)

Statius' technique of integrating the lament into the narrative is shown in his treatment of the dramatic situation after the return and death of Maeon. The Thebans proceed to the place where Tydeus struck down their compatriots (*Theb.* 3.114ff.). Most make the journey either to recover the corpses of the fallen or to console the mourners (114-18). The scene of unrestrained lamentation that follows is portrayed in the most graphic detail (120ff.). The purpose is to effect in the poet's audience a vicarious experience of inconsolable grief so they identify with the pathos of the women.

Statius' description of the mourners is remarkable for its hyperbolic conception and bears the evidence of declamatory influence. But he selects his details carefully in order to establish an atmosphere appropriate for the lamentable speech of Ide that follows. Under the gaze of the objectified figure of *Luctus atrox*, the mothers search for the corpses of their sons (125-28). Upon their discovery some of the mothers saturate their hair in the decay (129); others shut the eyes and cleanse the gaping wounds with their tears (129f.; cf. 173); yet others extract the darts or join the severed limbs together and affix the head to the shoulders (130-32). The particularity of the description is reminiscent of similar passages of morbidity in the works of Seneca (e.g., *Thy.* 721-43, *Oed.* 952-79) and Lucan (*Phars.* 2.178-85, 8.663-91).

The poet's attention then turns to the figure of Ide, whom he depicts in similar terms of horror (133ff.). While her dishevelled hair and lacerated cheeks portray her grief-stricken countenance, the extent of her suffering is shown when she examines and mourns over every corpse on the battlefield as if it were one of her sons (133-39). Statius further emphasises Ide's distress by likening her appearance to a Thessalian witch who wanders over the field looking for a corpse suitable for being raised from the dead (140-46). The picture would no doubt have made an even greater impact on the contemporary audience through the obvious reminiscence of the hideous Thessalian witch Erichtho in the *Pharsalia* (6.507-830).

The lament of Ide that follows serves as a fitting verbal manifestation of the grief experienced by the Theban mothers (*Theb.* 3.151-68). Since Ide's speech particularises the general sense of loss and sorrow that pervades the dramatic context, it reinforces and advances the narrative. Statius generates such emotion at the commencement of her lament that there is an intensification of the general tone of the narrative. This is accomplished primarily through a succession of rhetorical apostrophes, questions and exclamations that embellishes the style and gives the passage a heightened sense of urgency.

Ide begins her speech by apostrophising her sons (151f.):

hosne ego complexus genetrix, haec oscula, nati,
uestra tuor?

This address of the deceased with a subtle rebuke is commonplace in the
Statian lament. The transition from declarative statement in the narrative to
apostrophe in the opening line of her speech clearly distinguishes her lament
from the preceding narrative. There is implicit in her rhetorical question a
subtle hint of reproach directed at her sons; her subtle reproach is dramatically ironic, since earlier one of her sons reproaches Tydeus in similar but more
heated terms at the point of their deaths (2.641).

A distinctive feature of the *lamentatio* is the mourner's inculpation of
the gods. Ide faintly suggests this when she attributes the conjunctive
position of their corpses to personified Death (3.152f.). Her hesitancy over
which wounds and face to touch first emphasise her sense of loss (153f.).
But there is also an unmistakable element of egotism in her lament, for she
is bitterly disappointed that her sons have not achieved a fame prior to their
deaths that would increase her own renown (154-56). Ide had also hoped for
a better fate than for her sons to die obscurely on the battlefield without
glory (160-64). This expression of an unfulfilled desire is an element
characteristic of the lament in epic. Another common element is the
unrealised wish in which the mourner wishes either that she had not been
born, or had not given birth, or both. Ide's sorrow moves her to express
such a desire (157-60).

Ide's grief and sense of loss is genuine, although she betrays a
self-centred and self-indulgent attitude in her lament. Her lack of respect for
the manner of her sons' deaths does not prevent her from appreciating the
pious nature of their joint embrace. She ensures that her sons remain
unparted on the funeral pyre and that their ashes are mixed in the funerary
urn (165-68). The admiring tone of her concluding remarks suggest that the
anticipated consequences of mixing her son's ashes contrast favourably with
the direful commingling of Polynices' and Eteocles' remains (12.429ff.).

In the subsequent narrative other Theban women are shown mourning
in similar terms (3.169ff.). The realisation of the reader that Ide's lament
mirrors those of the other women maintains the atmosphere of pathos that
pervades the scene.

HYPSIPYLE (5.608-35)

Hypsipyle's search for her charge Opheltes (5.588ff.) is cast in terms similar to the search of Ide for her son. The hyperbolic nature of Statius' descriptive skill is shown especially in the concentration upon the mangled features of Opheltes' corpse. Resembling the gruesome description of Hippolytus' corpse in the *Metamorphoses* (15.524-29), the graphic portrayal of Opheltes' missing face and breast, flayed corpse, protruding brittle bones, and tendons immersed in fresh blood reaches a climax in the inflated pseudo-Ovidian expression *totumque in uulnere corpus* (5.596-98). The setting and tone for Hypsipyle's lament is further established by the subsequent skilful simile that likens Hypsipyle to the mother bird who returns to the nest to find her home and brood ravaged by a snake (599-604).

Hypsipyle's lament consists of the conventional *topoi*. One of the characteristic elements of the lament is the speaker's apostrophe of the victim by name and descriptive epithet. The substance of the epithets immediately establishes the attitude of the mourner toward her subject. In Hypsipyle's case the feeling is one of the deepest affection (608-10):

> o mihi desertae natorum dulcis imago,
> Archemore, o rerum et patriae solamen ademptae
> seruitiique decus . . . mea gaudia . . .

She then proceeds to contrast Opheltes' dire fate with the joy and consolation she had once known in his presence (611-19). This contrast between present and past circumstances, a customary feature of the Statian lament, immediately intensifies the atmosphere of pathos surrounding her plaint.

Hypsipyle's initial placing of blame on the gods displays the instinctive human urge to blame someone else other than oneself or the victim (620-22). This is quickly replaced by self-condemnation for her part in Opheltes' death (622-27):

> quos arguo diuos?
> ipsa ego te (quid enim timeam moritura fateri?)
> exposui Fatis. quae mentem insania traxit?
> tantane me tantae tenuere obliuia curae?
> dum patrios casus famaeque exorsa retracto
> ambitiosa meae (pietas haec magna fidesque!) . . .

126

The broken expression reveals the distress of Hypsipyle. Her informal lament is all the more appealing and convincing for its unpremeditated qualities and renders her more credible as a figure of pathos.

Hypsipyle understands that the death of Opheltes is compensation for the victim that she denied Venus by saving her husband Thoas (*exsolui tibi, Lemne, nefas*, 628). She is distraught over neglecting her duty to Opheltes and expresses a fervent wish for death (629-35):

> ferte, duces, meriti si qua est mihi gratia duri,
> si quis honos dictis, aut uos extinguite ferro,
> ne tristes dominos orbamque inimica reuisam
> Eurydicen, quamquam haud illi mea cura dolendo
> cesserit. hocne ferens onus inlaetabile matris
> transfundam gremio? quae—me prius ima sub umbras
> mergat humus!

The expression of a desire to bring harm to oneself is characteristic of the Statian lament. Hypsipyle can scarcely contemplate facing Opheltes' mother to inform her of the death. The skilful juxtaposition of the subsequent narrative describing her soiled appearance and thoughts of inculpation is representative of the Statian technique of interweaving speech and narrative (635-37).

EURYDICE, OPHELTES' MOTHER (6.138-73, 174-76, 180-84)

Eurydice's reaction to her son Opheltes' death is predictably violent (6.138ff.). Her long lament consists of the rhetorical qualities characteristic of this speech type. Short syntactic units of expression, parenthetical asides, rhetorical questions and exclamations predominate. The fragmented syntax suggests the unpremeditated flow of Eurydice's thoughts and sensations. This stream-of-consciousness effect helps the audience to identify more closely with the thoughts and feelings of the mourner and renders her more credible as a genuine figure of grief. The poet further enhances the appropriateness of Eurydice's lament by juxtaposing two brief passages of narrative (173, 177-79), each for a different purpose and each producing a different effect.

Eurydice never expected that she should have anything to fear from a Theban war (138-42):

non hoc Argolidum coetu circumdata matrum
speraui te, nate, sequi, nec talia demens
fingebam uotis annorum elementa tuorum,
nil saeuum reputans; etenim his in finibus aeui
unde ego bella tibi Thebasque ignara timerem?

Her words reflect not only her unfulfilled expectations for Opheltes through the contrast between past and present circumstances, but also the naïveté of women on both sides of the war who suffer undeservedly from its desolating effects.   There is inherent in her initial assessment of Opheltes' death a severe moral judgement on the effects of war upon the innocent, particularly those individuals who are most vulnerable.   It is a judgement that bears testimony to the tragic futility of war.

The instinctive reaction of Eurydice is to blame the gods for her suffering and the fate of Opheltes, who is the first to die in the war (143-48). Then she suddenly shifts the blame to Hypsipyle, whom she vituperates for her neglect of Opheltes (149ff.).   Eurydice understands that Opheltes is a surrogate victim for Thoas (150-54), who was saved by Hypsipyle when madness possessed the Argive women to slaughter their husbands (5.240ff.). Since Eurydice holds Hypsipyle primarily responsible for Opheltes' death, the loss of her son generates jealousy and anger rather than remorse.   She recalls enviously that Opheltes preferred Hypsipyle to herself (161f.) and that he was deprived of his real mother's affection while his nurse experienced a mother's joy in his complaints, laughter, tears and first words (163-67).

Eurydice's jealousy and anger leads her to reject the gifts of the Argive princes and demand that Hypsipyle join her on the funeral pyre (168-73). The subsequent descriptive narrative stresses the intensity of her grief and the extent of her resolve for vengeance against Hypsipyle (173).   After she repeats her demand and denies its cruelty (174-76), the narrative once again interrupts, suggesting the unreasonableness of her supplication and indicating a subtle shift in dramatic emphasis (177-80).   Eurydice resents Hypsipyle's lamentation (179)—the nurse is shown tearing at her hair and bosom (178)—but realises through the inaction of the princes that they will not grant her request for Hypsipyle's death.   So in her final words Eurydice attempts to deny the nurse even the privilege of publicly mourning her charge's death (180-84).   The simile that concludes the scene likens Eurydice to the grief-stricken mother of a young bullock who has been stolen away by a shepherd for sacrifice or a wild beast (186-92).   This further enhances the picture of desolation that is so characteristic of the lament in the *Thebaid*.

Since critics are so fond of pointing to the piety of women in the *Thebaid*, they generally discount the implications of Eurydice's display of jealousy and anger against Hypsipyle. There is admittedly a fine line between vindictiveness and righteous anger, but Eurydice's overpowering urge for revenge is scarcely the desire of a pious woman. Her overwhelming grief and resentment of Hypsipyle transmute into anger and jealousy; she is poisoned by these feelings in much the same way that Creon is consumed by indignation and bitterness in response to the death of Menoeceus.

EURYDICE, MENOECEUS' MOTHER (10.793-814)

The lament of Eurydice (10.793-814), Menoeceus' mother, resembles Ide's speech of mourning (3.151-68) in its reproachful tone. By the assent of the Theban populace Menoeceus is *auctorem pacis seruatoremque deumque* (10.684), but his mother perceives the significance of his death purely in personal terms. Eurydice did not nurture her son so that he should expiate the guilt of Thebes with his life (793f.). Because of her close relationship with the deceased, her violent grief obscures the heroic nature of her son's *Opfertod*.

The whole lament is ironic in a general sense because Eurydice is ignorant of Menoeceus' elevation to sacred status, a fact known to the Thebans and the reader or listener. Eurydice's use of the descriptive adjective *sacer* (804) to describe the madness that possessed her son further stresses the irony inherent in the dramatic situation; whereas she employs the adjective in an unfavourable sense ('execrable'), the poet's audience (cf. 650) and the Thebans would interpret it favourably ('sacred' [cf. 757]).

The instinctive reaction of Eurydice is to blame the gods for her son's unjust fate (795). She declares her moral innocence and protests that Jocasta's incestuous sons are undeservedly leaders and regents (796-801). Her words presage the deaths of Jocasta and her sons and are dramatically ironic, for the audience understands their import in a way that Eurydice cannot. She then shifts the blame from the gods directly to Menoeceus, identifying his death with her plight (802f.; cf. 804-806):

> tu, saeue Menoeceu,
> tu miseram ante omnes properasti extinguere matrem.

Eurydice perceives that the demand of the snake of Mars for an offering to ensure a Theban victory inspired Menoeceus to embrace death willingly (806-

10; cf. 612f.). Her assertion that her son's death is against the will of the Fates is a perceptive insight into the machinations of supernatural forces (809f.), since Menoeceus' death is but one incident in the plan of Jupiter, who elsewhere is portrayed as possessing power surpassing that of the Fates (1.213, 3.241f.). Menoeceus' death accords with the will of the supreme ruler, who just prior to the intervention of Virtus is shown in close companionship with the goddess (10.632ff.); thus the action of Virtus—despite the uncertainty of whether it is independent of or prompted directly by Jupiter (see 634f.)—in hastening the death of Menoeceus is best construed within the broader context of Jupiter's overriding control over the events on earth. Notwithstanding the supernatural imposition of death upon the youth (665-68) and the understandable concern of his mother over his ultimate fate (808f.), his sacrifice is still portrayed in the most heroic terms as a patriotic *Opfertod* worthy of his ascension to the stars (781f.).

Eurydice finishes her lament by echoing her earlier sentiment concerning Menoeceus (cf. 802-06), declaring that she should have feared her son rather than Capaneus and the Argives (811-814). The simile that concludes the scene is particularly moving and stresses the intensity of Eurydice's grief. She is like the dispirited tigress despoiled of her cubs lying in her lair, licking their traces on the warm stone and ignoring the flocks and herds who pass by (820-26).

ARGIA (12.322-48)

Argia's inspection of the corpses on the battlefield in the final book (288-90) resembles the search of the Theban women (3.127-28), Ide (3.137-39) and Ismenis (9.368-70) for their sons and husbands. When Argia finds Polynices, she falls over him, smothering his corpse with kisses and squeezing out the blood from his hair and attire (12.318-21; cf. 3.129).

The constituents of Argia's lament for her husband are commonplace (12.322ff.). The opening lines of the lament are reminiscent of the first section in Ismene's lament where she attempts to come to terms with her son's death (9.376ff.). There is explicit in Argia's address of her prostrate husband the contrast between his former proud mien as an Argive commander and his present bearing (12.322-24):

> hunc ego te, coniunx, ad debita regna profectum
> ductorem belli generumque potentis Adrasti
> aspicio, talisque tuis occurro triumphis?

So great is Argia's consternation that she scarcely comprehends that Polynices is deceased. She commands him to rise and lead her triumphantly into Thebes (325-28):

> huc attolle genas defectaque lumina: uenit
> ad Thebas Argia tuas; age, moenibus induc
> et patrios ostende lares et mutua redde
> hospitia.

She finally comes to her senses and realises that her husband is dead (328f.):

> heu quid ago? proiectus caespite nudo
> hoc patriae telluris habes?

Argia's observation that Polynices possesses only the actual ground he lies on is particularly pathetic and stresses the futility of his struggle to gain the Theban throne.

Argia briefly ponders on the ruinous consequences of her husband's feud with Eteocles and reprehends Jocasta and Antigone for not coming to mourn over Polynices (329-332). At first she recalls her attempt to dissuade Polynices from taking an active part in the war (333-35), then remembers that she had incited him to war (336f.; cf. 3.678-710):

> quid queror? ipsa dedi bellum maestumque rogaui
> ipsa patrem ut talem nunc te complexa tenerem.

These words of self-reproach are succeeded by an expression of gratitude to the gods for assisting her in finding Polynices' corpse (12.338-40). This inversion of the topical element of divine inculpation in the lament accentuates the pious qualities of this noble woman. The conventional expression of blame and condemnation that the mourner directs against a third party ensues; Argia's vituperation of the despotic Eteocles is especially virulent (340-43):

> ei mihi, sed quanto descendit vulnus hiatu!
> hoc frater? qua parte, precor, iacet ille nefandus
> praedator? vincam volucres (sit adire potestas)
> excludamque feras; an habet funestus et ignes?

Argia concludes her lament by resolving to bury Polynices (344-48):

sed nec te flammis inopem tua terra videbit:
ardebis lacrimasque feres quas ferre negatum
regibus, aeternumque tuo famulata sepulcro
durabit deserta fides, testisque dolorum
natus erit, parvoque torum Polynice fovebo.

These lines reveal that Argia has recovered her composure and sense of purpose. This is evidenced in her heroic determination to bury Polynices in accordance with human and divine law in the face of tyrannical opposition. She risks her life willingly in order to fulfil her obligation and discharge her duty to her husband. Argia displays a nobility and courage that easily surpasses the valour shown by the other Argive women; her unswerving devotion to Polynices serves as the supreme example of *pietas*. There is immanent in her lament and act of devotion a basic moral awareness of the individual's responsibility to other family and community members.

The mention of Argia and Polynices' son (347f.) evokes memories of Dido's famous reproach of Aeneas in the *Aeneid* in which the Carthaginian queen expresses a desire for a son to remind her of the Trojan leader in his absence (4.327-30). Unlike Dido, though, Argia is fortunate to have conceived a son whose features and manner resemble those of her partner; this factor alone makes the loss of Polynices easier to endure.

The Male Lament

The male lament is less common in heroic epic than the feminine lament. Menander cites Priam's ritual lament over the death of Hektor (*Il.* 22.416-28) as an early model for the ritual lament (*Epid.* Sp. 3.434.12-15). Another ritual lament in the *Iliad* is delivered by Achilleus over Patroklos (19.315-37). Informal laments in the *Aeneid* are spoken by Anchises for Marcellus (6.868-86), Mezentius over the corpse of his son Lausus (10.846-56), and Evander over the dead body of his son Pallas (11.152-81). All of these laments are accompanied by a violent display of grief on the part of the bereaved.

The laments of Polynices and Oedipus are the most noteworthy in the *Thebaid* and are of sufficient length to suggest certain distinctive characteristics. Overwhelming grief, self-condemnation, remorse, and reproach of the gods are conspicuous elements; the outstanding feature is the wish to commit suicide. The expression of the desire to take one's life is a variation upon the feminine wish for death. The active aspect of the male death wish contrasts with the passiveness of the feminine expression. Polynices and Oedipus follow up their suicide wishes with an actual attempt to take their lives, while the female mourner typically expresses a death wish intended either for herself or the individual whom she holds most responsible for the death of her loved one.

POLYNICES (9.49-72, 75F.)

When Polynices hears the news of Tydeus' death, he is paralysed with grief, scarcely managing to drag himself to the scene of his brother-in-law's death (9.36ff.). When his comrades point out Tydeus to him (45), he falls prostrate upon the corpse (47f.) and tearfully commences his lament (49-52):

> hasne tibi, armorum spes o suprema meorum,
> Oenide, grates, haec praemia digna rependi,
> funus ut inuisa Cadmi tellure iaceres
> sospite me?

The rhetorical question resembles the tone and sentiment of other introductory questions in the lamentable speeches of Ide (3.151-53), Ismenis (9.376f.), Eurydice (10.793f.), and Argia (12.322-24).

Polynices realises with the death of the heroic Tydeus that his dream of ascending the Theban throne is lost forever (52f.); the loss of his devoted friend renders meaningless the acquisition of the throne (54-56, 58-60). He orders his warriors to depart and leave him to face his brother alone (57, 59). Polynices is remorseful over involving Tydeus in his plan to gain power and holds himself directly responsible for his friend's death (60): *Tydea consumpsi!* He cites Tydeus' pledge of loyalty originating from their earlier brief confrontation and the heroic mission to Eteocles as examples of his friend's devotion (60-68). Polynices likens his bond of friendship with Tydeus to the friendship that exists between Theseus and Pirithous and between Telamon and Meleager (9.69), a comparison that echoes the advice of the rhetorician Menander (*Epid.* Sp. 3.396.15-18).

Like Ide in her lament over her sons (*Theb.* 3.153f.), Polynices pauses briefly in order to reflect on which wounds to touch first (9.69). He then shifts the blame for the death of Tydeus from himself to the gods, attributing the hero's death to divine causation, declaring that Jupiter and Mars are responsible for his fate (71f.):

(num fallor?) et ipse
inuidit pater et tota Mars impulit hasta.

The narrative that intervenes at this point depicts a lachrymatory Polynices wiping blood from Tydeus' face (73f.). This brief description of Polynices mourning over Tydeus' corpse enhances the atmosphere of loss and foretells a change in the direction of his lament. This is immediately confirmed when he cries, *tune meos hostes hucusque exosus, et ultra / sospes ego?* (75f.), and must be restrained from taking his life (76ff.). Polynices' attempt to take his own life is an indication of his difficulty in coping with the loss of his comrade and bearing the weight of his own guilt and self-condemnation. As noted above, Polynices' vain attempt to take his own life contrasts with the passive aspect of the feminine death wish. The ensuing narrative simile in which Polynices is likened to a bull lamenting the loss of his partner is especially effective in conveying the Theban's sorrow and despair (82-85).

OEDIPUS (11.605-26, 630F.)

Oedipus' lament is deserving of special attention. The description of the cadaverous Oedipus bursting forth from his profound darkness when he receives the news of his sons' deaths is visually graphic (11.580ff.). His grey beard and hair are filthy and stiff with decaying matter; his hair indurate with blood conceals his dreadful head; his eyes and cheeks are sunk deep into his head and obscure the traces of his ocular effosion (582-85). The subsequent simile comparing Oedipus to the pale Charon making his entrance to the world above accentuates the picture of morbidity (587-92).

Antigone supports the decrepit figure as they make way their way over fallen men and the instruments of war (586, 596-98). When Antigone's cry betrays her discovery of the corpses, Oedipus flings himself onto the bloody corpses, searching for the faces inside the casques (599f., 603). Finally he finds expression for his grief with a series of rhetorical questions, apostrophes, and exclamations that arrests instantly (605-09):

tarda meam, Pietas, longo post tempore mentem
percutis? estne sub hoc hominis clementia corde?
uincis io miserum, uincis, Natura, parentem!
en habeo gemitus lacrimaeque per arida serpunt
uulnera et in molles sequitur manus impia planctus.

These lines reveal that Oedipus is not only surprised at the depth of his feelings but also is repentant over having caused the death of his sons.

While Oedipus' speech mirrors the self-indulgent tone of Polynices' lament (9.49-72, 75f.) and lacks the implicit moralistic sentiment of Argia's lamentable speech (12.322-48), the blind man's self-condemnation and desire to punish himself underlines his feeling of guilt over his action of fomenting hatred between his sons and indirectly causing their deaths. The sincere expression of profound grief and the acceptance of responsibility for the deaths of his sons is evidence of Oedipus' deep regret. This display of remorse further suggests that Oedipus could bring himself to curse his sons only because he was under the influence of the Furies; now that the curse has been fulfilled, the Furies free him from their grip and he experiences true parental feelings. The previously obdurate Oedipus can scarcely believe that he has been reduced to tears and is amazed at his feelings of love and forgiveness.

Oedipus is unable to tell his sons apart and expresses a notable desire to do injury to himself (11.611-15):

> nec noscere natos
> adloquiumque aptare licet; dic, uirgo, precanti,
> quem teneo? quo nunc uestras ego saeuus honore
> prosequar inferias? o si fodienda redirent
> lumina et in uultus saeuire ex more potestas!

As shown previously, the desire to bring physical harm to oneself as a punishment is characteristic of the lament. The touch here is perhaps a bit extravagant, but is designed to arouse pathos and reflect the depth of Oedipus' grief. Just as Oedipus earlier inflicted upon himself a punishment that he deemed appropriate to his criminal acts of incest and murder, his wish to tear out his eyes illustrates that he views his rôle in precipitating the deaths of his sons as worthy of severe punishment.

The transference of culpability from one individual or group to another is a commonplace of the lament. Nevertheless, Oedipus' shifting of blame from himself to a host of human and divine characters is exceptional. He blames one of the gods for granting his execrable prayers against Polynices and Eteocles (617-19; cf. 1.56-87); furthermore, he holds Erinys, his mother, father, former kingdom and even his excised eyes responsible for his nefarious curse and prayer (619f.). Oedipus is aware that the sins of his forebears have been transmitted to him by his parents and that the deaths of his sons are a natural consequence of the guilt that he inherited from previous generations. Oedipus' fate and that of his sons are not entirely of his own making, for Jupiter merely brings to fruition through the instruments of fate what he has ordained.

There is considerable justification for Oedipus' attribution of blame to the Furies, since they are shown not only inspiring (cf. 1.73f.) and immediately carrying his curse into effect (88ff.) but also exerting a continuing and decisive influence over his actions (see esp. 1.60-72, 7.466-69); more generally, these demonic creatures are shown to be instrumental in bringing the plans of Jupiter and Pluto (see esp. 1.214-17, 8.34-79, respectively) to fruition through their infection of various human figures with *furor*, notably Oedipus and his sons (7.467-69).

Oedipus' attempt to absolve himself of blame for his sons' deaths on account of divine causation and inherited guilt is reasonable enough, given that he is shown to be inextricably entangled in the web of fate. At first glance it appears that the tenability of his argument is undermined to some extent because of his apparent incitement of Tisiphone and the infernal deities to vengeance on his behalf, but even at this moment he is shown to be under their control when uttering the curse against his sons (1.51f.); furthermore, he is exculpable to the degree that he is caught up in events beyond his control and is unable to exert any real influence over the fate of his sons.

Other cosmic forces are at work. Earlier Jupiter commands Mercury to accompany the shade of Laius to the upper world so that the spirit can instigate hatred in Eteocles for his brother and impel the regent to break the agreement of alternate rule with him (1.292-301). Since Oedipus is ignorant of the rôle of Laius' shade in hastening the deaths of Polynices and Eteocles, he expresses the hope that his father will receive him in Tartarus (11.622f.). While Oedipus has finally been able to forgive, it is impossible to know whether Laius' shade will prove capable of doing the same.

Reference to the touching of the deceased's body is frequently made in the Statian lament. Oedipus runs his hands across his sons' wounds, noting their hostile embrace and deep wounds (624). He implores them to release their grip of hatred on each other (625f.). The scene recalls the circumstances involving the twin sons of Ide, who embrace lovingly after being slain by Tydeus (2.629-43). Polynices and Eteocles embody qualities contraposed to those displayed by Ide's sons; while the former are models of treachery and hatred, the latter exemplify the virtues of brotherly love and devotion.

The narrative interrupts the speech of Oedipus at this juncture, just as it does toward the close of Polynices' lament (9.73f.), indicating a shift in direction and emphasis. Antigone anticipates the desire of her father to take his own life and removes the swords from his presence (11.627-30), whereupon he expresses his frustration and anger over his helplessness (630f.):

> ubi noxia tela?
> heu Furiae! num totum abiit in corpora ferrum?

The concluding exclamatory shouts and rhetorical questions echo the passionate outburst at the beginning of the lament. Antigone, whose speech and action elsewhere in the epic reveals her pious and heroic qualities, silently rejoices because her cruel father at last feels remorse and regret over his criminal deeds (633f.).

At the commencement of his lament, Oedipus accepts the responsibility for the deaths of his sons and is remorseful. His remorse changes to regret when he maintains that circumstances beyond his control incited him to curse them and pray for their destruction. As pointed out above, Oedipus' claim that he is a pawn of circumstance and fate has considerable merit; his declaration suggests that his wish for death toward the end of his lament is due more to his grief over losing his sons than guilt or remorse. Even so, his transformation from an embittered old man to an individual capable of feeling clearly impels him to seek death as a release from his emotional pain.

Consolation

The epic consolation is a verbal manifest of the psychological and practical necessity of the mourner to cease lamentation after a brief period of mourning so that he can resume living in the usual manner. The consolation is the culmination of the formal and public process of mourning in which a threnodist philosophises on various aspects involving the universality of death. One effect of the consolatory speech is to slow down the pace of the narrative and compel the listener to reflect on and identify with this most fundamental of all human sensations. Aletes' consolation actually enhances rather than assuages the sorrow of the Theban mourners (*Theb.* 3.179-213); however, his speech is particularly effective in heightening the atmosphere of loss and grief that pervades the dramatic situation because the speech arouses pathos for the unjust plight of the guiltless victims of the war.

The consolation in Homeric and Vergilian epic is generally more subdued in tone and therefore less elaborate than the lament. While the speaker of an epic lament is extremely distressed, the speaker of an epic consolation is usually fairly composed and philosophical. Such consolations are commonplace in Homeric epic. Quintilian remarks that the eloquence of Homer is revealed in his composition of consolatory speeches (*Inst.* 10.1.47). Although Achilleus' consolatory speech to Priam in reply to the Trojan king's request for the ransom of Hektor is perhaps the most celebrated example in the *Iliad* of Homer's skill in consolatory composition (24.518-51), the consolations of Hephaistos (1.586-94), Dione (5.382-415) and Achilleus (24.599-620) are particularly noteworthy for their mythological allusions. The latter speech of Achilleus merits considerable interest, since the reference to the slaughter of the sons and daughters by Apollo and Artemis (*Il.* 24.602-17, esp. 605-09) is echoed by Aletes in his consolatory speech in the *Thebaid* (3.191-94). Consolations are rare in the *Aeneid*. An outstanding example occurs when Jupiter consoles Hercules over the impending death of Pallas at the hands of Turnus (10.467-72).

ALETES (3.179-213)

The speech delivered by the aged Aletes is the sole consolation in the *Thebaid* (3.179-213). After Tydeus slays the Theban warriors sent by Eteocles to ambush him, the relatives of the men journey to the scene of the slaughter (114ff.). As the funeral pyres of the Theban men are kindled, Aletes delivers his consolatory speech to the relations of the victims (179ff.). Instead of the spontaneous outpouring of grief characteristic of the lament, there is generally a subdued tone, which is designed to assuage the misery and grief of the Thebans; the subdued tone also suggests the emotional exhaustion of the mourners. The simple declarative sentences that dominate the passage enhance the composed atmosphere.

Aletes commences his lament by philosophising on the circumstances concerning the past and present misfortunes of Thebes. Aletes blames the Fates for the past afflictions of the Theban race (179f.). He recounts the adverse circumstances that have plagued Thebes since its portentous founding when Cadmus sowed the dearth and the warriors who sprang up from the furrows turned upon each other (180-83): the deceit of Juno—whom Aletes describes as *iniqua* (184)—in persuading Semele to request Jupiter to reveal himself in his true form, whereupon she was destroyed by his thunderbolts (183-85); the slaying of Learchus by his father Athamas, who was maddened by Juno (185-88); and the killing of Pentheus by his mother Agave, who was driven mad by Dionysos (188-90). According to Aletes, only Apollo and Artemis' slaughter of Niobe's sons and daughters equals the present tragic circumstances (191-98). Aletes concludes this mitigative section of the consolation by reiterating his earlier claim that these misfortunes were engineered by the Fates (201-06) and adding that they were willed by Jupiter (206). There can be no doubt that Aletes holds the hostile gods directly responsible for the cruel suffering that Thebes has endured in the past. His criticism seems justified, since in most cases the victims are not actually guilty of any crime; even in the case of Pentheus, who suffers a cruel fate for refusing to accept the worship of Dionysos, his punishment—like that of the Lemnian women who neglect the worship of Venus (5.58ff.)—far outweighs the severity of his offence.

While Aletes attributes the previous ill fortune of the Thebans to divine causation, he holds Eteocles directly responsible for Thebes' present misfortune (206-09; cf. 214f.). At this juncture of the lament there is a transition in Aletes' demeanour from relative composure to violent emotion, from resigned acceptance of cruel supernatural power to tears of rage over human treachery. However, Aletes' passionate outburst inverts the condolent spirit and intent of the consolatory speech, for the consolation is designed to mitigate, not increase, the suffering of the afflicted. His prediction of a bloody war and desire for a proper burial while it is still possible can only serve to intensify the Thebans' grief and sense of loss (210-13). The ensuing narrative that describes him reviling Eteocles (214f.) shows the skill of Statius in shifting smoothly from speech to narrative.

Epikedion

ARGIVE TROOPS (8.174-207)

The brief *epikedion* that follows closely upon the descent of Amphiaraus to the underworld reflects the deep sorrow of the Argive warriors over their loss (8.174-207). Major features of the *epikedion* are the expression of grief, the praise of the deceased, and the consolation of the mourners. The four main sections of the funeral speech in honour of

Amphiaraus are: *prooemium* (174-76), praise of the priest's prophetic powers (177-83) and actions (183-88), consolation (189-194, 206-07), mourning and commemoration (195-205). Although the structure of the brief epic *epikedion* in honour of Amphiaraus does not conform strictly to the pattern of Statius' *epikedia* and *consolationes* in the *Silvae* or the *epitaphios* prescribed by Menander (*Epid. Sp.* 3.418.5-422.4) and pseudo-Dionysius (*Gen. Dem.* Rad. 277.6-283.19), the *topoi* resemble some of the elements that comprise these and other genres such as the *laudatio funebris, basilikos logos* (Men. *Epid. Sp.* 3.368.1-377.30), *paramuthetikos* (413.5-414.30), *monodia* (434.10-437.4) and various sepulchral epigrams. The common denominator of these genres is the praise of the dead. The funeral speech in honour of Amphiaraus is permeated with encomiastic elements attesting to his prophetic talents and prowess in battle.

Elements appearing in the funeral speech for the priest that are common to the prescriptions of the rhetoricians and the consolatory poems of Statius are (using *Silv.* 2.6 as an illustration): the reproach of the gods (*Theb.* 8.176; cf. Men. *Epid. Sp.* 3.435.9-14, *Silv.* 2.6.58-70), praise of the deceased's talents (*Theb.* 8.177-83; cf. Men. *Epid. Sp.* 3.420.9-24, ps.-Dion. Hal. *Gen. Dem.* Rad. 279.12-18, *Silv.* 2.6.21ff.), praise of the dead person's actions (*Theb.* 8.183-88; cf. Men. *Epid. Sp.* 3.420.24-27, *Silv.* 2.6.21-57), consolatory topics (*Theb.* 8.189-94, 206f.; cf. Men. *Epid. Sp.* 3.421.14-24, ps.-Dion. Hal. *Gen. Dem.* Rad. 281.2-283.10, *Silv.* 2.6.93-105), and mourning (*Theb.* 8.195-205; cf. Men. *Epid. Sp.* 3.420.4-9, 3.421.10-14, *Silv.* 2.6.58-93).

Speeches of Encouragement

There are two types of exhortative speeches in the *Thebaid*; they are the combat exhortation (*cohortatio* or *parakletikos*) and the noncombat exhortation. The first type is delivered by monarchs, warriors, a priest and a goddess and is a prominent feature in many of the battle scenes; the purpose of such a speech is to incite a group of loyal princes, warriors or citizens to combat. As in the *Aeneid*, there are no exhortations to battle addressed to individual warriors in the epic.

The other type of exhortation is nonviolent in persuasion; this type includes athletic as well as general speeches of encouragement. According to these definitions, there are fifteen combat exhortations and three noncombat exhortations in the *Thebaid*.

Combat Exhortations (Cohortationes)

The exhortatory war speech delivered by a commander-in-chief to his troops was a customary feature of ancient warfare. Heslop notes that '[a] harangue either before or in the middle of a battle is an obvious place to seek rhetorical effect since the speaker intends to rouse or revive his listeners; this type of oration will naturally be common in a heroic poem wherein fighting plays a large part'.[34] Hortatory speeches figure prominently in Homeric epic and in the lyric poems of Greek poets such as Tyrtaeus, a Spartan general of the seventh century BCE. The exhortative speeches of commanders-in-chief in the *Iliad* and of generals in Herodotus are prototypes of the *parakletikoi* and *cohortationes* of later annalists and historians. The traditional speech before battle in epic was adopted by Thucydides as an important element in his history; although he was the first to incorporate exhortative speeches by commanders to their troops into historical narrative as a standard practice, later historians such as Polybius, Livy and Tacitus followed his lead in the composition of their histories.

In the *Iliad* short speeches of encouragement are delivered on numerous occasions by commanders to their troops. The speeches of Hektor to the Trojans and their allies (15.486-99, 718-25) serve as models for this type. The commonplaces anticipate those in *parakletikoi* in historical composition, especially in the assumption of divine favour (*Il.* 15.488-93, 719, 724f.) and the glory of dying while fighting to save a homeland (496f.). Hortatory speeches by commanders prior to or during battle occur less frequently in the *Aeneid* than in the *Iliad*. Aeneas (*Aen.* 1.198-207, 2.348-54) and Turnus (*Aen.* 9.128-58, 10.279-84) each make only two exhortations to their troops. One of the most interesting is the speech of Pallas to the Arcadians (10.369-78), which echoes the exhortation of Aias to the Achaeans in *Iliad* 15.733-41. The *topoi* are similar to those appearing in historical *parakletikoi*: there are references to past deeds of bravery and battles won (369-71), an appeal to ancestry and patriotism (369-71, 374), observations on the disastrous consequences of defeat (372) and the absence of divine hostility (375), and a comparison between armies (375f.).

---

[34] Heslop (1962: pt. 1, 24).

SPEECH AND RHETORIC IN STATIUS' *THEBAID*

In the *Thebaid* the speech of encouragement is typically delivered by a commander or other person in a position of authority to his troops. Eteocles delivers three exhortative speeches to his warriors, one more than Adrastus and Thiodamas. The structure of this speech type is easy to discern. The *prooemium* usually consists of short references such as the superfluity of exhorting the troops (e.g., *Theb.* 7.375-78), the certainty of victory in the forthcoming battle (e.g., 10.21-23), or the favourable pronouncements of the gods (e.g., 10.189f.). Often the *prooemium* is omitted, particularly if there is some urgency in the proposal, as in Tydeus' exhortation to the Argive leaders (3.348ff.). Occasionally there is a *narratio* that provides the background for the proposal that follows, as in Tydeus' description of the ambush (356-60); however, the *narratio* is frequently dispensed with, presumably since the troops usually are aware of the circumstances concerning the exhortation. After the *propositio*, which is usually stated in clear and concise terms, comes the *probatio* (*tractatio*), a consideration of the main reasons for supporting the proposal. The last division of the combat exhortation is the *peroratio*; this section is extremely brief and usually consists either of a brief restatement of the proposal or a final appeal to the troops.

Reasons for adopting the proposal are variations on the traditional themes of divine favour, such as the favourable auspices and support of the gods (e.g., *Theb.* 7.380f., 10.23f., 10.192f., 10.213, 10.216f., 10.237, 10.267, 12.644-47); the rewards of victory or victory *as* the reward (e.g., 7.380f., 10.29, 10.34f., 10.192f., 10.243f.); the ease or certainty of victory (e.g., 3.360-62, 10.21, 10.29, 10.192f., 10.206-08, 10.214, 10.243f.); the justice of the cause and the unjust nature of the enemy's cause (e.g., 3.350f., 7.377f., 7.381-87, 10.19f., 10.644f., 10.648); ancestry, family and tradition, namely the strength or bravery of one's race and the glorious feats of one's ancestors (e.g., 3.349, 8.600f., 10.238f.); the superior strength of the allied forces in contrast to the weak and depleted forces of the enemy (e.g., 3.360-62, 10.24-35); injustice endured at the hands of the enemy (e.g., 9.12-19); and the ignominy of defeat (e.g., 2.620-23).

ETEOCLES (10.21-35), THIODAMAS (10.188-218)

The *topoi* of Eteocles' (10.21-35) and Thiodamas' (188-218) *cohortationes* are representative of this speech type. Eteocles delivers his cohortative speech to the Theban troops as they prepare to encircle the

142

Argive camp. He addresses his troops as *victores Danaum*, hoping to inspire them by suggesting they have for all intensive purposes won the war (21). The traditional arguments are employed: the gods are our allies (23f.); the forces of the enemy are depleted, since four of their leaders are dead (Tydeus, Amphiaraus, Hippomedon and Parthenopaeus) and those who survive (the elderly Adrastus, cowardly Polynices and crazed Capaneus) are scarcely to be feared (24-32); the reward of imminent victory are spoils and wealth (34f.).

A short while later Thiodamas incites the dispirited Argive troops to attack the Theban army, which has surrounded their camp, and declares that the auspices are favourable for an immediate assault (188ff.). In a speech dominated by short syntactic units of expression reflecting his prophetic frenzy, Thiodamas maintains that Amphiaraus has ordered such an attack on the sleeping Thebans to take place (190-95). The arguments for an attack are variations on the conventional exhortative themes of divine and auspicial favour (192f., 208, 213, 216-18), the rewards of victory (192f.), and the certainty and ease of success (214).

TYDEUS (3.348-65)

The combat exhortation of Tydeus (3.348-65) owes its scheme primarily to the impetus of the dramatic situation, namely, the ambush of the hero by the band of fifty warriors during his return journey from Thebes to Argos. After Tydeus successfully defends himself and returns to his adopted city, he finds Adrastus convoking a meeting with his princes (345ff.) The hero bursts into the palace and demands that Adrastus and the princes take up arms against the Theban enemy (348-53):

> arma, arma uiri, tuque optime Lernae
> ductor, magnanimum si quis tibi sanguis auorum,
> arma para! nusquam pietas, non gentibus aequum
> fas aut cura Iouis; melius legatus adissem
> Sauromatas rabidos seruatoremque cruentum
> Bebrycii nemoris.

In dispensing with the *prooemium* and proceeding immediately to the *propositio* and *partitio*, Tydeus shows his impetuous and violent nature. In appealing to the ancestry of the Argives and declaring that piety, justice and law have vanished from the earth, Tydeus attempts to demonstrate that the Argive cause is just.

After asserting that he is pleased to have gone on his mission because the guilt of Thebes has been exposed, Tydeus expresses additional justification for war in recounting the ambush (354-59):

> iuuat isse, iuuat, Thebasque nocentes
> explorasse manu; bello me, credite, bello,
> ceu turrem ualidam aut artam compagibus urbem,
> delecti insidiis instructique omnibus armis
> nocte doloque uiri nudum ignarumque locorum
> nequiquam clausere.

The *narratio* of events (356-60) is intended to provide the background to the *propositio*.

After briefly concluding the *narratio* by describing the disastrous consequences of the ambush for his attackers (359f.), Tydeus repeats his proposal and gives his reasons for recommending an immediate attack (360-62):

> nunc o nunc tempus in hostes,
> dum trepidi exanguesque metu, dum funera portant,
> nunc, socer, haec dum non manus excidit.

He is convinced that a quick assault upon the Thebans will bring success since they are frightened and weakened by his slaughter of the ambush party; despite his physical exhaustion and wounds, he expresses his eagerness to set out at once for Thebes (362-65).

ETEOCLES (7.375-90)

The exhortation of Eteocles to the Theban princes (7.375-90) is consistent with his dissembling and hypocritical nature. In the opening lines he feigns modesty and servility to his princes, professing that as a common soldier he would not refuse their command to fight in the forthcoming war (375f.). The stance of humility is scarcely credible in a figure like Eteocles, whose refusal to step down from the throne in violation of the agreement with his brother has precipitated the war in the first instance. The regent adds the commonplace assertion in speeches of this type that it is unnecessary to incite the princes to battle, since they have come unprompted to defend his righteous anger (377f.). In the case of Eteocles this claim is certainly baseless.

The familiar *topoi* of the *cohortatio* are evident: the gods are favourable to our cause (380f.); victory over the enemy will be your reward (380-81); and the cause is just (381-87). His words are dramatically ironic, since he is blind to the facts of the situation known to the reader: Jupiter and the Fates are hostile to his cause; defeat and death, not victory and glory, will ensue; and his cause is unjust and dishonourable. He holds his brother culpable entirely for the current situation. Eteocles concludes by reiterating his claim that assistance is given to him freely by the people and arguing that his army forbids him to abdicate the throne (387-90). Every element in the speech of the tyrant is intended to distort and misrepresent the circumstances leading up to the commencement of the war; his attempt to justify his cause in the war does not mask the real nature of the situation or conceal his true character.

The Divine Speaker

Speeches of encouragement addressed to groups of warriors are delivered infrequently in the *Iliad* (e.g., 4.509-13, 13.95-124), although a great many brief exhortations are made by the gods to individual warriors (e.g., 4.93-103, 13.47-58, 16.721-25). In the *Aeneid* there is one divine exhortation to a group of warriors (12.229-337), but no divinity exhorts a lone figure to battle.

PIETAS (11.478-81)

Pietas is the only deity in the *Thebaid* to deliver a speech of encouragement to a group of warriors (11.478-81); no individual warrior is exhorted to battle by a divinity in the epic. The goddess descends to earth in order to prevent the duel between Polynices and Eteocles from taking place (472ff.). She attempts to incite the troops on both sides to recommence their hostilities (478-81); however, Tisiphone upbraids and drives her from the battlefield and the duel between the brothers continues even more heatedly than before (484-96). Although there is no question that Pietas is a benevolent goddess associated with the powers of humanity and reason against supernatural forces of inhumanity and irrationality (cf. 457-63), it is significant that she feels compelled to exhort men to wage an unholy war in order to prevent an even worse crime of fratricide from being perpetrated.

The Vituperative Component

The commander-in-chief speech consisting of a vituperative component has its origin in the heroic tradition; the recipients of such an address are loyal chieftains, troops, or citizens. The ultimate purpose of the vituperative component is to provoke the addressee to assume an active rôle on the battlefield. In *Iliad* 8.228-31 Agamemnon chides his warriors for their cowardliness in pitched battle. Exhortative speeches with a vituperative component are also delivered by divinities to the warring sides they favour (e.g., *Il.* 13.95-124). In the *Aeneid* the vituperative words of Numanus to the Trojans (9.614-20) and Tarchon to the Etruscans (11.732-40) are designed to encourage their dispirited armies. The commanders heap scorn upon their troops by attributing effeminate qualities to them. Naturally the purpose of these exhortative speeches, as in Turnus' rebuke addressed to the Latins and Rutulians (11.459-61), is quite different from that of the discouraging taunts issued to the Trojans by their foes, including Turnus (12.99f.) and Iarbas (4.214-18), who also ascribe a womanish nature to the Phrygians.

The vituperative component is a significant feature of exhortations to battle delivered at public gatherings and assemblies in epic. Typical is the sarcastic rebuke that Turnus delivers to a public assembly of Latin and Rutulian citizens when they hesitate to engage the Trojans in combat (*Aen.* 11.459-61):

> immo . . . o ciues . . .
> cogite concilium et pacem laudate sedentes;
> illi armis in regna ruunt.

Similarly Capaneus delivers a scathing address to a crowd of Argive leaders and citizens that is intended to encourage the populace to instigate war against Thebes (*Theb.* 3.607-18).

CHROMIS (2.620-23), MENOECEUS (8.600-05)

Chromis and Menoeceus are successful in inspiring their Theban compatriots by shaming them to action. Rhetorical questions, exclamations, short sentences and clauses dominate their speeches. Chromis taunts the other members of the band sent by Eteocles to ambush Tydeus, declaring that the Argives will scarcely believe that Tydeus has vanquished so many warriors and exhorting them to fulfil their mission for Eteocles (2.620-23). Menoeceus chides his comrades who are slow to recover the body of Atys after the youth is struck down by Tydeus (8.600-05):

> pudeat, Cadmea iuuentus,
> terrigenas mentita patres! quo tenditis . . .,
> degeneres? meliusne iacet pro sanguine nostro
> hospes Atys? tantum hospes adhuc et coniugis ultor
> infelix nondum iste suae; nos pignora tanta
> prodimus?

Menoeceus' suggestion that his Theban compatriots bring disrepute to their ancestors by their inaction is a familiar *topos* of the epic exhortation.

CAPANEUS (3.607-18)

The address of Capaneus to a crowd of Argive leaders and citizens is one of the most rhetorically violent speeches in the *Thebaid* and is intended to encourage the populace to instigate war against Thebes (3.607-18); that Capaneus delivers such a speech is unsurprising, given his conceit and lack of reverence. The brute warrior is not the sort of hero to reserve his arrogance and insolence for his Theban adversaries alone; his speeches, mostly taunts and challenges, are directed with equal fearlessness to his friends, foes and even the Olympian gods. Capaneus' first and longest speech exemplifies his impetuous and arrogant nature. His primitive aspect and baser qualities are emphasised just prior to his oration when he is likened to the Cyclops and the Centaur (604f.).

Capaneus commences his speech by rebuking the mob for taking Amphiaraus' voluntary seclusion seriously and devoting undue attention to his oracular pronouncements (607-611). Capaneus accuses Amphiaraus publicly of cowardice, taunting him to practise ornithomancy and thereby reveal the future of the war (607ff.). The hero's irreverence is disclosed in his total disregard for Amphiaraus' standing in the community. Not only does Capaneus impute timidity to Amphiaraus (616), but he also refers to the priest as merely *unius ciuis* (607-09).

The hero's shamelessness is revealed further in his lack of deference for Apollo when he ascribes cowardice even to the god of prophecy and his priestess (611-15):

> non si ipse cauo sub uertice Cirrhae
> (quisquis is est, timidis famaeque ita uisus) Apollo
> mugiat insano penitus seclusus in antro,
> expectare queam dum pallida uirgo tremendas
> nuntiet ambages.

The suggestion of Apolline cowardice (611) in conjunction with the reference to *pallida uirgo* (614) assist in imparting an implicitly feminine tincture to Amphiaraus' character. Capaneus is so arrogant that he trusts only in his own courage and sword (*uirtus mihi numen et ensis / quem teneo!*, 615f.). The sentiment he expresses in this respect resembles his hubris in invoking his right arm as his god while slaying Hypseus (9.548-50). In both instances his words reveal a supreme self-confidence in his own capabilities and a corresponding contempt for and lack of faith in the gods.

Capaneus senses that the auspices that Amphiaraus has taken are unfavourable and he wishes to prejudice the crowd's judgement of Amphiaraus and his direful prophecy. He goads Amphiaraus into making a pronouncement in public by threatening to usurp his priestly function and make trial of the birds (3.616-18). The crowd are so infected with the martial enthusiasm of Capaneus that they encourage him in his reckless fury (618f.). Capaneus succeeds in disparaging Amphiaraus and achieving his primary aim of encouraging the Argive leaders and citizens to take up arms against Thebes.

Noncombat Exhortations

There are few hortatory speeches in the *Thebaid* in which the speaker does not attempt to incite the addressee to battle. Adrastus makes a brief athletic exhortation prior to the cestus contest in the funeral games. He asserts that the courage needed is closest to that of war itself (6.729f.). Exhortations to athletes are discussed in detail by pseudo-Dionysius (*Gen. Dem.* Rad. 283.20-292.23), who mentions that the purpose of such a speech is to motivate the athletes to perform greater feats, just as the purpose of the exhortative speech of a general is to inspire his army to victory (285.16-286.9).

Two extremely brief but uplifting exclamations are spoken by Argus and the Argive warriors who are led to water by Hypsipyle in *Thebaid* 4. Their cry *aquae!* (811f.) is followed by their undisciplined plunge into the waters of Langia.

Praise and Blame Speeches

The essential purpose of demonstrative oratory is to praise or blame some individual or group. The topics of this type of discourse naturally concern the virtues or vices of the person or group being praised or censured. There are specific qualities of character that are subsumed under these general topics. In the praise and blame speeches of the *Thebaid* the qualities most often mentioned are justice and injustice, gentleness and cruelty, courage and cowardice, affability and arrogance, temperance and immoderation, and wisdom and imprudence. Speakers typically will attempt either to eulogise their subjects by magnifying their virtues or will seek to disparage them by amplifying their vices.

There are relatively few informal speeches of praise and blame in the *Thebaid*; there are a number of brief vaunts but only one laudation. Vituperations, especially *uituperationes regum*, are the most important from a topical and thematic standpoint.

Laudation

There is considerable debate among scholars concerning the extent of Statius' debt to the rhetorical handbooks in his composition of the *Silvae*, but no critic disputes that encomiastic elements form a significant part of the poems. The encomiastic aspect is a relatively unimportant feature in Statius' technique of speech composition in the *Thebaid*.

A laudatory speech, particularly if it involves a god or hero, usually suggests a military or athletic superiority on the part of the individual addressed. The act of praising another involves a positive recognition and acceptance of the relative status, self-conception and accomplishments of the person to whom the praise or admiration is directed.

Eulogistic speeches are rare in epic. Only a handful of laudatory speeches in Homeric epic can be recognised as belonging to this type (e.g., *Il.* 8.281-91, *Od.* 11.553-62); no definite structure can be ascribed to them.

Perhaps the best known Homeric example of a speech of praise is the panegyric by Priam to Agamemnon in the teichoscopy (*Il.* 3.182-90); the general context is the praise of the might of Agamemnon's army.

HERCULES (8.502-16)

Hercules' address to the destructive war goddess Minerva is the only laudation in the *Thebaid* and his only speech (8.502-16). Statius did not employ the prescriptions of the rhetoricians in its composition, as few topical or thematic elements of the rhetorical *enkomion* can be discerned in Hercules' laudation. Tydeus' *aristeia* (457ff.) provides the general context for Hercules' laudation. The particular context involves Tydeus' clash with Haemon. Minerva assists Tydeus in his exploits (459), while Hercules champions Haemon (497-99). Minerva's and Hercules' support for their favourites results in a confrontation between the two divinities on the field of battle (500f.).

Hercules respectfully and calmly addresses the war goddess and plausibly attributes their chance meeting to the unrelenting wrath of Juno (502-04):

> fida soror, quaenam hunc belli caligine nobis
> congressum Fortuna tulit? num regia Iuno
> hoc molita nefas?

Hercules further claims that he would sooner face the thunderbolt and make war against Jupiter than offend Minerva (504-06):

> citius me fulmina contra
> (infandum!) ruere et magno bellare parenti
> aspiciat.

These lines portray his contempt for any action contravening the wishes of Minerva. Hercules breaks off from his intended statement of support for Haemon owing to his lineage in order to reassure Minerva that he will withdraw his support for him since the goddess aids his foe Tydeus (506f.):

> genus huic—sed mitto agnoscere, quando
> tu diuersa foues . . .

Hercules attempts to reinforce this impression of devotion to Minerva by claiming that he would withdraw his paternal support even for Hyllus and Amphitryon in deference to the aid the war-goddess gave him in his labours (507-12):

> . . . nec si ipsum comminus Hyllum
> Tydeos hasta tui Stygioque ex orbe remissum
> Amphitryona petat; teneo aeternumque tenebo,
> quantum haec, diua, manus, quotiens sudauerit aegis
> ista mihi, duris famulus dum casibus omnes
> lustro uagus terras.

The extent of Minerva's support for Hercules is shown in his admission that the goddess would have accompanied him on his trip to the underworld if this had been possible (512f.):

> ipsa (heu!) comes inuia mecum
> Tartara, ni superos Acheron excluderet, isses.

Hercules feels a strong sense of obligation to Minerva for the assistance she has given to him in the past. He acknowledges that the goddess is responsible for his admission to heaven (514f.). Hercules further displays his devotion to Minerva by offering her his native Thebes if she wishes to destroy the city (515). Finally he withdraws from the battlefield and prays for her pardon (*cedo equidem ueniamque precor*, 516).

Hercules' immense gratitude and respect for Minerva is shown clearly in his address. His sense of duty and obligation to the goddess is based on a rational assessment of the gifts she has bestowed upon him and the assistance she has given him; he is especially aware that he owes his divine status to Minerva's assistance. The hero acts in marked contrast to other prominent warriors in the epic such as Tydeus and Capaneus who lack the essential qualities of forbearance and equanimity; unparadoxically, those individuals are eventually driven by the Furies to perform insensate acts of violence.

Vaunts

A vaunt in epic is similar to a laudation; the difference is primarily one of address. While the laudation by definition is intended for another person or group, the speaker of a vaunt directs the praise toward himself in a vainglorious manner. The speaker usually flaunts a specific military or athletic victory or his prowess that is evident from such a victory in the face of his defeated, dying or dead foe, or to his own troops or companions. The vaunt reflects the speaker's feeling of superiority and enhances his self-confidence. In the *Iliad* the vaunt is usually spoken by a combatant who has vanquished an opponent in single combat; the person addressed is usually the dead or dying warrior. Polydamas boasts to himself when he strikes down Prothoenar (14.454-57), as does Automedon when he slays Aretos (17.538f.). Vaunts in epic are infrequent because the victor of a military or athletic contest generally elects to taunt his defeated opponent rather than boast over his victory.

Vaunts in the *Thebaid* are highly individualised, which suggests that their composition is influenced by the general narrative in which they appear. The suitability of the vaunts within the specific dramatic context and the broader scope of the epic are the primary determinants of their composition.

EUNAEUS (7.663-68)

The tone of Eunaeus' vaunt is typical of those delivered in the *Thebaid* (7.663-68). The description of the Bacchic priest emphasises just how ill suited he is for battle, for his appearance is youthful and his dress unmanly (652-61); the Theban is incapable of invoking fear in any man (652). Crazed by Bacchus, he runs through the battle field outside Thebes commanding that the Argive host refrain from attacking the city and claiming that the divine guidance and intervention of Apollo was critical to the founding of the city (663-65):

> prohibete manus, haec omine dextro
> moenia Cirrhaea monstrauit Apollo iuuenca;
> parcite, in haec ultro scopuli uenere uolentes.

Eunaeus claims that the Thebans are a sacred race descended from the gods (666-68):

> gens sacrata sumus: gener huic est Iuppiter urbi
> Gradiuusque socer; Bacchum haud mentimur alumnum
> et magnum Alciden.

The absurdity of his boast and of his presence at the commencement of hostilities between the Thebans and Argives are shown immediately when he confronts Capaneus in battle and his fate is sealed (668ff.). The unwarlike Eunaeus stands in stark contrast to the bellicose Capaneus. Their meeting on the battlefield is likened to a rabid lion joyfully leaping upon a youthful bullock or deer untried in combat; despite being assailed by hunters' spears, the lion focuses his attention on his prey unmindful of his wounds (670-74). In such an uneven contest there can be only one result; Capaneus hesitates only to taunt the priest before flinging his spear in a fatal blow (677ff.). The participation of the frail priest in war leads inevitably to his death, as in the case of the priest Amphiaraus later in the same book.

Vituperations

A vituperation consists of abusive language expressing contempt or scorn against another person. The primary object of a vituperation is to place a judgement of the most unrelenting kind upon an antagonist; in this type of speech the speaker usually describes qualities about his/her adversary that are unheroic or ignoble. The tone and content of the vituperation betrays an attitude of extreme superiority on the part of the speaker toward the addressee.

Ancient rhetoricians (e.g., Quint. *Inst.* 3.7.1-3, 3.7.19-25, ps.-Hermog. *Progymn.* Sp. 2.11.28-30) discuss the *uituperatio* (*psogos*) in conjunction with the *laudatio* (*enkomion*). While the *laudatio* is an occasion for praise, the *uituperatio* consists of censure and objurgation. Some rhetoricians of the Second Sophistic (e.g., Aphthon. *Progymn.* Sp. 2.36.7-19 [esp. 12-16], 2.40.14-17, Men. *Epid.* Sp. 3.368.1-377.30, 3.413.10f., 3.420.10-421.3) describe in considerable detail the various rules and divisions for the composition of the *laudatio* (and therefore the *uituperatio*). Although the vituperations in the *Thebaid* are not structurally patterned after the rhetorical *uituperatio* and portions of them cannot be assigned to the traditional *topoi*, they contain a preponderance of vituperative material. Elements that can be traced directly to the rhetorical treatises are the heavy vituperative tone and topical references to a subject's lack of certain virtues.

The Vituperatio Regis

The vituperations of the anonymous Theban (1.173-96), Maeon (3.59-77, 83-87) and Oedipus (11.677-707) are the longest and most important of their type in the *Thebaid*; they form a sub-group aptly named *uituperatio regis*.

The glorification of a king, emperor or other person of authority formed a significant division of epideictic rhetoric and literature. Menander's treatise, which includes the general rules for making this type of speech (*basilikos logos*), preserves the practice of earlier poets and rhetoricians (*Epid.* Sp. 3.368.1-377.30). The thematic elements of *Silvae* 4.1 (in which Statius eulogises Domitian on commencing his seventeenth consulship in 95 CE) mirror some of the *topoi* of Menander's *basilikos logos*, which indicates that Statius was well versed in the composition of regal panegyric.

While Alexander is frequently lauded by rhetoricians and philosophers throughout classical antiquity as an exemplar of monarchal virtue, Pliny's eulogy of Trajan in which the emperor is represented as the ideal sovereign shows the relevance of the practice to Roman conditions during the empire. The third oration of Dio Chrysostomus lists the personal qualities of a benevolent king whom he addresses as honesty, sincerity, moral virtue, a capacity for hard work, an appreciation of the arts, a fighting spirit, and the will and capability to protect all men.

The patterns and *topoi* prescribed for the *basilikos logos* and the *laudatio* were equally applicable to the composition of the *uituperatio regis*. Even as late as the fourth century CE Claudian modelled his invective against Rufinus loosely on the *topoi* and structural patterns outlined for the *uituperatio* by the rhetoricians of the Second Sophistic.

The vituperation of a regent or person of authority had actually been an established part of the heroic tradition since the time of Homer. An example from the *Iliad* is Thersites' diatribe against Agamemnon, in which the pathetic figure accuses the king of being avaricious, lustful and unworthy of command (2.225-42). The speech of vituperation in the *Thebaid* that portrays a monarch like Eteocles or Creon as a model of tyranny is the epic countertype of the rhetorical invective. Qualities imputed to these tyrants in the Statian *uituperatio regis* are naturally the converse of those virtues attributed to the philanthropic king whom Dio Chrysostomus addresses in his third oration.

The *topoi* of the Statian *uituperatio regis* (with matching references to other speech passages and the narrative) include the refusal of monarchs to allow proper burial of the dead (e.g., *Theb.* 11.677-82; cf. 3.96-98, 11.661-64, 12.94-102), the futility of adopting a servile approach to gain monarchal favour (e.g., 11.688-90; cf. 707-56), the inevitable suffering and death that is the ultimate reward of kingship (e.g., 3.75f., 11.679; cf. 1.34, 1.163f., 11.579, 11.654f.), the inherent timidity of institutional monarchy that is exposed upon accession (e.g., 11.684f.; cf. 3.5f.), the readiness of imperial henchmen to render physical violence (e.g., 3.83-85, 11.261f., 11.686f.; cf. 3.79-81), the destruction and suffering that subjects endure under the rule of a tyrant (e.g., 1.195f., 3.74f., 11.654f., 11.679; cf. 2.458-60, 11.269-82, 12.698f.), the inherent cruelty and arrogance of monarchs (e.g., 1.186-91; cf. 2.482-90, 3.214f., 11.305-08, 12.154-59, 12.174, 12.184-86, 12.677-81), the craving of tyrants for absolute power (e.g., 3.74f.), the disregard of tyrants for civil and divine law (e.g., 3.72; cf. 1.154), and the hatred of subjects for their monarchs (e.g., 11.294-96; cf. 2.480f.).

The theme of tyranny was popular among the declaimers of the early first century CE (e.g., Sen. *Controv.* 2.5, 3.6, 4.7, 5.8, 9.4), but the significance of the theme in the *Thebaid* goes far beyond the influence of declamation, for Statius' portrayal of monarchy in the *Thebaid* reflects unfavourably upon the imperial establishment. The frequent echoing of vituperative commonplaces in the speeches and surrounding narrative bears testimony to the consistency in the epic of the important idea of the pursuit and abuse of monarchal power.[35] Although the vituperation of a monarch in the *Thebaid* is lacking in the sophisticated topical patternisation that the rhetoricians prescribe for the composition of the *uituperatio* (e.g., Aphthon. *Progymn.* Sp. 2.36.7-19 [esp. 12-16], 2.40.14-17, Theon *Progymn.* Sp. 2.111.11-112.8), the speech on the misdeeds of Oedipus and his successors constitute the core of the Statian *uituperatio regis*.

ANONYMOUS THEBAN (1.173-96)

Statius incorporates vituperative elements into the second speech of the *Thebaid* (1.173-96). An anonymous Theban commences his vituperation of Polynices and Eteocles with a series of rhetorical questions lamenting the fate

---

[35] See chs. 2 and 4 of my *The Mythic Voice of Statius* (forthcoming).

of his people, who must endure the uncertainties and vagaries of alternate rule (173-77). A venomous apostrophe to Jupiter betrays his scorn of men and the gods (177-80):

> semperne vicissim
> exulibus seruire dabor? tibi, sumne deorum
> terrarumque sator, sociis hanc addere mentem
> sedit?

The anonymous Theban contrasts Eteocles' cruelty and arrogance with Polynices' gentleness and affability in the manner of the *synkresis* (cf. Aphthon. *Progymn.* Rabe 31.11f.), but notes cuttingly that the tyrant once possessed these traits as well (*Theb.* 1.186-91). Employing the ship as a metaphor for the fickle nature of fate, the Theban concludes his bitter attack on the brothers with a biting rhetorical flourish (191-96):

> nos uilis in omnes
> prompta manus casus, domino cuicumque parati.
> qualiter hinc gelidus Boreas, hinc nubifer Eurus
> uela trahunt, nutat mediae Fortuna carinae,
> (heu dubio suspensa metu tolerandaque nullis
> aspera sors populis!) hic imperat ille minatur.

Further emphasising the intensity of his indignation over the insufferable destiny of his compatriots is the parenthetic exclamation. The anonymous Theban can see no justification for the suffering of Thebes brought about by the brothers' decision to rule alternately, a policy that the narrative reveals is supernaturally motivated (cf. 123ff., esp. 138f.). The tone and sentiment of his speech is reminiscent of Thersites' hostile eloquence in the *Iliad* (2.225-42).

MAEON (3.59-77, 83-87)

When Tydeus routs and puts to death the Theban adversaries sent by Eteocles to ambush him on his return to Argos, he spares the augur Maeon (2.527ff.). Maeon had been forewarned earlier of the fateful consequences of the mission and had endeavoured unsuccessfully to deter Eteocles from sending the ambush party (690-95). Tydeus spares the life of Maeon so that the augur will return to Thebes and inform Eteocles of the result (697-703).

As Maeon approaches Thebes the next morning, the rumbling of the earth is a foreboding of the news he bears (3.37-39). The citizens detect Maeon's affliction at a distance (40). He is irate over the destiny accorded to him by the Fates and disconsolate that Tydeus has granted him the harsh punishment of life (41f.). The approach of Maeon is likened to a despondent shepherd returning to his master in order to convey the news of the herd's slaughter by savage wolves (45-48). Like the distraught herdsman, Maeon dreads bearing the calamitous news to his lord, pouring dust on himself in his mourning for his lost companions (49-52). When the mothers encounter Maeon at the gates of the city, they comprehend instantly in the lone figure the magnitude of the disaster that has befallen them (53-57). Their lamentation is compared to the last cry that the citizenry raise when their towns are opened to their conquerors or when a ship sinks in the open sea (55-57).

Immediately after Eteocles grants him an audience, Maeon commences his oration in an aggressive fashion (59ff.). His defiant words inject a dramatic vitality into the narrative. He asserts that Tydeus presents him as the sole unhappy survivor of the company sent to ambush Tydeus (59f.). Maeon professes that he is uncertain whether he owes his fate to divine will, Fortune, or the invincible power of Tydeus (60-62):

> siue haec sententia diuum,
> seu Fortuna fuit, seu, quod pudet ira fateri,
> uis inuicta uiri.

In maintaining that his destiny was cruelly determined by either the gods, Fortune or Tydeus, Maeon reveals the paradoxical nature of human fate. For Tydeus' action is consonant with Jupiter's divine plan and his resolution to eradicate the Theban house.

Maeon suggests that his pardon by Tydeus and his return to the city forebodes evil for Thebes (*mala protinus ales, / qua redeo*, 64f.). He would have preferred to join his comrades in death but is compelled to return against his will. He declares that neither tears nor cunning earned him the cruel pardon and dishonourable gift of light (65f.). The will of the gods and inexorable fate denied him the destiny of dying with his comrades (67-69). He is neither overzealous of life nor fearful of death (69-71).

Immediately after these assertions, Maeon commences the vituperative and prophetic segment of his oration. Maeon reviles Eteocles as a man of death and destruction, suggests that unfavourable omens portend destruction for Thebes, particularises the regent's present and future crimes, and forewarns Eteocles that the perpetual lamentation of his subjects and the spirits of Tydeus' victims will torment him (71-77):

> bellum infandum ominibusque negatam
> mouisti, funeste, aciem, dum pellere leges,
> et consanguineo gestis regnare superbus
> exule; te series orbarum excisa domorum
> planctibus adsiduis, te diro horrore uolantes
> quinquaginta animae circum noctesque diesque
> adsilient, neque enim ipse moror.

Maeon's account of Eteocles' criminal actions forms an important part of the *uituperatio regis*. Eteocles' insatiate craving for power is shown in the tyrant's initiation of an unholy war and his arrogant reign during his brother's exile. His iniquity and corruption of the legal process is demonstrated when he attempts to dispense with codified law.[36]

The speech interrupts at this point, revealing its dramatic effect upon Eteocles and his followers. Eteocles is predictably angered by his subject's audacity (77f.). Maeon has already unsheathed his sword when the tyrant's wicked liegemen Labdacus and Phlegyas prepare to attack him (79-81). He pauses momentarily to reflect on whether to take his own life before proclaiming (83-87):

> numquam tibi sanguinis huius
> ius erit aut magno feries imperdita Tydeo
> pectora; uado equidem exultans ereptaque fata
> insequor et comites feror expectatus ad umbras.
> te superis fratrique—

The aposiopesis prepares the auditor or reader for the subsequent description of his suicide.

Maeon determines to commit suicide rather than allow the timorous Eteocles to slay him, an event that would diminish his glorification. Maeon not only has no fear of impending death but in fact claims it publicly as his

---

[36] Maeon criticises Eteocles' lack of justice, temperance and wisdom, qualities intrinsic to the rhetorician's discussion of a tyrant's actions (Men. *Epid.* Sp. 3.375.6-376.23, esp. 375.6-8; cf. Men. *Epid.* Sp. 3.373.6-8, Theon *Progymn.* Sp. 2.112.2-8).

destiny. He seeks death voluntarily because he is convinced that destiny has ordained this particular moment for his death. The heroism shown by the pious augur affords a striking contrast to the pusillanimity displayed by Eteocles in dispatching fifty warriors to ambush Tydeus.

Although Maeon feels shame in being spared by Tydeus, he achieves a certain immortality in being spared by the superhuman figure; furthermore, he attains glory and honour in his defiant stance toward the truculent Eteocles and in boldly meeting his fate, as the poet's laudatory apostrophe stresses (99-102):

> tu tamen egregius fati mentisque nec umquam
> (sic dignum est) passure situm, qui comminus ausus
> uadere contemptum reges, quaque ampla ueniret
> libertas, sancire uiam.

This suicide scene is perhaps the most obvious Stoic reference in the entire epic. The use of *libertas* shows that Statius views Maeon's display of public defiance against the monarch as a blow against despotism and usurpation. The concept of *libertas* further suggests that the poet views Maeon's death as a release from the persecution of a tyrant, an attitude immanent in Stoicism. Stoics were particularly fond of citing Cato as an exemplar of Stoic virtue who committed suicide for this ennobling reason (e.g., Sen. *Ep.* 13f., Cic. *Tusc.* 1.30.74). The valorous deeds of Maeon reveal him as a hero whose qualities resemble those of the ideal Stoic figure.

Eteocles shows his moral pollution by refusing to permit the inhumation of Maeon; his attempt to afflict the augur's soul is an act of desperate vengeance that contravenes natural law. The monarch's profanatory act is an obvious precursor of his successor's inhumanity in the final book when Creon prohibits the burial of Polynices and the Argive host (94-102). In both cases Statius wishes to demonstrate that natural justice ultimately prevails over human injustice by ensuring that the corpses remain inviolate. Eteocles' attempt to avenge the insult to his pride fails as Maeon is admitted to the Elysian fields (3.108-11); furthermore, even the animals display a reverence for Maeon's corpse that is antithetic to the sensibilities of an impious tyrant: the wild beasts and birds leave the augur's body and clothes inviolate and guard his corpse (111-13).

OEDIPUS (11.677-707)

Creon, the successor of Oedipus, is the subject and recipient of a lengthy *uituperatio regis*. In book 11 Creon banishes Oedipus from Thebes because of his contaminative character after the death of the former monarch's sons. When he informs Oedipus of his decision (669-72), the old man's reply is predictably caustic, as shown in the preponderance of rhetorical questions and exclamatory statements in his vituperation. Oedipus stresses Creon's lack of courage, justice, temperance and wisdom, just as the anonymous Theban (1.186ff.) and Maeon (3.71ff.) do earlier in relation to Eteocles. Creon has only just become king, yet he wastes no time in following his successors' footsteps by acting malevolently; his refusal to allow the proper burial of the Argive dead is reminiscent of similar impious deeds performed by his cruel predecessors (11.677-82):

> iamne uacat saeuire, Creon? modo perfida regna
> fortunaeque locum nostrae, miserande, subisti,
> et tibi iam fas est regum calcare ruinas?
> iam tumulis uictos, socios iam moenibus arces?
> macte, potes digne Thebarum sceptra tueri:
> haec tua prima dies.

Oedipus demonstrates further that Creon has assumed the mantle of tyranny in the usual fashion of Theban monarchs. The blind man sarcastically asks Creon why he has so senselessly resorted to the timorous judgement of exile when far harsher punishments are available (682-85). Some liegeman would eagerly obey the monarch's command to decapitate him (685f.). While the reference to Creon's timidity recalls the faint-heartedness shown earlier by Eteocles (3.5f.), Oedipus' mention of the liegemen's eagerness to render physical violence recalls the preparedness of Eteocles' henchmen (3.79-81). Oedipus taunts Creon to slay him (*incipe!*, 11.688) and shows his indifference to the prospect of death in a succession of rhetorical questions. Even if he did attempt to conciliate Creon, the tyrant is unlikely to be moved by his plea (688-90). Creon can banish Oedipus from his palace and homeland, but the punishment that Oedipus has inflicted upon himself in the form of ocular effosion far surpasses in severity the punishment a wicked monarch can dispense (690-95; cf. 1.71f.):

mihine ulla minaris
supplicia, aut ullos reris superesse timores?
linquere tecta iubes? caelum terramque reliqui
sponte, atque ultricem crudelis in opra retorsi
non ullo cogente manum: quid tale iubere,
rex inimice, potes?

In a sense Oedipus has already pre-empted Creon's punishment because he is physically blind not just to the sight of Thebes but to heaven and earth. Oedipus has no fear of death or being denied a resting place in a foreign land (11.696-98); no fate is worse than the one he has already endured. However, the frail old man confesses with a pathetic touch that Thebes, his mother and his sons are still dear to him (699-701):

Oedipus is emboldened in his scornful reply to Creon because he knows that the monarch will suffer a fate similar to that of previous Theban monarchs (701-05):

habeas Thebana regasque
moenia, quo Cadmus, quo Laius omine rexit
quoque ego; sic thalamos, sic pignora fida capessas;
nec tibi sit uirtus Fortunam euadere dextra,
sed lucem deprensus ames.

Oedipus' blinding of himself is an act of self-retribution for his sins, but it also symbolises the commencement of his new rôle as a blind prophet. Just as he was able to divine that his sons would suffer for their sins, he is assured that Creon will endure a harsh punishment. The monarchs of Thebes are blind to the consequences of their wickedness, but the blind seer knows that no ruler's fate in Thebes is entirely his own. In the case of Creon this is especially true, since Creon's refusal to permit the burial of the corpses is inspired by Pluto and Tisiphone (8.72-74; cf. 12.590f.)

The Brief Vituperation

TISIPHONE (11.485-92)

The most noteworthy of the four brief vituperative speeches from a thematic standpoint in the *Thebaid* (5.491f., 11.259f., 11.485-92, 12.382-85) is spoken in the penultimate book when Pietas endeavours to prevent the duel between Polynices and Eteocles (457ff.). The benevolent goddess is momentarily successful, for she has a sudden and dramatic effect on the warriors who become conscious of their crime (474-76). Tisiphone dashes to the battlefield and enjoins noninterference upon her rival. She declares that the moment is due for violent retribution and that Pietas has procrastinated too long to exert her influence on impending events (485-87). In a series of questions Tisiphone argues that the series of crimes perpetrated by the Theban house demand natural vengeance (487-92):

> ubi tunc, cum bella cieret
> Bacchus et armatas furiarent orgia matres?
> aut ubi segnis eras, dum Martius impia serpens
> stagna bibit, dum Cadmus arat, dum uicta cadit Sphinx,
> dum rogat Oedipoden genitor, dum lampade nostra
> in thalamos Iocasta uenit?

This argument resembles the specious claim of Jupiter that the Thebans deserve to be punished for the crimes of their ancestors (cf. 1.227ff.). This is the only occasion in the epic where a divinity taunts another character. Tisiphone's reproach drives Pietas from the battlefield (11.492-96); in her absence the fighting resumes with greater intensity (497ff.). It is ironic that the goddess departs for Jupiter in order to complain about her treatment (496), since he is the prime mover behind the supernatural plan to eradicate the Theban house (1.224ff.).

CHAPTER 4

NONRHETORICAL-TYPE SPEECHES

Narrative Speeches

A narrative speech tells a story. The tale that Phoinix relates to Achilleus is the longest narrative speech in the *Iliad* (9.434-605). Odysseus' account of his adventures at the court of Alkinoos in the *Odyssey* is the longest and most famous narrative speech in Greek epic; in four books the hero recounts his experiences following the fall of Troy until his arrival at Kalypso's island (9.2-12.453). The longest and most celebrated narrative speech in Roman epic is the one that Aeneas relates to Dido in the *Aeneid* concerning the fall of Troy and his subsequent wanderings (2.3-3.715); his speech occupies almost two full books and is 1515 lines in length. There are numerous narrative speeches in Ovid's *Metamorphoses*, the longest being the story of Caenus told by Nestor (12.182-533). The narrative of the anonymous elder is the longest speech in Lucan's *Pharsalia* (2.68-232). The longest narrative speeches in each of the three Flavian epics are the story of the Lemnian massacre told by Hypsipyle (Stat. *Theb.* 4.49-498), the tale of Jupiter's love for Io and her wanderings recounted by Orpheus (Val. Flac. *Argon.* 4.351-421), and the story related by Marus to Serranus of the Roman army's struggle with a monstrous serpent (Sil. Ital. *Pun.* 6.118-293).

ADRASTUS (1.557-672), HYPSIPYLE (5.49-498)

There are two important narrative speeches in the *Thebaid*. Since they consist of a recounting of events in chronological sequence, their plots are simple; however, the simplicity of the stories belies their balanced and sophisticated concentric (or recessed panel) structure. Unlike those in Homeric and Vergilian epic, they are not delivered by the main protagonists in the epic. In book 1 Adrastus relates the tale of Coroebus to Polynices and Tydeus (557-672); in the fifth book Hypsipyle recounts the story of the Lemnian massacre to Adrastus and the Argive warriors (49-498). After Aeneas' speech to Dido in the *Aeneid*, Hypsipyle's narrative is the longest

163

in Roman epic. Both narrative speeches are essential to the meaning of the *Thebaid*, since they connect with other sections through the paralleling of episodes, foreshadowing of events, evocation of reminiscences, and repetition of motifs in the main narrative. Their real importance lies in their ability to underscore and elaborate upon important issues concerning supernatural malevolence and human suffering.[1]

The narratives of Adrastus and Hypsipyle reveal an internal structure governed by nonrhetorical conditions. The balanced arrangement of the events described in these speeches is a reflexion of the care that Statius takes in composing the *Thebaid*. Their concentric structure (i.e., ABCDCBA type) centres on incidents highlighting the *pietas* of the main protagonists in the face of pervasive supernatural hostility. The speeches are not architecturally symmetrical in a strict technical sense, since the number of lines in each section does not always correspond to the number of lines in its counterpart; however, it would be unreasonable to expect them to correspond in every case.

The recessed panel structure of the Coroebus story (1.557-668) takes the form of ABCDEFEDCBA; the chiastic arrangement depicts the series of disastrous events that afflict Argos and the eventual restoration of harmony and order. Coroebus' heroic action in slaying the monster Poine occupies the central panel (F: 604-26), juxtaposed by displays of divine retribution (E: 596-604, 627-35), demands for death (D: 590-95, 636f.), scenes of arrival (C: 562-90, 638-61) and harmony (B: *ante* 562, 661-66); there are also the *prooemium* and *peroratio* (A: 557-61, 666-68). There is a progression from harmony to discord back to concordance, a pattern that corresponds to the Hypsipyle digression and the movement of the poem as a whole.

The concentric structure of the long narrative speech of Hypsipyle (5.28-498) is intricate and complex (ABCDEFGFEDCBA). The content of the entire digression is carefully arranged for maximum effect around the *pietas* of Hypsipyle. Just as the Coroebus story centres on Coroebus' bravery in slaying the monster *Poine* (1.557-668), the heroic action of Hypsipyle in rescuing her father from the frenzied Lemnian women is the focus of the digression and occupies the central panel (G: 5.240-95), juxtaposed by scenes of divinely infused *furor* and release from *furor* (F: 195-240, 296-334), arrivals of the Lemnian men and Argonauts in Lemnos (E: 170-94,

---

[1] For a full treatment of these speeches, see ch. 1 of my *The Mythic Voice of Statius* (forthcoming).

335-444), divine infection of women with hatred and love (D: 85-169, 445-67), departure of the Lemnian men and Argonauts from Lemnos (C: 75-84, 468-85), marital and civil disharmony in Lemnos (B: 57-74, 486-92), and harmony in Lemnos (A: 49-56, 493-98). The concentric structure illustrates the vicissitudes of fortune experienced by the Lemnians for their failure to worship Venus. The fluctuating fortunes of the Lemnian women are reminiscent of the changing fortunes of the Argives in the Coroebus story and resemble the frequent change in circumstances of the Argives and Thebans in the main narrative.

Descriptive Speeches

Descriptive scenes are an important element in the narrative pattern of the *Thebaid*.[2] The relatively few speeches that consist of description are delivered by priests and servants. The majority of descriptions in the speeches are dynamic rather than static, meaning that the figures depicted in the scenes are moving and interacting with each other.[3] There are four speeches of description given by priests (3.502-15, 516-45, 519-35, 553-78); all are important in that they relate to events recounted or alluded to elsewhere, but Amphiaraus' description of the sanguineous conflict between the eagles and swans is the most significant (3.516-45). There are three descriptive speeches given by servants (7.254-89; 7.294-358, 363-73; 12.246-54); the most important are spoken by Phorbas from a Theban watch-tower (7.254-89; 7.294-358, 363-73).

AMPHIARAUS (3.516-45)

In the third book Adrastus encharges Amphiaraus and Melampus to read the future (449ff.). After first engaging in haruspicy unsuccessfully, the priests journey to Mount Aphesas to make trial of the birds. The descriptive speeches that follow of Melampus and Amphiaraus create a structural pause between the emotional scene of Tydeus' return to Argos (53ff.) and the ravings of Capaneus (607ff.) in the third book. The speeches serve to

---

[2] The most notable of these descriptions are the *concilium deorum* (1.197ff.) and the palace of sleep (10.84ff.).

[3] The only speech of static description is given by Menoetes (12.246-54).

illustrate rather than narrate a fictitious scene that is appropriate to the context and relevant to other events and themes advanced in the narrative.

In these descriptive speeches the effect of the careful accumulation of descriptive details that are closely connected with episodes and characters in the main narrative is to stimulate the intellect of the reader or listener. Another effect of these speeches is to arouse the imagination and emotions of the audience. This would have been especially true of an audience in the first century CE, who would have followed the scene of augury involving Melampus and Amphiaraus with great interest. So great was the Roman demand for and interest in augury that Statius could scarcely fail to include such a scene in his epic.

Amphiaraus first prays Jupiter to send clear signs of what the Fates hold for Argos and Thebes (3.489-96). The prophets take the auspices and Melampus is the first to describe the terrible portents. His speech consists of a description of the inauspicious movements of the birds (502-05). The birds of favourable omen—the raven of Apollo, eagle of Jupiter, and owl of Minerva—are nowhere to be seen (506-08). Instead birds of prey—hawks, vultures and owls—and other monstrous creatures of flight, including the screech-owl and horned owl with its funeral chant, viciously rend each other's faces with their curved talons (508-15).

The general signs of foreboding described by Melampus concerning the fate of Argos is followed by the speech of Amphiaraus portending the defeat of Argos (516-45). He gives a detailed description of a gory fight that occurs between seven eagles representing the Argive princes and a group of swans denoting the Thebans. The attack of the eagles upon the swans parallels the Argive attack upon Thebes. At first the eagles have the advantage, but then Jupiter ensures that the swans gain the ascendancy and prevail over their opponents (530ff.); similarly, the anger of Jupiter in the main narrative prompts the god to bring about a Theban victory after the Argives gain the upper hand early in the war.

The fate of the eagles anticipates the tragic lot of the Seven. One of the eagles, representing Capaneus, dies instantly after catching fire from a sudden flash of the sun (*hic excelsa petens subita face solis inarsit / summisitque animos*, 3.539f.); this spectacle parallels the scene in which Capaneus is struck and consumed by Jupiter's thunderbolt (10.921-39). Another eagle, with tender wings, pursues and is overwhelmed by stronger birds (*illum uestigia adortum / maiorum uolucrum tenerae deponitis alae*, 3.540f.), just as the young Parthenopaeus pursues and is vanquished by warriors much more powerful and experienced than him (9.683ff.). A third eagle, which falls clinging to his opponent (*hic hosti implicitus pariter ruit*, 3.542), foreshadows the deaths of Polynices and Eteocles, who slay each other and then die in each other's embrace (11.540-73). The action of yet another eagle in abandoning his flock (*hunc fuga retro / uoluit agens sociae linquentiam fata cateruae*, 3.542f.) anticipates the action of Adrastus, who flees from the field just prior to the commencement of the brothers' duel (11.439-43). An eagle overwhelmed by a rain-cloud (*hic nimbo glomeratus obit*, 3.544) foreshadows the death of Hippomedon, who is overwhelmed by the river Ismene (9.315ff.), while the anthropophagous death of Tydeus (8.760f.) is foreshadowed in the action of an eagle who devours a swan (*hic praepete uiua / pascitur inmoriens*, 3.544f.). Finally, Amphiaraus recognises a falling eagle as symbolic of his own death in the coming war (*illum . . . qui cadit, agnosco*, 546f.).

PHORBAS (7.254-89; 7.294-358, 363-73)

These speeches are spoken by Phorbas to Antigone from a Theban watch-tower. In this scene the poet introduces a *teichoskopia*, an episode that originated in Homeric epic (*Il.* 3.161ff.) and was later used by dramatists such as Euripides (*Phoen.* 88ff.). In the *Iliad* Priam asks Helen to identify from the walls of Troy the Achaean warriors visible on the plain below (3.161ff.). The request of Priam seems unnecessary, since he must have known the Achaean warriors by sight after almost ten years of war, but the catalogue serves the function of introducing the Greeks to the bard's audience.

Six books precede Phorbas' identification of the Thebans in the *Thebaid*. Admittedly, this number of books should have been sufficient to present the personalities of Theban heroes who were to take part in the coming war, but nevertheless the poet utilises the form of the Homeric *teichoskopia* to avoid presenting the Theban heroes to his audience in a manner that recalls the earlier catalogue of the Argives at the commencement of the fourth book (38ff.). The poet blends elements into the speeches of Phorbas that connect with events and characters in other sections of the poem. The references to a number of warriors by name who play a rôle later in the war effectively links the catalogue with the rest of the poem.

Antigone asks her faithful attendant Phorbas to identify the Theban troops visible from the tower (7.247-52). Phorbas names the many cities whose warriors flock to support the Theban cause (260f., 265-75, 282-85). The first warrior to be mentioned specifically is the commander Dryas (255ff.), who will later kill Parthenopaeus (9.841-74) and be struck down in retribution (9.875f.), presumably by Diana, given the goddess' enmity of his father Orion (*procul, oro, paternum / omen et innuptae uetus excidat ira Dianae*, 7.256-58). The naming of Eurymedon (7.262-65) anticipates his rôle in the defence of Thebes (8.356, 11.32). Amphion' appearance as the leader of a rustic band of warriors (7.271-79) foreshadows his confrontation with Parthenopaeus (9.778ff.), who in the Argive catalogue is shown leading the rustic Arcadians to war (4.254ff.).

Antigone takes advantage of a short break in the flow of Phorbas' catalogue (7.290) and asks about two warriors she spots in the distance (291ff.). So similar in aspect and manner are they that Antigone imagines them to be brothers (291-93) and expresses the wish that her brothers could mirror the affection shown by the pair (293). Phorbas tells her that the two warriors are Lapithaon and Alatreus, who are actually father and son (296ff.). When the nymph Dercetis was inflamed with passion and possessed Lapithaon, the son she bore was not much younger than her lover (303f.). The concord evident between them is an emotional inversion of the triangular relationship existing between Oedipus and his sons. When Lapithaon and Alatreus appear later in book 11 (34-38), the bond between them is as strong as ever, while the mutual enmity that exists between Eteocles and Polynices is shortly to erupt in a violent and fatal confrontation on the battlefield.

Phorbas subsequently steers Antigone's attention to the imposing figure of Hypseus, who is the son of the river god Asopus (7.309ff.). The river god challenged the authority and might of Jupiter when that god made off with his daughter Aegina (319-25). That the scene is linked with the subsequent narrative in a number of ways is plain. The defiant attitude of Asopus (320-29) mirrors the rebellious attitude shown by Capaneus—who significantly is the slayer of Hypseus (9.546-65)—just prior to his death in book 10 (899ff.). Furthermore, the scene foreshadows the fatal struggle of Hippomedon with the river god Ismenos in the ninth book (446ff.). It is after the death of Hippomedon that Hypseus commits his daring but fateful deed of recovering the helmet of Hippomedon and displaying it to the Thebans, whereupon he is promptly struck down by Capaneus (9.540-65).

After Phorbas mentions the many cities that are under the command of Hypseus and Iphitus (7.330-55), he recalls the death of Laius (355-58). The thought of the dead regent momentarily saddens him and he breaks off from his catalogue (359-62). He regains his composure sufficiently to name Clonis and the sons of Abas (363-71), but desists from continuing when he sees that Eteocles is about to address his troops (372f.).

Soliloquies

It is commonly known that exercises in which the speaker impersonated an imaginary or historical figure by indulging in soliloquy formed an indispensable component of a rhetorician's studies. Soliloquies are also an important constituent of classical epic, where they are used to reveal the private thoughts and emotions of the characters and thereby assist in defining their personalities. Soliloquists either talk or think aloud to themselves, although thoughts that are not actually intended to be spoken aloud are best described as internalised lines of dialogue. Epic soliloquies (or monologues) traditionally serve to explain the conduct of characters and to furnish them with motives for their actions. In addition to serving as a means of character description, soliloquies also provide information directly to the audience about the dramatic situation.

Soliloquies render the poet's task easier in relating the inner thoughts and feelings of important characters in critical situations without the dramatic inexpedience of engaging in a long narrative description. The poet's use of direct speech in epic in order to portray the thoughts, feelings and sense impressions of soliloquisers in significant moments of crisis is dramatically more effective in revealing the psychology of the characters than merely describing their emotions to the auditor or reader. The psychophysical state of the monologists in the *Thebaid* ranges widely across the emotional spectrum: anxiety, anguish, guilt, shame, doubt, anger, sadness, astonishment, faith and duty.[4] Tropes and figures employed by Statius in order to depict these emotions include the exclamation, parenthesis and the rhetorical question.

An analysis of the content of the soliloquies in Statian epic reveals that the speakers either reflect on a course of action that has been taken or deliberate and resolve on what course of action should be taken in a moment

---

[4] Duty is not normally considered to be an emotion, but is used here in the sense of the passionate devotion that one may have for another individual or cause, as in Argia's profound sense of responsibility toward her husband (4.196ff.).

of crisis. The monologues serve the recognised dramatic function of materialising the internal dialogue between the soliloquisers and their alter egos; this internal discourse discloses the characters' most intimate feelings. In mirroring the private emotions and thoughts of prominent figures in the epic, the soliloquies provide insight into the personalities of the speakers. Since the speakers are alone, their thoughts are presumed to be an expression of their true feelings.

As in Homeric and Vergilian epic, the speakers of soliloquies in the *Thebaid* are prominent figures, ranging from Theban royalty to Olympian gods. Statius uses the monologue less frequently than Homer and Vergil; Jupiter, Apollo, Bacchus, Eteocles, Capaneus and Argia each soliloquise on only one occasion. The monologues of the gods are in the main less complex psychically than those of Vergil and in their measured deliberation mirror the Homeric soliloquies, while those of the mortals resemble the Vergilian soliloquies in emotional intensity and complexity of moods.

No soliloquy in the *Thebaid* extends to twelve lines and the average length is under eight lines. Like the monologues in Homeric epic, they are introduced by verbs of saying or similar phrases in which the verb of speaking is understood. The soliloquies of Eteocles, Argia, Jupiter and Capaneus are spoken, while those of Bacchus and Apollo are introduced by the elliptic phrase (i.e., they are either spoken or understood to have been voiced). Like Vergil, Statius does not employ the Homeric monologue in which a warrior debates whether to stand up to the enemy and fight or withdraw from the encounter (e.g., *Il.* 11.404-10, *Od.* 5.356-64).

ETEOCLES (3.6F., 9-18)

One of Eteocles' shortest yet psychologically most compelling speeches is his emotive monologue at the start of book 3. In this interior monologue Eteocles reveals his apprehension about his plot to assassinate Tydeus, who has set out for Argos after failing to convince the king that he should abandon the Theban throne to Polynices. The speech falls between Tydeus' victory over his Theban adversaries and Maeon's report of the failed mission and subsequent suicide before Eteocles; the interposition of the monologue serves to emphasise that Eteocles is responsible for the assassination plot and must ultimately bear the consequences for ordering such a wicked and cowardly mission. He is anxious and guilt-ridden over the crime he has ordered his men to perpetrate and fearful of the mission failing.

The *moderator perfidus* (*Theb*. 3.1) contemplates over the failure of his Theban troops in returning to the city (6f.). He commences his soliloquy in the Homeric manner by employing an emotionally charged exclamation (cf. *Il*. 11.404, 17.91, *Od*. 5.298) and reflecting on the possible reasons for the delay of the Thebans (*Theb*. 3.6-12):

> 'ei mihi' . . .
> 'unde morae?' (nam prona ratus facilemque tot armis
> Tydea, nec numero uirtutem animumque rependit)
> 'num regio diuersa uiae? num missus ab Argis
> subsidio globus? an sceleris data fama per urbes
> finitimas? paucosne, pater Gradiue, manuue
> legimus indecores?'

Unable to find a reason for the apparent lack of the mission's success with the involvement of valiant soldiers like Chromis, Dorylas and the Thespians, Eteocles betrays his fear in an unconscious comparison with the prowess of Tydeus and unwittingly presages Thebes' impending downfall through a negative anticipation of the mission's result (12-18):

> at enim fortissimus illic
> et Chromis et Dorylas et nostris turribus aequi
> Thespiadae totos raperent mihi funditus Argos.
> nec tamen ille meis, reor, impenetrabilis armis
> aere gerens solidoque datos adamante lacertos
> uenerat; heu segnes, quorum labor haeret in uno,
> si conserta manus.

The tyrant's betrayal of his private thoughts and emotions define the essential elements of his personality and specifically reinforces key aspects of his confused state of mind that Statius brings to the audience's attention in the simple narrative surrounding the soliloquy. The nautical simile that follows Eteocles' speech likens the tyrant's anguish to the despairing helmsman in a storm at sea (22-32); the simile functions to reinforce both the effect of Eteocles' monologue and the surrounding narrative describing his confused and distressed state.

ARGIA (4.200-10)

Before Argia makes her first speech in the *Thebaid*, Statius has shown her to be an exemplar of virtue, propriety and humility (1.533-39), qualities that she continues to bear as a loyal and dutiful wife after her marriage to Polynices. In her soliloquy in 4.200-10, Argia relinquishes to Eriphyle the fateful necklace of Harmonia that Polynices had presented to her earlier as a bridal gift (2.265-67). Argia's sense of loyalty and decency prompt her not to take pleasure in beautifying herself while her husband is at war (4.200ff.).

The rhetorical question abnegating her ownership of the necklace and the interposition of the parenthetic exclamation *infandum!* reveals the exemplary qualities of a virtuous wife who abstains from pleasure in her husband's absence (204-06):

> scilicet (infandum!), cum tu cludare minanti
> casside ferratusque sones, ego diuitis aurum
> Harmoniae dotale geram?

If her husband should return safely and she become queen, then more rightly could she then adorn herself after paying homage to the gods (206-09). She concludes her monologue by disposing of her necklace to anyone who can claim and wear it while her husband is at war (209f.).

Earlier at Argia's wedding Eriphyle is seized with a fierce jealousy over Argia's possession of the necklace and seeks eagerly to acquire it (2.299-305). Eriphyle's prominent position in Argive society as the husband of Amphiaraus means that she is worthy of the necklace's acquisition (304), but her vanity, jealousy and fateful determination to obtain and wear it contrasts with the simple nobility of Argia in relinquishing the necklace. Moreover, while Eriphyle is so impious that she has no compunction about sacrificing her husband Amphiaraus in war, Argia shares her husband's burden through self-abnegation. Argia's monologue bears graphic witness to the heroic and magnanimous qualities that she displays elsewhere in her devotion to Polynices.

BACCHUS (4.669-78)

Bacchus' first speech is his monologue in book 4 where he reflects upon the threat to himself and his race in his native city (669ff.) Bacchus blames Argos and her patron goddess Juno for instigating war between the

Thebans and Argives, citing the goddess' jealousy over his mother's affair with Jupiter and his subsequent violent birth (671-675):

> hoc mihi saeuum
> Argos et indomitae bellum ciet ira nouercae.
> usque adeone parum cineri data mater iniquo
> natalesque rogi quaeque ipse micantia sensi
> fulgura?

The rhetorical question reveals the contemptuous regard that Bacchus has for Juno in her unrelenting rage against his city. The patron god of Thebes maintains that Argos' attack is impious and unwarranted because she has not engaged in any inimical action against Thebes (675f.). He resolves to delay Argos' attack upon Thebes (677; cf. 678, 684ff.).

The importance of Bacchus' monologue lies in his implicit recognition that he cannot change the course of events set down by Jupiter but only delay their fulfilment, an idea that is central to the theme of Jovian control of human fate and reiterated elsewhere in the epic. When Bacchus expostulates to Jupiter over the fate of Thebes, Jupiter conveniently tells Bacchus: *inmoto deducimur orbe / Fatorum* (7.197f.).[5]

APOLLO (6.372-83)

Apollo's soliloquy precedes the chariot race in the funeral games of book 6. Upon catching sight of Admetus and Amphiaraus in the field of competitors, he wonders which god has promoted athletic rivalry between his equally devoted and beloved seers (6.372-75). The god briefly recounts episodes illustrating their loyalty and obedience to him and the prophetic art (375-78). He observes that Admetus is more deserving of first place on account of his deeds. However, Apollo notes that Amphiaraus is destined for an early death while Admetus is assured of a long life (380f.). For Amphiaraus there are no joys left, for he shall perish in the war (381f.); Apollo's own oracle has prophesied his seer's death (383).

The soliloquy is significant for its mood of fatalism and sombre atmosphere. The god's speech shows that Amphiaraus' fate is inseparably linked with the chain of events that leads to the destruction of Thebes.

---

[5] On the relationship between Jupiter and the Fates, see ch. 1 of my *The Mythic Voice of Statius* (forthcoming).

Apollo's monologue acquires additional significance later when he intervenes in the chariot race and ensures the seer of victory. The god understands that he is impotent in the sense that he can do nothing to alter Amphiaraus' fate, but he is still able to bring Amphiaraus considerable honour commensurate with his position before his death. This divine intervention almost causes the death of Polynices and presages his own eventual destruction. The scene also serves as a reminder that as Apollo's single-minded determination to grant Amphiaraus his victory almost causes the death of an Argive comrade, so Polynices' obsession for power leads to the deaths of many of his compatriots.

CAPANEUS (10.845-47) AND JUPITER (10.909f.)

Capaneus' challenge to the authority of Jupiter and the other Olympian gods provides the context for two brief soliloquies in book 10. Capaneus declares his resolve to ascend the Theban ramparts to the same tower where Menoeceus heroically sacrificed himself to the Theban cause (10.845f.); in his typical brazen fashion, he says he will perform this act in order to test the worth of the Apolline oracle (847; cf. 666-68).

Encouraged by the widespread devastation he is able to effect from his position on the tower, Capaneus belittles the power of the gods and mocks the fulminous deeds of Jupiter (899-906). The lesser gods are enraged by his arrogance (907), but Jupiter merely laughs at him (907f.). Jupiter is not angered by Capaneus' bold challenge because it represents no serious threat to his power; nor is there any pity in his attitude toward his human challenger. The god merely reflects exclamatively on the giants' brazen challenge to the authority of the gods in Phlegra where he struck them down with lightning and wonders in amazement how man can be so bold as to challenge his power (909f.).

Although Jupiter addresses Capaneus in his soliloquy, the god does not intend for Capaneus to hear or respond to his rhetorical question; the speech is intended to inform the reader what is passing through Jupiter's mind. Capaneus naturally is doomed by his impetuosity and his violent death serves to illustrate the futility of challenging the power of the gods, particularly that of Jupiter, the supreme ruler. Jupiter's monologue shows him responding calmly to Capaneus' threat, supremely confident in the power he wields. The subsequent narrative reveals there is nothing particularly righteous about Capaneus' display of valour (11.1f.):

174

postquam magnanimus furias uirtutis iniquae
consumpsit Capaneus . . .

It seems as if his senseless challenge is not to be viewed as a heroic act, since it is shown to be inspired by the Furies at the behest of the malevolent Pluto (8.76f.; cf. 10.831-33); the favourable reception of Capaneus' shade in the underworld recalls the rôle of Pluto in engineering the challenge and further discredits the deed.

Apostrophes

In an apostrophic speech the speaker addresses a person who is absent as if he were physically present. The apostrophe is always violently emotional in expression and tone and is conducive to the elevated style of Statian epic. Fontanier describes this aspect of the apostrophe suitably when he says:[6]

> [Q]u'est-ce qui peut donner lieu à l'*Apostrophe*? Ce n'est ni la réflexion, ni la pensée toute nue, ni une simple idée: ce n'est que le sentiment, et que le sentiment excité dans le cœur jusqu'à éclater et à se répandre au dehors comme de lui-même. L'*Apostrophe* en général ne serait que froide et insipide, si elle ne s'annonçait comme l'expression d'une émotion vive ou profonde, comme l'élan spontané d'une âme fortement affectée.

Fontanier is referring to the figure of apostrophe in his description, but his comments are equally valid for the apostrophic speech.

The apostrophe differs from the lament mainly in that the absent person addressed is not deceased and is not being mourned. But like the lament, the apostrophe reveals itself in a spontaneous outburst of passion that reflects the heightened emotional state of the speaker. This intensity and immediacy of emotion, characteristic of the apostrophe, enlivens the narrative and increases the pathos of the dramatic situation. Rhetorical questions, anaphora, exclamations such as *o!*, *heu!*, *en!*, *io!* and *ecce!*, short sentences and clauses, some strung together by coordinating conjunctions such as *et*, *sive*, *an* or *si*, abound in the majority of apostrophic speeches. Since a speaker

---

[6] Fontanier (1968: 372).

can maintain a highly charged emotional state only for a short period of time, apostrophes are characteristically short. The majority of those in the *Thebaid* are under the average of 7.5 lines in length; they appear mainly in the last third of the epic. Most apostrophes are delivered by humans, but a few are spoken by supernatural powers.

ANONYMOUS SHADE (2.19-25)

The scene for the apostrophic speech of the anonymous shade in book 2 is one of infernal coldness, stagnation, fetidity, bareness, pallidity and gloom (1ff.). Mercury accompanies Laius to the upper world at Jupiter's behest so that the ghost can incite Eteocles to break his agreement of alternate rule with Polynices. Laius still bears the fatal wound he incurred as the result of his chance meeting with Oedipus. The patricide has sped events inexorably on their way to a fateful conclusion for the royal house of Thebes.

One of the shades in the underworld, who had offended the gods and now suffers the dire consequences, catches sight of Laius being escorted to the world above (16-18). Filled with bitterness, hatred and envy, the shade (who resembles the anonymous Theban; cf. 1.171ff.) reproaches Laius, citing three supernatural beings who could be responsible for his ascent (2.19-22):

> uade . . . o felix, quoscumque uocaris in usus,
> seu Iouis imperio, seu maior adegit Erinys
> ire diem contra, seu te furiata sacerdos
> Thessalis arcano iubet emigrare sepulcro . . .

The connexion of Jupiter with one of the Furies and a Thessalian witch suggests that his actions resemble those of the infernal powers. All three supernatural figures actually play an important rôle on the occasions that Laius ascends to the upper world. Whereas Jupiter commands Mercury to raise the shade of Laius so that he can move Eteocles to hatred of his brother (1.285-302), one of the Furies has filled the spirit of Laius with hatred and a desire for revenge. The reference to necromancy prognosticates the second coming of Laius at the behest of Tiresias (4.604ff.). The anonymous shade is envious of Laius' return to the upper world, for the former regent will gaze upon the sky, sun, green earth and pure rivers that he left behind previously (cf. 2.23f.); however, the shade declares that this will only make

Laius more despondent when he has to return to the gloomy confines of the world below (25).

PIETAS (11.465-70, 471)

Pietas' address to Nature in the antepenultimate book is typical of the apostrophe for its tone. Her complaint against Nature is invested with great feeling. Pietas rhetorically asks why Nature created her in opposition to the passions of men and the gods and cries out that she is longer reverenced (11.465-67). She suggests excitedly that it is the innate streak of fury within man that predisposes him to internecine strife (468-70):

o furor, o homines diraeque Prometheos artes!
quam bene post Pyrrham tellus pontusque uacabant!
en mortale genus!

Her brief speech highlights the ascendancy of death and destruction over the forces of piety and love in Thebes.

ARGIA (12.209-19) AND ANTIGONE (12.437-46)

The apostrophes of Argia to Polynices (209-19) and Antigone to her brothers (437-46) in the final book are notable for their emotional violence, compact expression and rhetorical figures. After Argia leaves her companions to search for and bury her husband's corpse in defiance of Creon's decree, she declares that she will not wait for the possibility of aid from Theseus to ensure that he is buried (12.209-12). Argia resolves to risk her own life to bury Polynices and reproaches herself for delaying so long (212-18). The love and devotion that Argia shows for her husband in this apostrophe highlights her noble and pious nature. The apostrophe of Antigone is spoken after she and Argia unwittingly mix the ashes of Eteocles with Polynices' corpse and a violent conflagration erupts (429ff.). Antigone expresses her horror and appeals to the spirits of her brothers to cease their enmity (437-46).

Challenges

Challenges in the *Thebaid* are issued by speakers directly or indirectly calling upon their opponents to take part in combat or an athletic contest. The challenges that are issued in the *Thebaid* are short monologues, averaging under four and one-half lines in length; no challenge extends to nine lines. The incisive manner of this type of speech resembles the challenges in the *Aeneid*, whereas in the *Iliad* challenges are longer and more numerous. Most of the challenges in the *Thebaid* occur in battle scenes, the exceptions being Hippomedon's and Capaneus' athletic challenges to the Achaean warriors in the funeral games in book 6. There are only eight speeches of challenge in the *Thebaid* made by four characters; Tydeus and Capaneus each make three speeches of this type. The prominent stylistic features of the challenge are anaphora and repetition, exclamation and the rhetorical question.

The constituents of the challenge in the *Thebaid* are the challenger, the opponent who is the recipient of the challenge, and the actual issuance of the challenge. All challenges are military or athletic and are characterised by brevity reminiscent of challenges in Vergilian epic. The challenges are not always precise in their formulation, but the intention of the speakers is nevertheless unmistakable (e.g., 5.565-70). Those of the effeminate Crenaeus (9.340-43) and of the impulsive Capaneus (10.899-906) prove to be ill-judged, resulting immediately in their deaths. Those of Tydeus (2.547-49, 8.664-72, 8.677-79), Hippomedon (6.656-59) and Capaneus (6.734-37) are accompanied by deeds that help promote and define their heroic and aggressive personalities. Challenges are characteristically fiery and are the principal ingredient of many of their dramatic contexts. They are successful only when the speakers display a heroic prowess equal to the purpose and force of their declamatory outbursts.

HIPPOMEDON (6.656-59), CAPANEUS (6.734-37)

Athletic challenges are issued during the funeral games in book 6. After Adrastus calls for contestants in the discus, a number of Achaeans come forward, including Hippomedon, who in his right hand carries a much heavier discus than those of his competitors (6.646-56). Hippomedon is not only physically imposing (654) but also vainglorious, as his subsequent challenge illustrates. He challenges the Achaean warriors to take their throws in the event with his disc, scorning the quoits of the other competitors; he then casually flings his own a considerable distance (656-61). The brutish Capaneus makes the other athletic challenge in the funeral games. When the cestus contest is announced, he issues a challenge to the Achaean warriors and expresses hopes that an Aonian will meet his challenge, for he maintains that he does not wish to slay a warrior of his own Argive stock in the contest and have his courage sullied with the blood of a compatriot (734-37); this claim is belied a little later by his desire to slay his clever opponent Alcidimas (819-22).

TYDEUS (8.664-72, 677-79)

Two of Tydeus' challenges are issued during his *aristeia* in book 8. He pours scorn upon the Thebans as he wreaks havoc upon them and puts them to flight. The purpose of his mocking is to drive the Thebans to accept his challenge in combat. Tydeus rhetorically asks the Thebans why they flee him, sardonically reminds the Theban warriors of his monomachy during which he killed fifty of their comrades, and invites them to avenge their comrades' deaths (8.664-68). He ridicules the Thebans for their unwillingness to accept his challenge and asks where he might find Eteocles (668-72), referring ironically to the monarch as *egregius dux* (672).

At this juncture Tydeus catches sight of Eteocles in battle and rushes to meet him. Tydeus' respectful address of the king is again ironic (677): *Aoniae rex o iustissime gentis. . . .* Under the guise of deference Tydeus reveals his intense contempt for Eteocles. The sneering taunt is intended to drive the king to accept his subsequent challenge, which he delivers in the form of a stinging rhetorical question. Tydeus remarks that Eteocles has been avoiding a confrontation in open combat and suggests that the king would rather wait for the relative safety of night (678f.).

CAPANEUS (10.899-906)

Capaneus' challenges are remarkable for their boldness. His challenge of Jupiter and the Olympian gods during his assault on Thebes is typical of his temerity (10.899-906). Furor (832) has possessed Capaneus, just as Pluto ordained (cf. 8.76f.); crazed by his success against his Theban foes, he dares to challenge the power and authority of the gods (10.832ff.). He wonders aloud if there is no patron deity of Thebes that will meet his challenge

(899f.), then specifically asks for Bacchus and Hercules, taunting the gods by referring to them as *infandae segnes telluris alumni* (900f.). Capaneus argues that any gods of lesser repute are an affront to his standing (901). He dares to claim that he can withstand Jupiter's burning light and challenges the god directly (903-05):

> en cineres Semelaeaque busta tenentur!
> nunc age, nunc totis in me conitere flammis,
> Iuppiter!

Capaneus then taunts Jupiter by imputing cowardice to him: the hero suggests that the god is braver at frightening Semele and demolishing the Theban walls he helped his *socer* Cadmus build (905f.). The demeaning references to Bacchus, Hercules and Jupiter reveal the extent of Capaneus' contempt for the higher powers.

Taunts

The taunt of an opponent is a significant and familiar component in the battle scenes of the *Thebaid*. A taunt is a brief speech in which someone is made the object of reproach, derision, or scorn. This type of speech is designed either to provoke an adversary in battle or to bring some inglorious deed or fact such as impending death to the opponent's attention. The taunt usually betrays an attitude of superiority on the part of the speaker, although sometimes a general defensiveness on the part of the speaker is apparent.

It is unsurprising that there is a wide range of taunts in the *Iliad*, given the many opportunities for taunts arising out of martial circumstances. This is unsurprising, given the many opportunities for taunts arising out of martial circumstances in the *Iliad*. When Aeneas meets Achilleus on the battlefield (*Il.* 20.176ff.), Aeneas declares to Achilleus that both his comrades and the Greeks have so many taunts to utter that a ship of one hundred benches could not sustain them (246f.). The Trojan further observes that mortals possess a ready and facile tongue capable of all manner of speech; whatever words a man has spoken he will hear in turn (248-50). In Homeric epic the taunt is usually spoken by a combatant who has vanquished an opponent in single combat; the person addressed is usually the dead or dying warrior. Sometimes the taunt is made after the wounding of an opponent; notable instances occur when Pandaros (*Il.* 5.102-05, 284f.) and Paris (*Il.* 11.380-83) believe themselves to be victors in their duels. Occasionally a combatant reveals an urge to taunt a dying warrior, for example, when Hektor vanquishes Patroklos (*Il.* 16.830-42). A taunt can follow the flight of a warrior from battle or even take place during the approach of a combatant; when the latter occurs, the speaker's intention is to boost his own morale during the ensuing engagement. There is also the taunt that is delivered to an ally or compatriot (e.g., 1.159, 225).

The taunt figures less prominently in the *Aeneid*, since fighting between the Trojans and the Rutulians, their main antagonists, is restricted primarily to books 9, 10 and 12. An element of sarcasm is no less apparent in the taunts of Aeneas and the Trojans than in those of their opposition. There are some notable examples of Trojan disdain for their opponents. When Aeneas seeks vengeance for Pallas' death and roams the battlefield searching for victims in order to vent his rage (10.510ff.), he taunts his opponents in a sarcastic and insulting manner reminiscent of the Homeric manner. In a scene as cruel as that of any in Homeric epic, Aeneas ignores Tarquitus' plea for mercy, lops off his head, kicks the corpse and vindictively proclaims that it will remain forever unburied (557-60). Aeneas' reproach is faithful to the heroic tradition, for his harsh sentiments mirror the scathing victory speeches of Odysseus (11.452-54) and Achilleus (21.122-24) with their avian and piscine references in the *Iliad*; the thalassic component (*Aen.* 10.559f.) is commonplace in taunts in Homeric epic (e.g., *Il.* 16.745, 21.122-35). Only a moment later Aeneas confronts the fallen Lucagus with a contemptuous taunt (*Aen.* 10.592-94) reminiscent of Patroklos' mocking of Kebriones (*Il.* 16.745-50). When Lucagus' brother pleads for his life, Aeneas sneers at him and plunges his swordpoint into his opponent's breast (10.597ff.).

The taunts issued in the *Thebaid* lie firmly within the heroic tradition. As in Homeric and Vergilian epic, they are spoken in battle when the fighting is most intense; they are particularly frequent in the last third of the epic where Argive and Theban warriors engage each other in individual combat. Taunts in battle scenes in the *Thebaid* characteristically are invested with great intensity of emotion, particularly contempt and odium for the opposition. The evidence reveals that taunts consist of corresponding elements and are delivered prior to or during individual or group combat, when one is on the verge of winning or losing, or even after the defeat of the enemy. They are generally shorter in the *Thebaid* than in Homeric epic; in length they approximate those of the *Aeneid*. The seventeen taunts are on average under four and one-half lines in length.

Most of the taunts are issued by leading Argive heroes such as Capaneus (*Theb.* 7.677-79, 9.557-59, 10.873-77, 10.925f.), Hippomedon (9.137-39, 294-301, 476-80), Tydeus (2.661-68, 8.472f., 8.582f.) and Polynices (11.548-51, 568-72) against their Theban opponents in *monomachiae*. The only warriors on the Theban side to deliver taunts are Periphas' brother (2.641), Amphion (9.779-87) and Eteocles (9.96-103). Unlike the great Olympians in Homer (*Il.* 4.7-19: Zeus to Hera; 21.394-99: Ares to Athene) and Vergil (10.607-10: Jupiter to Juno), none of the Olympian deities in the *Thebaid* feels moved to utter a taunt against a god equal in stature to his/her own. There is nothing to compare with Athene's taunt of Ares in battle in the *Iliad* (21.410-14) or even the comparatively mild but ironic taunt of Jupiter addressed to Juno in the *Aeneid* (10.607-10).

Not only do Olympians in Statian epic avoid taunting each other, but also no member of the divine family feels threatened enough to taunt lesser beings in order to unsettle them to his/her own advantage. While the latter case holds true for the *Aeneid*, there are a number of occasions in Homer where the Olympian gods taunt humans and lesser deities (e.g., *Il.* 5.440-42: Apollo to Diomedes, 16.707-09: Apollo to Patroklos). Furthermore, while Olympian and lesser deities employ the taunt to unbalance their divine and human foes in the *Iliad*, this speech type is not employed for this purpose by minor divinities in Vergilian and Statian epic.[7]

Circumstances occasionally arise in the *Thebaid* that lend themselves to the promulgation of an Olympian taunt to a minor deity or human antagonist. One such opportunity presents itself to Jupiter in book 10 when Capaneus foolishly challenges the fulminous power of the chief god (883ff.). Jupiter is moved just enough to reflect briefly on the madness of the hero and the human race before calmly striking him down (907ff.). Through the conspicuous absence of an Olympian taunt in the *Thebaid*, Statius suggests the incontrovertible preeminence of the Olympian deities.

Taunts in epic are characteristically issued prior to the commencement of hostilities between individual combatants or opposing armies. The taunt issued under these circumstances is designed to enhance the confidence of the speaker while it enervates the resolve and strength of the opponent. The attitude of superiority that accompanies the delivery of a taunt occasionally

---

[7] Although Tisiphone vituperates Pietas and achieves the same result (*Theb.* 11.484-92).

suggests a general apprehensiveness on the part of the speaker about the impending duel; this is implicit, for example, in Parthenopaeus' taunt directed at Amphion (*Theb.* 9.790-800). Taunts that are made just before or after the termination of hostilities between two opponents occur frequently in epic. Such taunts invariably are spoken when one of the combatants is at the point of death or already bereft of life; the speaker is almost always the victor in the contest. The victory taunt delivered at the close of combat is a spontaneous expression of the speaker's feeling of superiority over his foe. From a psychological perspective the favourable outcome enhances the self-assurance of the victor and serves to confirm his feeling of invulnerability in battle.

In the eleventh book of the *Aeneid*, as noted above, Aeneas often mocks his foes after vanquishing them in combat. In the *Iliad* Achilleus repeatedly taunts his opponents after injuring or slaying them (20.389-92, 21.122-135, 21.184-99). The most celebrated instance occurs when the hero strikes Hektor with his spear through the neck (*Il.* 22.326ff.). As Hektor falls to the ground fatally injured, Achilleus stands over his body and sneers at him, calling him a fool (333). Another notable illustration of the Homeric practice of taunting occurs after Patroklos hurls a stone at Kebriones, charioteer of Hektor and a son of Priam (16.734ff.). The object crushes the skull of Kebriones; his eyes fall upon the dust-ridden earth; and his body plunges to the ground as his spirit relinquishes its hold over him. Patroklos mocks Kebriones as he lies in the dust, likening his fall from the chariot to a diver leaping from a ship in search of oysters at sea (745-50). After Patroklos delivers the deathblow to Kebriones, he vies with Hektor for possession of the corpse (751ff.). Patroklos and his Achaean compatriots prove superior until Apollo enters the fray. Subsequently the god strikes Patroklos across the back; Euphorbos spears him; and Hektor thrusts a spear through his belly. As Patroklos lies dying, Hektor taunts the Achaean for his failed promise to plunder Troy and bear away the Trojan women as captives, professing that he will abandon his corpse to the vultures (830ff.). Patroklos' taunt of exultation proves to be premature when he is vanquished by the Trojan forces with the assistance of Apollo.

Victory taunts in Homeric epic are occasionally made by the successful combatant after the death of his opponent. They are addressed either to the vanquished warrior or his compatriots. Patroklos' taunt of Kebriones (*Il.* 16.745-50) and those of Achilleus to Lykaon (21.122-135) and Asteropaios (21.184-89) are directed at the deceased victims. Deiphobos is the object of

Idomeneus' taunt after slaying Alkathoos (13.446-54), while Menelaos directs his insulting ridicule to the Trojans and Zeus after dispatching Peisandros (13.620-39). In the *Aeneid* Turnus taunts the Arcadians after taking the life of Pallas (10.491-95) and mocks Eumedes after dealing the herald a deathblow with his own sword (12.359-61). A few taunts in the *Thebaid* are issued by the subjugator to his rival just at the moment of his death or immediately afterward (8.472-73, 9.557-59, 12.779-81).

Not only are taunts exchanged between warring parties at the commencement and culmination of hostilities in the *Thebaid*, but also combat sequences where a warrior delivers a taunt to an adversary or a group of opposing warriors in the midst of a violent confrontation are an equally essential component of the battle narrative. Once again the precedent for this originates from the Homeric practice. While there are frequent and lengthy exchanges of taunts in the thick of battle in the *Iliad*, taunts are fewer in number and shorter in length in the *Aeneid*. The vitriolic taunts of Aeneas are typical of those uttered in the extreme heat of combat (*Aen.* 10.557-60, 592-94, 599f.).

Given the heroic framework of the *Thebaid*, it is unsurprising that the exchange of taunts between individual and group combatants figure heavily in the battle narrative of the *Thebaid*. As in Homeric and Vergilian epic, taunts are frequently made before the commencement of hostilities between individual combatants or opposing armies, toward the culmination of combat proceedings, and during the most heated part of the conflict. The notable features of this speech type are the provocative and derisive tone, the projection of confidence or the appearance of superiority that occasionally betrays the speaker's apprehensiveness, and the thalassic and feminine constituents. The violent emotional current immanent in the exchange of taunts provides the foundation for many of the most effective dramatic situations that arise in the narrative.

TYDEUS (2.661-68, 8.582F.)

During the battle between Tydeus and the fifty Theban warriors sent against him by Eteocles, the hero wreaks destruction among his foes (2.532ff.). After his brutal slaying of Menoetes, Tydeus pursues his remaining assailants and bitterly taunts them (661-68):

> non haec trieterica uobis
> nox patrio de more uenit, non orgia Cadmi

cernitis aut auidas Bacchum scelerare parentes.
nebridas et fragiles thyrsos portare putastis
imbellem ad sonitum maribusque incognita ueris
foeda Celaenaea committere proelia buxo?
hic aliae caedes, alius furor: ite sub umbras,
o timidi paucique!

The salient feature of his taunt is the imputation of feminine qualities to the Theban race (660ff.). Tydeus regards the Thebans, whose women are especially devoted to the *orgia* of Bacchus, as distinctively feminine in character. As the hero notes toward the close of his taunt, the degree of madness that infects the Thebans in their worship of Bacchus does not compare with the intense *furor* that gains hold of him; the fifty Theban warriors are simply no match for him.

Tydeus is foolishly challenged by the youthful and naïve Atys during the hero's *aristeia* (8.578ff.). The Calydonian is encouraged by the prospect of a favourable outcome in an unequal contest and laughs at Atys, taunting him for his feeble endeavours. He further reproaches the youth for his reckless daring (*improbe*, 582), intimating that he will acquire fame because of his death at the hands of a distinguished warrior (*uideo, magnum cupis . . . leti / nomen*, 582f.). This notion is derived from the heroic ideal in which an individual can achieve immortality through death, provided his conqueror possesses a superhuman stature (e.g., *Aen.* 10.829f., 11.688f., Ov. *Met.* 12.80f.). After this suggestion Tydeus deals the youth a deathblow by lightly flinging his spear and striking him in the groin (8.583-86).

CAPANEUS (7.677-79, 10.873F., 10.925F.)

Capaneus issues a taunt prior to single combat at the commencement of hostilities between the Argive and Theban forces (7.621ff.). The intrepid warrior confronts the maddened priest Eunaeus in unequal combat (668ff.), deriding Eunaeus' fragile demeanour before dispatching him with his spear (677-79):

. . . quid femineis ululatibus . . .
terrificas, moriture, uiros? utinam ipse ueniret
cui furis! haec Tyriis cane matribus!

Capaneus' reference to the womanish traits of the priest is typical of the prominence that the feminine constituent assumes in some epic taunts.

One of the most conspicuous taunts is spoken in the antepenultimate book by Capaneus. The intrepid hero storms Thebes unperturbed by the Theban forces and oblivious to the projectiles hurled against him (10.848ff.); his formidable presence is likened to a river gradually loosening a bridge from its base (864-69). He towers over Thebes and terrifies the inhabitants with his prodigious frame, ridiculing the size of Thebes' towers and walls and referring scornfully to the mythical founding of the City (873-77). The maddened colossus proceeds to dismantle the walls of the City and lapidate its temples and homes until with supreme arrogance he foolishly challenges Jupiter (899-906) and sneers at the force of the omnipotent god's thunderbolt (925f.). This affront finally moves Jupiter to strike Capaneus down in his folly even while the hero speaks.

HIPPOMEDON (9.137-39, 294-301, 476-80)

Hippomedon, a fearless warrior in the mould of Capaneus, makes three taunts in the ninth book during his *aristeia*. He cuts off the hand of Leonteus while taunting him (9.133ff.), taunts the combative Panemus after slaying his twin brother Thespiades (292ff.), and derisively dismisses the considerable fluviatile power of Ismenos as an aberration of an effeminate predisposition after the river furiously attacks him (476-80).

POLYNICES (11.548-51, 568-72)

There is one scene in the *Thebaid* where a combatant delivers an exultant taunt prematurely. The most significant monomachy in the epic takes place in the penultimate book when Polynices duels with Eteocles and injures him (497ff.). Eteocles retreats as his strength diminishes and feigns death in a fall, whereupon Polynices believes that he is victorious and taunts his brother (548-51):

> quo retrahis, germane, gradus? hoc languida somno,
> hoc regnis effeta quies, hoc longa sub umbra
> imperia! exilio rebusque exercita egens
> membra uides; disce arma pati nec fidere laetis.

Polynices' spontaneous expression of exultation at the moment of his apparent triumph reveals his cruelty and vindictiveness. He imagines that he has finally achieved his goal of becoming king. But the ostensible fulfilment of his ambition does not assuage his spiteful anger against his brother. The exile attempts to strip the dying regent of his armour, but Eteocles summons his failing strength and plunges his sword into Polynices' heart (557-67).

Under similar circumstances in Homeric and Vergilian epic the victor customarily delivers a speech of exultation in which he taunts his opponent for his inferiority, condemning him as a wretched and contemptible creature. However, Statius introduces an interesting psychological twist to the situation. Instead of having Eteocles articulate the standard heroic taunt after his fatal stabbing of Polynices, the poet has the exile issue a final rebuke in his death throes (568-72):

> uiuisne an adhuc manet ira superstes,
> perfide, nec sedes umquam meriture quietas?
> huc mecum ad manes! illic quoque pacta reposcam,
> si modo Agenorei stat Cnosia iudicis urna,
> qua reges punire datur.

Venini and Vessey observe that the tone of the exile's venomous effusion contrasts dramatically with his final words of penitence and consanguineous sentimentalism in Euripides' *Phoenissae* (1444-53).[8]

Polynices' uncompromising and rancorous speech reveals that he is as shameless and implacable as his brother. The subsequent apostrophe of the poet stresses the joint criminality of the brothers (*Theb.* 11.574f.):

> ite truces animae funestaque Tartara leto
> polluite et cunctas Erebi consumite poenas!

Notwithstanding the intervention of malevolent supernatural forces who drive Eteocles and Polynices to destruction (cf. 576), Statius clearly intends to demonstrate that the brothers' malevolence and flagitiousness render them equally culpable and deserving of death.

Despite the deaths of both antagonists in the duel and the absence of an anticipated taunt by Eteocles, the scene is typically heroic in its inspiration and formulation. As in the meeting between Paris and Menelaos in the *Iliad*

---

[8] Venini (1961b: 397), Vessey (1973: 278f.).

(3.340ff.), the spectacle matches in single combat the two individuals most responsible for the war. The decisive duel between the leading warriors on each side still involved in the war resembles the momentous epic monomachy between Aeneas and Turnus (*Aen.* 12.710ff.). One of the curious features of heroic epic is that *decisive* monomachies between the main antagonists take place only after much depletory bloodshed between the armies and a growing lack of resolve in both camps (e.g., *Il.* 22.131ff., *Aen.* 11.708ff.); the idea of the most powerful warriors from both sides meeting in single combat or in small group combat in order to resolve a conflict may originate from actual historical occurrences.[9] In the *Thebaid* the inevitable duel between Polynices and Eteocles takes place after the exhausted forces are deadlocked.

THESEUS (12.779-81)

The most notable taunt among those issued in the *Thebaid* by the subjugator to his rival just at or immediately after the moment of his death is spoken by Theseus when he encounters Creon on the battleground in the final book. A frenzied Creon threatens the Athenian king and hurls his shaft harmlessly at his opponent (12.761-68). Theseus laughs at Creon, briefly apostrophises the Argive spirits, then unhesitatingly fells and kills Creon with his spear (768-78). As the Athenian regent despoils his corpse he taunts (779-81):

> iamne dare extinctis iustos . . . hostibus ignes,
> iam uictos operire placet? uade atra dature
> supplicia, extremique tamen secure sepulcri.

These lines reveal the intensity of Theseus' passionate outburst against Creon for his refusal to permit the burial of Polynices and the Argive troops. A basic moral judgement consisting of the duty of man to observe natural law pervades the theme of his taunt. Despite his indignation Theseus grants the Theban his burial; his righteous words contrast with those of Creon when he prohibits the burial of the Argive corpses (12.94-102; cf. 11.661-64).

---

[9] Gluck (1964: 25 and n. 3).

Threats

In the *Thebaid* few speeches are dominated by expressions of intent to inflict injury or death upon an adversary. Surprisingly, there are no threats that are actually spoken in the heat of battle; only one threat is delivered prior to individual combat (12.761-66). In the majority of cases threats are delivered before public or regal audiences (2.452-67, 3.648-69, 5.656-60, 5.672-79). The speakers are either deities or humans of considerable stature. The most conspicuous stylistic feature of the threat is the exploded period, consisting of short, abrupt clauses and uneven expression (e.g., 2.462-67, 5.656-60). Rhetorical questions and exclamations predominate, enhancing the atmosphere of emotional violence.

The threats of Tydeus (2.452-67) and Capaneus (3.648-69) are the most important on account of their psychological portrayal of the heroes. The only deities to issue threats are Pluto and Diana. The underworld god threatens Amphiaraus during his descent to the underworld (8.84f.), while Diana threatens the future slayer of her son Parthenopaeus with death (9.663-67).

TYDEUS (2.452-67)

When Eteocles is in the process of rejecting Tydeus' demand that he step down from the Theban throne in accordance with the pact of alternate rule he had made with his brother (2.415-51), the Argive hero violently interrupts the regent's speech to objurgate him. A threatening tone pervades his heated reply. Tydeus roars that Eteocles will pay deservedly with his life for his refusal to abdicate the throne (453-58). He predicts death and destruction for the inhabitants of Thebes (458-61):

> ast horum miseret, quos sanguine uiles
> coniugibus natisque infanda ad proelia raptos
> proicis excidio, bone rex. o quanta Cithaeron
> funera sanguineusque uadis, Ismene, rotabis!

Tydeus' address of Eteocles as *bone rex* is of course ironic. The hero also unwittingly presages his impending slaughter of the band of warriors treacherously despatched by Eteocles to kill him on his return to Argos; the lives of Theban men are thrown away needlessly by the regent when he sends his troops to a horrid death.

Tydeus threatens the regent again with death before departing hastily from the court (462ff.). His passionate speech and threatening manner emphasise his predisposition toward unrestrained violence, a tendency that becomes manifest in an ignominious death accompanied by his divinely motivated anthropophagy (8.716ff., esp. 751ff.).

CAPANEUS (3.648-69)

Capaneus illustrates the same tendency toward violence in book 3 when he threatens Amphiaraus (648ff.) after the prophet has prophesied internecine warfare between Argos and Thebes (620ff., esp. 640ff.).[10] Ironically he accuses the priest of being infected with *furor* (3.648f., 661f.), whereas it is in fact Capaneus who is maddened by his desire for war (cf. 668f.). He discredits Amphiaraus' priestly function and declares that the gods pay no attention to human prayers (652-60). In a telling *sententia* he asserts that the gods exist only because man created them in his fear (*primus in orbe deos fecit timor!*, 661). Capaneus further warns Amphiaraus to stay clear of him once the day for battle arrives (662-66). The insulting and menacing tone of his speech highlights the violent and blasphemous aspects of his character.

Commands

Thirty speeches in the *Thebaid* take the form of commands. Naturally enough, the majority of commands are issued by deities and monarchs; other commands are spoken by warriors and priests. Most are very brief in length; over one-half are four lines or less in length. The demanding tone of the command allows for little, if any attempt at persuasion; when the command also involves an attempt to persuade, the tone is usually threatening. Deliberations frequently are imperatival in tone even if they consist primarily of arguments and promises (e.g., *Theb.* 2.102-19). On the other hand, the distinguishing feature of the command is its lack of persuasive elements; hence its brevity. Another notable feature of this speech type is the sense of great urgency that is often conveyed through the varied sentence

---

[10] Legras (1905: 293) maintains incorrectly that this speech is deliberative.

structure and extensive use of figures. Since there is only one command that can be held with any degree of certainty not to have been obeyed (10.492), this speech type is unquestionably the most effective in the *Thebaid*.

The commands of Jupiter (1.285-302, 3.229-52, 7.6-33) and Pluto (8.34-79) are the longest and most important in the *Thebaid*. The most obvious function of these commands is the advancement of the narrative, but the rôle they play in defining the gods' personalities and adorning the narrative is just as important. Jupiter and his brother reveal themselves in their commands as cruel and unrelenting deities who are bent on the destruction of humanity. The embellishment of the narrative through the use of vigorous language and the generation of emotion in these commands does much to enhance the oppressive mood and atmosphere of the scenes in which they are spoken.

Other important commands are delivered by the pious but occasionally ineffectual Adrastus; somewhat surprisingly, he issues six commands, more than any other regent, while tyrannical monarchs such as Eteocles and Creon deliver only one command between them in direct speech (11.669-72). The commands of Adrastus are brief, averaging a few lines in length. Among the most interesting and significant is the command he addresses to Agreus and Polynices (6.914-19) during the funeral games.

JUPITER (1.285-302, 3.229-52, 7.6-33)

At the council of the gods in book 1 Jupiter dismisses Juno's plea not to involve Argos in the punishment of Thebes, maintaining that Venus and Bacchus would argue in a similar manner on behalf of Thebes if they were given the opportunity (1.285-89). The king of the gods swears that his oath to punish Thebes and Argos is irrevocable (290-92). He orders Mercury to convey the message to Pluto that the spirit of Laius be allowed to ascend to the world above so that he can incite Eteocles to violate the compact of alternate rule he has made with Polynices (292ff.).

Jupiter observes that the spirit of Laius will find it easy to convince Eteocles that he should retain the throne because the tyrant already desires this on his own (299-301). Jupiter asserts that Eteocles would deny Polynices the throne without his intervention. If this were in fact the case, there would be—naturally and paradoxically—a harmony between the will of Eteocles and the destiny that Jupiter marks out for him. Jupiter would like the other deities to believe that even without his intervention in the affairs of the brothers that Eteocles would attempt to retain the throne. However, this is not the impression of the monarch that Statius attempts to convey early in the poem. The narrative portrays Eteocles as a victim of forces beyond his control (*pro gnara nihil mortalia fati / corda sui!*, 2.92f.) and the shade of Laius rebukes him for his inactivity and apparent lack of concern for his own safety (102f.). Eteocles is not intending at this point to undertake any action to deprive his brother of the throne and it is only the direct intervention of Jupiter and the Furies that brings the pair into conflict. Even though Jupiter claims that the Theban and Argive races have a genetic predisposition toward criminality and immorality (1.227), he makes clear that the events to take place are directly the result of his own will (*hinc causae irarum, certo reliqua ordine ducam*, 302).

Another important command of Jupiter (3.229-52) emphasises his ultimate control over proceedings in Thebes and Argos. Jupiter summons Mars, who has been in Thrace destroying people and cities (220f.). As Mars stands before Jupiter panting and with his sword dripping blood from his slaughter of the Thracians (227ff.), Jupiter orders the war-god to depart for Argos and incite the city's inhabitants to hatred and martial violence against Thebes (213-33). Jupiter is portrayed as an omnipotent and unrelenting power when he allows Mars to consume the cities in war (234f.); his malevolence is further revealed when he is shown to be the direct cause of Eteocles' ambush of Tydeus, which is the incident that sparks Argos to march against Thebes (235-38).

After commanding Mars to add credibility to Tydeus' tale of slaughter and betrayal (239), Jupiter further enjoins noninterference on the gods (239-41), telling them that no amount of effort or attempt at persuasion can alter the course of destiny (241-43):

> sic Fata mihi nigraeque Sororum
> iurauere colus: manet haec ab origine mundi
> fixa dies bello, populique in proelia nati.

If the hour for war were firmly established at the very moment of the world's conception, as Jupiter claims (242f.), then the possibility of him attempting to change the course of destiny would be removed and he would be cleared of all responsibility. As this is precisely what Jupiter wants the Olympians to believe, his purpose his served by feigning powerlessness before the Fates. However, he suggests his own authority over the Fates when he observes, *Fata mihi iurauerunt* (241f.); in addition, his claim to impotence is undercut in the narrative (*uocem Fata secuntur*, 1.213) and is never confirmed by other speakers. The atmosphere of inevitable doom and destruction is further enhanced by Jupiter's threat to destroy single-handedly the two cities if any gods intervene in his scheme (3.244-52). The suggestion that Jupiter is capable of destroying the two cities on his own is testimony to his preeminent rôle in the universal order. But the outstanding feature of the threat is its tone, which is remarkable for its violent conception and demonstrates the extent of the supreme ruler's uncompassionate and vengeful disposition.

In the seventh book Jupiter commands Mercury again to descend to earth (cf. 1.285-302), on this occasion to bid Mars to incite the Argives to violence against Thebes (6ff.). His speech is tetrapartite in structure: the command to Mercury (6-14); the *narratio*, a survey of the situation (14-21); a reference to the destructive potentialities of Mars (22-26); and a threat to transmute his war-making powers into a force of peace and beneficence (27-33).

Although the Argives are intent on going to Thebes (6.914-19, 7.100-03), Jupiter is piqued because of their brief stay in Nemea and the apparent inaction of Mars in instigating war between Argos and Thebes. Earlier Jupiter had commanded Mars to provoke war between the two cities (3.29-39). The reappearance of Jupiter in a scene where he once again exhorts Mars to fulfil his duty reminds the reader of his critical rôle in the events leading up to the war.

Jupiter's reference to the powers and conduct of Mars is illuminating (7.22-25):

> at si ipsi rabies ferrique insana voluptas
> qua tumet, inmeritas cineri dabit impius urbes
> ferrum ignemque ferens, implorantesque Tonantem
> sternet humi populos miserumque exhauriet orbem.

This imagined scene of desolation is precisely what Jupiter threatens to bring about in his speech before the Olympian council in the first book (242-46). His words afford a heightened sense of foreboding to the scene, for through the agency of Mars the innocent citizens of many cities, not only of Thebes and Argos, will die and their homes will be destroyed. This is a direct acknowledgement by Jupiter that his determination to punish Thebes and Argos for the crimes of their ancestors will result in the deaths of many innocent victims. In spite of his seemingly incomparable powers, Jupiter seems unwilling to prevent this needless death and suffering. But he is more than willing to dispossess an extremely powerful deity of his powers if his command is ignored.

PLUTO (8.34-79)

Pluto, Jupiter's infernal counterpart, is indignant when the underworld is intruded upon at the end of book 7. Pluto protests vigorously against what he supposes to be an invasion of his territory and a violation of his sovereignty by one of his brothers (8.34-79). The opening lines of his speech are indicative of the animosity he displays toward his brothers throughout his speech (34-38). The infernal ruler maintains that his brothers should not infringe upon his domain since he was granted sovereignty over the underworld in the drawing of lots (38-46). He threatens to retaliate against his brothers by subverting the established order of the universe, remonstrates against the hostile attitude of his brothers, and takes exception to the intrusion upon his territory by various animated figures such as Pirithous, Theseus and Hercules (46-56). His treatment of Orpheus and Proserpina is notable for its violence (57-62):

> Odrysiis etiam pudet (heu!) patuisse querelis
> Tartar: uidi egomet blanda inter carmina turpes
> Eumenidum lacrimas iterataque pensa Sororum;
> me quoque—sed durae melior uiolentia legis.
> ast ego uix unum, nec celsa ad sidera, furto
> ausus iter Siculo rapui conubia campo.

The violence of his stern law that reclaims Eurydice for his world and his rape of Proserpina attest to his ruthless and vindictive nature. Yet the infernal ruler considers the decree of Jupiter depriving him of Proserpina for six months of the year to be unjust (63f.):

> nec licuisse ferunt; iniustaeque a Ioue leges
> protinus, et sectum genetrix mihi computat annum.

These lines reveal a sullen attitude brought about by his inability to possess Proserpina for the entire year.

The final section of the speech is especially significant not only in terms of advancing the action but also in signposting the poet's intentions in order to arouse expectation and maintain interest in the narrative. Pluto dispatches Tisiphone to avenge the challenge to his authority and foredooms the Argive and Theban heroes (65ff.). He predestines the fratricidal confrontation between Eteocles and Polynices (8.69-71; cf. 11.387ff.), the anthropophagous act of Tydeus (8.71f.; cf. 751ff.), the refusal of Creon to allow the burial of the Argive corpses (8.72-74; cf. 11.661-64), and the challenge of Capaneus to the authority of Jupiter (8.76-77; cf. 10.831ff.). The rôle of Pluto in predetermining the horrible fates of these figures shows the importance of his position in a universe portrayed as hostile to the human situation. He is the infernal counterpart of Jupiter and co-instigator of human violence and destruction. It is partly through the unwitting agency of Pluto, who himself acts in concert with the Furies, that Jupiter is able to bring his plan for the extirpation of the royal houses to fruition.

ADRASTUS (6.914-19)

Toward the close of the funeral games, Polynices and Agreus step forward to compete in the sword fight (6.912ff.). Adrastus intervenes and forbids any fighting to take place, telling the contestants to save their strength for the war that lies ahead (914-19):

> manet ingens copia leti,
> o iuuenes! servate animos auidumque furorem
> sanguinis aduersi. tuque o, quem propter auita
> iugera, dilectas cui desolauimus urbes,
> ne, precor, ante aciem ius tantum casibus esse
> fraternisque sinas (abigant hoc numina!) uotis.

This sounds reasonable enough under the circumstances, but his words are full of tragic irony, because they carry one meaning to him and another to those who are in a better position to appreciate their true significance. The reader knows that Adrastus and Polynices are soon to become victims of Jupiter's plan. All too true for the coming war as a whole are the words *manet ingens copia leti* (914); Polynices will possess a mad desire for the blood of Eteocles as he does for Agreus' (915f.; cf. 11.387ff.); and the cities and fields will be laid bare in a sense not foreseen by the monarch (916f.). The connexion between the elements of this brief command and subsequent events is indicative of the care that the poet takes in integrating each speech into the narrative and thematic infrastructure of the poem.

PARTHENOPAEUS (9.885-908)

The most pathetic of all commands in the epic is delivered in the throes of death by the youthful warrior Parthenopaeus. As he is carried from the battlefield in the arms of his comrades, he orders his faithful servant Dorceus to console his mother and convey a message to her acknowledging his fault in taking up arms against the enemy (9.885-97). In his youthful innocence he has proven incapable of understanding the dangers of warfare until it is too late.

The poet adds an especially pathetic touch when Parthenopaeus bewails the fact that his mother will wait for his return in vain (895-97) and is absent at the moment of his death (898-99); he then offers her a lock of hair in place of his body (900-05). A subtle touch of youthful ignorance forms a fitting climax to one of the most pathetic scenes in the epic (906f.):

> haec autem primis arma infelicia castris
> ure, uel ingratae crimen suspende Dianae.

Parthenopaeus is unaware that the solicitous Diana has assisted him in every conceivable way; the final, tragic irony is that it makes no difference.

Oracular and Prophetic Speeches

Interpretations of omens and oracles, speeches of prophecy, and oracular pronouncements are prominent features in epic poetry. Most prophecies in the *Iliad* involve in some way the fate of Achilleus (e.g., 8.469-77, 18.86-96, 24.130-32), while those in the *Odyssey* are concerned in some way with the trials of Odysseus and his eventual triumph over Penelope's suitors on his return to Ithaca (e.g., 1.194-205, 5.29-42, 11.100-37). The majority of prophecies in the *Aeneid* involve the destiny of Aeneas and the fate of the Trojans (e.g., 1.257-96, 3.374-562, 7.124-57).

There are eight oracular and prophetic speeches in the *Thebaid*. Most are delivered by priests and priestesses; others are spoken by the ghost of Laius and Apollo, the god of prophecy. Since all these speeches are concerned in some way with death and destruction, they underscore the central themes of war, violence and suffering in the epic; more specifically, they emphasise the inutility of divine revelation and the hopelessness of man's position. Most of the speeches contain omens warning of impending disaster, but these are disregarded, misunderstood, misinterpreted or acted upon to little or no purpose.

Since the oracular and prophetic speeches point forward to events in the narrative, they arouse and increase the audience's sense of expectation. The inevitable fulfilment of prophecies illustrates the causal relationship between speech and dramatic narrative in different sections of the epic. This unity of speech and narrative is one of the important organising principles in the work.

The distinguishing feature of the oracular interpretation is a descriptive passage recounting what events the speaker foresees. In prophetic speeches events are foretold without any description of the vision or omens that may appear to the speaker. In the *Thebaid* the oracular pronouncement or proclamation is delivered by a priest or priestess of Apollo; the outstanding feature is the formal proclamation that a certain event will take place or that some human action must be performed in accordance with the will of the Fates.

AMPHIARAUS (3.620-47)

The most significant of oracular interpretations is spoken in book 3 when Capaneus provokes a reluctant Amphiaraus to emerge from his chamber and divulge the findings of his auspice-taking (607ff.), although the priest denies this in the first part of his address to the Argive citizens (620-23).[11] Amphiaraus maintains that destiny has a different fate in store for him than to suffer bodily at the hands of Capaneus (623f.), adding that it is his love for the people and the inspiration of Apollo that compels him to reveal his oracle, which remains silent only on the fate of the insane Capaneus (625-28). The priest wonders what has prompted the Argives to forsake their homes, rush headlong toward certain death, and compelled him to seek council with the gods when they could have remained in ignorance about their dire fate (629-37). He then relates the events he foresaw earlier that portend death and destruction for both sides (640-42).

Amphiaraus concludes by imploring the Argives to cast aside their arms, but then realises that the gods do not permit them to do this in their frenzy and that his attempt to forestall inevitable doom is futile (643-47).

---

[11] Legras (1905: 283) wrongly considers this speech to be deliberative.

The prophetic ability of Amphiaraus proves to be of no value to him or his compatriots, since he is unable to save Argos or himself from destruction. Neither the priest nor the Argives are able to exert any real measure of control over their lives; their lack of free will epitomises the hopeless plight of human figures in the *Thebaid* and contributes much to the despairing tone.

SHADE OF LAIUS (4.626-44)

After the shade of Laius appears to Tiresias and Manto (4.604ff.), the Theban priest beseeches him to prophesy the result of the war (620f.). Laius commences by asking why he has been chosen to foretell the future and lays bitter complaint against Oedipus (626-34). He announces that he will divulge only what Lachesis and Megaera permit him to reveal about the outcome of the war (635f.). He predicts the defeat of the Argives, the descent of Amphiaraus to the underworld, the violent death of Capaneus, the deaths of many brave heroes, and Eteocles' refusal to permit burial of the Argive corpses (637-41).

But it is the last part of his prophecy that proves perplexing to Tiresias and Manto. According to Laius, Thebes will be victorious, but it is Oedipus who will gain the final triumph, not Eteocles (641-44):

> certa est uictoria Thebis,
> ne trepida, nec regna ferox germanus habebit
> sed Furiae; geminumque nefas miserosque per enses
> (ei mihi!) crudelis uincit pater.

The reference to the possession of Thebes by the Furies shows that the city's inhabitants have little control over their own lives and are being manipulated by superhuman forces.

The shade of Laius departs, leaving the priest and priestess confused about the true import of his pronouncement (644f.). His words of prophecy are full of tragic irony, since they carry a foreboding meaning not comprehended by Tiresias and Manto but understood by the audience; the irony is effective in engaging and maintaining the interest of the audience in the action. The war will bring a hollow victory for Thebes, since the supernaturally inspired wish of Oedipus will be fulfilled in the mutually destructive duel between her two most prominent citizens.

PRIESTESS (5.647), AMPHIARAUS (5.733-52)

When Lycurgus receives the new of Archemorus' death in book 5, he recalls the words of Jupiter's oracle (5.647): *prima, Lycurge, dabis Dircaeo funera bello*. The king refuses to participate in any unholy war, but this does not alter the course of his son's fate. Later in the same book Amphiaraus informs the Argives that the death of Archemorus is just one occurrence in a series of ordained events that will ultimately lead to death and destruction (735-40). The priest reveals that Apollo has decreed that the Argives are to put aside their arms and tearlessly pay honour to the new deity Archemorus (740-52).[12]

Questions

There are eleven interrogatory speeches in the *Thebaid*. Ten of these are intended to elicit information from the addressee by means of simple (or direct) questions; one other consists merely of a rhetorical question (11.258f.). Naturally most of the interrogatory speeches are only a few lines in length. Interrogatory speeches consisting of simple questions usually seek information about the location, identity, ancestry or origin of the addressee or a third party (e.g., 1.438-46, 7.490-92, 12.366f.). Others of this type seek to obtain different types of general information from the addressee (e.g., 2.334-52, 3.546, 7.77-80). Few of these speeches are significant in a thematic sense; the speech of Argia to Polynices (2.334-52) is the most important.

ARGIA (2.334-52)

Argia's questioning of Polynices forms the longest interrogatory speech in the epic. She asks her husband what thoughts he entertains of leaving Argos (2.334f.). Argia perceives that her husband yearns for the throne of Thebes, but knows that Eteocles will not make way for him without a violent struggle, as the unfavourable signs and her ominous dreams suggest

---

[12] Legras (1905: 283) incorrectly maintains that this oracular pronouncement (5.733-52) is a funeral oration (*logos epitaphios*), while Vessey (1973: 319 n. 3) considers it to be a prayer.

(345-51). Argia concludes by asking again where he intends to travel, then betrays her insecure feelings by suggesting that he may be returning to a love in Thebes (351f.).

Responsions

Responsions are frequently made to various types of speeches in the *Thebaid*. The majority of responses are to deliberative speeches and simple questions; there are relatively few replies to threats (12.689-92), challenges (389-92) and responsions (393-95). There are seventeen responsions to deliberations in the epic; just over one-half of them are positive.[13] Responsions to simple questions (brief in themselves) are characteristically short, averaging under six lines in length; there are eight replies to questions. The majority supply information requested by the interrogator concerning identity, ancestry and origin (e.g., 1.452-65, 5.29-39, 12.374-80).

Eteocles' responsion (2.415-51) to the deliberation of Tydeus is of special significance in defining the personality of the monarch, while the responsions of Mars (3.295-316) and Jupiter (7.195-221) to the deliberative speeches of Venus and Bacchus, respectively, are central to an understanding of the concept of fate in the epic. The most notable sequence of responsions to questions are those of Tydeus and Polynices (1.448ff.), who are called upon by Adrastus to give the reason for their quarrel at the entrance to the palace and to divulge their identities (438-46).

---

[13] A positive response to a deliberation is one in which the respondent agrees to comply with the request of the persuader or, if the request cannot be met, attempts to reassure the persuader, console him, or assuage his fears. In a negative response the speaker directly refuses to consent to the persuader's request or replies in a negative fashion to the proposal. On the basis of these definitions there are nine positive replies to deliberations: *Theb.* 2.176-88 (Tydeus), 2.189-97 (Polynices), 2.356-62 (Polynices), 3.388-93 (Adrastus), 3.712-20 (Adrastus), 4.776-85 (Hypsipyle), 10.360-63 (Dymas), 10.679f. (Menoeceus), 10.722-34 (Menoeceus); there are eight negative responsions: 2.415-51 (Eteocles), 2.655-59 (Tydeus), 3.295-316 (Mars), 6.819-22 (Capaneus), 10.436-38, 441 (Dymas), 10.588 (Thebans), 11.298-308 (Eteocles), 12.374-80 (Argia).

ETEOCLES (2.415-51)

In book 2 Tydeus warns Eteocles to surrender the throne in favour of
Polynices (393-409). In the narrative preceding the response of Eteocles, the
monarch is likened to a snake who is angered and prepares to strike back at
its foe (411-15). Despite the anger welling up inside of him, Eteocles is able
to reply in an accomplished manner to the accusations of Tydeus (415ff.).
He displays all the cunning of a professional rhetorician in attempting to
justify his claim to the throne. The reasoning is specious at best, but he
presents his arguments skilfully. In rejecting Polynices' claim to the throne,
which he asserts is founded on violence, Eteocles carefully adduces reasons
for retaining his position as monarch and for denying the office to Polynices.
The main features of Eteocles' responsion are a rejection of Tydeus' demand,
a declaration of his right to wear the crown, and finally the justification for
his claim. The speech is entirely consistent with the portrayal of Eteocles as
an unscrupulous and scheming tyrant.

Eteocles declares that if he had not already been forewarned of
Polynices' dissension, the boldness and threatening posture of Tydeus alone
would have served as a reflexion of Polynices' enmity and a presentiment of
conflict (415-20). Eteocles further accuses Tydeus of having little regard for
justice and equity, but professes to excuse him for his irreverence because
the legate is merely following instructions (420-24). The regent declares that
he has every right to keep the throne, since Tydeus' claim on behalf of
Polynices is based on threats of violence rather than trust or peace (424-29).
The pharisaical claims of Eteocles are a gross attempt at moral deception,
since he has violated the agreement of alternate rule with his brother that had
been based upon mutual trust.

Furthermore, Eteocles maintains that he does not begrudge the lot of
Polynices, who should be content to have married into Argive royalty and to
rule over wealthy Argos (430-33, 436-38); however, Eteocles asserts that he
should be permitted to rule over Thebes, the poorer of the two kingdoms
(433-36). He asserts that Argia, accustomed to the luxury of Argos, would
be unable to endure the simple life of Thebes, even though his sisters would
look after her needs (438-40); she would also be offended by the unsightli-
ness of his grief-stricken mother and the cries of his accursed father
(440-42).

Eteocles next employs the predictable but spurious argument of a tyrant
that his subjects are accustomed to his rule and should be spared the

201

uncertainty brought about by a change of monarchs (442-45); this is essentially an argument involving expedience (*utile*) and ease (*facile*). He claims his people would suffer punishment if he were to step down from the throne (446-48); this is certainly true, since Polynices is shown earlier taking note of his opponents so that he can take action against them after he gains power in Thebes (316-19). Eteocles argues further that the citizens of Thebes would scarcely permit him to relinquish the throne even if he was willing to do so (449-51). This final claim on the devotion and loyalty of his subjects is unfounded, since the enmity of the Theban people for Eteocles has already been confirmed in the narrative.

MARS (3.295-316)

As Mars hastens to carry out Jupiter's command to incite the Argives to war (3.260ff.), the war god confronts Venus, who attempts to dissuade him from acting unfavourably toward Thebes by reminding him that the citizens of the city are descended from an earlier union between the two divinities that bore Harmonia, wife of Cadmus (263-91). Mars does not allow her to finish her impassioned plea, but leaps down from his chariot to embrace and comfort her (291ff.). The war-god invokes her affectionately, acknowledges her power and the hold she has over him, and maintains vigorously that he has not forgotten their union nor her loyalty to him (295-303). He tells Venus, however, that he must fulfil his duty in accordance with the admonition of the Fates and the decree of highest Jupiter (304ff.). In an undisguised gibe at her husband, he asserts parenthetically that Vulcan would be unequal to the task assigned to him by Jupiter (305f.).

Mars contends that the power of Jupiter is so great that he dare not refuse to execute his commands; in any event, he declares, the course of fate cannot be altered (306-12), an argument of convenience that resembles the one Jupiter employs earlier (241-43). The war-god understands that any attempt to oppose the decree of Jupiter would ultimately prove futile (cf. 304f.). However, he knows that he has a limited degree of freedom to exercise his power, provided that his actions are in accordance with the will of Jupiter. Therefore Mars is able to promise Venus that he will assist the Theban forces on the battlefield in the forthcoming war with Argos (312-15); he believes that he can do this because his action does not contravene the wishes of the Fates (316; cf. 304f.), whereas the narrative reveals that Jupiter is in fact the supreme arbiter of human destiny.

JUPITER (7.195-221)

The aforementioned scene is recalled later when Bacchus entreats Jupiter to spare Thebes and tries to convince him of the injustice of his scheme to eradicate the royal house (7.155-92). Jupiter commences his reply by rejecting the accusation of Bacchus that he has chosen Argos as a foe for Thebes because of Juno's hatred (195-97); rather, he suggests, the immutable decrees of the Fates and the evil deeds of ancestors have precipitated war (197f.):

> inmoto deducimur orbe
> Fatorum; ueteres seraeque in proelia causae.

This is one of two occasions in the poem in which Jupiter portrays himself as being subordinate to the Fates; the other occasion is in his command to Mars and the other Olympians (3.241-43). While an early passage in the narrative (1.213) and later references by various speakers to Jupiter establish his universal supremacy (e.g., 3.471, 488), the comments of other figures suggest that he is the co-executor or superintender of fate (e.g., 304f., 316) but never, as he claims, the subordinate of the Fates.

Jupiter adopts a sympathetic and merciful stance toward mankind, maintaining that he is sparing of human blood and has seldom used the thunderbolt to assert his supremacy over the earth (7.199-202). He professes that he is saddened by the loss of so many lives and is annoyed by the need to give so many bodies fresh life (205f.). Furthermore, he suggests that he is reluctant to punish Thebes and Argos for their crimes and says that he will maintain his composure in the face of false accusations by Thebes and Bacchus (208-10); finally, he denies that he bears any resentment toward the sons of Oedipus (215f.). However, the episodes he cites of his retributive rôle in the universe—the annihilation of the Lapithae (203f.), the destruction of ancient Calydon (204f.), the future eradication of the royal house of Thebes (207f.)—tend to undermine considerably the credibility of his claims.

The argument of Jupiter that the Thebans are eager to blame the gods for their destiny (209) recalls the sentiment he expresses in the opening speech of the *Odyssey* (1.32-34). In the *Thebaid* Jupiter asserts that the sacrifice of the sons of Oedipus are demanded by the powers of divine and natural law in retribution for the crimes of his Dorian ancestors (7.216-18; cf. 208f.):

> rogat hoc tellusque polusque
> et pietas et laesa fides naturaque et ipsi
> Eumenidum mores.

Jupiter suggests that Bacchus has little basis for arguing his case for Thebes on moral grounds, since Pentheus endured a harsh fate for committing a crime less serious than those perpetrated by Oedipus, yet Bacchus did not mourn or protest his death (211-14). In fact Bacchus' incitation of the Theban women to their gruesome dismemberment of Pentheus is yet another instance of supernatural cruelty where the punishment appears to exceed by far the magnitude of the offence committed.

Jupiter does offer some measure of consolation and assurance to Bacchus by telling him that he has decided Thebes will survive for the time being, although Argos will not go unavenged (219-21):

> non hoc statui sub tempore rebus
> occasum Aoniis, ueniet suspectior aetas
> ultoresque alii.

These lines demonstrate the supremacy of Jupiter over the affairs of men, point toward the supernaturally engineered destruction of the city, and belie his earlier claims that he has no control over the fate of Thebes. Despite his claims to the contrary, Jupiter is no god of mercy. In view of the unrelenting nature of Jupiter and the harsh inexorability of his plan, it is futile for Bacchus to object to the severe fate that the divine ruler has imposed upon Thebes. Jupiter naturally rejects the view that holds the gods responsible for the fate of Thebes and predictably attributes the crimes of the Thebans to the genetic defects of their race (cf. 1.227ff.).

CHAPTER 5

THE REVELATION OF CHARACTER IN THE SPEECHES

Characterisation and the Speeches

Unquestionably one of the most important functions of the speeches in Statian epic is their revelation of character, perhaps superseded only by their crucial rôle in helping to unfold the plot. In chapter 2 it is argued briefly that many of the speeches help to define the personalities and attitudes of the characters generally and to furnish psychological and emotional characterisations of the speakers at specific points of the text. In the *Thebaid* the speeches almost always suit the personalities of the human characters as described in the narrative and revealed in their actions (cf. Hor. *Ars P.* 114-24, Quint. *Inst.* 3.8.13), except when supernatural intervention drives these figures to speak and act out of character. Statius draws attention through speech to certain characteristics and plays down or ignores others in order to reveal character in a light consistent with the aims of his work; the use of direct speech enables him to do this without appearing to intrude in the reader's perception of character. In some dramatic situations he breaks this illusion of authorial objectivity by intervening directly through the use of descriptive narrative, epithets and editorial comment.

Naturally the way the various characters speak and think is central to understanding the main issues of the *Thebaid*, especially the idea of supernatural control over human action. In examining the personalities of various human figures in the epic it is important especially not to lose sight of those instances where the higher powers provoke or inspire many of the human figures to behave in a manner inconsistent with their usual or unaffected (i.e., uninfluenced) character. Equally it is worthwhile to recall the obvious point prior to undertaking any analysis of character in the epic that the magniloquent versified speech of the leading and minor figures is quite unlike the natural speech of ordinary persons, but this elevated style of speech well reflects the high social position of the various speakers.

Speeches naturally reflect not only the differing circumstances and possibilities but also the broad range of feelings of the various characters in specific dramatic situations. The integration of speeches into the narrative is particularly effective in those dramatic situations where feelings run high, since in a dramatic sense the speeches are far more effective than mere narrative in conveying the depth and wide range of divine and human emotions. The expression of emotions in the speeches is one of the means that the poet uses to manipulate the audience's perception of his characters. If the poet infuses emotion carefully into the speeches at the appropriate points, then the audience may well respond in a manner that will serve the ends of his creative work, even if this is only in its identification with or rejection of certain sentiments of the speaker. This is not as improbable as it may at first appear, given that the ancient rhetoricians themselves believed that the vicarious arousal of an audience's emotions was realisable through the careful incorporation of emotionally charged passages into the speeches (e.g., Cic. *De Or.* 2.185ff.). Naturally in Statius some emotions are intrinsic to particular speakers who have a tendency to deliver certain types of speeches. A warrior such as Tydeus makes a number of battle speeches, namely taunts, challenges and threats, and these are quite different from the types of speeches made by women and other figures in the epic.

A number of critics argue that the characterisations of Statius tend to be stylised and stereotyped.[1] Recently Vessey goes so far as to argue that the function of the characters is essentially symbolic in that each serves to point up a particular side of human nature.[2] On the surface this may appear

---

[1] The judgement of Butler (1909: 218f.) is particularly harsh. He refers to the various characters in the *Thebaid* as 'featureless', 'colourless', 'uninteresting', or 'too rhetorical', and asserts that Statius 'fails in his portrayal of life and character'. Dimsdale (1915: 461) holds that the 'characters are but shadowy. Tydeus *alone* is drawn in clear and vigorous lines' (my emphasis). Watkiss (1966: 85, 183) asserts that Statius stresses certain aspects of the characters' personalities to the extent that they become types of persons rather than dynamic characters. Vessey (1971: 376, 1973: 65-66, 1982: 577f.) maintains that Statius employs a figural technique and proceeds to criticise Statius' presentation of character for its typification and lack of individualisation.

[2] Vessey (1973: 65). This is the result of Vessey's overemphasis on the effect of Stoic philosophy upon Statius' presentation of character. According to Vessey (1971: 376; 1973: 58f., 65f.), Statius paints the characters in the *Thebaid* mainly in Stoic terms, which means there can be little or no variation in the portrayal of their personalities. Vessey (1971: 376; 1973: 58f.) attributes an alleged lack of variety in Statian characterisation to his Stoic background. For a general criticism of the views of Vessey on characterisation in the *Thebaid*, see Ahl (1974: 143f.). Vessey (1971: 375) also errs in suggesting that the 'narrative [of the *Thebaid*] shows a trend toward psychological motivation; events spring

to be the case, since in the characterising process the poet concentrates on specific traits in individuals that are of interest to him and relevant to his central themes. However, this consistency in the conduct and disposition of the different characters does not automatically preclude individuality or complexity in characterisation; in fact successful characterisation involves the proficient blending of conventional and particular elements. In most cases in the *Thebaid* the expression of character in the speeches aids in establishing the broad and salient characteristics of the speakers as well helping to define their individual characteristics.

Most of the major and some of the minor human characters in the *Thebaid* are round or tridimensional, meaning they are presented in some depth. Some characters respond in a variety of ways to the different situations that confront them; unsurprisingly, the speeches of these characters reveal a complex set of attitudes. The usually peaceloving Adrastus is driven to an insatiable lust for slaughter and bloodshed. The complex character of Polynices ranges from extreme cruelty and vindictiveness to an affectionate concern for his wife Argia. He is perhaps the most memorable figure in the epic because of his various individualistic and typical characteristics; he has a great many unique personal qualities but is also portrayed as a typically corrupt aspirant to the throne. It is this blending of the particular and universal that makes Polynices such a successful character from a dramatic standpoint. To varying degrees the other human figures discussed in this chapter, with the notable exception of Hippomedon and perhaps Tiresias, are a blend of particular and typical characteristics; unlike duodimensional characters, these round or tridimensional characters lack pure consistency in their attitudes as revealed in their speeches and actions. Statius emphasises the dominant personality traits of these characters, but he is also careful to draw attention to other aspects of their personalities.

Notwithstanding the generally complex treatment of human characterisation in the poem, some of the divine and human figures show the same consistency of character. Jupiter and the other gods generally require duodimensional treatment, since they are portrayed almost exclusively in

---

from the inner nature of [Statius'] characters, not from external causes'. This could not be further from the case: most of the events in the poem are instigated by supernatural forces who further their designs by acting directly upon various human characters; see ch. 1 of my *The Mythic Voice of Statius* (forthcoming).

monochromatic terms;[3] with the exception of Pietas and a few others, the supernatural powers tend toward malevolence and injustice in their treatment of mankind except when they look after the interests of particular favourites. Not all the human characters in the epic are deserving of tridimensional treatment. Although Hippomedon is an extraordinary figure, he is essentially a flat or stock character, since his personality shows virtually no depth or variation and is based upon only a few dominant characteristics. Capaneus comes close to being a flat character for the same reasons in spite of his supernaturally inspired challenge of Jupiter, an act that can be viewed as an extension of his previous demonstrations of antipathy toward the gods.

Some of the uninformed critical comments concerning the alleged stereotypy and simplicity of Statian characterisation stem from a failure to appreciate the complexity and evolution of character in the *Thebaid*. A flat character such as Hippomedon is almost certainly static and is unlikely to change, since there are only a very small number of characteristics that can be altered effectively and any personality change that does occur must be credible. But a round character such as Polynices or Adrastus may be either static or dynamic; such a figure may develop little if any during the course of events or he may undergo a radical transformation of character. Sometimes a character such as Eteocles or Oedipus may undergo a dramatic change in personality, but this can easily be overlooked if the transformation occurs quite early or late in proceedings.

Many of the leading human figures in the *Thebaid* are dynamic because their inner characters change, even if this is only because the higher powers act upon them or release them from their control.[4] Amphiaraus is depicted as a pious and peaceloving priest until the gods set upon him and fill him with a desire for war and an insatiable bloodlust. Oedipus is portrayed as bitter and vindictive when he is under the control of the Furies, but is an entirely different person when these powers leave him alone. This transition

---

[3] The term 'monochromatic' is used by Vessey (1973: 65). The difference between Vessey's view and mine is that he believes most of the major characters are presented consistently, whereas this is clearly not the case, as shown in the discussion in this chapter. Vessey (1982: 577f.) appears to moderate his views somewhat on Statian characterisation when he concedes there is a small measure of ambiguity in some of the presentations of character in the *Thebaid*, namely those of Tydeus and Polynices, and maintains that the portrayal of women by the poet is more skilful than his depiction of men.

[4] Of course, as Schetter (1960: 123) notes, none of the figures in the *Thebaid* undergoes the type of sustained development of character that Aeneas experiences in Vergil.

in the personalities of the various characters occurs at many different points in the progression of the narrative. Both Oedipus and Amphiaraus undergo a radical transformation of character just prior to their final appearances, but a character such as Eteocles is barely allowed to show even a hint of his real nature before he is set upon by supernatural forces. Nevertheless even Eteocles is a dynamic character because his personality is transmuted by the actions of these external forces upon him.

Speech, including thought represented as speech, is the most direct and probably therefore the best key to understanding the personalities and motivation of the major characters, especially given the large percentage (35.4) of the text devoted to *oratio recta*. But it should be stressed that direct speech is only one of the techniques that Statius employs in the portrayal of character in the *Thebaid*. His presentation of character consists of the blending of at least three additional elements: the narrative exposition of character; the physical description of persons, including their reaction to events and speeches; and the narration of physical actions. In many instances the poet draws attention to the character of a speaker or addressee by describing his manner and physical characteristics just before (e.g., 1.390-400, 3.598-607), during (e.g., 6.173, 12.92f.), or after a speech (e.g., 11.249-56, 632f.). A thorough examination of the personalities of the various figures in the *Thebaid* would easily form the basis for a complete study in itself.[5] In this chapter the discussion of characterisation is devoted mainly to those aspects of personality that are revealed in the speeches. In the discussion of various characters below greatest attention is given to those individuals who deliver the most speeches; the obvious advantage of this approach generally is that it is possible to explore more fully the relationship between the speeches and the narrative description of character; more specifically, it is easier to determine if the presentation of character in the speeches is consistent or inconsistent with the narrative presentation of character.

---

[5] For instance, see the critical works of ten Kate (1955) and Kabsch (1968), which treat the major characters in the epic, or the monographs of Götting (1969), Klinnert (1970) and Schubert (1984), which are devoted mainly to analyses of the rôles played by one or two characters.

Speakers and Addressees

There are eighty-one characters who deliver speeches in the *Thebaid*; these supernatural and divine figures make 265 speeches totalling 3,448 1/12 lines;[6] the average length of each speech is thirteen lines. Naturally the number of speeches each character makes affords an indication of their relative prominence in the epic. There are twelve characters who each deliver at least seven speeches; the speeches of these figures total 141, just over fifty-three per cent of the speeches in the epic. It has often been argued that the *Thebaid* lacks a central character, which is true, but Tydeus and Adrastus together figure in one out of every 5.8 speeches made. They speak more frequently and more lines than any of the other central characters. Adrastus makes only two fewer speeches than Tydeus and speaks more lines than any other figure except Hypsipyle, who speaks almost five hundred lines in only five speeches. Other important speakers are Jupiter, the rest of the Seven (Eteocles, Amphiaraus, Hippomedon, Parthenopaeus, Capaneus), Polynices, Creon, Argia, Antigone and Tiresias; less prominent speakers are Oedipus, Theseus and Jocasta.

A further measure of the significance of the rôles of the various characters in the epic is the extent to which they figure in speech situations as addressees rather than merely as speakers. Eteocles and Polynices are addressed more times (twenty) than any other characters. Tydeus (fourteen), Adrastus (thirteen), Jupiter (twelve) and Antigone (nine) are addressed less often. The Argive warriors are addressed a surprising seventeen times and the Theban warriors on fifteen different occasions, although they speak together only three speeches. Tydeus and Adrastus speak or are addressed thirty-eight and thirty-five times, respectively, slightly more than Polynices (thirty-three) and Eteocles (thirty) and significantly more than the Argive warriors (twenty), Jupiter, Argia (nineteen) and Antigone (eighteen).[7]

---

[6] For a complete list of the characters and their speeches, see stat. app. 3, tables 8 and 9.

[7] See stat. app. 6, table 13 for the statistics on other central characters.

Divine Speakers

Nineteen supernatural figures in the epic make forty-five speeches;[8] these speeches total 611 1/2 lines and average 13.6 lines.[9] Jupiter and Bacchus are the only deities to deliver five or more speeches, but a host of deities make three speeches each.[10] The speeches and actions of the vast majority of supernatural powers reveal their proclivity to cruelty and injustice.

Jupiter

The omnipotent deity makes more speeches than any other divinity, yet he delivers only seven of the forty-five divine speeches in the epic;[11] his speeches total 142 1/4 lines and average over twenty lines. Some critics refer to Jupiter as a kind, compassionate and fair-minded supernatural power;[12] however, his actions and speeches portray him as anything but a benevolent, merciful and just god. The speeches of this deity are among the most important in the *Thebaid*. He reveals himself in his speeches as an omnipotent, misanthropic, dissimulating, cruel and uncompassionate deity. His speeches (1.214-47, 1.285-302, 3.229-52, 7.6-33) play a critical rôle in three of the most important scenes in the epic and emphasise his determination to bring about the destruction of Thebes and Argos.

In the first scene on Olympus (1.197-311) he maintains that the inherent criminality of man is deserving of divine retribution, but the list of alleged human crimes he catalogues (227-47)—especially those of Cadmus, Agave and Tantalus—seriously undercut his argument that man deserves to be punished for his wickedness, since the offences were either committed

---

[8] Forty-six speeches including the deliberation of Amphiaraus' spirit recounted by Thiodamas to the Achaean leaders (10.206-11).

[9] These totals exclude the 4 1/2-line inserted speech of Amphiaraus' spirit (10.206-11).

[10] See stat. app. 3, table 8 for a complete list of speeches made by supernatural figures (including spirits other than Amphiaraus' spirit).

[11] Lipscomb (1909: 19) maintains that Jupiter delivers eight speeches but does not list them.

[12] Gossage (1969: 80f.; 1972: 195, 200), Vessey (1973: 82-91, 165-67); cf. Kabsch (1968: 114-28, 130).

unknowingly, inspired largely by the gods, or have already been avenged; furthermore, there appears to be little reason why innocent descendants should be made to suffer for the transgressions of previous generations. In an attempt to conceal his real motives, Jupiter contrives an argument based on the necessity of punishing man for his crimes, but he sorely fails to convince. His pathetic attempt to defend his unwarranted punishment of the innocent Argive citizenry (243-47, esp. 285-87) exposes his insincerity and highlights his inherent cruelty.

Jupiter reveals himself as a vindictive and merciless deity especially in his commands. The deity orders Mercury to accompany Laius to the upper world where the shade is to inspire Eteocles to retain the throne (1.292-302) in violation of the brothers' pact of alternate rule. He also commands Mars to inflame the Argives to war (3.229-35), acknowledges his causative rôle in the perpetration of the treacherous ambush of Tydeus (235-36), and threatens to destroy the two cities on his own if any of the gods interfere in his scheme (244-52). Jupiter refers to the Theban ambush of Tydeus as the crime of Eteocles even though he admits responsibility for instigating the incident (235-37). His threat is evidence not only of his universal supremacy but also of his general hostility and cruelty toward mankind, since he could easily single out individuals for punishment if he so wished (e.g., 10.907-39).

Later Jupiter feels compelled to command Mercury to descend to earth once again and bid Mars to incite the Argives to violence against Thebes (7.6-33). He appears to acknowledge unwittingly that his plan to punish Thebes and Argos for past crimes will result in the deaths of many present-day inhabitants who are entirely innocent of any wrong-doing (22-25, esp. 23). Despite his seemingly invincible powers, Jupiter shows no interest in preventing this needless waste of human life. But his threat to transmute the war-making powers of Mars into a force of peace and beneficence (27-33) demonstrates that he is more than willing to dispossess the war-god of his powers if his order is ignored; this threat of Jupiter directed against one of the most powerful deities demonstrates not only that he has the power to punish just those human figures who might be guilty of wrong-doing but also that he has no genuine interest in restricting his punishment of mankind to this group.

The deceitful and uncompassionate nature of Jupiter is further emphasised in his dissembling reply (7.195-221) to the argument of Bacchus that his plan to eradicate the Theban royal house is unjust (155-92). Jupiter maintains that he has no control over the course of destiny (197f.), is able to control his rage easily (199), is sparing of human blood (199f.), rarely makes use of the thunderbolt (200-02), is saddened by the loss of human lives and annoyed by the need to reanimate so many bodies (205f.), is reluctant to punish Thebes and Argos (208-10), and bears no resentment toward the sons of Oedipus (215f.). But the incidents he cites of his retributive rôle (203-08) and his actions elsewhere in the epic demonstrate the fallacy of his claim to the personal qualities of benevolence and moderation.

Jupiter orders a cloud to be spread over the earth just prior to the duel between Eteocles and Polynices so that the Olympian deities will not be able to watch the deathly struggle between the brothers (11.122-33). Although he feigns horror at the prospect of such an impious crime being committed and that the gods must not be contaminated by the sight of the dual fratricide, he does nothing whatsoever to prevent the duel that his brother and the Furies instigate (8.69f., 12.136ff.). Yet there is no question that he possesses the power to prevent the fratricide from occurring. When Capaneus mocks the fulminous deeds of Jupiter (902-06), the monologue of the deity shows him responding calmly to Capaneus' threat, supremely confident in the fulminous power wields.

Other Divinities

Other prominent deities include Bacchus, Mars, Tisiphone, Apollo, Venus and Diana. As discussed in chapters 3 and 4, an analysis of the speeches and actions of these deities reveals that their attitude toward mankind is generally one of malevolence and hostility, sometimes merely indifference, although on a few occasions they show concern for a favourite city or human figure.

Human Speakers

Sixty-two of the characters who deliver speeches in the epic are human, either individuals or groups; the speeches of these figures total 219 and constitute over four-fifths of those delivered in the epic.[13] Eleven of the twelve most prominent speakers in the epic are human and they are responsible for making over one-half of the speeches. These characters are

---

[13] For a complete list of speeches by human figures, see stat. app. 3, table 9.

(in order of the number of speeches given, including inserted discourses): Tydeus (twenty-four), Adrastus (twenty-two), Capaneus (fourteen), Polynices (thirteen), Argia (twelve), Eteocles (ten), Antigone (nine), Amphiaraus (eight),[14] Creon, Tiresias and Hippomedon (seven). Other speakers who assume important rôles in various scenes of the *Thebaid* are Oedipus, Theseus, Parthenopaeus, Jocasta and Hypsipyle; each of these characters makes at least four speeches.

Monarchs

This grouping of human figures, including aspirants to the throne and former regents (but not Laius' spirit), makes sixty-three speeches totalling 768 11/12 lines; the average length of each speech is 12.2 lines. Adrastus is portrayed generally in a favourable light, but the picture that emerges of other monarchal characters from an analysis of their speeches and actions is predominantly negative; notwithstanding, the poet establishes clearly that the irrational and violent behaviour of these figures is inspired largely by malevolent supernatural powers who are determined to eradicate the royal houses of Thebes and Argos.

Adrastus

Adrastus is one of the most prominent figures in the *Thebaid*. The Argive monarch delivers more speeches (twenty-two) than any other figure except Tydeus and speaks more lines (296 1/3) than anyone except Hypsipyle; the average length of his speeches is 13.5 lines. He is also addressed thirteen times. Through his speeches he is portrayed mostly as a benevolent, just, temperate, peaceloving and pious regent; however, he is not, as some critics maintain, a Stoic sage.[15]

Adrastus is not eager for war and shows his determination to forestall or delay the commencement of hostilities between his city and Thebes. This is evident especially in his speech to Polynices after Tydeus returns from his unsuccessful mission to Thebes (3.388-93, esp. 393). His obvious lack of enthusiasm for martial violence places him directly in opposition to the wishes of the gods and his own people for war (cf. 407-49). After the

---

[14] Excluding his spirit's deliberative speech reported by Thiodamas (10.206-11).

[15] So Aricò (1972: 131), Vessey (1973: 98); *contra* Ahl (1974: 143; 1986: 2810).

failure of Tydeus' mission the monarch decides that Amphiaraus should conduct an augury in order to reveal the future (449-52), whereupon the priest prophesies a disastrous result to the war and attempts to dissuade the populace from undertaking it without success (620-77).

The supreme instance of his peacemaking rôle occurs during the single combat between Polynices and Eteocles. After the duel commences Adrastus intervenes and urges the brothers to stop their bloody fight (11.429-35); in a supreme act of selflessness he even offers his throne to Polynices if the prince will refrain from further fighting (11.433-35), but his attempt to prevent the fratricide fails and he flees from the scene (435-46). The various peacemaking efforts of Adrastus can be cited as evidence of his weakness and irresolution as a monarch,[16] but even a cursory examination of the matter immediately exposes the superficiality of such an assertion. Adrastus is unable to prevent war or the fratricide, but these events are instigated directly by the gods, particularly Jupiter, Mars and the Furies. The monarch can hardly be accused fairly of being weak and vacillating when his attempts to prevent violence from occurring are hindered by the gods. The occasions on which he promotes the cause of peace without success exemplifies the inability of humankind to exert any meaningful control over its own destiny in the face of overwhelming supernatural opposition.

When the higher powers do not interfere or inflame the situation, Adrastus reveals himself to be totally in control of his subjects and his faculties. On a number of occasions Adrastus plays the rôle of peacemaker successfully. One-third of his speeches are delivered in dramatic situations where he intervenes to prevent an outbreak of violence and bloodshed. He intervenes to calm Tydeus and Polynices when they are brawling at the royal portals (1.438-46); persuades the exiled princes to cease quarrelling and to become friends (1.468-73); restores order along with Amphiaraus to a potentially explosive situation when Lycurgus threatens to slay Hypsipyle (5.669-71); calms his troops when they attack the Nemean palace because of their mistaken belief that Lycurgus is taking Hypsipyle to her death (5.701-03); and exhorts his warriors to restrain the raging Capaneus from overwhelming Alcidimas during the funeral games (6.809-12).

Adrastus reveals himself as a pious and god-fearing monarch in his speeches, particularly his prayers. This is evident especially in the praises he sings to Apollo and his humble plea for divine favour (1.682-720, esp.

---

[16] Cf. Vessey (1973: 315).

696-720) immediately after recounting the Coroebus tale (557-672). Elsewhere he is deeply emotional and respectful in his invocation of Nox (1.498-510), is reverential and ingratiating toward Hypsipyle, whom he mistakes for a goddess (4.753-71), and displays a pious attitude in his prayer to the newly deified Archemorus (7.93-103). But the prayers of the monarch are notable for their ignorance and are full of dramatic irony. In his prayer to Nox (1.498-510) he is unaware of the true significance of Tydeus and Polynices' arrival in Argos; his plea to Apollo for divine favour (1.696-720) will go unheeded and his army will not return triumphantly to Argos (cf. 4.768f.); and his appeal for success in the war against Thebes similarly will go unfulfilled (7.96-103).

The final picture that emerges of Adrastus is not *entirely* favourable.[17] Not only does the monarch seem unaware of the pervasive hostility of the supernatural powers toward mankind, but also he is unable to withstand completely the violent influences of the gods. He ignores the omens that portend disaster for Argos by warring against Thebes (cf. 3.456-58, 499-551, 619-47), although perhaps the only other choice available to him was to stay behind in Argos while his army marched on Thebes. There are two noteworthy situations where Adrastus shows a remarkable lack of self-restraint. When Thiodamas assures the Argive troops of success in the nocturnal attack upon the Theban camp (10.188-218), the monarch is caught up in the enthusiasm that sweeps over the men. He delivers two combat exhortations inciting his warriors to violence against the Thebans (10.236-44, 266-68) even while he acknowledges the fraudulent and treacherous nature of the mission (241f.); after the massacre his appetite for bloodshed appears unsatiated as he urges his troops onward toward the walls of Thebes (487). Adrastus becomes possessed totally by *furor* and demonstrates that even he is not entirely immune to the base madness for slaughter that infects the rest of his troops in the war. Although the fury of Adrastus cannot be attributed directly to Juno since she does not incite him to madness, it must be pointed out that she inflames the priest Thiodamas so successfully that the effect on the rest of the Argives, including Adrastus, is equally dramatic (10.219-21).

---

[17] *Contra* Watkiss (1966: 66), who maintains that Statius takes extreme care in his presentation of Adrastus as a peaceloving and wise monarch to prevent corruption of this portrayal.

Polynices

Polynices delivers thirteen speeches in the epic totalling 119 1/6 lines and is addressed twenty times. Almost one-half of the speeches the prince makes are responsions; he also makes two deliberations and two taunts. The character of Polynices is complex and requires three-dimensional treatment. His most important speeches are his lament over Tydeus (9.49-72, 75f.) and his deliberations of the Argives (3.367-81) and Adrastus (11.155-92). Although the other speeches of the prince are generally brief, every line is carefully contrived to reveal the various aspects of his character.[18]

The prince is capable of dishonesty and deceit, as revealed in the artfully deceptive speech that he delivers to the Argives after the return of Tydeus from Thebes (3.367-81). When Tydeus exhorts the Argives to war (348-65), Polynices plays upon the alarm of the councillors and skilfully manipulates the situation to gain maximum support for his cause. The exile feigns anger over his brother's treatment of Tydeus and professes his shame in endangering his comrade's life by permitting him to go to Thebes to present his claim to the throne (368-70). Polynices' offer to return to Thebes to meet his fate and his claim that he never intended to involve Thebes in his fate (372-74, 378) lacks any semblance of honesty or credibility. His arrogance, cunning, obsession for power, and revengeful and envious spirit are apparent in this speech.

The spontaneous exultation of Polynices at the moment of his apparent triumph over his brother (11.548-51, 557-60) is a further demonstration of his cruelty and vindictiveness; even the apparent fulfilment of his ambition to gain the Theban throne does not assuage his spiteful anger against Eteocles. The final taunt of the exile over Eteocles at the moment of their deaths (568-72) is uncompromising and rancorous and reveals that Polynices is as shameless and implacable as his brother.[19]

---

[18] Watkiss (1966: 62, 64) strangely refers to Polynices as a 'colourless' character; however, his personality does not lack variety or interest, as his speeches and actions show.

[19] *Contra* Legras (1905: 212), ten Kate (1955: 53ff.) and Schetter (1960: 117), who consider Polynices to be superior to Eteocles in temperament. Gossage (1972: 205) observes that Polynices is a more varied character than Eteocles and suggests that the prince arouses greater sympathy than the monarch for his cause. Both of these are valid points, but Statius is intent upon stressing that Polynices possesses the same capacity for cruel leadership as his brother.

Polynices is shown to be totally preoccupied with the acquisition of monarchal power. As soon as he goes into voluntary exile his arrogance prompts him to entertain thoughts of replacing his brother on the Theban throne (1.312-23). His desire for power remains undiminished despite the considerable wealth and standing in the royal hierarchy of Argos that his marriage to Argia brings him (2.307-15). The care he takes in distinguishing between his supporters and his opponents in preparation for the day he ascends the throne reveals that he is a potential tyrant in the mould of his brother (316-19; cf. 448). Similarly the unwillingness of Polynices to share his place of refuge with Tydeus in front of the royal palace after their arrival in Thebes (401ff.) suggests that he would be no more willing than his brother to relinquish the reigns of power.

In a number of instances Polynices is prevented from acting in accordance with his real wishes. Much emphasis in the text is placed upon the dominant rôle of the higher powers in inciting Polynices to hatred, jealousy and suspicion of his brother and in stimulating his lust for power (1.123ff., 7.467f.), even though this appears in no way to lessen his culpability for perpetrating deeds that are inspired by supernatural forces. Nevertheless it is apparent that Polynices is driven to seize power violently from his brother mainly through the instigation of Jupiter and the Furies; similarly the prince only shows a desire to slay his brother after the infernal goddesses act upon him (11.57ff., esp. 150-54, 197-203, 208f., 383-89) at the behest of Pluto (8.69-71). He is depicted only as being uncertain whether to commit suicide or take flight (11.138f.), but the Furies intervene on three occasions to incite him to violence against his brother. Megaera intervenes and infuses him with the urge to slay Eteocles and to seek death in his kinsman's blood (150-54). When Adrastus begins to calm his rage, Megaera physically hurls him onto his horse to search for his brother (196-204). Antigone again softens Polynices (382-87), but when Tisiphone pushes Eteocles through the Theban gates to confront him, Megaera incites the exile against his brother and even guides the reins of his horse toward his foe (403-05). Polynices is rendered powerless by these infernal powers and is unable to exert any meaningful control over his actions.

In addition to these supernatural factors that appear to lessen the responsibility of Polynices for his violent actions, there is another side to the prince that is all too often ignored or played down by the critics. His hesitation to reveal his background to Adrastus suggests that he is anything but proud of his ancestry (1.448-50, 465; cf. 676-81). The joy of Polynices is genuine when he expresses his gratitude to Adrastus for offering his daughters in marriage to him and Tydeus (2.189-97); he shows a tender and anxious concern for his wife Argia (2.356-62, 4.89-92); and his affection for and devotion to his sister Antigone is said to be greater than his desire for power or love of his country (cf. 12.394-97). When Polynices discovers that Tydeus is dead, he is paralysed with grief (9.39-45). He is genuinely remorseful over involving Tydeus in his plan to gain power and holds himself responsible for his friend's death (60) as well as the gods (71f.). The attempt of Polynices to take his own life (76f.) reflects his grief over the loss of his comrade and his difficulty in bearing the weight of his own guilt and self-recrimination. It is unfortunate for Polynices that he comes to appreciate the nobility and unselfishness of Tydeus only when his faithful comrade is dead. In a later speech to Adrastus (11.155-92) he also shows genuine regret for the devastation and suffering he has brought to Argos. These speeches betray the violent emotions and guilt of the prince, but his awareness of the rôle of the gods in conspiring to implicate him in the doom of Argos is given considerable thematic emphasis (9.71f., 11.188f.).

Eteocles

Eteocles makes ten speeches totalling 126 1/6 lines and is addressed the same number of times as Polynices (twenty). His speeches and actions reveal him as a cruel, perfidious and hypocritical tyrant; although prone to fear (e.g., 4.406-09), he is portrayed as a capable military leader (cf. 7.390-92, 688). The first speech of the Theban monarch (2.393-409), which is directed at Tydeus who warns the monarch to abdicate in favour of Polynices, draws attention to his negative qualities. Eteocles accuses Tydeus of having little regard for justice and fairness (420-23), an assertion that is certainly hypocritical since the monarch himself shows no concern for justice and equity. He declares that he has a right to keep the throne because the claim of Polynices is based on threats of violence rather than trust or peace (424-29); this claim is extremely ironic since he violates the agreement of alternate rule with his brother that is been based upon mutual trust and orders the treacherous ambush of Tydeus on his return to Thebes (cf. 482ff.). Eteocles reveals a callous and mocking attitude toward Polynices and Argia (430-42) when he maintains that his brother should be content to rule over wealthy Argos (430-33) and that his wife, accustomed to the luxury of Argos, would be unable to endure the simple life of Thebes (438-40). The false concern of Eteocles for his subjects and his unfounded claim to their love and gratitude are further evidence of his dissembling and deceitful nature.

The most revealing speech of Eteocles from a psychological standpoint is his interior monologue in which he betrays his apprehension and guilt about his plot to assassinate Tydeus and his fear that the mission might fail (3.6f., 9-18). Eteocles does not express any of the concern for the welfare of his men that a monarch reasonably might be expected to show; rather, he displays only a selfish anxiety for the mission's apparent lack of success and the potential consequences of its failure. The profound solicitude and egotism evident in his private thoughts are fundamental attributes of his character. The situation that confronts Eteocles is personally unacceptable and invokes a curious blend of mental anguish, frustration, hopelessness, guilt, shame and determination in the tyrant.

Eteocles' combat exhortations to his warriors are a reflexion of his predisposition toward hypocrisy, deception and pretence. This is well illustrated when he encourages his troops to recover the corpse of Tydeus by appealing to their moral sense of justice over the anthropophagy of this hero (9.12-24). In an earlier exhortation (7.375-90) he feigns humility (375f.) and maintains that his subjects and army support him (377f.), a claim that lacks any semblance of credibility. Every element in this exhortation is calculated to justify and advance his position as monarch, but this attempt to distort and misrepresent the situation only serves to reveal the true character of this tyrant.

Other speeches are consistent with the unfavourable picture that emerges of Eteocles. He taunts Hippomedon and accuses him of shamelessness in protecting the corpse of Tydeus (9.96-103), yet shows no hint of shame over his own crimes. He shows supreme confidence in his own fighting capabilities in speeches to Creon (11.308) and Eteocles (391f.). In the former speech he accuses his uncle of concealing his ambition to gain the throne, which is hypocritical given the nature of his own desire to maintain his position. His prayers to Jupiter (11.210-25, 248f.) are characterised by a tragic ignorance of the plot of Jupiter to destroy him, as shown in his mistaken belief that the chief god sides with Thebes and his cause (esp. 217-21; cf. 248f.)

The personality of Eteocles appears to be determined mainly by the gods who influence and govern his behaviour. It is significant that he is depicted as a helpless victim of supernatural forces without any control over his own destiny (cf. 92f.). Eteocles clearly has no chance to exercise his own free will in the matter of his abdication since Jupiter determines for him that he will not relinquish the throne to his brother (1.292-302; cf. 2.93-127). Later his decision to set an ambush for Tydeus is inspired by Jupiter, who claims responsibility for the crime (3.234-38). Before Eteocles is set upon by these powers there is no specific indication that he would refuse to abide by his agreement of alternate rule with Polynices, a pact that is effected through the intervention of Tisiphone (1.123ff.). Indeed the contentment of Eteocles with his lot and unconcern about the future (2.92f.) stand in marked contrast to his horror-stricken state and anxious resolve to retain the throne after he is set upon by the spirit of Laius (89-133, esp. 123f.). Later Tisiphone incites Eteocles against his brother and father, thereby precipitating the outbreak of war between the Thebans and Argives (7.467f.).

Other incidents attest to the dominant rôle of the gods in motivating or interfering with the actions of Eteocles, especially in relation to the mutual fratricide that is instigated by Pluto (cf. 8.69-71) and carried out through the agency of the Furies (cf. 8.69-71, 11.57ff.). Tisiphone diverts the sacrificial prayer of Eteocles to Jupiter (11.205-09), shoves the Theban monarch through the gates of Thebes to meet Polynices in single combat (387-92; cf. 268), and drives him onto the plain toward his brother to meet his divinely ordained end. Without the disastrous intervention of Jupiter, Pluto and Tisiphone in the affairs of the brothers, there is no real evidence to suggest that Eteocles would not have shared joint or alternate power with Polynices, for much of the motivation for his actions would be missing.

Creon

The seven speeches of Creon are all spoken in the last triad of the poem; the average length of the speeches is 14.7 lines. Creon shows little faith or trust in supernatural powers in his first speech (10.690-718). He is distrustful of Tiresias, whom he believes is conspiring with Eteocles to send Menoeceus to death through a false oracular pronouncement (694-703). Creon would much prefer his son to return to face the dangers of the battlefield rather than to sacrifice himself without real cause (711-18). Later he denounces Eteocles (11.269-96) and suggests that Tiresias should conceive another oracle to bring death to his other son Haemon (288-93), a repetition of his belief that the oracle demanding the death of Menoeceus is devised by

Eteocles as a ruse to rid himself of a potential rival to the throne. His bitter denunciation of Eteocles, whom he believes should accept the challenge of Polynices to meet in single combat (11.262ff.), betrays a hint of his hubris, power lust, violent potentiality and desire to exact revenge for the death of his son.

The predisposition of Creon toward arrogance, cruelty and vengeance is confirmed upon gaining power when he prohibits the burial of the Argive corpses (11.661-64, 12.94-104) and banishes Oedipus from Thebes (11.669-72, 750-54; cf. 755f.). His ban on the burial of Polynices and the Argive dead contrasts with his earlier alleged concern for the Theban corpses lying unburied on the battlefield (276f.). This hypocritical lack of compassion for the dead and moral insensibility is accompanied by a corresponding loss of affection for Menoeceus and illustrates the dramatic deterioration of his character immediately upon his accession to the throne. This change in the character of Creon appears to originate from the fact of his accession, which arouses within him vindictive feelings of great intensity and a corresponding lack of compassion and humanity (654-64, esp. 661), as shown in his desire to avenge the death of his son by denying burial to Polynices and the Argive corpses. Notwithstanding, the behaviour of Creon in outlawing the burial of the dead is shown to be inspired directly by the Furies in response to the command of Pluto (8.72-74; cf. 12.590f., 696f.). Later speeches by Creon, especially his threat of Theseus (12.761-66), demonstrate further the deterioration of his personality.

Oedipus

The legendary monarch of Thebes delivers four speeches totalling just over eighty-seven lines. The most important from a causative standpoint is the curse he utters against his sons (1.56-87); this speech is often cited as evidence of his inhumane and vengeful tendencies. But the preceding narrative shows that the former monarch is under the influence of the Furies when he curses his sons (1.51f.; cf. 11.617-19). The opening lines of the curse reveal that he has been subject to the pervasive influence of the Furies since his birth (60-72). The Furies inspire him to slay his father (1.64-66; cf. 73f., 2.10, 11.491) and sleep with his mother (1.68-70, 11.491f.). He continues to be subject to the influence of these malevolent powers (e.g., 7.466-69, esp. 468f.) until after the death of his sons when he is released from their grip (cf. 11.599ff., esp. 617-21). At this point he becomes a totally changed person and experiences true parental feelings of profound grief and remorse. This transformation of character from an embittered to a remorseful old man is most evident in his lament over the corpses of his sons (11.605-26, 630f.) and his desire to take his own life (627-30).

Theseus

The four brief speeches of Theseus emphasise his extreme righteousness and determination to ensure that the Argives receive their due rites of burial (esp. 12.590-98, 642-48). But the superficially favourable characteristics of this figure and the admirable aspects of his cause are more than offset by his terrifying manner and appearance (665-76, esp. 672-74), blunt speech (e.g., 779-81), eagerness for the slaughter of war (595), incitement of the Athenian troops to violence and bloodshed (642-48), martial arrogance (cf. 736f.), destructive actions on the battlefield (741-51), lack of any compassion for or show of mercy toward his Theban counterpart (cf. 768-82), and comparison and links with the supernatural powers (649-55, 733-36; cf. 606-10).

Warriors

The four most prominent warriors in the epic are Tydeus, Capaneus, Hippomedon and Parthenopaeus, who between them deliver forty-nine speeches. The average length of these speeches is only 6.8 lines; this is because over one-half of them are combat speeches, namely challenges, taunts, threats, exhortations and vaunts, which are themselves brief by nature. The speeches and actions of these figures reveal their heroic qualities of courage, devotion and loyalty to family and friends, tremendous fighting prowess, impetuosity, arrogance, occasional insolence and, with the exception of Parthenopaeus, immense physical strength.

Tydeus

Tydeus figures more often in speech situations than any other character in the *Thebaid*, speaking or being addressed thirty-eight times. This Calydonian hero also makes more speeches than any other figure (twenty-four) and speaks more verses (186 1/3) than any character except Hypsipyle and Adrastus. However, the speeches of Tydeus are shorter in length (ave.

7.8 lines) than those of any character except Capaneus (5.4) and Hippomedon (4.2). The Calydonian is revealed as a powerful figure whose outstanding qualities, particularly his heroic prowess and steadfast devotion to his friends, are offset by his impetuosity and lack of restraint. The *types* of speeches he delivers reflect his hostile and aggressive personality; his speeches comprise threats, taunts, challenges, commands, a cohortation and a vaunt and are significant for their psychological portrayal of the hero. Passionate speeches and a threatening manner emphasise his predisposition toward unrestrained violence. His most important speeches are directed to Adrastus (2.176-88), Eteocles (2.393-409, 452-67), Minerva (715-42), and the Argive troops (3.348-65, 7.539-59).

When Tydeus arrives at the Theban court to persuade Eteocles to abide by his agreement of alternate rule with Polynices and step down from the throne (2.389ff.), he rudely dispenses with the customary ingratiatory references and launches a scathing attack upon the regent (393-409). He is entirely unmindful of Eteocles' position in failing to address him in a respectful manner and the hostile and threatening tone of his speech is its outstanding feature. After Eteocles refuses to accede to Tydeus' demand that he step down from the Theban throne, the Argive hero violently interrupts the regent's speech to threaten him (452-67). Again a threatening tone pervades his heated reply. When Tydeus returns to Argos (3.345ff.), he can scarcely restrain himself as he burst in upon the royal council and without even the customary formalities to urge war upon the city (348-65).

Other speeches strengthen this impression of an impetuous and violent personality. He is the first to reply fully to Adrastus when the regent asks him and Polynices to explain the reason for their quarrel (1.452-65) and he responds before the Theban exile in accepting Adrastus' offer of marriage to his daughters (2.176-88). In his challenges and taunts he pours scorn upon his Theban adversaries (2.547-49, 2.661-68, 8.664-72) and shows utter contempt for Eteocles (8.677-79). Tydeus is merciless toward his foes, as shown in his taunt of Idas in battle (8.472f.) and in his rejection of Menoetes' plea for mercy in the ambush scene (2.655-59). In this latter scene he spares the life of Maeon (697-703) at the behest of Minerva, but his mercilessness and martial prowess is evident in his mass slaying of forty-nine Theban warriors prior to this intervention (529ff.). The hero betrays a streak of supreme arrogance when he taunts the youthful Atys (8.582f.) and refuses to plunder the corpse of his opponent whom he deems scarcely worthy of his attention (588f.). His vainglorious boast during the funeral games for Opheltes (2.906-08) further stresses this hubristic aspect of his character.

In his final speech Tydeus asks his Argive comrades to bring the head of Melanippus to him (8.735-44) and is portrayed as being content merely to gaze upon his foe's head (751-57). The subsequent anthropophagy is often cited as evidence of his unnatural cruelty and dreadful barbarism.[20] However, the text emphasises that Pluto (8.71f.) and Tisiphone (8.757f., 8.760-62, 11.85-88) are responsible for driving Tydeus to feed upon the head of his slayer, an action that offends the sensibilities of Minerva (8.762-66), whose intention it was to confer immortality upon the hero in recognition of his devotion to her and his physical prowess (758f.).

Tydeus is as devoted to his favourite deity and his friends as he is merciless against his enemies. His prayers to Minerva reveal his sincere devotion to the goddess (2.715-42, 8.588-91) and his comminatory speeches to Lycurgus (5.663f., 672-79) and Capaneus (6.816f.), which accompany his defence of Hypsipyle and Alcidimas, respectively, are evidence of his loyalty to his friends and allies. He is devoted completely to the cause of Polynices and displays unswerving loyalty to his comrade, as shown especially in his challenge of Eteocles (8.677-79) and the hostile words he directs toward Jocasta and her daughters (7.539-59, 612-14), who earlier attempt to dissuade Polynices from marching on Thebes.

Capaneus

The fourteen speeches of this *magnanimus* hero and *superum contemptor* (3.602, 9.550), like those of Hippomedon, are extremely brief, averaging 5.4 lines in length. Capaneus' speeches and accompanying actions stamp him not only as an impetuous, arrogant, shameless, even insolent figure, but also as an extremely brave and loyal warrior. His contempt for the malevolent supernatural powers has its righteous element, as shown in his refusal to participate in the cowardly nocturnal attack (10.258f.) upon the Theban camp that is inspired and aided directly by the gods (see esp. 79-82, 146-55; cf. 160-63, 188-218). In his heroic defiance and challenge of the gods he is shown to be striking an impressive but futile blow against supernatural tyranny and injustice.[21]

---

[20] E.g., Glaesener (1899: 104), ten Kate (1955: 91).

[21] *Contra* Farron (1979-80: 35), who describes Capaneus as 'the villain *par excellence*'.

The speeches of this immensely powerful and physically imposing hero consist mainly of taunts and challenges and are directed with equal fearlessness to his foes, friends and even the Olympian gods. The majority of these speeches are accompanied by fearless deeds that help to define his heroic and aggressive personality. He taunts the frail Eunaeus (7.677-79) just before striking him down, exhorts the Argive warriors to open warfare against Thebes (10.482-86) while storming the gates of the city, and declares his intention to test the worth of the Apolline oracle by ascending the Theban walls to the same tower where Menoeceus sacrificed himself to the Theban cause (845-47; cf. 666-68).

His challenge directed at the Achaeans to send one of their warriors to meet him in the cestus event during the funeral games contains a threat of death (6.734-37); when the Spartan Alcidimas accepts his challenge and fells him, Capaneus becomes incensed and expresses the desire to carry out his threat against his smaller but composed and more skilful opponent (819-22). Capaneus' threat against Alcidimas resembles Epeius' challenge in the *Iliad* where he predicts that his antagonist in the boxing contest will suffer a brutal death (23.667-75). However, there is a important difference in the respective challenges of Epeius and Capaneus. Epeius does not literally mean what he says, for he is chivalrous in his defeat of his opponent Euryalus (*Il.* 23.689ff.), but Capaneus fully intends to kill his Spartan opponent Alcidimas and is prevented from doing so only through the spirited intervention of Adrastus, Hippomedon and Tydeus (*Theb.* 6.813ff.). In this scene Capaneus displays the personal qualities of compelling arrogance, lack of restraint and proclivity to madness that constitute the essence of his character and ultimately lead to his death. Alcidimas' adroitness and intelligence contrast with the crazed state and brutal tactics of Capaneus and enable the Spartan to survive his stronger opponent.

The narrative preceding the initial appearance of Capaneus draws attention to his primitive aspect and baser qualities as well as his immense physical strength and huge frame in the comparison of this hero with a Centaur and Cyclops (3.604f.; cf. 4.165-77, 10.853ff.). The blustering and threatening tone of his first two and longest speeches betray his arrogance, recklessness and irreverence (3.607-18, 648f.). His extremely violent speeches to Amphiaraus and the Argive mob are designed to bring the priest into disrepute and to incite the citizens to take up arms against Thebes. The shamelessness and irreverence of this brute hero toward Amphiaraus in this scene is a reflexion of his contempt for the gods and their representatives on earth, the priests and priestesses.

The hubris of Capaneus is evident especially in his expression of trust only in his own courage and sword (3.615f.):

> uirtus mihi numen et ensis
> quem teneo!

This same arrogance can be seen in his invocation of his right arm, a speech that shows too his disdain of the higher powers (9.548-50):

> ades o mihi, dextera, tantum
> tu praesens bellis et ineuitabile numen,
> te uoco, te solam superum contemptor adoro.

Capaneus' invocation occurs just prior to his taunt (557-59) and slaying of Hypseus, who mocks him, but it must be stressed that his slaying of the Theban warrior is motivated primarily by a sense of devotion to Hippomedon, as his apostrophe of the Mycenaean hero shows (562-65). The heroic qualities of Capaneus are shown in his avengement of Hypseus' plundering of Hippomedon's corpse, his recovery of his comrade's body from the battlefield, and his fiery and valorous disposition. Later he expresses complete confidence in his ability to wage battle (10.485f.):

> sunt et mihi prouida dextrae
> omina et horrendi stricto mucrone furores.

These speeches of Capaneus betray a supreme belief in his own capabilities and a corresponding contempt for and lack of faith in the gods, who reveal themselves for the most part as cruel and unjust powers through their hostility or indifference toward mankind. Heroism and arrogance are the dominant characteristics of his personality; these qualities are entirely compatible, for the loyalty he shows toward his friends is equalled only by his contempt for his antagonists, divine and human.

The challenges of this bellicose figure are remarkable for their boldness and self-glorification. His challenge (10.899-906) and taunts (873-77, 925f.) directed against the Thebans, Jupiter and the other Olympians during his assault on Thebes exemplify his temerity and self-conceit. Capaneus is naturally doomed by his impetuosity and his violent death serves as a demonstration of the futility of challenging the cruel exercise of divine power and authority. Notwithstanding, his insane challenge is shown to be instigated by the Furies at the behest of Pluto in revenge for the imagined intrusion of Jupiter upon his infernal domain (8.33ff. [esp. 76f.], 11.88-91; cf. 10.831-33). Capaneus' defiant challenge (5.565-70) and attendant slaying of the serpent sacred to Jupiter (570-78) is further evidence of his vanity and utter contempt for the gods.

Hippomedon

This Mycenaean hero of immense physical size and strength delivers seven speeches averaging over four lines in length. During the funeral games for Opheltes he challenges the Achaean warriors to use his heavy disk in the discus event (6.656-59), then proceeds to hurl it far beyond the distances reached by the other competitors. He shows a great devotion to his friends and allies. Along with Tydeus he restrains physically the crazed Capaneus who threatens to overwhelm Alcidimas in the boxing match and reminds him that the Spartan is a comrade in arms (6.816f.). As he defends bravely the corpse of Tydeus against the Thebans who strive to recover it, he cuts off the hand of Leonteus who attempts to drag the corpse away and taunts the unfortunate warrior (9.137-39); later he encourages Tydeus' steed to avenge the death of his master (211-17). His taunt of Panemus (9.294-301), reproach of the river-god Ismenos (476-80), and prayer to Mars seeking death by the sword rather than by drowning (506-10) further reflect his heroic stature. Hippomedon shows himself to be supreme in battle until Ismenos attacks and weakens him so greatly that finally he succumbs to a shower of missles from the Theban forces arrayed against him (446ff.).

Parthenopaeus

This young Arcadian makes four speeches averaging just under eleven lines in length. Parthenopaeus serves as a tragic example of the youthful warrior who in his boyish innocence and enthusiasm for the imagined glory of war (9.683-99, esp. 683, 694-99) does not appreciate its real dangers until it is too late (cf. 885-97). He is the favourite of Diana, patron goddess of Atalanta, his mother. When the youth appeals reverently to her for victory in the foot-race (6.633-37), the goddess ensures that he is triumphant and he races across the plain, scarcely touching the earth with his feet (638-45).

Similarly she acts upon him so that he is scarcely recognisable as he races across the battlefield, leaving a stream of fallen bodies in his path (9.726ff.) and taunting his opponents with uncharacteristic rancour (e.g., 790-800). When Diana disguises herself as his trusty manservant Dorceus and urges him to refrain from further fighting (811-14), he declares his devotion to the goddess and his mother and intention of paying homage to them (815-19). After Parthenopaeus is wounded mortally (867ff.), the youth orders Dorceus to console his mother and convey a message of sorrow and regret to her for partaking in the war at such an early age (885-907).

Women

Fifteen human women deliver forty-three speeches (including inserted discourses) totalling 1050 11/12 lines, not quite one-third of the total number of lines spoken in the epic;[22] the average length of the speeches is twenty-five lines[23] (versus 10.8 for the rest of the speeches). With some minor exceptions, notably in the case of Eriphyle, these characters incarnate the virtuous qualities of womanhood. Their speeches and actions are consistent with this portrayal of women as exemplars of nobility, courage, humility, piety and familial devotion.

Argia

This daughter of Adrastus and wife of Polynices makes eleven unrecounted speeches averaging 11.7 lines in length; eight of these speeches are delivered in the final book. She is portrayed as the archetypal pious and devoted wife. Prior to her first speech and marriage to Polynices her virtue and humility are evident in a meeting with her future husband (1.533-39).

After her marriage Argia displays an anxious concern over his welfare, realising that his desire to acquire power in Thebes will result in violence and bloodshed (2.334-52). She approaches Adrastus and asks him to declare war on Thebes (3.687ff.), realising that she may well come to regret her plea (707-10). Although this request of Argia seems to be inconsistent with her

---

[22] When divine characters are included, women speak 1258 1/2 lines (including inserted speeches), over one-third of the total number of speech lines.

[23] The average length is 14.1 lines, excluding the long narrative of Hypsipyle (5.49-498) and recounted speeches therein.

usual character and is a tragic error of judgement, which she later has cause to regret (cf. 12.336f.), her urgent appeal actually highlights her humanity since it is based mainly on familial and marital reasons and is motivated out of pity for the misfortune of her husband and an appreciation of the justice of his cause (cf. 3.696-98).

The soliloquy of Argia as her husband departs with the Argive army for Thebes demonstrates the simple heroism, nobility and piety of this woman (4.200-10). She decides to relinquish the fateful necklace of Harmonia that Polynices earlier had presented to her as a bridal gift, believing that it is inappropriate to take pleasure in beautifying herself while Polynices is at war (200-06). Out of a sense of devotion to her husband Argia decides to share his burden by abstaining from any form of pleasure during his absence.

Nowhere are the heroic qualities of Argia and her unswerving devotion to Polynices more in evidence than after his death. She resolves to travel to Thebes, allegedly to plead for the burial of the Argive dead (12.196-204), but actually to bury Polynices, as her apostrophe establishes (12.209-19). On her approach to Thebes she invokes the City and asks for assistance in recovering the corpse of her husband so that she can give him a proper burial (12.256f.). This action is represented not only as the supreme example of *pietas* and conjugal devotion but also as a direct challenge of supernatural and monarchal tyranny (cf. 12.184-86).

The lament of Argia over Polynices emphasises further her pious and noble qualities. She is reverent toward the gods in her expression of gratitude for their help in recovering the corpse of her husband (338-40) and shows her devotion to him by reiterating her resolve to inhume his body (344-48). When the soldiers of Thebes discover her joint attempt with Antigone to bury Polynices, she again shows her heroic qualities by claiming responsibility for the deed (12.452ff., esp. 458f.). She risks her life willingly in defiance of the gods and Creon in order to ensure that her husband his buried in accordance with the higher law of nature, a law that consists of each individual showing a sense of duty and moral responsibility to other family and community members.

Antigone

Like her sister-in-law Argia, Antigone is portrayed generally as a noble, courageous and pious woman. She delivers nine speeches averaging over eight lines in length; seven of these speeches are made in the last two books. She does not make her first speech until the second half of the poem, but appears early in the poem when she escorts Polynices from Thebes in his self-enforced exile (2.313f.). Antigone has conflicting feelings about whom to favour in the war (cf. 8.613-15), as shown in her support of the cause of Polynices (615) and desire for a Theban victory (cf. 7.247-49).

Antigone intervenes twice in attempting to prevent martial and fraternal violence. She appeals tearfully to Polynices not to undertake war against Thebes (7.535f.) and makes a despairing plea to dissuade him from meeting his brother in single combat (11.363-82). After the death of Polynices she shows a sense of loving devotion and moral obligation to her brother when she escapes from her Theban guards and hurries to the battlefield outside of Thebes in order to bury his corpse in defiance of her uncle (12.349ff.); yet so strong is her sense of moral responsibility that she feels compelled to confess her shame to Argia in not coming earlier to bury her brother (382-85). Antigone expresses her horror and urges the spirits of her brothers to cease their hatred after she and Argia mix their ashes unwittingly and a violent conflagration erupts (429ff.). When the Theban guards are awakened by the tremor, she is no less heroic than her sister-in-law in claiming responsibility for the burial attempt and seeking the promised punishment of death (447-63).

Despite the past crimes of her father Oedipus, Antigone remains completely devoted to him. It is true that she assumes a pitiably obsequious stance in importuning Creon to permit Oedipus to remain in Thebes (11.708-39), but this is motivated primarily out of a sense of duty to her father, just as she is galvanised by the injustice of Creon and sisterly devotion into ensuring that Polynices receives his due rites of burial (cf. 12.349ff.). This sense of duty to her father is evident immediately after the death of her brothers when Argia is the sole figure to come to the aid of Oedipus. She guides him to the corpses of his sons (11.586ff.) and must prevent her grief-stricken father from taking his life (627-30); she is numb with sorrow herself but even so is pleased to see that her father is capable of feeling grief and remorse (632f.).

Jocasta

Jocasta makes four speeches averaging nearly fifteen lines in length. The two important speeches of this legendary queen portray her as a peaceloving figure through her attempts to forestall the outbreak of war and the dual fratricide (7.497-527, 11.329-53). As Jocasta departs from Thebes for the Argive camp, her unsightly and disfigured appearance betrays her sorrowful and mournful state, yet she maintains a majestic sense of presence that is likened to the most ancient of the Furies (7.474-78). Although she is so frail that she must be supported by her daughters, her frenzied determination is evident as her pace seems to overreach her strength (479-81). Jocasta demands admittance to the Argive camp (483-85) and is filled with anger and grief as she searches for and confronts her son (490-92, 496). She attempts to persuade Polynices to negotiate his claim to the Theban throne with Eteocles instead of striving to gain power by forceful means (7.497-527). The former Theban queen is ashamed of and remorseful over her fateful marriage to Oedipus and the birth of her sons (514). Her speech draws attention to the special significance of the family relationship (esp. 503-06, 520-27) and her willingness to forgive her son even for his madness (515). Ultimately her plea fails as it must under the supernatural governance of events in Argos (cf. 466-69), notwithstanding the sudden and dramatic impact it has upon Polynices and the Argive troops (528-38).

When Jocasta hears news of the impending duel between her sons, she confronts Eteocles in a manner far less dignified and considerably more excitable (11.315-20) than her previous approach to Polynices (7.490-92); the old woman is so invigorated by her grief and despair that neither her attendants nor daughters can keep step with her (11.321-23). She makes a final, desperate attempt to dissuade the Theban monarch from meeting his brother in single combat (329-53), although she appears to realise that the impending duel is inspired by one of the Furies and is therefore beyond her power to prevent (329-31). After the mutual fratricide takes place, she is so overcome by grief and a sense of personal loss brought about by a lifetime of misfortune that she ends her own life (634-37).

Hypsipyle

Hypsipyle makes only four unrecounted speeches yet speaks more lines (496 11/12) than any other figure; her narrative speech to Adrastus is the longest in the epic (449 5/6). The exiled queen of Lemnos and devoted attendant of Opheltes retains a noble and dignified presence despite her dishevelled appearance (4.747ff.). The callous disregard of Hypsipyle for the safety of the infant Opheltes, whom she abandons while she leads the

Argives to the waters of Langia (778ff.), is inconsistent with the generally favourable portrayal of her in the poem, but the narrative stresses that the Fates are responsible for ensuring that her negligent action takes place (780). She is grief-stricken over the death of her charge (5.588ff., esp. 608-35) and accepts responsibility for his death (622-27), although she realises that the gods have played their rôle in bringing about his death (620-22).

In her account of events on Lemnos Hypsipyle reveals the nobility and moral superiority of her character not only generally through her immunity to the destructive influences of hostile supernatural powers and her refusal to submit psychologically to these demoniac forces, but also specifically through her refusal to take part in the divinely instigated massacre of the men and children of Lemnos (cf. 195ff.) and her rescue of her father Thoas (240-51, 265ff.). Her steadfast devotion to her father stands in marked contrast to the behaviour of the other Lemnian women, who are unable to withstand the malign power of the gods.

Priests and Priestesses

The speeches and actions of the seven priests and priestesses show them generally to be pious and devoted to the gods, although occasionally they are inspired by the higher powers (e.g., 10.160ff.) to speak violently (e.g., 188-218, 269-91) and perform gory deeds (e.g., 266ff.). Amphiaraus and Tiresias deliver fifteen of the twenty-six speeches made by priests and priestesses in the epic.[24]

Amphiaraus

The nine speeches of this pious priest total just over 152 lines.[25] Amphiaraus first appears when Adrastus asks him to conduct an augury and reveal the outcome of a future war with Thebes (3.449-52). The priest invokes Jupiter reverentially and asks for an indication from the chief god regarding the fate of Argos (471-96). He is so agitated by the portents of war (547-51) he describes to Melampus (516-45) that he retreats into isolation and refuses to reveal his findings (570-75). After Mars inflames the

---

[24] Excluding the deliberation of Amphiaraus' spirit reported by Thiodamas to the Achaean leaders (10.206-11).

[25] These totals include the recounted speech of Amphiaraus' spirit (10.206-11).

Argive populace to war (575-97), he is motivated out of love for his people to come forth and try to dissuade them from taking up arms against Thebes (620-45), but then realises the futility of attempting to avert a conflict instigated by the higher powers (646f.). The pious qualities of this priest are emphasised further when he urges Lycurgus to refrain from violence against Hypsipyle (5.669-71) and informs the Argives they must hold obsequies for Opheltes (733-52).

Amphiaraus is against the war, but his resolve weakens under the violent attack of Atropos upon his will and the action of his wife Eriphyle, who foredooms her husband through her acquisition of the fateful gold necklace (4.187-95, 211-13). Under this influence of Atropos (189f.) and the watchful eye of Tisiphone (211-13) he drives off to war in his chariot, presenting a conspicuous and fearsome sight with his spear and shield (214-45, esp. 221f.). Apollo intervenes to bring him glory in the chariot race (6.491ff.) and in the great war (7.692ff.). Amphiaraus is aware of the overwhelming presence of Apollo (cf. 779f.) as he is borne into the middle of the first battle (698f.). Succumbing completely to the inspiration of Apollo while under the protection and guidance of various deities (695-98, 702-04, 736-59; cf. 779f.), Amphiaraus is filled with an insatiable craving for the violence and bloodshed of war (703-11; cf. 711-22). His character is so transmuted that he even slays a fellow priest of Apollo against his own will (715f.). Apollo saves Amphiaraus from the spear of Hypseus (736f.) and guides the chariot of his favourite priest across the field even as he drives him to slay a host of warriors in quick succession (738-70, esp. 752f.). Clearly the supernatural powers exert such control over Amphiaraus that he is unable to exercise any real measure of free will over his own actions.

In his speeches to Apollo (7.779-88) and Pluto (8.90-122) the Argive priest displays a hitherto unseen desire to vengeance against his wife for betraying him (7.787f., 8.104, 120-22). Later his shade spurs Thiodamas into exhorting the Argives successfully to enter the Theban camp and slaughter the enemy in their sleep (10.206-11). These actions are entirely inconsistent with the former character of Amphiaraus and are attributable to the harmful influence of supernatural powers. Prior to the imposition of divine will upon him, the speeches and actions of the priest reveal a strong moral character; afterward he appears mainly as a figure bent on violence and revenge.

Tiresias

This Theban priest makes seven speeches averaging just under thirteen lines in length. Tiresias delivers his speeches during the important scenes of necromancy (4.414-645) and capnomancy (10.589-627). He approaches Pluto and the infernal deities with a simple feeling of dependence and a simple request to allow the shades of the dead to return to the light (4.473-87). Only a moment later Tiresias angrily rebukes the infernal goddesses when his request is not granted immediately, believing that they do not treat him seriously because he refuses to practise sorcery (501-11). His threat to use a hidden power that he claims to possess (512-18) betrays the agitated mental state of a pious but frustrated priest who momentarily feels neglected by the gods. The other speeches of Tiresias show the priest practising his arts (4.536-48, 4.583-602, 4.610-24, 10.592-98, 10.610-15).

An examination of the characterising function of the speeches in the *Thebaid* reveals that the characterisation of human and divine figures is generally more complex than most critics realise. It is true that the personalities of human figures achieve a remarkable consistency in the speeches and narrative of the poem, but there is a often a dramatic change in their characters when they are made subject to the influence of supernatural powers. In general a certain pattern of behaviour and attitude emerges among the various human characters in the speeches and narrative, then is undermined by the later speeches and actions of these figures in reaction to the harmful influences of the supernatural powers or the absence of these forces, and this phenomenon finally is perceived as a pattern of the entire characterising process in the epic.

CHAPTER 6

ELEMENTS OF STYLE IN THE SPEECHES

Use and Types of Stylistic Elements

Elements of style such as sound complexes of consonants and vowels and figures of speech and thought are important poetic tools in producing special effects in the speeches of the *Thebaid*, thereby enhancing the effectiveness of speeches and underscoring—or undercutting—their themes. This chapter is concerned with the functional qualities of the various stylistic devices, in particular the way they create texture and tone in particular speeches and infuse them with an element of dramatic vitality. The texture of the speeches consists of those elements such as rhyme, metre and tone that are not concerned with the external structure of the speeches (the traditional elements that constitute the various speech types). The tone of the speeches is roughly equivalent to the mood or atmosphere that is created by the various poetic and rhetorical devices; tone or mood is created by varying combinations of stylistic devices such as alliteration, assonance, rhyme, rhetorical repetition, metre and rhythm.

Studying rhetorical handbooks such as Quintilian's *Institutio Oratoria* and the *Rhetorica ad Herennium* was an important means of instruction in the new schools of rhetoric; they are heavily laden with references to every type of rhetorical device conceivable. Quintilian treats over one hundred of these (*Inst.* 9.1-3), while *Rhetorica ad Herennium* discusses sixty-four (4.18-69).[1] Quintilian cautions his students against the poets' excessive use of rhetorical figures (*Inst.* 9.3.101; cf. 9.3.27). The critic must exercise some care in dealing with Statius' use of them. The particular figures as well as the frequency and circumstances of their use are important factors for consideration. Simply because the handbooks quote verses from the poets as examples of figures of speech does not mean that their copious use in the *Thebaid* is intentionally rhetorical. In this chapter special attention is paid

---

[1] However, other rhetoricians such as Seneca were sparing in their citation and discussion of figures, perhaps because they were so well known.

236

to some of the poetic and rhetorical devices treated in the *Institutio Oratoria* that contribute to the creation of special effects in the speeches of Statius.

Statius would no doubt have been instructed in the use best suited for a particular figure, a training designed for the orator but whose purpose served the poet equally as well. But the ancient commentators did not approach the matter of a poet's use of rhetorical figures with the same attitude. Eusebius in Macrobius' *Saturnalia* argued that Vergil's use of a range of figures shows that he was very much an orator, and his colleagues agreed with him (4.6). This preoccupation with figures of speech and rhetorical precepts shows just how ingrained rhetoric was as an institution. The rules for their use by poets and rhetoricians was important part of their training in the schools (Quint. *Inst.* 8.5.35). Judging by Quintilian's preoccupation with tropes and figures, he regarded them as the chief part of *ornatus*.

Although Daniels concedes that many of the figures of Statius are beautiful, he criticises the poet for an alleged lack of striking originality in their use.[2] Notwithstanding, Statius uses tropes and figures in the *Thebaid* to amplify, clarify and communicate the feelings and emotions of the various characters in specific dramatic situations. He employs a wide variety of these stylistic devices in order to depict psychic and physical states of the speakers, whose emotions range widely across the emotional spectrum. This generation of emotion in the speeches through the use of such forceful tropes and figures as hyperbole, apostrophe, the rhetorical question and exclamation not only embellishes the style but also affords a heightened sense of dramatic urgency.

No doubt Statius' use of these stylistic devices was often conscious, sometimes partly or perhaps even entirely subconscious, but in the end it is unimportant whether they were employed intentionally or instinctively, since the poet would have been well aware of the aural and emotional effects they produced in either case. Nor is it really possible to distinguish with certainty whether various stylistic devices are rightly to be considered poetic or rhetorical, since they are common to the practice of poetry and rhetoric. For instance, Statius makes frequent use of the so-called rhetorical question in the composition of the speeches, but its use can be viewed as a natural means of human expression in a tense dramatic situation.

---

[2] Daniels (1905: 14). Daniels refers to some lines in the *Thebaid* that depend heavily on the *Aeneid* for their formation as 'poetry comparable to the merest tyro'!

Ancient rhetoricians often disagree with each other concerning the definition and categorisation of various tropes and figures. Unable to distinguish with precision between a trope and a figure,[3] they engage in interminable disputes over their number and type (cf. Quint. *Inst.* 8.6.1, 9.1.10). Quintilian himself is no exception in this respect. After examining the difficulty inherent in attempting a system of classification, he distinguishes trope from figure (9.1.1-9). The term of trope is employed to designate the transference of an expression from its standard and central meaning to another for the purpose of ornamentation or, as most grammarians define a trope, as the transference of a word from its proper place to one which it does not rightly belong (9.1.4; cf. 8.6.1); for the purposes of the discussion in this chapter a trope is considered to be the use of a word or phrase in a sense that departs from its literal or proper meaning. According to Quintilian, a figure is the appellation used when the expression is manipulated in an unusual or uncommon manner (9.1.4f.); a little further on he adds to this by defining a figure as *arte aliqua nouata forma dicendi* (14).

Quintilian's differentiation between trope and figure is relatively simple, although it is not without its difficulties. He essentially considers a trope a change in the meaning of a word or phrase, while a figure involves the creation of a distinctive effect in deviating from the usual use of an expression without a real change in the meaning of the words. But Quintilian himself perceives the problems inherent in his rigorous distinction between trope and figure. It is often difficult to distinguish between a trope and a figure, since *translatis uerbis quam propriis figuratur oratio* (9.1.9). Quintilian recognises that his convenient definition is not equally applicable to all situations in which a rhetorical figure is employed (cf. 9.2.2f.). Consequently he observes that irony is as much a figure of thought as a trope and that periphrasis, hyperbaton and onomatopoeia are considered by some to be figures of speech rather than tropes (9.1.3).

After Quintilian elaborates on his distinction between trope and figure, he examines the difference between figures of thought and speech. Figures of thought are those of the mind, feeling or imagination, while figures of speech are concerned with words, diction, elocution, expression or style

---

[3] For instance, the *Rhetorica ad Herennium* (4.31.42) does not separate a trope from a figure. However, Cicero does distinguish between them, noting that the Greeks were responsible for their division (*Brut.* 18.69).

(9.1.17). He emphasises the practical aspects of the use of figures. They contribute to the credibility of an argument, affect the minds of the judge unwittingly, arouse emotion, effect in the audience a favourable disposition toward the orator's cause, aid in relieving monotony, and help to clarify the issue with circumspection (19-21). Quintilian divides figures of thought into three classes according to their effect on the auditor. There are figures that make the argument clearer and more cogent (9.2.6), those that excite the emotions (26), and those that elevate the style of the speaker (96).

Prior to his treatment of the figures of speech, Quintilian divides them into two types. The first is grammatical and is styled the system of language, while the second is rhetorical and is concerned with the disposition of words (9.3.2). These figures serve to attract and maintain the attention of the audience, while arousing them intermittently with an especially striking figure. If they are employed with moderation and variety, their effect is charming and inducing to the auditor (27).

Notwithstanding the difficulties inherent in Quintilian's definition and classification of poetic and rhetorical devices such as tropes and figures, he is the only rhetorician in the first century CE to attempt such a classification; therefore his treatment of them is followed closely here in examining their usage and function in the speeches of the *Thebaid*. The discussion in this chapter is devoted mainly to those devices that appeal to Statius mainly on account of their striking or arresting qualities.[4]

Alliteration and Onomatopoeia

The study of word sounds—'verbal music', to use Bateson's phrase,[5] or 'audial imagery', to use Knight's term[6]—is a controversial subject because of the subjectivity involved in assessing the effect of certain vowel and consonant sounds upon the meaning of a particular passage. There are simply no hard and fast rules governing the study of sound values. Much

---

[4] The separate discussions of some of these devices are somewhat truncated (e.g., ellipsis and aposiopesis), but further examples of their use can be found elsewhere in this chapter and in the discussions of individual speeches in chs. 3 and 4; see also index of speech and rhetorical subjects.

[5] Bateson (1966: 21-23).

[6] Knight (1966: 303).

depends on the effect in a given passage of a particular sounds, which in another context might suggest a different sense or meaning. The sounds of closely associated or clashing letters, syllables and words in successive verses often create an onomatopoeic effect, appropriately referred to by Wilkinson as 'expressiveness',[7] in which the meaning is suggested as much in the sounds, rhythm and rhyme of the lines as in the literal meaning of the words.[8]

The figure alliteration and trope onomatopoeia are two of the more useful devices that the imperial poet had at his disposal to create sound effects in the speeches. Alliteration is not specifically mentioned in the rhetorical treatises, but is nevertheless a popular figure among the rhetoricians and poets.[9] The occurrence of the close repetition of identical consonant or vowel sounds in successive or nearly apposite words or syllables comes closest to the figure of *adnominatio*, which Quintilian unnecessarily categorises in a group distinct from figures of thought and speech. The function of this third class of figures is to attract and arouse the audience through the similarity and contrast of diction (*Inst.* 9.3.66). *Rhetorica ad Herennium* refers to alliteration only in the context of excessive figures that should be avoided (4.12.18). Onomatopoeia is in the strict sense the creation of a word that imitates a sound (cf. Quint. *Inst.* 8.6.31f.).[10] In an extended sense the trope becomes a subtle device of a discerning poet in which the sounds of the words not only suggest and reinforce their meaning but also the verses themselves convey their meaning in the effect produced.

Alliteration is used frequently and with great skill by Statius at the beginning of words and of consonants and vowel sounds within words in speeches to create tone and atmosphere. The highly alliterative quality of his verse is evident in one of the early speeches in the poem when Jupiter bids Mercury to convey a message to Pluto; the force of the command is suggested in the close association of harsh consonants (1.292-95; my italics):

---

[7] Wilkinson (1963: 49).

[8] Excellent comments on verbal music and expressiveness appear in Marouzeau (1954: 1-86), Herescu (1960), Knight (1966: 296-308), Wilkinson (1963: 1-88), Watkiss (1966: 332-47).

[9] On alliteration in Roman literature, see Marouzeau (1954: 45-50), Herescu (1960: 129-34) and Wilkinson (1963: 25-28).

[10] On onomatopoeia see Marouzeau (1954: 24-39 [*expressivité*]) and Wilkinson (1963: 46-85 [expressiveness]).

> quare im*p*iger ali*s*
> *p*ortante*s* *p*raecede Noto*s*, Cyllenia *p*role*s*,
> aera *p*er liquidum regni*s*que inl*ap*su*s* *o*paci*s*
> dic *p*atruo . . .

The stammering *p* and hissing *s* sounds—especially the sibilant at the close of each line—convey something of the sonal power of Jupiter's words.

Statius' skilful use of alliteration is evident especially in his composition of strongly emotional speeches such as those of mourning and consolation. In the lament of Ide over her twin sons (3.151-68), Statius skilfully uses sound, as shown in the alliteration of *l*—particularly in the onomatopoeic *ululata* (158)—and careful placement of long vowels, in order to suggest her sense of loss and strengthen the unity of the passage by echoing its meaning (157-60; emphasis mine):

> at quanto me*l*ius dextraque in sorte iugatae,
> quis steri*l*es tha*l*ami nu*ll*oque u*l*u*l*ata do*l*ore
> respexit *L*ucina domum! mihi quippe ma*l*orum
> causa *l*abor.

Immediately afterward in the same speech the predominance of the doleful *s* and *m* sounds along with the unsonorous vowel *i*, which Dionysius of Halicarnassus considers particularly inelegant (*Rhet.* 14.143; cf. Quint. *Inst.* 9.4.34), are extremely effective in conveying the extent of her grief and disappointment (3.160-64; my italics):

> cau*s*a labor; *s*ed nec belloru*m* *i*n luce patent*i*
> con*s*picu*i* fat*i*s aeternaque gent*i*bu*s* au*s*i
> quae*s*i*s*ti*s* *mis*erae uulnu*s* *m*e*m*orab*i*le *m*atr*i*,
> *s*ed *m*orte*m* obscura*m* nu*m*erosaque funera pa*ss*i,
> heu quantu*s* furto cruor et *s*ine laude iaceti*s*!

The emotional effect of the pathetic command of the dying Parthenopaeus (9.885-907) to his trusty manservant Dorceus is enhanced through the dexterous use of sound, particularly the *i* vowels (885-97; italics mine):

> lab*i*mur, *i*, m*i*seram, Dorceu, solare parentem.
> *i*lla qu*i*dem, *si* uera ferunt praesag*i*a curae,
> aut somno iam tr*i*ste nefas aut om*i*ne u*i*dit.
> tu tamen arte p*i*a trep*i*dam suspende d*i*uque

241

dec*i*p*i*to; neu tu sub*i*tus neue arma tenent*i*
ueuer*i*s, et tandem, cum iam cogere fater*i*,
d*i*c: meru*i*, genetr*i*x, poenas; *i*nu*i*ta capesse:
arma puer rapu*i*, nec te ret*i*nente qu*i*eu*i*,
nec t*i*bi soll*i*c*i*tae tandem *i*nter bella peperc*i*.
u*i*ue *i*g*i*tur pot*i*usque an*i*m*i*s *i*rascere nostr*i*s
et iam pone metus. frustra de colle Lyca*ei*
anx*i*a prospectas, s*i* quis per nub*i*la longe
aut sonus aut nostro sublatus ab agm*i*ne pulu*i*s.

The short *i* and long *i* sounds—especially at the end of the lines—help to give his utterance a mournful tone. This sound pattern is continued in the concluding section of the speech (900-907; my italics):

hunc tamen, orba parens, *crinem*, . . .
. . . *hunc* toto capies pro corpore *crinem*,
comere quem frustra me ded*i*gnante solebas.
hu*i*c dab*i*s exequ*i*as, atque *i*nter iusta memento,
ne qu*i*s *i*nexpert*i*s hebetet mea tela lacert*i*s
d*i*lectosque canes ull*i*s agat amplius antr*i*s.
haec autem prim*i*s arma *i*nfel*i*c*i*a castr*i*s
ure, uel *i*ngratae cr*i*men suspende D*i*anae.

The plaintive tone of the short and long *i*'s is complemented by the striking anaphora of *hunc* and repetition of *crinem* in consecutive lines (900f.). The balanced, parallel structure of the attributive adjectives and nouns ending in *-is* in three successive lines (904-06) further heightens the plaintive effect. Significantly, the concluding line (908) of the speech (and of the book) does not continue with this pattern of grammatical parallelism. The discordant effect created by the failure to satisfy the reader's sense of expectancy draws attention to the inaccuracy of Parthenopaeus' reference to Diana as *ingrata*.

A plaintive effect is produced in the prophetic speech of Amphiaraus, who relates to the Argives the direful events he foresees when taking the auspices (3.640-42; my emphasis):

uidi ingentis portenta ruinae,
uidi homin*um* diu*um*que metus hilar*em*que Megaer*em*
et Lachesin putri uacuant*em* saecula penso.

242

The doleful-sounding suffixes *-um* and *-em* combine with the frequent long syllables and anaphora of *uidi* to produce a sorrowful and solemn effect, greatly enhancing the despairing tone of his speech.

The long vowel *o* is skilfully used in the prayer of the Bacchic queen to her god (4.383-404). As desperation and panic reigns in Thebes, the frenzied priestess rushes through and fills the anxious city with frantic cries (384-89; my emphasis):

> . . . tu nunc horrente sub Arc*o*
> bellica ferrat*o* rapidus quatis Ismara thyrs*o*
> pampineumque iubes nemus inreptare Lycurg*o*,
> aut tumidum Gangen aut claustra nouissima Rubrae
> Tethy*os* Eoasque dom*os* flagrante triumph*o*
> perfuris . . .

The rhyming long *o* sound, especially at the close of the lines, is expressive of the wild shrieking usually associated with the female worship of Bacchus.

S and *x* sounds (often accompanied by anaphora, *adiectio* or polyptoton), owing to their harshness (cf. Quint. *Inst.* 9.4.37f.), are used with great effect by Statius to express the hostility of the speaker, as in Eurydice's inculpatory invocation of Menoeceus (10.802f.; my emphasis):

> *tu*, *s*aeue Menoeceu,
> *tu* mi*s*eram ante omne*s* properas*t*i e*x*tinguere matrem.

The venomous apostrophe of the anonymous Theban (1.173-96) is marked by a series of sibilant and double consonants, producing an alliterative effect that reflects his scorn of men and the gods (177-80; emphasis mine):

> *s*emperne uici*ss*im
> e*x*ulibu*s s*eruite dabor? tibi, *s*umne deorum
> terrarumque *s*ator, *s*ocii*s* hanc addere mentem
> *s*edit?

Similarly the frequency of the hissing *s*, *ss* and *x* sounds in the lines comprising Diana's threat expresses her hostility toward the Theban warrior—as yet unknown (cf. 9.875f.)—who will slay Parthenopaeus (9.663-67; italics mine):

'*sed* decu*s* extremum mi*s*ero' confu*s*a uici*s*sim
uirgo refert, 'duraeque licet *s*olacia morti
quaerere, nec fugiet poena*s* quicumque nefandam
in*s*onti*s* pueri *s*celerarit *s*anguine de*x*tram
impiu*s*, et no*s*tri*s* fa*s* *s*it *s*aeuire *s*agittis.'

The animosity of Maeon, the sole survivor of the party dispatched by
Eteocles to slay Tydeus, is revealed in the opening lines of his vituperation
of the monarch through the skilful use of alliteration and other stylistic
devices (3.60-62; my italics):

> *siue* haec *s*enten*t*ia di*uu*m,
> *seu* Fortuna fu*i*t, *seu*, quod pudet *i*ra fater*i*,
> *uis* *i*nu*i*cta *u*ir*i*.

The alliteration of *u* and sibilant *s*, the assonance of *i*, and the anaphora of
seu (with *siue*) are extremely effective in stressing Maeon's indignation over
his humiliating fate and his contempt for the monarch.[11]

Alliteration plays an important rôle in the outburst of Adrastus over
Capaneus' threatened slaying of Alcidimas in the cestus contest (6.809-12;
emphasis mine):

> *ite*, oro, *s*ocii, *f*urit, *ite*, *o*pponite dext*r*as,
> *f*estinate, *f*urit, *p*almamque et *p*raemia *ferte*!
> non *p*rius, *ef*racto quam mi*s*ceat o*ss*a ce*r*ebro,
> ab*s*istet, uideo; moritu*r*um au*ferte* Lacona.

The alliteration of the labial spirant *f* and mute *p*, the frequency of the
sibilant *s* (especially the double *s*) and rolling *r* sounds, the abrupt, detached
expression, and the repetition of *ite*, *furit* and *ferte* combine to create a
powerful impression of his alarm.

Assonance, Rhyme and Homeoteleuton

Quintilian argues that it is a fault to end a series of sentences (or lines)
with similar cadences, endings and inflexions (*Inst.* 9.4.42f.). He holds this

---

[11] Cf. Snijder (1968: 71 *ad* 3.62).

view probably because he realises that highly inflected languages such as Latin and Greek naturally tend toward assonance and rhyme and therefore these effects appear to require little skill to produce on the part of the poet. Notwithstanding, Quintilian discusses various types of play upon verbal resemblances in his rhetorical treatise (9.3.75-80). Assonance, rhyme and homeoteleuton are three of the more important stylistic elements used by Statius to create tone and atmosphere in the speeches of the *Thebaid*, yet this appears to have gone largely unnoticed by critics. Critics often find it difficult to distinguish between these stylistic elements,[12] but essentially assonance involves the close repetition of similar vowel sounds,[13] rhyme the duplication of terminal sounds at the close of successive lines,[14] and simple homeoteleuton the repetition of identical sounds or words within a single line or series of verses.[15]

Statius uses assonantal and rhyming patterns to produce a powerful and skilful effect in the speech of Pluto to his absent brothers (8.34-79; emphasis added):

quae super*um* labes inimic*um* impegit Auerno
aethera? quis rupit tenebras uitaeque silentes
admonet? unde minae? uter haec mihi proelia fratr*um*?
congredior, pereant aged*um* discrimina rer*um*.
nam cui dulce magis? magno me tertia uict*um*
deiecit fortuna polo, mund*umque* nocent*em*
seruo; nec iste meus: diris *quin* peruius astris
inspicit*ur*. tumidusne meas regnat*or* Olympi
explorat uires? habeo iam quassa Gigant*um*
uincula et aetheri*um* cupidos exire sub ax*em*

---

[12] For discussions on the difference between assonance, rhyme and homeoteleuton, see Herescu (1960: 136f., 157f. n. 1); cf. Marouzeau (1954: 58) and Wilkinson (1963: 32 n.). On the confusion between rhyme and homeoteleuton, see Herescu (1960: 136 n. 1, 170-73).

[13] On assonance in Roman literature, see Herescu (1960: 135-66) and Wilkinson (1963: 28-31).

[14] On rhyme see Marouzeau (1954: 58-65), Herescu (1960: 167-80) and Wilkinson (1963: 32-34). Wilkinson (1963: 32 n.) considers rhyme not only to occur between the ends of verses but also between the main caesura and close of the line. Marouzeau (1954: 59) appears to hold the same view, judging by the examples of rhyme he gives from Horace (*Ars P.* 99f., 344), although Herescu (1960: 136 n. 1) rightly notes that verse 344 does not in fact rhyme.

[15] On homeoteleuton see Marouzeau (1954: 51-58) and Herescu (1960: 136, 169-73).

Titanas miser*um*que patr*em*: quid me otia maesta
saeuus et implacid*am* prohibet perferre quiet*em*
amiss*um*que odisse diem? pand*am* omnia regna,
si placet, et Stygio praetex*am* Hyperiona cael*o*.
Arcada nec superis (quid enim mihi nuntius ambas
it*que* redit*que* domos?) emitt*am* et utrum*que* teneb*o*
Tyndariden. cur autem auidis Ixiona frang*o*
uerticibus? *cur* non expectant Tantalon undae?
anne profanatum totiens Chaos hospite uiu*o*
perpetiar? me Pirithoi temerari*us* ardor
temptat et audaci Theseus iurat*us* amico,
me ferus Alcides tum cum custode remot*o*
ferrea Cerbereae tacuerunt limina portae;
Odrysiis etiam pudet (heu!) patuisse querel*is*
Tartar: uidi egomet blanda inter carmina turp*es*
Eumenidum lacrimas iterat*aque* pensa Sororum;
me quo*que*—sed durae melior violentia leg*is*.
ast ego uix unum, nec celsa ad sidera, furt*o*
ausus iter Siculo rapui conubia camp*o*:
nec licuisse ferunt; iniustaeque a Ioue leg*es*
protinus, et sectum genetrix mihi computat annum.
sed quid ego haec? i, Tartareas ulciscere sed*es*,
Tisiphone; si quando nouis asperrima monstr*is*,
triste, insuetum, ingens, quod nondum viderit aether,
ede nefas, quod mirer ego inuideant*que* soror*es*.
at*que* adeo *fratres* (nostri*que* haec omina sunt*o*
prima odii), *fratres* alterna in uulnera laet*o*
Marte ruant; sit *qui* rabidarum more ferar*um*
mandat atrox hostile caput, *qui*que igne suprem*o*
arceat exanim*es* et manibus aethera nud*is*
commaculet: iuuet ista ferum spectare Tonant*em*.
praeterea ne sola furor mea regna lacessat,
quaere d*eis* qui bella ferat, *qui* fulmin*is* ign*es*
infest*um*que Iou*em* clipeo fu*m*ante repellat.
faxo haud sit cunctis leuior metus atra mouere
Tartara frondenti quam iungere Pelion Ossae.

This speech is marked by rhetorical devices emphasising the considerable anger of the infernal ruler: a preponderance of short disjunctive sentences and clauses; figures such as the rhetorical question, exclamation, parenthesis, aposiopesis and anaphora; and the repetition of the enclitic *-que* and suffixes

246

-o and *-am*. The varied, disjointed expression is characteristic of Pluto's entire speech and reflects the disordered state of his mind.

But it is mainly the poet's use of assonance or rhyme in virtually every line of the speech that attracts our attention. The echoing of duplicate or similar sounds (or words), especially *-um* and *-em*, *-o* (or *-or*), and *-es* and *-is* at the close of successive or near-consecutive lines, is particularly effective in stressing the indignation of the infernal deity:

fratr*um* (36)	cael*o* (47)	querell*is* (57)
rer*um* (37)	teneb*o* (49)	turp*es* (58)
uict*um* (38)	frang*o* (50)	leg*is* (60)
nocent*em* (39)	uiu*o* (52)	leg*es* (63)
Gigant*um* (42)	ard*or* (53)	sed*es* (65)
ax*em* (43)	amic*o* (54)	monstr*is* (66)
quiet*em* (45)	remot*o* (55)	soror*es* (68)
	furt*o* (61)	nud*is* (73)
ferar*um* (71)	camp*o* (62)	ign*es* (76)
Tonant*em* (74)		
	sunt*o* (69)	
	laet*o* (70)	
	suprem*o* (72)	

as is the repetition or echoing of syllabic or suffixal sounds (or words) in or nearly in the same metrical position in consecutive or near-successive lines:

super*um* . . . inimic*um* (34)	mundum*que* (39)
aged*um* . . . rer*um* (37)	diris *quin* (40)
mundu*m*que nocent*em* (39)	
aetheri*um* . . . ax*em* (43)	implacid*am* (45)
miser*um*que patr*em* (44)	pand*am* (46)
implacid*am* . . . quiet*em* (45)	praetex*am* (47)
amiss*um* . . . pand*am* (46)	emitt*am* (49)

cur (50)	temerari*us* (53)	*fratres* (69)	*qui* (71)
cur (51)	iurat*us* (54)	*fratres* (70)	*qui*que (72)

or even within the same line or pair of lines:

inspicit*ur* . . . regnat*or* (41)

itque reditque . . . utrumque (49)

iterataque . . . quoque (59, 60)

inuideantque . . . atque . . . nostrique (68, 69)

exanimes . . . nudis (73)

deis . . . fulminis ignes (76)

qui . . . qui (76)

infestumque Iovem . . . fumante (77)

The internal harmony of these lines gives added force to the speech and provides further evidence of the poet's skill in hexametric composition. Statius also takes special care to link the speech closely with the subsequent narrative through the echoing of identical or similar sounds. The repetition or echoing of *qui* and the suffixes *-que*, *-is* and *-es* continues into the subsequent narrative (80f., especially the triple near-repetition *qui . . . qui . . . atque*) and helps to create a sense of continuity in the transition between speech and narrative passages.

Rhetorical Repetition

Alliteration, assonance, rhyme and metre involve repetition, but the focus in this section is on the repetition of syllables, words or phrases in Statian speeches.[16] Quintilian notes that the repetition of words creates an impression of force (*Inst.* 9.1.33, 9.3.29). The closely related figures of *adiectio*, the simple repetition of a key or emphatic word (9.3.28), anaphora, the repetition of a word or phrase at the beginning of successive lines or clauses (cf. 9.3.30), and polyptoton, the use of a word in different cases (9.3.37; cf. 9.1.34), are a few of the frequent iterative devices that Statius uses in order to add force and clarity to the speeches. Quintilian does not

---

[16] See Watkiss (1966: 322-31) on Statius' use of rhetorical repetition in the *Thebaid*; on rhetorical repetition in Roman literature, see Marouzeau (1954: 261-76) and Herescu (1960: 181-203).

actually mention the name anaphora, but describes the figure as a practical device to effect force and emphasis (9.3.30);[17] this point is perspicuous, since the repetition of an initial word or phrase is naturally emphatic.

A few examples will suffice to illustrate how Statius employs these figures to secure emphasis in his speeches. In Jupiter's apostrophe of Oedipus, *adiectio*, anaphora and other sonal repetitions combine to create a powerful impression reflecting the imperious personality and resolve of the speaker (*Theb.* 1.239-41; my emphasis):

> *iam iam* rata uota tulisti,
> dire senex. *meruere tuae, meruere t*enebr*ae*
> ultorem sperare Iouem.

The sense of force and urgency in the denunciatory outburst of Creon to Eteocles (11.269-95) is enhanced through the succession of anaphorae of *hos* (276f.), *redde* (279f.), *ubi* (280f.) and *hostia* (283f.). As can be seen from this example, rhetorical repetition is a useful device to help convey odium. The anaphora of the sibilant *his* is particularly effective in conveying the extent of Capaneus' contempt for the gods (10.925f.). Similarly the anaphora of the hissing *seu* (2.20f.) and the rhyming of the conjunction with voiceless *heu* (23) adds force to the acrid tone of the speech of the anonymous shade to Laius (19-23). In other speeches the desperation of Atalanta to Diana is enhanced through the anaphora of *sed* (9.615, 618); the self-conceit of Capaneus is stressed in his invocation to his right arm by the anaphora and polyptoton of *tu* (9.548-50), figures customarily employed for solemn effect in the formal prayer; and the anaphora of *dum* greatly adds to the force of Tisiphone's reproach of Pietas, which drives the benevolent goddess from the battlefield (11.487-92).

Statius illustrates the utility of rhetorical repetition when he makes frequent use of the enclitic *-que* in a passage from the speech of Jocasta to Polynices in which she attempts to dissuade him from undertaking war against Thebes (7.501-08; italics mine):

> longae tua iussa cohortes
> expectant, multo*que* latus praefulgurat ense.
> a miserae matres! hunc te noctes*que* dies*que*

---

[17] Compare the definition and treatment of this figure given in *Rhet. Her.* 4.13.19 (=*repetitio*).

deflebam? si uerba tamen monitus*que* tuorum
dignaris, dum castra silent suspensa*que* bellum
horrescit pietas, genetrix iubeo*que* rogo*que*:
i mecum patrios*que* deos arsura*que* saltem
tecta uide, fratrem*que* . . .

Rhetorical repetition is naturally employed by Statius in conjunction with other stylistic devices to create this sense of power and emphasis in the speeches of his characters. An excellent example occurs in the combat exhortation of Tydeus to the Argives (3.348-65). The exclamatory tone of the speech, terse fragmented syntax, *adiectiones* and anaphorae (*arma*, 348, 350; *iuuat*, 354, 355; *bello*, 355; *nunc*, 360; *dum*, 362), the simple or near repetition of final verse syllables (349-53), and the echoing of similar sounds within the same (*-em*, *-am*, 356) or successive lines (*-que*, *-quiquam*, 358f.) combine to create a sense of urgency to the situation and to stress the force of his words.

Rhetorical Question

Certainly one of the most common figures of thought is the *interrogatio*, or rhetorical question. It receives a comprehensive treatment from Quintilian (*Inst.* 9.2.6-16; cf. Aq. Roman. *De Fig.* Halm 25.26-26.2, *Rhet. Her.* 4.25.22), no doubt because of its popularity. The purpose of the figure is to create a stylistic effect and add emphasis to a point the speaker is making in his argument. Its use is a matter of some importance in the *Thebaid*, since it features heavily in the speeches. The discussion here will be devoted mainly to some general observations by Quintilian and some examples from the *Thebaid* illustrating their use.

Quintilian observes that the *interrogatio* stresses the point of the speaker (*Inst.* 9.2.7) and draws to the attention of everyone what cannot be rightly denied (8). The rhetorical question can make a reply difficult to produce on the part of the adversary (8f.); incite odium in the audience for the opponent (9); excite pity (9); embarrass the opposition and incapacitate him so that he is unable to engage in deception (9); serve as a means for the expression of indignation (10), admiration (10), a command (11) or a deliberative conception (11f.); further dissimulation where required (14); and produce a pleasing effect when the question is answered immediately by the speaker (14). Quintilian notes that there are other uses of this figure, but does not attempt to treat them (16).

Statius uses the rhetorical question in the *Thebaid* primarily to emphasise the speaker's point. The effect of the figure is stylistic and emphatic; by the use of the *interrogatio*, the speaker intends to make a deeper impression on the auditor than he could by making a direct statement. This type of question is not designed to induce a reply directly but to impress upon the mind of the hearer that there is only one possible, obvious answer. Statius often uses the rhetorical question to express the indignation of a speaker (cf. Quint. *Inst.* 9.2.10). The frequent succession of rhetorical questions in *oratio recta* in the *Thebaid* often conveys the impression of violent, spontaneous emotion and is instrumental in creating the declamatory tone that characterises many of the speeches. The use of the *interrogatio* is a common means of exciting pity (cf. Quint. *Inst.* 9.2.9), particularly in apostrophes and speeches of mourning and consolation.

There is one rhetorical question to every 7.8 lines of speech, or on average 1.7 per speech.[18] The frequency of rhetorical questions in many of the speech passages gives them a marked rhetorical bent. According to Clarke, there are between two and three rhetorical questions to every one hundred lines of speech in the *Iliad*, while he estimates there are between nine and ten in the *Aeneid*.[19] He provides no evidence to sustain his figures, so they are not worth much. But he is probably right in suggesting that the use of the figure *interrogatio* in epic increases in line with the greater rhetorical propensities of the late Republic and early Empire.[20]

---

[18] There are over five hundred questions in the *Thebaid* (519); for the statistical breakdown see stat. app. 12, table 26. Ninety-eight per cent of these questions are rhetorical (507). Eighty-seven per cent of rhetorical questions are spoken (442); see stat. app. 12, table 27 for a list of rhetorical questions in speeches; for a similar list of rhetorical questions in (non-speech) narrative, see stat. app. 12, table 28.

All of the direct questions in the epic occur in speeches. A direct or simple question is designed to elicit information (cf. Quint. *Inst.* 9.2.6f.), as in *Theb.* 1.443f. where Adrastus asks Polynices and Tydeus, *sed prodite tandem / unde orti, quo fertis iter, quae iurgia?* While there are twelve such questions actually spoken by various characters, no direct questions appear in the (non-speech) narrative of the *Thebaid*. See stat. app. 12, table 29 for a list of the direct questions in the speeches.

[19] Clarke (1949: 24).

[20] Clarke (1949: 24f.).

There are many speech passages in the *Thebaid* where a succession of rhetorical questions gives a marked rhetorical effect. The speeches that contain an abundance of rhetorical questions are generally laments or impassioned deliberations.[21] The series of mostly brief *interrogationes* in the deliberative speech of Amphiaraus (3.620-47) betrays the anxiety of the Argive priest over the mad rush of his compatriots to war (629-35):

> quo, miseri, fatis superisque obstantibus arma,
> quo rapitis? quae uos Furiarum uerbera caecos
> exagitant? adeone animarum taedet? et Argos
> exosi? nil dulce domi? nulla omina curae?
> quid me Persei secreta ad culmina montis
> ire gradu trepido superumque inrumpere coetus
> egistis?

Successive rhetorical questions combine with an emotionally charged proemial exclamation (*ei mihi*, 3.6) and the interposing narrative (7f.) to reveal the anxiety of Eteocles over the failure of his troops to return from their mission against Tydeus (6-12):

> 'ei mihi' . . .
> 'unde morae?' (nam prona ratus facilemque tot armis
> Tydea, nec numero uirtutem animumque rependit)
> 'num regio diuersa uiae? num missus ab Argis
> subsidio globus? an sceleris data fama per urbes
> finitimas? paucosne, pater Gradiue, manuue
> legimus indecores?'

Rhetorical questions are sometimes used in the *Thebaid* to arouse sympathy (cf. Quint. *Inst.* 9.2.9). In a prayer to Mars, Hippomedon employs a series of independent clauses consisting of rhetorical questions and an exclamation (9.506-10):

---

[21] Some of the more notable speeches tinged with this rhetorical effect are made by the anonymous Theban (1.173-96), Venus (3.269-91), Amphiaraus (3.620-47), Polyxo (5.104-29, 132-42), Hypsipyle (5.608-35), Eurydice (6.138-83), Bacchus (7.144-92), Jocasta (7.497-527), Pluto (8.34-79), Argive troops (8.174-207), Polynices (9.49-76), Ismenis (9.376-98), Creon (10.690-718, 11.269-96), Menoeceus' mother (10.793-814), Jocasta (11.329-53), Oedipus (11.605-31, 677-707), Antigone (11.708-39) and Argia (12.322-48).

fluuione (pudet!), Mars inclyte, merges
hanc animam, segnesque lacus et stagna subibo
ceu pecoris custos, subiti torrentis iniquis
interceptus aquis? adeone occumbere ferro
non merui?

The rhetorical questions and interjectional exclamation, which convey the extent of Hippomedon's alarm over his inglorious fate through the excited and broken effect they create, help to elicit a sympathetic response from Juno to no avail (cf. 510ff.).

An illustration of the use of a string of rhetorical questions to arouse sympathy occurs when Venus poses a series of these questions to Mars stressing the injustice of his intended action of arousing the Argives to war against Thebes (3.269-91, esp. 269-74; my emphasis):

bella etiam in Thebas, socer o pulcherrime, *bella*
ipse paras ferroque tuos abolere nepotes?
nec genus Harmoniae *nec* te conubia caelo
festa *nec hae* quicquam lacrimae, furibundae, morantur?
criminis *haec* merces? *hoc* fama pudorque relictus,
hoc mihi Lemniacae de te meruere catenae?

As can be seen from these passages, rhetorical questions rarely appear in isolation from other rhetorical devices in the speeches.[22] Here the effect of the *interrogationes* drawing attention to the anxious concern of Venus over the plight of Thebes is heightened through the repetition of *bella* and *nec*, polyptoton of *hic*, and litotes of *at non*. Subsequent rhetorical questions (282f., 288-90), exclamations (275f., 286), aposiopeses (280, 291) and the repetition of *solum* (281) further emphasise the solicitude of the goddess.

Exclamation and Apostrophe

The exclamation is a figure of thought whose function is to excite the auditor or reader through the simulation of anger, happiness, fear, admiration, amazement, grief, indignation, a wish or some other emotion (Quint.

---

[22] On the use of the rhetorical question with various stylistic devices, see below, pp. 264ff.

Inst. 9.2.27).[23] This forceful figure is commonplace in the speeches of the *Thebaid*. A few examples will suffice to illustrate its use. The parenthetic exclamation in the speech of the anonymous Theban (*Theb.* 1.173-96) emphasises the intensity of his indignation over the insufferable destiny of his compatriots (195f.):

> heu dubio suspensa metu tolerandaque nullis
> aspera sors populis!

In the speech of Amphiaraus to Pluto the simple exclamatory ethical dative is particularly effective in portraying the extent of the deceased priest's despair (8.111f.):

> ei mihi! nil ex me sociis patriaeque relictum,
> uel captum Thebis.

Later in the same book the parenthetic exclamation of Hercules in his speech to Minerva reveals his contempt for any action contravening her wishes and those of Jupiter (504-06):

> citius me fulmina contra
> (infandum!) ruere et magno bellare parenti
> aspiciat.

A few lines later an exclamation reveals the intensity of Hercules' sense of duty to Minerva for the assistance she has brought him (512f.):

> ipsa (heu!) comes inuia mecum
> Tartara, ni superos Acheron excluderet, isses.

Exclamatory sentences in the consolatory speech of Aletes to the Thebans (3.179-213) show that Aletes has suddenly become inflamed with passion (210-13; my emphasis):

> *quantus* equis *quantus*que uiris in puluere crasso
> sudor! io *quanti* crudele rubebitis amnes!

---

[23] See Marouzeau (1954: 214f.) for uses of this figure in Roman literature.

uiderit haec bello uiridis manus: ast ego doner
dum licet igne meo terraque insternar auita!

The repetition of the exclamatory adjective *quantus* further stresses his indignation over the unmerited suffering that the innocent citizenry will endure on account of their perverse monarch.

Closely related to the exclamation is the figure of apostrophe, which is a digression in a speech where the speaker turns away to address a specific individual who is absent (*Inst.* 9.2.38; cf. 9.3.24-26).[24] The appellation is also applied to a situation in which a statement diverts the auditor from the matter under examination (9.2.39). The apostrophe, like the exclamation, is associated with the expression of deep conviction and sincere emotion (unless deception is the main aim of the speaker, as in Jupiter's apostrophe of Oedipus during his Olympian address, *Theb.* 1.239-41), but it has a more specific utility than the exclamation; this is because the apostrophe is almost always directed in a relatively coherent manner toward a particular individual or object, whereas the exclamation is generally a spontaneous and direction-less form of emotional expression. This figure is employed commonly in the epic narrative of Statius, less often in the speeches of his characters.[25] A sole illustration of its use with the exclamation in the speeches occurs in Tydeus' apostrophising of Melanippus (8.739-41):

---

[24] *Rhetorica ad Herennium* does not distinguish between the figures of exclamation and apostrophe; they are discussed under the heading *exclamatio* (4.15.22).

[25] Apostrophes in the speeches of the *Thebaid* include 1.178-80, 1.222f., 1.239-241, 1.582-86, 1.596-99, 1.624-26, 2.460f., 3.211, 3.379-81, 3.513, 3.607f., 3.637-40, 4.514-16, 5.628, 5.628-30, 7.20, 7.282-87, 7.334f., 7.340f., 7.343-46, 7.355f., 7.370, 8.588f., 8.739-41, 9.22, 11.605f., 11.607, 12.561, 12.562, 12.593f. Watkiss (1966: 309) claims that there are fifty-six apostrophes in the *Thebaid*, of which forty-three are those of the poet (*q. v.* Watkiss [1966: 488 n. 2]). For a complete catalogue of the apostrophes in the epic, see Hampel (1908: 48-50). On Statius' use of apostrophe, see Hampel (1908: 48-51), Fortgens (1934: *ad* 6.141, 144ff.), Mulder (1954: 193f. *ad* 2.266), Snijder (1968: 72 *ad* 3.64, 83 *ad* 3.99), Watkiss (1966: 308-21) and Williams (1972: 91 *ad* 10.498). Hampel (1908: 51) estimates that there is one apostrophe in every 111 lines in Statian epic. According to Hampel (1908: 41, 51), there is one apostrophe in every 180 verses in Vergil's *Aeneid* and *Georgics*, one per 120 lines in Ovid's *Metamorphoses*, one apostrophe per fifty-six lines in Lucan, one in every 108 verses in Silius Italicus, and one per ninety-three lines in Valerius Flaccus.

caput, o caput, o mihi si quis
apportet, Melanippe, tuum! nam uolueris aruis,
fido equidem, nec me uirtus suprema fefellit.

Simile and Metaphor

Under the terms of the definition given at the beginning of this chapter, figures suggesting a comparison between two objects are tropes; hence simile and metaphor are perhaps the most obvious tropes, although Quintilian does not include the former in his list.[26] Quintilian observes that the simile is useful in helping to prove an argument and in making an illustration more vivid (*Inst.* 8.3.72; cf. *Rhet. Her.* 4.45.59). A simile more specifically involves a comparison between two essentially dissimilar objects on the basis of a similarity in one or more aspects (*Rhet. Her.* 4.45.59). When the resemblances between the objects compared are exact, the simile is known more precisely as *redditio contraria* or ἀνταπόδοσις (Quint. *Inst.* 8.3.77-81). Although the simile is a common trope in the *Thebaid*,[27] it far more often appears in the narrative than in the speeches, where it is used commonly to stress the theme and enhance the mood of particular scenes.[28] The simile in the narrative speech of Hypsipyle is an example of ἀνταπόδοσις (*Theb.* 5.231-35). Here Hypsipyle likens the action of Lycaste who is forced by her mother to slay her brother Cydimus to a tamed wild beast who hesitates to assume its native disposition despite being goaded and beaten.

A metaphor differs essentially from a simile in that it merges into one the two objects being compared.[29] Quintilian defines metaphor as the

---

[26] Quintilian discusses four different types of similes in a group distinct from tropes, thought and speech (*Inst.* 9.3.75f.).

[27] The number of similes that critics record in the *Thebaid* ranges from 179 to 210. Watkiss (1966: 228) cites the figure of 179 (cf. Watkiss 1966: 482 n. 2); Holland (1973: 49) counts 191; Williams (1972: 37 *ad* 10.13f.) mentions 193; Legras (1905: 295) asserts that there are 195 (193 excluding the spurious lines 6.229-33, 719-21; cf. Burck 1979: 347); and Obrycki (1975: 353) says there are 'okolo 210'.

[28] The Statian simile generally plays a valuable rôle in embellishing the narrative and in serving as a significant comment upon the dramatic situation. *Contra* Butler (1909: 225 n. 1), Steele (1918: 91), Summers (1920: 34f.); cf. Dimsdale (1915: 462).

[29] On metaphor see Quint. *Inst.* 8.6.4-18, Cic. *De Orat.* 3.38.155-70, *Orat.* 24.81f., 27.92-94, 60.201f. and Demetr. *Eloc.* 78-89.

transference of a noun or verb from the place where it belongs to another where an appropriate word is lacking or the transferred word is preferable (*Inst.* 8.6.5). The metaphor is used for purposes of necessity, clarification, ornamentation and the elicitation of emotions (8.6.6, 19).[30] Quintilian's conception of metaphor is much narrower than the contemporary understanding of this trope. Today the understanding of metaphor involves not merely the simple substitution of one word for another but extends to the comparison between two unlike objects by identification, the substitution of one for the other, or the ascription of one or more qualities of one object to the other. Nevertheless, Quintilian's limitative conception of metaphor does not prevent him from recognising its effect as being pleasant and elegant, since he regards the metaphor as easily the most commanding and beautiful of tropes (8.6.4f.). He points out further that it adds to the copiousness of language by interchanging and borrowing words and providing an appellation for every object and occurrence (8.6.5). In Statius' *Thebaid* the phrase *puppemque insana flagellat arbor* (*Theb.* 5.373f.) is an excellent example of Quintilian's fourth type of metaphor in which an abstract or inanimate object is invested with animate qualities (cf. Quint. *Inst.* 8.6.11).[31]

Synecdoche, Metonymy and Antonomasia

The closely related tropes of synecdoche, metonymy and antonomasia are used by Statius with great effect in the speeches. Synecdoche is the representation of a whole object by one of its parts. According to Quintilian, this trope affords variety to language by our perception of many objects from a single entity, the substitution of the whole for one of its parts, the species for the genus, the cause for the effect, or the reverse (*Inst.* 8.6.19; cf. Cic. *De Orat.* 3.42.168, *Rhet. Her.* 4.44f.). Quintilian observes that the use of synecdoche is more common among the poets than the rhetoricians (*Inst.* 8.6.19f.). On the whole Quintilian's discussion of this trope is rather unsatisfactory because he limits its function to variety. In his treatment he does not consider that in order for synecdoche to be effective the part representing the whole must be significant and directly relevant to the topic

---

[30] See Marouzeau (1954: 147-52) on the use of this trope in Roman literature.

[31] On Statius' use of metaphor, see Wilson (1898) and Watkiss (1966: 274-92).

under discussion. Examples from the speeches in the *Thebaid* are *limina* for *domus* (3.609) and *auro* for *casside aurata* (708).[32]

Quintilian notes that metonymy is closely related to synecdoche and describes the former as the substitution of a word or name for another closely related term (*Inst.* 8.6.23; cf. *De Orat.* 27.92-94). The trope was commonly used by rhetoricians and by advocates in the courts, but the poets used the figure still more liberally (cf. *Inst.* 8.6.24f.). Quintilian adduces examples of different types of metonymy, but a sole example from the *Thebaid* of the type that signifies one entity for another is *post manes* (10.351) for *post mortem* in the speech of Hopleus to Dymas.[33]

Antonomasia is the opposite of metonymy and a close relative of synecdoche. The trope is the substitution of an epithet or a description of the most prominent characteristics of an individual (Quint. *Inst.* 8.6.29). Its use was rare among the orators but was a regular feature of the poets (8.6.29f.). Examples of antonomasia from the speeches in the *Thebaid* are Aletes' reference to Niobe as *impia Tantalis* (3.192f.) and the reference by Ornytus to the Sirens as *Sicilos deos* (12.156f.).[34]

Periphrastic Expression

Periphrasis, closely connected to the aforementioned tropes of synecdoche, metonymy and antonomasia, involves the use of a number of words where one or few would suffice equally as well in conveying the meaning (Quint. *Inst.* 8.6.59; cf. *Rhet. Her.* 4.32.43, Beda *De Trop.* Halm 614.1-8). Although the trope does have a practical use in avoiding the indecorous point, its main purpose is ornamental (*Inst.* 8.6.59f.). Quintilian observes that periphrasis appears frequently in poetry and oratory, although with greater restraint in the latter discipline (61). Although he considers the use of periphrasis to be solely ornamental, the trope is an effective device when used with restraint and for the specific end of clarifying a meaning or the immediate context. Periphrasis can also aid in achieving an elevated style but when used to an excessive degree can become bombastic in its effect.

---

[32] See Lunderstedt (1913) and Watkiss (1966: 293ff.) on the use of synecdoche by Statius.

[33] See Watkiss (1966: 293ff.) on Statius' use of metonymy in the *Thebaid*.

[34] On the use of antonomasia by Statius, see Watkiss (1966: 296-98).

When this happens it is known as περισσολογία and becomes a stylistic impediment (61). An example of periphrasis in the *Thebaid* occurs when Adrastus describes the deaths of Argos' inhabitants in this pleonastic manner (1.632f.):[35]

> labuntur dulces animae, Mors fila Sororum
> ense metit captamque tenens fert manibus urbem.

Rhetorical Exaggeration

Hyperbole is one of the most popular tropes of Statius, for it abundantly suits his extravagant style. Quintilian defines this trope as *decens ueri superiectio* (*Inst.* 8.6.67). Hyperbole can be employed for conscious exaggeration or diminution in several different ways (68). The poet or can express more or less than the actual facts warrant; elevate or attenuate his theme by the employment of a simile, comparison, indication or metaphor; and even heighten the effect by adding another hyperbole (8.6.67-70, 73; cf. Cic. *De Orat.* 3.53, Beda *De Trop.* Halm 615.27-30). Quintilian cautions against the excessive use of this trope but notes despairingly that a lack of discretion in its employment has already led to numerous faults in style (*Inst.* 8.6.73f.). The exaggeration of facts must not be taken to an extreme or the presentation will lack credibility (74). Hyperbole is an effective device in raising laughter, if that is what is intended; if not, the poet will only make himself appear fatuous (74f.). The trope is a virtue when the topic is unnatural, for amplification is effective when the language matches or surpasses the exceptional circumstances of the subject (76). The real value of the trope lies in the transference of real or imagined emotion inherent in the situation to the auditor or reader. Hyperbole is *de rigeur* in Statian speeches. A simple illustration of this trope occurs in Aletes' speech of consolation to the Thebans when he refers to Niobe as being *innumeris . . . circumfusa ruinis* (*Theb.* 3.193).

---

[35] Statius' use of periphrasis prompts Curtius (1953: 276) to make the laughable assertion that 'the abuse of periphrase *begins* with Statius' (my emphasis) and to cite *Theb.* 10.841f. as alleged evidence of this abuse: *innumerosque gradus gemina latus arbore clusos, / aerium sibi portat iter. . . .*

Emphasis is treated by Quintilian in his sections on tropes and figures (*Inst.* 8.3.83-86, 9.2.3, 9.2.64). The trope reveals a deeper meaning than what is actually revealed in a literal sense by the language. According to Quintilian, there are two types of emphasis: one has more meaning than what it expresses (9.2.3) and corresponds to the modern usage of the figure that is achieved by hyperbole; the other kind means something that it does not actually express and involves the intentional omission of a key word or phrase (64).[36] Emphasis is a figure of thought when the concern is not purely verbal or semantic but extends to the poet's treatment of a broader issue or theme. Emphasis is more striking as a figure of thought because the implied comparison or contrast is less specific than when it functions as a trope. A sole example of Statius' tropical use of emphasis to indicate more than what is actually said is Hypsipyle's description of the Lemnian women slaying their husbands (*Theb.* 5.202): *inuasere nefas.*

Verbal Irony

Quintilian considers irony to be both a trope and a figure of thought. In irony the literal meaning of the words is the opposite of what the speaker actually intends to convey. If this verbal conflict is brief, then the irony is a trope. But if the speaker constructs a passage in which the appearance belies the reality of the circumstances, then the attendant irony is a figure of thought (cf. *Inst.* 9.1.3, 9.2.44-46; Aq. Roman. *De Fig.* Halm 24.21-24) and is closely related to emphasis.[37] In either case the poet intends for the reader to discern the hidden intent beneath the literal meaning. An example of verbal irony as a trope occurs in the *Thebaid* when Venus addresses Mars as *socer o pulcherrime* (3.269).

---

[36] For an extensive treatment of this figure, see *Rhet. Her.* 4.53.67, where the author gives examples being effected by *exsuperatio, ambiguum, consequentia, abscisio* and *similitudo.*

[37] On different types of irony, see Quint. *Inst.* 9.2.47-51 and Jul. Rufin. *De Fig.* 1-7 Halm 38.3-40.18.

Antithetic Expression

Antithesis is perhaps the figure most frequently employed by the postclassical poets. Quintilian is unsure whether to regard it as a figure of thought or a figure of speech. But he attempts to draw the distinction in terms of universals and particulars. Antithesis is more a figure of speech when it involves the contrasting relation between words and clauses and their suggestive meanings; when the figure admits the consideration of a sentential idea or general theme, it is closer to a figure of thought (*Inst.* 9.2.101).[38] In either case the careful counterpoising of one expression against another for emphasis and piquancy is central to the figure's function, as in the scene Thiodamas addresses the Argives as they prepare to attack the Thebans who lay sleeping in their camp (*Theb.* 10.270f.; my emphasis):

> Argolicas *hi*ne ausi obsidere portas,
> *hi* seruare *uiros*?

Antithesis is also apparent in the consolatory speech of Aletes to the Thebans (3.206f.; italics mine):

> nunc *regis iniqui*
> ob noxam *inmeritos* patriae tot culmina *ciues*
> exuimus . . .

Ellipsis and Aposiopesis

Quintilian observes that ellipsis is sometimes mistaken for aposiopesis (*Inst.* 9.3.60). Ellipsis is a common figure of speech among the poets and rhetoricians.[39] The figure occurs when the word omitted is easily inferred from the context (9.3.58; cf. *Rhet. Her.* 4.30.41, 4.54.67). This omission

---

[38] Quintilian discusses antithesis as a figure of thought in *Inst.* 9.2.110f. and as a figure of speech in 9.3.81f. Other references to antithesis occur in *Rhet. Her.* 4.45.58, Cic. *Orat.* 39.135, Jul. Rufin. *De Fig.* 37 Halm 47.16-26, *De Schem. Lex.* 13 Halm 51.9-15, Demetr. *Eloc.* 22-26, 171f., 247, 250.

[39] On ellipsis see Marouzeau (1954: 216f.).

of a word vital to the correct grammatical structure of a sentence emphasises the statement by virtue of the condensed effect. A sole illustration of this figure occurs in the speech of Amphiaraus to the Argives where there is the frequent omission of the copulative verb in a series of rhetorical questions (*Theb.* 3.629-35).[40]

Statius often uses the closely related figure of aposiopesis in the speeches.[41] The figure is used to show strong emotion or anger, to give the appearance of anxiety or scrupulousness, or as a means of transition (Quint. *Inst.* 9.2.54f.). This is done by the conscious failure to complete a sentence, as in the aforementioned speech of Amphiaraus when he breaks off suddenly in resignation from his plea to the Argives to refrain from war (*Theb.* 3.646f.):

> sed quid uana cano, quid fixos arceo casus?
> ibimus—

Later the preponderance of abrupt interruptions in the priest's speech to Pluto betrays his distressed state (8.94, 96, 105f., 108).

Another instance occurs when Hercules breaks off from his intended statement of support for Haemon in order to reassure Minerva that he will withdraw his support for the youth since the goddess aids his foe Tydeus (8.506f.):

> genus huic—sed mitto agnoscere, quando
> tu diuersa foues . . .

The aposiopesis heightens the effect of Hercules' anxiety.

Personification and Deification

Prosopopoeia is either a figure or a trope, although the distinction is not always easy to make. Generally when the device involves the endowment of inanimate objects with human qualities it more closely approaches

---

[40] See above, p. 252 for these verses.

[41] E.g., 1.460, 3.87, 3.280, 3.291, 4.517f., 8.60, 8.506, 10.729, 12.301. On Statius' use of aposiopesis, see Williams (1972: 113f. *ad* 10.688).

a figure. Additionally the use of the figure involves the investiture of certain concepts and abstractions with human shape, character and feelings in order to achieve a particular effect and purpose (cf. Quint. *Inst.* 9.2.29-37, Cic. *De Orat.* 3.53.205).[42] Statius often uses personified and deified abstracts for thematic purposes in his epic narrative, less frequently in the speeches.[43] A sole illustration of this purpose in the narrative speech of Hypsipyle occurs in the description of the displacement of the deified abstractions Amores (*Theb.* 5.70) and Hymen (71) with Odia (73), Furor (74) and Discordia (74); the investiture of these forces with supernatural sensibilities reinforces the impression conveyed in the main narrative of the pervasive hostility of the higher powers toward humanity.

Metrical Structure and Verse Rhythm

The manipulation of the metre is one of the important poetic devices that Statius uses to create special effects in the speeches; this variation in the pace of the metre contributes substantially to their tone and atmosphere.[44] Verse with a predominance of spondees naturally conveys an atmosphere of stateliness, impressiveness, solemnity and majesty or a sense of sluggishness, listlessness and inertia (cf. Quint. *Inst.* 9.4.42, 87f., 91), depending on the narrative context of the speech. An illustration of the poetic utility of the spondaic line to illustrate the former sense occurs in the solemn invocation of Thiodamas to the Earth (*Theb.* 8.303):

. . . o hōmī|nūm dī|uūmque aē|tērnă crĕ|ātrĭx.

The heavy spondaic pattern of the opening line immediately attests to the sombre and sacred atmosphere of the prayer.

---

[42] See Volkmann (1885: 280, 312) and Marouzeau (1954: 209) for uses of this figure in classical literature.

[43] For discussions on Statius' use of personification, see Fortgens (1934: *ad* 6.27), Lewis (1936: 49-55), Schetter (1960: 27f.), Snijder (1968: 90), Williams (1972: 106f. *ad* 10.633) and Burgess (1978: 137-43).

[44] On Statius' usage of metre in the *Thebaid*, see Müller (1861), Moerner (1890), Schubert (1913), Brass (1923) and Watkiss (1966: 374-88). For analyses of metrical structure and verse rhythm in classical literature, see Marouzeau (1954: 301-21) and Wilkinson (1963: 89-134).

Just as a succession of spondees slows the tempo of a speech, so a series of dactyls increases the verbal pace and creates an impression of speed, haste and quickness or a sense of panic, urgency and consternation (cf. Quint. *Inst.* 9.4.91f.). The opening verses of Creon's speech to Eteocles demonstrates the usefulness of the dactylic pattern to convey the latter sense (11.269-72):

'ĭbĭs', ă|ĭt, 'nĕqŭe | te ūltĕrĭ|ūs frāt|rēmqŭe dŭ|cēmqŭe,
pēssĭmĕ, | fūnĕrĭ|būs pătrĭ|āe lăcrĭ|mīsqŭe pŏ|tēntĕm,
Eūmĕnĭ|dūm bēl|līqŭe rĕ|ūm, pătĭ|ēmŭr ĭ|nūltĭ.
sāt tŭă | nōn aē|quīs lŭĭ|mūs pĕr|iūrĭă | dĭuīs.'

Dactyls predominate in these lines, as they do throughout the speech of Creon. The rapid succession of dactyls and the resultant heterodyne effect reinforce the sense of Creon's alarm and desperation over the possibility that Eteocles might not accept the challenge of his brother to meet in single combat. There are only six spondees in these first four lines and only forty-four in the entire speech of almost twenty-eight lines (269-96).[45]

Blending the Elements

A stylistic device rarely produces a special effect on its own. On almost every occasion poetic and rhetorical elements join to create a particular effect suited to the narrative context of the speech. The speech passages presented in this section for examination are just a few of the many in the *Thebaid* that could be cited as evidence of this combinative phenomenon.

The rhetorical elements of style in the brief *cohortatio* of Thiodamas reinforce the impression conveyed by the content of his moral depravation. As the Argive troops prepare to massacre the dormant Thebans, the priest exhorts them (10.269-71; my italics):

cernitis expositas turpi marcore cohortes?
pro pudor! Argolicas hinc ausi obsidere portas,
hi seruare uiros?

---

[45] Cf. Watkiss (1966: 376).

The stylistic devices—rhetorical questions, exclamation, repetition of *hi*, antithesis of *hi* and *uiros*, short syntactic units of expression, the staccato effect produced by the repetition of the voiced liquid *r*, and alliteration of the double consonant *x* and dental spirant *s* suggesting his contempt for the dormant Thebans—are particularly effective in portraying the frenzied emotional state of Thiodamas.

Later in the same book Creon attempts to dissuade his Menoeceus from returning to Thebes to meet his fate and exhorts his son to return to battle (690-718). The most notable feature of this speech is its pathetic sense of importunity, which is enhanced by the anaphorae of *cur* (692), *ne* (696; cf. 703, 708) and *i* (713f.), polyptoton of *quis* (690f.) and *ille* (702f.), close repetition of the enclitic *-que* (694f., 712; cf. 704, 709, 714, 717, 718 [narr.]), antithesis of *hic* and *ibi* (711), and the varied, disjointed sentence structure (esp. in 691-96, 703-08, 711-15).

The elements of style in the dissembling speech of Polynices to the Argives (3.367-81) are extremely effective in arousing the anger and pity of the men. Various devices exert a powerful ethical and emotional appeal and are instrumental in persuading the Argives of the righteousness of his cause. These include the frequent assonance of the vowel *i* in the opening lines (3.367-69), repetition of words similar in sound at the same juncture in successive lines (*mihi* and *mei*, 369f.) and within the same line (*me* and *mei*, 370), anaphorae of *quam* (375f.) and *hunc* (379f.), repetition of *nec* (373f.) and *tibi* (380), partial likeness of the phrases *nec me* (374) and *non me* (376), frequent repetition of the suffixal vowels *-o* (367f., 370, 374f., 377-79, 382) and *-i* (369-71, 373, 375, 378, 380), apostrophe (*germane, tibi*, 380), *extenuatio* (374-76; cf. Quint. *Inst.* 9.1.28, 9.2.3), parenthesis (374), exclamations (367-70) and rhetorical question (369).

In a later speech of the exiled prince a profusion of rhetorical elements combine to betray his violent emotions and guilt over the woe he has brought to Argos (11.155-92). The jagged and uneven expression (esp. 165-70, 188-92), parentheses and aposiopeses (11.165-69, 188-92), anaphorae of *non si* (170f.) and *uidi* (175f.), anastrophe of *me propter* (175), repetition of *nec* (179f.), exclamations (166, 187) and rhetorical questions (168, 173f., 182, 185) are particularly striking.

The deliberations of Jocasta are remarkable for their use of stylistic devices and striking effects. In an attempt to avert war she makes two impassioned appeals to her sons (7.497-527, 11.329-53). The opening lines of her speech to Polynices clearly reflect the extent of her grief and anger over his bellicose intentions (7.497-504; my italics):

> *quid* molle*s* la*c*rima*s* *u*ene*r*anda*que* nom*i*na fing*is*,
> *r*ex A*r*gi*u*e, m*i*h*i*? *quid* colla am*p*le*x*ibus amb*is*
> *i*n*u*isam*que* te*r*is fe*r*rato *p*ecto*r*e mat*r*em?
> t*u*ne *i*lle e*x*ilio *u*ag*u*s et m*i*se*r*ab*i*lis ho*sp*e*s*?
> quem non *p*e*r*mo*u*e*as*? longae t*u*a i*u*ssa coho*r*t*es*
> e*x*pectant, m*u*lto*que* lat*u*s *p*raefulgurat en*se*.
> *a* mise*r*ae mat*r*es! hunc te nocte*sque* die*sque*
> deflebam?

Harsh single and double consonants—*s*, *ss*, *x*, *r* and *p*—convey an impression of Jocasta's anger, as do the abrupt -*a* and -*e* (or enclitic -*que*) suffixes. The slight rhyme of the long and short *i* and *u* and the alliteration of the semivowels *i* and *u* are particularly effective in giving expression to the wailing accompanying her speech. The exclamation *a miserae matres!* emphasises the affliction and suffering of all mothers who lose their sons in war, while the profusion of rhetorical questions, anaphora of *quid*, and repetition of the suffixes -*is* and -*es* (assonance) at the end of the lines further enhance the passionate and plaintive effect produced by the careful combination of sounds in this passage. Later rhetorical questions (508, 511f., 523f.), exclamations (515, 521f.), parentheses (508, 514f., 522f.), anaphora of *aut* (510), the echoing of the enclitic particle -*ne* in the same line (511), and the repetition of the enclitic conjunction -*que* (esp. 520f.) emphasise her anguish.

Perhaps the single most conspicuous stylistic feature of the entire speech is the frequent repetition of identical or similar sounds in or nearly in the same metrical position in consecutive or near-successive lines. The enclitic -*que* just mentioned appears seventeen times in the entire passage, ten times in lines 502-08, and is placed at virtually the same point of the fifth foot in lines 503-07. The suffix -*es* occurs at the close of six out of eight verses in lines 510-17, on three occasions preceded by an adjective containing the suffix -*e*. Furthermore, the suffix -*um* in the final word of line 504 is repeated at the same point in the succeeding verse, while the concluding syllable -*em* in line 507 is repeated at the end of the next line. The resultant sound effects seem intentional and are evidence of Statius' consummate skill in versification.

Later Jocasta approaches Eteocles and makes a final, desperate plea in a vain attempt to avert his impending duel with Polynices (11.329-53). The intensity of her violent emotional outburst is even greater than in her earlier appeal to Polynices (7.497-527) and is reflected especially in the rhetorical questions and exclamations that predominate in the opening section of the speech (329-38). The brusque and uneven expression produces a spasmodic and excited effect that faithfully reflects the extent of her emotional distress.

Argia's lament over the corpse of Polynices contains a preponderance of stylistic elements (12.322-48). Her vituperation of the despotic Eteocles is especially virulent and this is reflected in the variety of rhetorical and poetic devices that dominate this section of her lament (340-43; emphasis mine):

> ei mihi, sed quanto descendit uulnus hiatu!
> hoc frater? qua parte, precor, iacet ille nefandus
> praedator? uincam uolucres (sit adire potestas)
> excludamque feras; an habet funestus et ignes?

Abrupt exclamations and rhetorical questions, adversative conjunctions and a parenthetic insertion are particularly effective in portraying the intensity of Argia's contempt and hatred for Eteocles. The frequency of the dental fricative s, guttural mute c and q, and labial mute p accentuates this attitude of hostility, while the assonance of the vowels i and u and alliteration of the semivowels i and u suggest the wailing accompanying her lament. Simple repetition or echoing of certain syllabic and suffixal sounds—some in or nearly in the same metrical position—in successive lines further emphasises Argia's enmity toward Eteocles:

quanto (340),	uulnus (340),	frater (341),
qua (341)	nefandus (341),	precor (341),
	funestus (343)	praedator (342)
uolucres (342),	uincam (342),	potestas (342),
ignes (343)	excludamque (343)	feras (343)

The final section of the lament continues with this pattern of verbal repetition (344-48; my emphasis):

> sed nec te flammis inopem tua terra uidebit:
> ardebis lacrimasque feres quas ferre negatum
> regibus, aeternumque tuo famulata sepulcro

durab*it* deserta fides, testis*que* dol*orum*
natus er*it*, paru*oque* t*orum* Polynice foueb*o*.

Again this duplication or echoing of identical or similar sounds in or nearly in the same metrical position in successive or near-consecutive lines—

arde*bis* (345),	lacrimas*que* (345)	durab*it* (347)
regi*bus* (346)	aeternum*que* (346)	natus er*it* (348)
	testis*que* (347)	
dol*orum* (347)	paru*oque* (348)	
t*orum* (348)	aliam*que* (349)	

tu*o* . . . sepulcr*o* (346)
paru*oque* . . . foueb*o* (348)

—or even within the same line:

lacrimas*que feres quas ferre* (345)

—produces a skilful and vigorous effect. The internal harmony of these lines suggests that Argia has recovered her composure and sense of purpose toward the end of her lament. The further repetition of the enclitic *-que* in the narrative following the speech (349) has the effect of linking the speech more closely with the sorrowful context.

Rhetorical questions, exclamations and abbreviated syntax are often combined in the speeches to indicate deep emotion, thereby helping the speeches to stand out from the usually less intense narrative into which they are inserted. In the laments of Hypsipyle over Opheltes (5.608-35 [esp. 622-27], 6.138-73, 174-76, 180-83), the preponderance of rhetorical questions, exclamations—particularly those that are parenthetical—and short disjunctive sentences greatly emphasise Hypsipyle's distress. The spontaneous nature of Hypsipyle's emotional outburst is shown in the spasmodic effect of her uneven expression.

Similarly the distress of Atlanta in her speech to Diana (9.608-35) is highlighted through the use of these same elements in her attempt to elicit the sympathy of the goddess for Parthenopaeus (627-30):

quid in nostris, nemoralis Delia, siluis
Maenades hostiles Thebanaque numina regnant?

ei mihi! cur penitus (simque augur cassa futuri!),
cur penitus magnoque interpretor omine quercum?

The effect of the two rhetorical questions (627f., 630), the exclamatory ethical dative (629), the parenthetic exclamation (629) and the jagged syntax furnishes the impression that Diana's passionate and despairing outburst of sympathetic concern for her son is spontaneous.

Rhetorical questions, exclamations and abbreviated syntax are frequently accompanied by rhetorical repetition, as in the apostrophes of Argia and Antigone and the deliberation of Evadne in the final book. These speeches are remarkable for their emotional violence, compact expression and rhetorical figures. In the apostrophe of Argia to Polynices (12.209-19), rhetorical repetition (esp. anaphorae: *an-*, 209, *an*, 211; *si*, 214, *heu si*, 216), rhetorical questions (209-11, 212f., 217f.), exclamations (211 [parenthetic], 216), and the jagged effect of the syntax are particularly effective in conveying her excited state and the magnitude of her misery. Similarly rhetorical questions (12.438f., 440f., 443f.), exclamations (439f., 442f.), rhetorical repetition (esp. anaphorae: *iam*, 443, 445; *hoc*, 445f.), and the staccato effect of the short clauses and sentences are the outstanding stylistic features in the apostrophe of Antigone to her brothers (437-46). When Evadne, wife of Capaneus, pleads with Theseus on behalf of the Argive women for assistance in burying their dead husbands (12.546-86), the rhetorical questions (550f., 561f., 573), exclamations (550, 561), anaphorae of *ubi* (561f.), *si* (581) and *semper* (585), repetition of the enclitic *-que* (esp. 555-58, 560, 571f.) and pointed effect (esp. 555f., 561f., 573) combine to give an added sense of conviction, urgency and persuasive force to her speech.

Aposiopesis often appears with rhetorical questions, exclamations and rhetorical repetition to create a strongly emotional effect, as in the speeches of Amphiaraus and Bacchus. In the oracular and prophetic speech of Amphiaraus to the Argives (3.620-47), these elements are particularly effective in conveying the priest's emotional excitement, which finally gives way to a feeling of resignation at the end of his speech (643-46; italics mine):

proicite arma manu: deus ecce furentibus obstat,
ecce deus! miseri, *quid* pulchrum sanguine uicto
Aoniam et diri saturare noualia Cadmi?

> sed *quid* uana cano, *quid* fixos arceo casus?
> ibimus—

A pathetic effect is created in the deliberation of Bacchus to Jupiter (7.155-92) through the profusion of rhetorical questions (155-57, 161f., 164f., 172-74, 180f., 188), exclamations (175-77, 182) and aposiopeses (158f., 174, 183, 189).

Rhetorical questions and repetition are combined with other stylistic elements such as rhyme, alliteration and hyperbole to convey excitement, odium and anger, among other emotions. In Capaneus' taunt of the Thebans, the hero ridicules the size of Thebes' towers and refers scornfully to the mythical founding of the city (10.873-77):

> humilesne Amphionis arces,
> pro pudor, *hi* faciles, carmenque imbelle secut*i*,
> *hi*, mentita diu Thebarum fabula, mur*i*?
> et quid tam egregium prosternere moenia moll*i*
> structa lyra?

The rhetorical questions, exclamation, anaphora of *hi*, and rhyming of the final syllable are expressive of his excited state. The contempt of Capaneus for the gods is highlighted in his challenge of Jupiter (899-906) by a series of taunting rhetorical questions (899-903, 905f.), repetition of *nunc* (904), and harsh alliteration of the labial consonants at the beginning of words and within words (905f.). In the challenge of Tydeus to the Thebans (8.664-72), the force of his anger is effected through the profusion of rhetorical questions (664, 668f., 671f.), occasional exclamatory statements (667f., 670), rhetorical repetition, namely *adiectio* (*totidem*, 667) and anaphora (*nulline*, 668), and rhetorical exaggeration (esp. 667f.).

The passages cited in this chapter are only a few of the many instances that can be adduced to illustrate the masterly ability of Statius in using sounds, figures, rhyme, metre and other stylistic devices to create various poetic and rhetorical effects in the speeches. While his use of them is extensive, this does not mean automatically that rhetorical influence is inherent, for these elements of style are the common property of ancient poets and orators. But they are an important means of manipulating the tone of his material and in creating special effects, a process in itself often described as rhetorical. Since the frequent use of these stylistic devices by Statius is characteristic in the main of postclassical poets, it is not so much their appearance in the speeches that attracts our attention but rather his skilful use of them.

AFTERWORD

Statius has been considered to be more of a rhetorician than a poet with respect to the major design elements of his work as well as the rhetorical aspects of his speeches.[1] It is true that the *Thebaid* does operate in the rhetorical mode, but the poet shifts moods, as can be seen in the quiet moments that punctuate the narrative. There are those who have judged the *Thebaid* unfavourably mainly on the basis of its rhetorical qualities, as if the epic somehow loses its worth and meaning because of this rhetoricalness.[2] While Statius' vigorous style and heightened use of language may seem quite artificially rhetorical to modern critical sensibilities, it is important to realise that a learned and sophisticated audience in the first century CE, with their very fine-tuned sensibilities of rhetoric, would not have found the complex, ornate, paratactic expression unnatural or unappealing. Certainly rhetoric is an important organisational element in terms of form and style, but it is nonsensical to criticise the poem because of its strong presence. The rhetoric is functional as well as ornamental.

This study has attempted to show that Statius skilfully adapts the conventions of rhetoric and uses its resources in order to achieve his artistic aims, for it has been seen that even the violent and aggressive emotionalism of the speeches is turned to good effect and is entirely consistent with his thematic intentions. The poet is far more concerned with ideas and issues than rhetoric. In this regard the speeches function as an integral part of the *Thebaid*, since an understanding of the speeches is central to appreciating its major themes.

The natural affinity of Roman rhetoric and poetic and their mutual debt makes it difficult for the critic to determine generally whether particular speeches, figures, learned allusions and descriptions in Statian epic arise naturally out of dramatic circumstances or are the products of either an unconscious imitation of rhetoric or an intentional adaptation of poetic models. In the case of the speeches it is especially difficult to ascertain the

---

[1] E.g., Schanz (1913: 160).

[2] E.g., Schwabe (1892: 117), Daniels (1905: 12), Mozley (1928: x), Laidlaw (1951: 144), Mendell (1967: 127).

extent of their debt to rhetoric, since it has been shown that even when their forms are faithful to the rhetorical tradition this similarity does not preclude a significance germane to the dramatic circumstances and a meaning critical to the central thematics of the epic. Furthermore, although some of the speeches can be described as rhetorical on account of their grandiloquent and forceful expression and the similarity of their form with the structure and *topoi* of their rhetorical counterparts (e.g., speeches of mourning and consolation), even the prescriptions for some of these speech types are based on poetic *exempla*. The traditional form, constituent elements and phrasing of some of the speeches are rhetorical, but the relevance of these rhetorical-type speeches to the epic narrative shows that Statius did not compose them strictly according to the prescriptions of the handbooks; the structure, *topoi*, language and figures of the speeches are manipulated with equal purpose in order to achieve the desired artistic effects.

Although an attempt has been made in this study to trace the debt of Statius to the treatises of the rhetoricians in the composition of his epic speeches, the more important task has been to examine the manner in which Statius incorporates conventional elements of rhetoric into the speeches in order to achieve certain effects. Although it is not always easy to distinguish between those elements of the speeches that owe their origins to the rhetorical tradition and those aspects of their composition that are nonrhetorical, this study has demonstrated that rhetorical and nonrhetorical material form a natural and indispensable part of the poetic armoury of Statius; the skill, imagination, experience and intuition of the poet is evident in the way he uses these resources to meet the dramatic, thematic and tonal requirements of the epic narrative. There is a strong thematic relationship between the speeches and the narrative, since even those speeches that appear to be estranged from the rest of the text are seen upon closer analysis to be essential to the meaning of the epic.

Since the education and training of Statius prepared him for a career as a poet or an orator, the treatment of the speech passages in the *Thebaid* deserves special attention from the critic. The number, weighting and form of the speeches in the *Thebaid* immediately draws attention to their importance as an essential instrument of poetic craftsmanship. In a critical sense the speeches function to explore and clarify thematic issues, establish tone and mood, vary the level of emotional intensity in the narrative, emphasise the epic circumstances, vary the pace of the narrative, present and treat the causes of events, provide motivation for subsequent action, define personalities and present information. Ultimately the speeches serve to reveal the thoughts and feelings of the poet on the human condition. It is through a careful examination of their form, function and meaning that the contemporary critic attains a greater understanding and appreciation of the poet and his craft.

A CATALOGUE OF THE SPEECHES

These Statistical Appendices comprise thirty-one tables presenting evidence on individual speeches, including their classification; the speeches of the major and minor characters; disguised characters' speeches; collective and tandem speeches; gods, humans and objects of address; inserted speeches; monologues and speech clusters; speeches commencing, concluding or interrupted in midline by narrative; opening, interposing and closing formulas to speeches; potential speeches in true and virtual *oratio obliqua*; rhetorical and simple (direct) questions in speech and narrative; the speeches in the *Achilleid*; and the speeches in the *Silvae*.

Throughout the Statistical Appendices, the following abbreviations identify the different classes of speech:

Apo		Apostrophe
Cha		Challenge
Com		Command
Del		Deliberative Speech
Des		Descriptive Speech
Enc		Speech of Encouragement
	(Coh)	Combat Exhortation (*Cohortatio*)
	(Exh)	Noncombat Exhortation
For		Forensic Oration
Gre		Greeting
M&C		Speech of Mourning or Consolation
	(Lam)	Lament
	(Con)	Consolation
	(Epi)	*Epikedion*
Nar		Narrative Speech
O&P		Oracular or Prophetic Speech
	(Int)	Interpretation of Omens or Oracle
	(Ora)	Oracular Pronouncement
	(Pro)	Prophecy

P&B	Praise or Blame Speech
(Lau)	Laudation
(Vau)	Vaunt
(Vit)	Vituperation
Pra	Prayer
Que	Question
Res	Responsion
(to Cha)	to Challenge
(to Del)	to Deliberative Speech
(to Gre)	to Greeting
(to Que)	to Question
(to Res)	to Responsion
(to Thr)	to Threat
Sol	Soliloquy
Tau	Taunt
Tha	Thanksgiving
Thr	Threat

Some speeches in the epics and occasional poetry of Statius appear in clusters; the cluster indicates the grouping of which the speech forms a part. Speeches are in dialogues, trialogues or tetralogues. The number following the colon signifies the number of the speech in the colloquy; for example, T:6 indicates that the speech is the sixth made in the trialogue. Monologues are shown as an 'M', general interlocution by an 'I'. A dialogue is represented by a 'D', a trialogue by a 'T', and a tetralogue by a 'Te'.

STATISTICAL APPENDIX 1

THE SPEECHES IN THE *THEBAID*

Table 1. Speech Totals for the Thebaid

Book No.	No. of Speeches	No. of speeches over ave. length (13 ll.)	Pct. of speeches over ave. length (13 ll.)	Lines of speech	Lines of text[1]	Pct. of direct speech	Ave. length of speech	Frequency of occurrence (speech per lines of text)	Longest speech	Shortest speech
1	15²	8²	53.3²	339 7/12	720	47.2	22.6²	48.0²	115 5/6²	3/4
2	20	7	35.0	221 1/12	743	29.8	11.1	37.2	36 5/12	5/6
3	20	14	70.0	351 1/2	721	48.8	17.6	36.1	35	5/12
4	18	11	61.1	264 1/4	850	31.3	14.7	47.2	26	1/6
5	19²	5²	26.3²	551 1/6	753	73.2	29.0²	39.6²	449 5/6²	3/4
6	15	1	0.7	96 11/12	946	10.2	6.5	63.0	42 5/6	1/6
7	21	8	38.1	331 11/12	823	40.3	15.8	39.2	75 7/12	2
8	15	6	40.0	221 5/12	766	28.9	14.8	51.1	45	1 1/6
9	30	4	13.3	264 1/4	907	29.1	8.8	30.2	27 5/12	1/6
10	35²	4²	11.4²	240 1/2	939	25.6	6.9²	26.8²	31²	7/12
11	31	9	29.0	335 2/3	761	44.1	10.8	24.5	38	7/12
12	26²	4²	15.4²	229 5/6	819	28.1	8.8²	31.5²	41	1/6
Total	265²	81²	30.6²	3448 1/12	9748	35.4	13.0²	36.8²	449 5/6²	1/6

---

[1] The text of the *Thebaid* is edited by Hill (1983), who has restored the verses removed by Klinnert (1973).

[2] Including recounted speeches. *Figures not footnoted in this table do not include reported speeches.*

Table 2. Conspectus of the Thebaid *by Speeches*

No.	Line Nos.	Lines of Verse	Speech Type[4]	Cluster:[3] Speech No.	Addressor(s)	Addressee(s)

BOOK ONE

1-87: Invocation of the emperor Domitian. The blind Oedipus prays to Tisiphone and invokes a curse upon his sons.

(1)	56-87	32	Pra	M	Oedipus	Underworld gods

88-196: Tisiphone hears Oedipus' entreaty and hastens to Thebes. Polynices and Eteocles agree to reign in alternate years. Eteocles wins the draw and his brother departs from the city.

(2)	173-96	23 1/3	P&B (Vit)	M	A Theban	Thebans, Jupiter

197-282: Jupiter declares that Argos and Thebes will be pitted against each other in internecine warfare; Juno opposes Jupiter's contrivance of war.

(3)	214-47	34	For	D:1	Jupiter	Olympian gods
(4)	250-82	32 7/12	For	D:2	Juno	Jupiter

283-302: Jupiter dismisses Juno's objections against his plans for Argos' implication in war; he sends Mercury to Pluto in order to effect a violation of the pact of alternate rule between Eteocles and Polynices.

(5)	285-302	16 3/4	Com	D:3, M[5]	Jupiter	Juno, Mercury

303-446: Mercury departs to fulfil Jupiter's command. Polynices journeys to Argos and finds refuge before Adrastus' palace during a storm. Polynices and Tydeus meet and engage in combat before Adrastus bids them to stop.

(6)	438-46	8 5/12	Que	T:1	Adrastus	Tydeus and Polynices

447-556: Adrastus acknowledges Polynices and Tydeus as his appointed sons-in-law and summons his daughters.

(7)	448-50	1 3/4	Res (to Que)	T:2	Tydeus and Polynices	Adrastus
(8)	452-65	13	Res (to Que)	T:3	Tydeus	Adrastus
(9)	465	3/4	Res (to Que)	T:4	Polynices	Adrastus
(10)	468-73	5 5/12	Del	T:5	Adrastus	Tydeus and Polynices
(11)	498-510	12 7/12	Pra	M	Adrastus	Nox, Fortuna

---

[3] For a discussion of the cluster, see pp. 16f.

[4] For a discussion of the speech type, see pp. 8f.

[5] Jupiter replies to Juno's persuasion, then commands Mercury in what is the primary purpose of his speech.

STATISTICAL APPENDIX 1

No.	Line Nos.	Lines of Verse	Speech Type	Cluster: Speech No.	Addressor(s)	Addressee(s)
557-672: Adrastus relates the tale of Coroebus to Polynices and Tydeus.						
(12)	557-672	96 5/6[6]	Nar	T:6	Adrastus	Polynices and Tydeus
(13)	643-61	19	Pra	M	Coroebus	Apollo
673-720: Polynices confesses his ancestry; Adrastus invokes Apollo.						
(14)	676-81	5 7/12	Res (to Que)	T:7	Polynices	Adrastus
(15)	682-720	37 7/12	Pra	T:8, M[7]	Adrastus	Polynices, Apollo

BOOK TWO

No.	Line Nos.	Lines of Verse	Speech Type	Cluster: Speech No.	Addressor(s)	Addressee(s)
31-133: Laius appears to Eteocles and urges him to violate his pact of alternate rule with Polynices.						
(1)	19-25	6 5/6	Apo	M	A Shade	Laius
(2)	102-19	18	Del	M	Ghost of Laius[8]	Eteocles
134-305: Adrastus offers his daughters in marriage to Tydeus and Polynices, who wed Deipyle and Argia amid dire portents.						
(3)	152-72	21	Del	T:1	Adrastus	Tydeus and Polynices
(4)	176-88	12 1/4	Res (to Del)	T:2	Tydeus	Adrastus
(5)	189-97	8 5/12	Res (to Del)	T:3	Polynices	Adrastus
306-74: Polynices ponders his loss of rule. Argia betrays her anxiety over her husband's desire to return to Thebes. Tydeus volunteers to go to Thebes and press Eteocles to honour his promise and step down from the throne.						
(6)	334-52	17 11/12	Que	D:1	Argia	Polynices
(7)	356-62	7	Res (to Que)	D:2	Polynices	Argia
375-481: Tydeus arrives in Thebes and demands that Eteocles abandon the throne; Eteocles spurns Tydeus.						
(8)	393-409	17	Del	D:1	Tydeus	Eteocles
(9)	415-51	36 5/12	Res (to Del)	D:2	Eteocles	Tydeus
(10)	452-67	14 1/12	Thr	D:3	Tydeus	Eteocles
482-643: Eteocles lays an ambush for Tydeus, who routs his Theban adversaries.						
(11)	535	5/6	Que	M	Tydeus	Theban warriors
(12)	547-49	2 5/12	Cha	M	Tydeus	Theban warriors
(13)	620-23	3 3/4	Enc (Coh)	M	Chromis	Theban warriors

---

[6] Excluding the speech of Coroebus recounted by Adrastus (1.643-61).

[7] Adrastus briefly addresses Polynices before making a prayer of moderate length.

[8] Disguised as Tiresias.

No.	Line Nos.	Lines of Verse	Speech Type	Cluster: Speech No.	Addressor(s)	Addressee(s)
(14)	641	5/6	Tau	M	Brother of Periphas (*sine nomine*)	Tydeus

644-81: Menoetes unsuccessfully seeks a reprieve from death at the hands of Tydeus.

No.	Line Nos.	Lines of Verse	Speech Type	Cluster: Speech No.	Addressor(s)	Addressee(s)
(15)	649-54	5	Del	D:1	Menoetes	Tydeus
(16)	655-59	3 1/3	Res (to Del)	D:2	Tydeus	Menoetes
(17)	661-68	7	Tau	M	Tydeus	Theban warriors

682-742: Tydeus is dissuaded by Minerva from vaunting his victory before Thebes and pays homage to the goddess.

No.	Line Nos.	Lines of Verse	Speech Type	Cluster: Speech No.	Addressor(s)	Addressee(s)
(18)	686-90	4	Com	M	Minerva	Tydeus
(19)	697-703	7	Com	M	Tydeus	Maeon
(20)	715-42	28	Pra	M	Tydeus	Minerva

BOOK THREE

1-113: Maeon informs Eteocles of Tydeus' victory and commits suicide.

No.	Line Nos.	Lines of Verse	Speech Type	Cluster: Speech No.	Addressor(s)	Addressee(s)
(1)	6-7, 9-18	9 5/6	Sol	M	Eteocles	-------
(2)	59-77, 83-87	22 7/12	P&B (Vit)	M	Maeon	Eteocles

114-217: The Thebans inhume their dead; Aletes denounces Eteocles.

No.	Line Nos.	Lines of Verse	Speech Type	Cluster: Speech No.	Addressor(s)	Addressee(s)
(3)	151-68	18	M&C (Lam)	M	Ide	Ide's sons[9]
(4)	179-213	35	M&C (Con)	M	Aletes	Thebans

218-52: Jupiter commands Mars to incite Thebes and Argos to war.

No.	Line Nos.	Lines of Verse	Speech Type	Cluster: Speech No.	Addressor(s)	Addressee(s)
(5)	229-52	23 7/12	Com	M	Jupiter	Mars, Olympian gods

253-323: Venus accosts Mars for his ensuing rôle in inciting conflict between Thebes and Argos; Mars rebuffs her.

No.	Line Nos.	Lines of Verse	Speech Type	Cluster: Speech No.	Addressor(s)	Addressee(s)
(6)	269-91	22 5/12	Del	D:1	Venus	Mars
(7)	295-316	21 7/12	Res (to Del)	D:2	Mars	Venus

325-439: Tydeus returns to Argos and exhorts the Argives to war. Polynices craftily assumes the guilt for his brother's heinous deed, while Adrastus disavows Polynices' complicity in any evil-doing.

No.	Line Nos.	Lines of Verse	Speech Type	Cluster: Speech No.	Addressor(s)	Addressee(s)
(8)	348-65	17 1/4	Enc (Coh)	M	Tydeus	Argives and Adrastus

---

[9] Names not mentioned.

STATISTICAL APPENDIX 1

No.	Line Nos.	Lines of Verse	Speech Type	Cluster: Speech No.	Addressor(s)	Addressee(s)
(9)	367-81	13 1/2	Del	D:1	Polynices	Eteocles, Argives, Tydeus
(10)	388-93	5 5/6	Res (to Del)	D:2	Adrastus	Polynices

440-565: Adrastus encharges Amphiaraus and Melampus to read the future. The prophets take the auspices and are terrified by the dire portents.

(11)	471-96	25 7/12	Pra	M	Amphiaraus	Jupiter
(12)	502-515	14	Des	D:1	Melampus	Amphiaraus, Apollo
(13)	516-45	29 3/4	Des	D:2	Amphiaraus	Melampus
(14)	546	5/12	Que	D:3	Melampus[10]	Amphiaraus
(15)	546f.	1	Res (to Que)	D:4	Amphiaraus	Melampus

566-677: Amphiaraus refuses to divulge the findings of his auspice-taking. Capaneus impels the priest to prognosticate internecine warfare between Thebes and Argos. Argos declares her support for war.

(16)	607-18	10 5/6	Enc (Coh)	D:1	Capaneus	Achaeans, Amphiaraus
(17)	620-47	26 11/12	O&P (Int)	D:2	Amphiaraus	Achaeans
(18)	648-69	21	Thr	D:3	Capaneus	Amphiaraus

678-721: Argia bewails Polynices' plight and is relieved by Adrastus.

(19)	687-710	24	Del	D:1	Argia	Adrastus
(20)	712-20	8 5/12	Res (to Del)	D:2	Adrastus	Argia

BOOK FOUR

1-344: The catalogue of the Argive armies.

(1)	200-10	10 5/6	Sol	M	Argia	-------
(2)	318-40	22 7/12	Del	M	Atalanta	Parthenopaeus

345-405: Desperation and panic in Thebes.

(3)	383-404	21 7/12	Pra	M	Queen of the Bacchantes	Bacchus

---

[10] This speech could be assigned equally well to Amphiaraus, who would ask the question rhetorically, suggesting to Melampus that his imminent death is not sufficient cause to shed tears. The editors are evenly divided on the matter. Some modern editors such as Garrod (1906), Klotz (1908) and Mozley (1928) assign this question to Melampus, while others such as Snijder (1968) and Hill (1983) follow the ancient commentator Lactantius Placidius (ed. Jahnke [1898]) and Barth (1664) in ascribing it to Amphiaraus. Amphiaraus or Melampus weep, in any case, because of the knowledge of Amphiaraus' impending death. For an exposition of the problems inherent in assigning this speech, see Snijder (1968: 218f.).

No.	Line Nos.	Lines of Verse	Speech Type	Cluster: Speech No.	Addressor(s)	Addressee(s)

406-645: Tiresias and Manto exercise necromancy to find out the result of the ensuing conflict; their efforts prove inconclusive.

No.	Line Nos.	Lines of Verse	Speech Type	Cluster: Speech No.	Addressor(s)	Addressee(s)
(4)	473-87	15	Pra	M	Tiresias	Pluto
(5)	501-18	18 1/12	Pra	T:1	Tiresias	Underworld goddesses
(6)	519-35	17	Des	T:2	Manto	Tiresias
(7)	536-48	12 5/6	Com	T:3	Tiresias	Manto
(8)	553-78	26	Des	T:4	Manto	Tiresias
(9)	583-602	18 3/4	O&P (Int)	T:5	Tiresias	Manto
(10)	610-24	14 1/4	Del	T:6	Tiresias	Ghost of Laius
(11)	626-44	18 2/3	O&P (Pro)	T:7	Ghost of Laius	Tiresias, Eteocles

646-729: Bacchus enjoins the water nymphs to desiccate the earth in order to detain the Argives; the nymphs, with the exception of the nymph of Langia, effect widespread drought.

No.	Line Nos.	Lines of Verse	Speech Type	Cluster: Speech No.	Addressor(s)	Addressee(s)
(12)	669-78	8 1/4	Sol	M	Bacchus	-------
(13)	684-96	12 5/6	Com	M	Bacchus	Water nymphs

730-850: The Argives come upon Hypsipyle, slave girl of Lycurgus; she rescues them from an ignominious end.

No.	Line Nos.	Lines of Verse	Speech Type	Cluster: Speech No.	Addressor(s)	Addressee(s)
(14)	753-71	19	Pra	D:1	Adrastus	Hypsipyle
(15)	776-85	9 1/4	Res (to Del)	D:2	Hypsipyle	Adrastus
(16)	811	1/6	Enc (Exh)	M	Argus	Argive warriors
(17)	812	1/6	Enc (Exh)	I	Argive warriors	*inter se*
(18)	832-50	19	Pra	M	An Argive chieftain	Nymph of Langia

BOOK FIVE

31-39: The Argive host drink their fill of the Lerna. Adrastus entreats Hypsipyle successfully to divulge her ancestry.

No.	Line Nos.	Lines of Verse	Speech Type	Cluster: Speech No.	Addressor(s)	Addressee(s)
(1)	20-27	7 5/6	Que	D:3	Adrastus	Hypsipyle
(2)	29-39	10 7/12	Res (to Que)	D:4	Hypsipyle	Adrastus

40-498: Adrastus beseeches Hypsipyle to narrate her tale of woe; she relates the story of the Lemnian massacre.

No.	Line Nos.	Lines of Verse	Speech Type	Cluster: Speech No.	Addressor(s)	Addressee(s)
(3)	43-47	5	Del	D:5	Adrastus	Hypsipyle

No.	Line Nos.	Lines of Verse	Speech Type	Cluster: Speech No.	Addressor(s)	Addressee(s)
(4)	49-498	396 1/12[11]	Nar	D:6	Hypsipyle	Adrastus and Argive warriors
(5)	104-29, 132-36, 137, 139-42	34 1/6[12]	Del	M	Polyxo	Lemnian women
(6)	136, 137f.	2 1/4	Com	M	Venus	Polyxo
(7)	245-47	2 1/6	Del	M	Hypsipyle	Thoas
(8)	271-84	13 1/6	Com	M	Bacchus	Thoas, Hypsipyle
(9)	491f.	2	P&B (Vit)	I	Lemnian crowd	*inter se*

499-637: A serpent strikes down Opheltes. Hypsipyle bewails her charge's death, while Capaneus slays the serpent.

(10)	565-70	4 5/6	Cha	M	Capaneus	Serpent
(11)	608-35	27 1/4	M&C (Lam)	M	Hypsipyle	Opheltes

638-79: Lycurgus threatens Hypsipyle with death, but the Argives rescue her.

(12)	647	1	O&P (Ora)	M	Priestess	Lycurgus
(13)	656-60	4	Thr	Te:1	Lycurgus	Argive princes
(14)	663f.	3/4	Com	Te:2	Tydeus	Lycurgus
(15)	669-71	1 7/12	Com	Te:3	Adrastus and Amphiaraus	Lycurgus and Tydeus
(16)	672-79	7 5/6	Thr	Te:4	Tydeus	Lycurgus

680-709: The safety of Lycurgus is threatened, but Adrastus calms the Argive host.

(17)	681-89	8 1/3	O&P (Pro)	Te:5	Lycurgus	Tydeus
(18)	701-03	2 1/3	Com	M	Adrastus	Argive warriors

710-52: Hypsipyle recognises her sons Lemnos and Thoas. Amphiaraus urges the Argives to pay honour to Opheltes.

(19)	733-52	20	O&P (Ora)	M	Amphiaraus	Adrastus and Argive princes

---

[11] Excluding the persuasive speech of Polyxo to the Lemnian women recounted by Hypsipyle (5.104-29, 132-42), the speech of persuasion by Hypsipyle to Thoas recounted by Hypsipyle (245-47), Bacchus' command to Hypsipyle reported by Hypsipyle (271-84), and the vituperative comments of the *vulgus* related by Hypsipyle (491f.).

[12] Excluding Venus' command to Polyxo reported by Polyxo to Hypsipyle (136, 137f.: a speech within a speech within a speech).

No.	Line Nos.	Lines of Verse	Speech Type	Cluster: Speech No.	Addressor(s)	Addressee(s)

BOOK SIX

1-295: The funeral rites of Opheltes. Assembling of the crowd at the funeral games of Opheltes; description of the games site.

No.	Line Nos.	Lines of Verse	Speech Type	Cluster: Speech No.	Addressor(s)	Addressee(s)
(1)	138-73, 174-76, 180-84	42 5/6	M&C (Lam)	M	Eurydice (Opheltes' mother)	Opheltes
(2)	197-201	4 7/12	Pra	M	Lycurgus	Jupiter

296-549: The chariot race. Catalogue of contestants; the race commences; Polynices falls from Arion; victory of Amphiaraus.

No.	Line Nos.	Lines of Verse	Speech Type	Cluster: Speech No.	Addressor(s)	Addressee(s)
(3)	319f.	1 1/4	Com	M	Adrastus	Polynices
(4)	372-83	11 3/4	Sol	M	Apollo	-------

550-645: Foot race. The fraudulent action of Idas in winning; Adrastus enjoins the race to be re-contested; Parthenopaeus wins easily.

No.	Line Nos.	Lines of Verse	Speech Type	Cluster: Speech No.	Addressor(s)	Addressee(s)
(5)	618	1/6	Enc (Coh)	I	Arcadian warriors	*inter se*
(6)	627-30	3 5/12	Com	M	Adrastus	Idas and other running contestants
(7)	633-37	5	Pra	M	Parthenopaeus	Diana

646-730: Discus. Disappointment of Phlegyas; Hippomedon easily defeats his adversaries.

No.	Line Nos.	Lines of Verse	Speech Type	Cluster: Speech No.	Addressor(s)	Addressee(s)
(8)	656-59	2 5/12	Cha	M	Hippomedon	Achaean warriors
(9)	726-30	4 5/6	Enc (Exh)	M	Adrastus	Phlegyas, Achaean competitors

731-825: Cestus. Capaneus overwhelms Alcidimas, but Hippomedon and Tydeus must prevent him from slaying his Spartan opponent.

No.	Line Nos.	Lines of Verse	Speech Type	Cluster: Speech No.	Addressor(s)	Addressee(s)
(10)	734-37	3 2/3	Cha	M	Capaneus	Achaean warriors
(11)	809-12	4	Com	M	Adrastus	Achaean warriors
(12)	816f.	1 7/12	Del	T:1	Tydeus and Hippomedon	Capaneus
(13)	819-22	3 1/4	Res (to Del)	T:2	Capaneus	Tydeus and Hippomedon

826-910: Wrestling. Tydeus defeats Aygellus in a spirited contest.

No.	Line Nos.	Lines of Verse	Speech Type	Cluster: Speech No.	Addressor(s)	Addressee(s)
(14)	906-08	2 7/12	P&B (Vau)	M	Tydeus	Tydeus' companions

912-46: Sword fighting and archery. Adrastus forbids Polynices and Agreus from fighting and awards both competitors golden helmets. The Argives puzzle over the portent of Adrastus' arrows.

No.	Line Nos.	Lines of Verse	Speech Type	Cluster: Speech No.	Addressor(s)	Addressee(s)
(15)	914-19	5 7/12	Com	M	Adrastus	Agreus and Polynices

No.	Line Nos.	Lines of Verse	Speech Type	Cluster: Speech No.	Addressor(s)	Addressee(s)

BOOK SEVEN

1-144: Jupiter sends Mercury to order Mars to sow the seeds of war.

(1)	6-33	28	Com	M	Jupiter	Mercury
(2)	77-80	4	Que	M	Mars	Mercury
(3)	93-103	10 1/4	Pra	M	Adrastus	Opheltes
(4)	123-26	3 1/6	Que	I	Argive crowd	*inter se*

145-242: Bacchus expostulates to Jupiter over the fate of Thebes; the lord of the universe expounds the origins of the war to Bacchus.

(5)	155-92	38	Del	D:1	Bacchus	Jupiter
(6)	195-221	26 5/12	Res (to Del)	D:2	Jupiter	Bacchus

243-373: Phorbas catalogues the Theban troops for Antigone.

(7)	247-52	5 7/12	Del	D:1	Antigone	Phorbas
(8)	254-89	36	Des	D:2	Phorbas	Antigone
(9)	291-93	3	Que	D:3	Antigone	Phorbas
(10)	294-358, 363-73	75 7/12	Des	D:4	Phorbas	Antigone

374-469: Eteocles exhorts his troops to defend Thebes. The Argive host approaches Thebes while inside the city panic reigns.

(11)	375-90	15 5/12	Enc (Coh)	M	Eteocles	Theban troops

470-533: Jocasta attempts to effect a last-minute settlement between her sons.

(12)	483-85	2	Del	M	Jocasta	Argive warriors
(13)	490-92	2 1/4	Que	M	Jocasta	Argive princes
(14)	497-527	30 1/4	Del	D:1	Jocasta	Polynices, Argive warriors

534-627: Tydeus dissuades the troops from accepting Jocasta's proposal and she flees from the camp.

(15)	539-59	20 5/12	Del	D:2	Tydeus	Argive warriors, Jocasta, Polynices
(16)	612-14	2 5/12	Com	D:3	Tydeus	Jocasta, Antigone and Ismene

628-87: The war commences. Capaneus slays Eunaeus.

(17)	663-68	5 1/6	P&B (Vau)	D:1	Eunaeus	Argive warriors
(18)	677-79	2 1/4	Tau	D:2	Capaneus	Eunaeus

688-823: The aristeia *and death of Amphiaraus.*

(19)	730-35	5 5/6	Pra	M	Hypseus	Asopus
(20)	772-77	5 11/12	Com	D:1	Apollo	Amphiaraus

No.	Line Nos.	Lines of Verse	Speech Type	Cluster: Speech No.	Addressor(s)	Addressee(s)
(21)	779-88	10	Pra	D:2	Amphiaraus	Apollo

BOOK EIGHT

1-126: Pluto threatens the deceased Amphiaraus on his arrival in the underworld, whereupon the seer successfully conciliates the god.

(1)	34-79	45	Com	M	Pluto	Underworld deities and Tisiphone
(2)	84f.	1 5/12	Thr	D:1	Pluto	Amphiaraus
(3)	90-122	33	Pra	D:2	Amphiaraus	Pluto

127-341: The Argives report the circumstances of Amphiaraus' death to Adrastus, who is horror-stricken. The Argives mourn the augur's death.

(4)	138-50	12 1/4	Del	M	Palaemon	Adrastus
(5)	174-207	34	M&C (Epi)	I	Argive troops	*inter se*
(6)	303-38	35 1/2	Pra	M	Thiodamas	Tellus

342-496: General fighting breaks out; the commencement of Tydeus'aristeia.

(7)	472f.	1 7/12	Tau	M	Tydeus	Idas

497-535: Hercules confronts Minerva on the field of battle but withdraws in her favour.

(8)	502-16	14 7/12	P&B (Lau)	M	Hercules	Minerva

536-606: Tydeus slays and wounds Atys. Menoeceus shames the Thebans into action.

(9)	582f.	1 1/6	Tau	M	Tydeus	Atys
(10)	588-91	3 7/12	Pra	M	Tydeus	Minerva
(11)	600-05	5 1/4	Enc (Coh)	M	Menoeceus	Theban warriors

607-54: Ismene and Antigone lament their ancestry; Ismene mourns over the dying Atys.

(12)	622-35	13 7/12	Nar	M	Ismene	Antigone

655-766: Tydeus continues to wreak havoc upon the Thebans until Melanippus' spear strikes him down.

(13)	664-72	8 5/12	Cha	M	Tydeus	Theban warriors
(14)	677-79	2 5/6	Cha	M	Tydeus	Eteocles
(15)	735-44	9 1/4	Del	M	Tydeus	Argive warriors

BOOK NINE

31-86: Polynices grieves over the death of Tydeus.

(1)	12-24	11 5/6	Enc (Coh)	M	Eteocles	Theban warriors
(2)	49-72, 75f.	25 1/6	M&C (Lam)	M	Polynices	Tydeus

No.	Line Nos.	Lines of Verse	Speech Type	Cluster: Speech No.	Addressor(s)	Addressee(s)

86-195: The Argives and Thebans fight over Tydeus' corpse.

No.	Line Nos.	Lines of Verse	Speech Type	Cluster: Speech No.	Addressor(s)	Addressee(s)
(3)	96-103	7 7/12	Tau	M	Eteocles	Hippomedon
(4)	137-39	2 1/3	Tau	M	Hippomedon	Leonteus
(5)	157-165, 166-68	9 1/3	Del	M	Tisiphone[13]	Hippomedon

196-314: Hippomedon drives the Thebans into the River Ismenos.

(6)	211-17	6 7/12	Del	M	Hippomedon	Tydeus' steed
(7)	294-301	7 5/6	Tau	M	Hippomedon	Panemus

315-50: Crenaeus challenges Hippomedon and is quickly struck down, but appeals to his mother Ismenis while in his death throes.

(8)	340-43	3 1/6	Cha	M	Crenaeus	Hippomedon
(9)	350	1/6	Apo	D:1	Crenaeus	Ismenis

351-445: Ismenis laments her son Crenaeus' death. Ismenos hears her and resolves to bring about Hippomedon's demise.

(10)	356	1/6	Apo	D:2	Ismenis	Crenaeus
(11)	376-98	23	M&C (Lam)	D:3	Ismenis	Crenaeus
(12)	421-45	24 5/6	Apo	M	Ismenos	Jupiter, Bacchus, Hippomedon

446-539: Ismenos overwhelms Hippomedon. Juno successfully pleads with Jupiter to intervene on Hippomedon's behalf, but the hero is weakened and falls to the Thebans' projectiles.

(13)	476-80	4 7/12	Tau	M	Hippomedon	Ismenos
(14)	506-10	4	Pra	M	Hippomedon	Mars
(15)	511-19	8 1/6	Del	M	Juno	Jupiter

540-64: Hypseus plunders Hippomedon's corpse but is struck down by Capaneus.

(16)	544-46	2 1/6	P&B (Vau)	M	Hypseus	Aonian warrriors
(17)	548-50	2 7/12	Pra	M	Capaneus	Capaneus' right arm
(18)	557-59	2 5/12	Tau	M	Capaneus	Hypseus
(19)	562-65	3 5/6	Apo	M	Capaneus	Hippomedon

570-682: Atalanta fears for her son Parthenopaeus. She determines to exact vengeance for his death and implores Diana for help; the goddess is told by Apollo that his death is imminent.

(20)	608-35	27 5/12	Pra	M	Atalanta	Diana
(21)	650-62	12 3/4	O&P (Int)	D:1	Apollo	Diana
(22)	663-67	4 1/3	Thr	D:2	Diana	Apollo

---

[13] Disguised as Halys the Inachian.

No.	Line Nos.	Lines of Verse	Speech Type	Cluster: Speech No.	Addressor(s)	Addressee(s)

683-775: The aristeia of Parthenopaeus.

| (23) | 713-25 | 12 1/12 | Apo | M | Diana | Menoeceus |

776-807: Amphion taunts Parthenopaeus.

| (24) | 779-87 | 8 3/4 | Tau | D:1 | Amphion | Parthenopaeus |
| (25) | 790-800 | 11 | Tau | D:2 | Parthenopaeus | Amphion |

808-20: Diana, disguised as Dorceus, appeals unsuccessfully to Parthenopaeus to withdraw from the battleground.

| (26) | 812-14 | 2 7/12 | Del | D:1 | Diana[14] | Parthenopaeus |
| (27) | 815-19 | 5 | Del | D:2 | Parthenopaeus | Diana[14] |

821-40: Venus successfully beseeches Mars to drive Diana from the battlefield.

| (28) | 825-30 | 5 7/12 | Del | M | Venus | Mars |
| (29) | 835-37 | 2 7/12 | Com | M | Mars | Diana |

841-907: Mars wreaks havoc on the troops. Parthenopaeus is fallen and instructs Dorceus to console his mother.

| (30) | 885-900, 901-07 | 22 5/12 | Com | M | Parthenopaeus | Dorceus |

BOOK TEN

1-48: Assembling of the Theban troops and the encirclement of the Argive camp.

| (1) | 21-35 | 14 1/4 | Enc (Coh) | M | Eteocles | Theban warriors |

49-155: The Argive matrons appeal to Juno against Thebes. The goddess has Iris impose a deep sleep upon the Thebans.

| (2) | 67-69 | 3 | Pra | M | Argolic mothers | Juno |
| (3) | 126-31 | 6 | Com | M | Iris | Somnus |

156-261: Thiodamas successfully exhorts the Argive chieftains to attack the Theban troops during the night.

(4)	188-218	26 1/2[15]	Enc (Coh)	M	Thiodamas	Achaean leaders
(5)	206-11	4 1/2	Del	M	Amphiaraus' spirit	Thiodamas
(6)	236-44	8 7/12	Enc (Coh)	M	Adrastus	Achaean warriors

---

[14] Diana disguises herself as Dorceus, Parthenopaeus' charge.

[15] Excluding the speech of Amphiaraus' spirit (10.206-11).

288

STATISTICAL APPENDIX 1

No.	Line Nos.	Lines of Verse	Speech Type	Cluster: Speech No.	Addressor(s)	Addressee(s)

262-347: The Argive army enters the Theban camp and wreaks destruction.

No.	Line Nos.	Lines of Verse	Speech Type	Cluster: Speech No.	Addressor(s)	Addressee(s)
(7)	266-68	1 11/12	Enc (Coh)	M	Adrastus	Achaean warriors
(8)	269-71	2 5/12	Enc (Coh)	M	Thiodamas	Achaean warriors
(9)	330-35	5 7/12	Del	M	Actor	Thiodamas
(10)	337-45	9	Pra	M	Thiodamas	Apollo

348-448: The devotion and deaths of Hopleus and Dymas: the pair attempt unsuccessfully to recover the bodies of Parthenopaeus and Tydeus.

No.	Line Nos.	Lines of Verse	Speech Type	Cluster: Speech No.	Addressor(s)	Addressee(s)
(11)	351-59[16]	9	Del	D:1	Hopleus	Dymas
(12)	360-63	3 1/2	Res (to Del)	D:2	Dymas	Hopleus
(13)	365-70	5	Pra	M	Dymas	Cynthia
(14)	393	7/12	Com	M	Amphion	Dymas and Hopleus
(15)	423-30	7 5/12	Del	D:1	Dymas	Theban warriors
(16)	431-34	3 3/4	Del	D:2	Amphion	Dymas
(17)	436-38, 441	3 5/12	Res (to Del)	D:3	Dymas	Amphion

449-551: The Thebans bar the gates of Thebes and defend their city against the advancing Argive army.

No.	Line Nos.	Lines of Verse	Speech Type	Cluster: Speech No.	Addressor(s)	Addressee(s)
(18)	482-86	4 7/12	Enc (Coh)	M	Capaneus	Argive warriors
(19)	492	1	Com	M	Megareus	Theban sentry

552-627: Panic, despair and rebellious thoughts predominate in Thebes. The oracular pronouncement of Tiresias and Creon's reaction.

No.	Line Nos.	Lines of Verse	Speech Type	Cluster: Speech No.	Addressor(s)	Addressee(s)
(20)	584-87[17]	2 5/12	Del	D:1	Thebans	Thebans
(21)	588[17]	5/6	Res (to Del)	D:2	Thebans	Thebans
(22)	592-98	5 1/2	Com	M	Tiresias	Theban altar maid
(23)	610-15	6	O&P (Ora)	M	Tiresias	Thebans

628-737: Virtus, disguised as Manto the prophetess, informs Menoeceus of his fate. He willingly accepts his destiny and departs for Thebes despite the protestations of his parents.

No.	Line Nos.	Lines of Verse	Speech Type	Cluster: Speech No.	Addressor(s)	Addressee(s)
(24)	662-71	10	Del	D:1	Virtus[18]	Menoeceus
(25)	680f.	1 7/12	Res (to Del)	D:2	Menoeceus	Virtus[18]
(26)	690-718	28 5/12	Del	D:1	Creon	Menoeceus
(27)	722-34	12 5/12	Res (to Del)	D:2	Menoeceus	Creon

---

[16] See p. 16 for a brief examination of the imagined speech in 10.355 that Hopleus has Tydeus' mother utter to Dymas.

[17] Lipscomb (1909: 45) also contends that these collective speeches are two separate discourses. They could less accurately be interpreted as a single discourse spoken by two groups of Thebans in turn.

[18] Disguised as Manto the prophetess.

No.	Line Nos.	Lines of Verse	Speech Type	Cluster: Speech No.	Addressor(s)	Addressee(s)
738-826: Menoeceus sacrifices himself for the Theban cause.						
(28)	762-73	12	Pra	M	Menoeceus	Battle gods and Apollo
(29)	793-814	22	M&C (Lam)	M	Eurydice (Menoeceus' mother)	Menoeceus
827-82: The aristeia of Capaneus.						
(30)	845-47	2 11/12	Sol	M	Capaneus	Argive warriors
(31)	873-77	3 5/6	Tau	M	Capaneus	Thebans
883-939: Capaneus challenges the gods and is struck down by Jupiter.						
(32)	888f.	1 1/2	Apo	M	Bacchus	Jupiter
(33)	899-906	7 3/4	Cha	M	Capaneus	Olympian gods and Jupiter
(34)	909f.	1 1/2	Sol	M	Jupiter	Capaneus
(35)	925f.	1 5/6	Tau	M	Capaneus	Jupiter and Olympian gods (*oblique*)

BOOK ELEVEN

1-112: The Argives rout the Thebans. Tisiphone and Megaera agree on a strategy to effect a grisly end to the war.

(1)	76-112	37	Del	M	Tisiphone	Megaera

113-35: Jupiter abandons Thebes to the forces of the underworld.

(2)	122-33	12	Com	M	Jupiter	Olympian gods

136-204: Polynices resolves to challenge Eteocles for the Theban crown. Adrastus unsuccessfully attempts to dissuade Polynices from his determined course of action.

(3)	155-92	38	Del	M	Polynices	Adrastus
(4)	201f.	1 1/6	Com	M	Megaera[19]	Polynices

205-56: Aegyptus interrupts Eteocles' portentous sacrifice to Jupiter in order to convey Polynices' challenge.

(5)	210-25	16	Pra	M	Eteocles	Jupiter
(6)	242-45	4	Del	M	Aegyptus	Eteocles
(7)	248f.[20]	1 1/6	Pra	M	Eteocles	Jupiter

---

[19] Disguised as Phereclus.

[20] Although these verses could be held to be a continuation of Eteocles' prayer from 11.225, it is better to consider them as constituting a separate speech of the monarch, especially since there are

STATISTICAL APPENDIX 1

No.	Line Nos.	Lines of Verse	Speech Type	Cluster: Speech No.	Addressor(s)	Addressee(s)

257-314: Eteocles' associates attempt to dissuade him from meeting Polynices in combat, but goaded by Creon, he accepts his brother's challenge.

(8)	257f.[21]	7/12	Del	M	Companion of Eteocles (1)	Eteocles
(9)	258f.[21]	1	Que	M	Companion of Eteocles (2)	Eteocles
(10)	259f.[21]	1 2/3	P&B (Vit)	M	Companion of Eteocles (3)	Eteocles
(11)	260-62[21]	1 5/12	Del	M	Companion of Eteocles (4)	Eteocles
(12)	269-96	27 5/6	Del	D:1	Creon	Eteocles
(13)	298-308	10 1/3	Res (to Del)	D:2	Eteocles	Creon

315-53: Jocasta upbraids Eteocles for accepting Polynices' challenge to a duel.

(14)	329-53	25	Del	M	Jocasta	Eteocles

354-423: Antigone beseeches Polynices to abandon his challenge of Eteocles. The brothers rush on to the field of battle to commence the duel.

(15)	363-82	19 1/6	Del	M	Antigone	Polynices
(16)	389-92	3 1/3	Res (to Cha)	D:1	Eteocles	Polynices
(17)	393-95	2 5/6	Res (to Res)	D:2	Polynices	Eteocles

424-56: Adrastus entreats Polynices and Eteocles to abandon their duel.

(18)	429-35	5 2/3	Del	M	Adrastus	Polynices and Eteocles

457-81: Pietas unsuccessfully endeavours to prevent the contest between Polynices and Eteocles.

(19)	465-70, 471	5 1/3	Apo	M	Pietas	Natura
(20)	478-81	3 5/12	Enc (Coh)	M	Pietas[22]	Argive and Theban warriors

482-96: Tisiphone ensures that the duel eventuates between Polynices and Eteocles.

(21)	484-92	8 1/6	P&B (Vit)	M	Tisiphone	Pietas

---

two potential speeches in *oratio obliqua* (231, 232f.) and one actual speech (242-45) that is delivered after Eteocles' words in lines 210-25 and before the commencement of his brief prayer in lines 248f.

[21] There are four short comments here made by Eteocles' companions. I have chosen to consider them as four separate speeches by various individuals of the kings' cortege; they could less satisfactorily be considered as one speech made by the group.

[22] Disguised as a male warrior.

No.	Line Nos.	Lines of Verse	Speech Type	Cluster: Speech No.	Addressor(s)	Addressee(s)

497-579: The contest between and deaths of Polynices and Eteocles.

(22)	504-08	5	Pra	M	Polynices	Underworld gods
(23)	548-51	4	Tau	M	Polynices	Eteocles
(24)	557-60	2 5/6	Com	M	Polynices	Argive companions
(25)	568-72	4 1/3	Tau	M	Polynices	Eteocles

580-647: The affliction of Oedipus and Jocasta.

| (26) | 594f. | 1 1/3 | Del | M | Oedipus | Antigone |
| (27) | 605-26, 630f. | 23 5/12 | M&C (Lam) | M | Oedipus | Eteocles and Polynices |

648-754: Creon banishes Oedipus despite the former king's protestations.

(28)	669-72	3 7/12	Com	T:1	Creon	Oedipus
(29)	677-707	30 5/12	P&B (Vit)	T:2	Oedipus	Creon
(30)	708-39	31	Del	T:3	Antigone	Creon
(31)	750-54	4 2/3	Res (to Del)	T:4	Creon	Antigone

BOOK TWELVE

1-104: Funeral rites of the Thebans. Creon prohibits the burial of Polynices and the Argive troops.

| (1) | 72-92, 94-102 | 29 1/4 | M&C (Lam) | M | Creon | Menoeceus |

105-72: The Argive women start out for Thebes. They encounter Ornytus, who tells them of Creon's decree forbidding burial of their husbands, and set out for Athens to seek the assistance of Theseus.

| (2) | 149-66 | 17 7/12 | Del | M | Ornytus | Widows of Argive leaders |

173-290: Argia determines to bury Polynices; attended by Menoetes, she separates herself by a ruse from the Argive women and starts out for Thebes.

(3)	196-204	8 1/3	Del	M	Argia	Argive widows
(4)	209-19	10 1/12	Apo	M	Argia	Polynices, Ornytus
(5)	246-54	9	Des	M	Menoetes	Argia
(6)	256-67	11 1/4	Pra	M	Argia	Thebes

291-311: Juno entreats the moon goddess Cynthia to assist Argia in her search for Polynices' body.

| (7) | 299-308 | 10 | Del | M | Juno | Diana |

No.	Line Nos.	Lines of Verse	Speech Type	Cluster: Speech No.	Addressor(s)	Addressee(s)
312-48: Argia finds and laments over her husband's corpse.						
(8)	322-48	24 1/4[23]	M&C (Lam)	M	Argia	Polynices
(9)	333-35	2 3/4	Del	M	Argia	Polynices
349-408: Antigone comes upon Argia and mourns with her in commiseration over their fate. Menoetes chides them to complete their mission of Polynices' burial.						
(10)	366f.	1 1/12	Que	T:1	Antigone	Argia
(11)	374-80	6 5/12	Res (to Que)	T:2	Argia	Antigone
(12)	382-85	3 1/6	P&B (Vit)	T:3	Antigone	Argia
(13)	392-404	12 1/4	Nar	T:4	Argia	Antigone
(14)	406-08	3	Del	T:5	Menoetes	Argia and Antigone
409-46: Argia and Antigone unwittingly mix the ashes of the brothers and are stunned by the sight of cinerary enmity.						
(15)	437-46	10	Apo	M	Antigone	Argia, Eteocles, Polynices
447-63: Creon's troops arrest Argia and Antigone.						
(16)	458	1/4	Del	M	Antigone[24]	Theban warriors
(17)	458	1/6	Del	M	Argia	Theban warriors
(18)	459	1/4	Del	M	Antigone	Theban warriors
(19)	459	1/3	Del	M	Argia	Theban warriors
464-586: The mourners descend upon Athens and supplicate at the altar of Clementia. The Argive women appeal to Theseus for vengeance and assistance in burying their dead.						
(20)	546-86	41	Del	M	Evadne	Theseus
587-638: Theseus agrees to assist the Argive women. Men from neighbouring areas flock to join Theseus' army.						
(21)	590-98	8 3/4	Com	M	Theseus	Creon, Phegeus
639-76: Theseus exhorts his troops, then sets out for Thebes.						
(22)	642-48	7	Enc (Coh)	M	Theseus	Attic troops
677-708: Creon accepts Theseus' challenge; the Thebans reluctantly prepare for battle.						
(23)	689-92	3 1/4	Res (to Thr)	M	Creon	Phegeus

---

[23] Excluding the recounted deliberation of Argia to Polynices (12.333-35).

[24] See p. 302, n. 58.

No.	Line Nos.	Lines of Verse	Speech Type	Cluster: Speech No.	Addressor(s)	Addressee(s)

709-819: Theseus and his army descend upon Thebes and wreak destruction. Theseus meets and kills Creon. The Athenians and Thebans conclude a peace treaty. Statius' concluding sentiment on the fate of his epic.

(24)	761-66	5 11/12	Thr	D:1	Creon	Theseus
(25)	771-73	1 7/12	Pra	M	Theseus	Argive deified souls
(26)	779-81	2 11/12	Tau	D:2	Theseus	Creon

CLASSIFICATION OF SPEECHES IN THE *THEBAID*

Table 3. Totals for Speech Types[1]

Speech type	No. of speeches	Lines	Ave. length of speech	Divine speakers[2]	Human speakers[3]	Monologic speeches	Dialogic speeches	Trialogic speeches	Tetralogic speeches	General interlocutory speeches
Apo	10	74 5/6	7.5	6	4	8	2	0	0	0
Cha	8	35 1/2	4.4	0	4	8	0	0	0	0
Com	30[4,5]	259 1/12[5]	8.6[5]	9[5]	11	24[5]	3	2	2	0
Del	56[5]	709 1/12[5]	12.7[5]	7	28[5]	31[5]	19	6	0	0
Des	7	207 1/3	29.6	0	5	1	4	2	0	0
Enc	18	142 5/6	7.9[5]	1	11	15	1	0	0	2
For	2	66 7/12	33.3	2	0	0	2	0	0	0
M&C	11	306 11/12	27.9[5]	1	10	9	1	0	0	1
Nar	4	591 1/2[5]	147.9[5]	0	4	1	1	2	0	0
O&P	8	112 5/12	14.1	2	4	3	2	2	1	0
P&B	11[5]	115 5/6[5]	10.5[5]	2	9[5]	7	1	2	0	1[5]
Pra	31[4,5]	453 1/6[5]	14.6[5]	0	22[5]	27[5]	3	2	0	0
Que	11	49 11/12	4.5	1	8	4	4	2	0	1
Res	28	227 5/12	8.1	2	12	1[6]	18	9	0	0
Sol	6	45 1/12	7.7	3	3	6	0	0	0	0

---

[1] Including recounted speeches, except in the final totals for the number of lines and average length of speech (columns three and four, respectively).

[2] Including semi-divine figures.

[3] Including groups and spirits of the dead.

[4] This figure is less than the total of monologic and clustered speeches, because some speeches of this speech type partake of more than one cluster.

[5] This figure takes account of the inserted speeches in its determination.

[6] Cf. p. 309, n. 107.

Speech type	No. of speeches	Lines	Ave. length of speech	Divine speakers	Human speakers	Monologic speeches	Dialogic speeches	Trialogic speeches	Tetralogic speeches	General interlocutory speeches
Tau	17	74 1/4	4.4	0	9	13	5	0	0	0
Thr	7	58 7/12	8.4	2	4	0	5	0	2	0
Total	265[7]	3448 1/12[8]	13.0[7,9]	19[7,10]	62[7,10]	158[7,11]	71	29	5	5[7]

Table 4. Speech Types by Book

Book	Apo	Cha	Com	Del	Des	Enc	For	M&C	Nar	O&P	P&B	Pra	Que	Res	Sol	Tau	Thr	Total
1	0	0	1	1	0	0	2	0	1	0	1	4	1	4	0	0	0	15
2	1	1	2	4	0	1	0	0	0	0	0	1	2	5	0	2	1	20
3	0	0	1	3	2	2	0	2	0	1	1	1	1	4	1	0	1	20
4	0	0	2	2	2	2	0	0	0	2	0	5	0	1	2	0	0	18
5	0	1	5	3	0	0	0	1	1	3	1	0	1	1	0	0	2	19
6	0	2	4	1	0	2	0	1	0	0	1	2	0	1	1	0	0	15
7	0	0	3	5	2	1	0	0	0	0	1	3	4	1	0	1	0	21
8	0	2	1	2	0	1	0	1	1	0	1	3	0	0	0	2	1	15
9	5	1	2	6	0	1	0	2	0	1	1	3	0	0	0	7	1	30
10	1	1	4	8	0	6	0	1	0	1	0	4	0	5	2	2	0	35
11	1	0	4	11	0	1	0	1	0	0	3	3	1	4	0	2	0	31
12	2	0	1	10	1	1	0	2	1	0	1	2	1	2	0	1	1	26
Total	10	8	30	56	7	18	2	11	4	8	11	31	11	28	6	17	7	265

---

[7] See p. 295, n. 5.

[8] This figure is less than the total number of lines in this column, because the verses of inserted speeches are counted twice in determining the figure for each speech type but only once in the final total.

[9] There are 13.4 lines per speech, not counting inserted speeches.

[10] This figure counts each speaker or group of speakers only once, although he/she/it may have spoken in more than one speech type.

[11] This figure includes one speech that is also dialogic (1.285-302) and a second speech that is also trialogic (682-720).

296

Table 5. Catalogue of Speeches by Types

No.	Book/Lines	Lines of Verse	Addressor(s)	Addressee(s)	Cluster: Speech No.
			APOSTROPHES		
(1)	2.19-25	6 5/6	A shade	Laius	M
(2)	9.350	1/6	Crenaeus[12]	Ismenis	D:1
(3)	9.356	1/6	Ismenis[13]	Crenaeus	D:2
(4)	9.421-45	24 5/6	Ismenos	Jupiter, Bacchus, Hippomedon[14]	M
(5)	9.562-65	3 5/6	Capaneus	Hippomedon	M
(6)	9.713-25	12 1/12	Diana	Menoeceus	M
(7)	10.888f.[15]	1 1/2	Bacchus	Jupiter	M
(8)	11.465-70, 471	5 1/3	Pietas[16]	Natura	M
(9)	12.209-19	10 1/12	Argia[17]	Polynices, Ornytus	M
(10)	12.437-46	10	Antigone	Argia, Eteocles, Polynices	M
			CHALLENGES		
(1)	2.547-49	2 5/12	Tydeus	Theban warriors	M
(2)	5.565-70	4 5/6	Capaneus	Serpent	M
(3)	6.656-59[18]	2 5/12	Hippomedon	Achaean warriors	M
(4)	6.734-37	3 2/3	Capaneus	Achaean warriors	M
(5)	8.664-72	8 5/12	Tydeus[19]	Theban warriors	M
(6)	8.677-79	2 5/6	Tydeus[20]	Eteocles	M
(7)	9.340-43	3 1/6	Crenaeus	Hippomedon	M

---

[12] Crenaeus invokes his mother for assistance in the form of a brief apostrophe.

[13] Ismenis apostrophises Crenaeus but he is unable to reply.

[14] The demigod's primary address is Jupiter, but he also addresses Bacchus and Hippomedon.

[15] Although this speech consists of a series of questions, its tone and purpose is clearly lamentative.

[16] Pietas apostrophises Natura, then makes a resolution to descend to the field of battle to restore peace.

[17] Argia concludes her apostrophe to Polynices with a brief apostrophic address to Ornytus, a wounded Argive soldier whom she met earlier (12.141ff.).

[18] An athletic challenge.

[19] Tydeus taunts the Thebans to incite them to accept his challenge in combat.

[20] Tydeus taunts Eteocles to accept his challenge.

No.	Book/Lines	Lines of Verse	Addressor(s)	Addressee(s)	Cluster: Speech No.
(8)	10.899-906	7 3/4	Capaneus[21]	Jupiter and Olympian gods	M

COMMANDS

No.	Book/Lines	Lines of Verse	Addressor(s)	Addressee(s)	Cluster: Speech No.
(1)	1.285-302	16 3/4	Jupiter	Juno, Mercury[22]	D:3, M[22]
(2)	2.686-90	4	Minerva	Tydeus	M
(3)	2.697-703	7	Tydeus[23]	Maeon	M
(4)	3.229-52	23 7/12	Jupiter[24]	Mars, Olympian gods	M
(5)	4.536-48	12 5/6	Tiresias	Manto	T:3
(6)	4.684-96	12 5/6	Bacchus	Water nymphs	M
(7)	5.136, 137f.	2 1/4	Venus	Polyxo	M
(8)	5.271-84	13 1/6	Bacchus	Thoas, Hypsipyle	M
(9)	5.663f.	3/4	Tydeus[25]	Lycurgus	Te:2
(10)	5.669-71[26]	1 7/12	Adrastus and Amphiaraus	Lycurgus and Tydeus	Te:3
(11)	5.701-03	2 1/3	Adrastus	Argive warriors	M
(12)	6.319f.[27]	1 1/4	Adrastus	Polynices	M
(13)	6.627-30	3 5/12	Adrastus	Idas and other running contestants	M
(14)	6.809-12	4	Adrastus	Achaean warriors	M
(15)	6.914-19	5 7/12	Adrastus	Agreus and Polynices	M
(16)	7.6-33	28	Jupiter	Mercury	M
(17)	7.612-14	2 5/12	Tydeus	Jocasta, Antigone and and Ismene	D:3
(18)	7.772-77	5 11/12	Apollo	Amphiaraus	D:1

[21] Capaneus taunts the Olympians in his challenge to their power and authority.

[22] Jupiter replies to Juno's persuasion, then commands Mercury in what is the primary purpose of his speech.

[23] Tydeus commands Maeon to carry his challenge of war directed at the Thebans to Eteocles.

[24] Jupiter orders Mars and prophesies on the future of Thebes, but the central purpose of his speech is to enjoin noninterference on the gods in the ensuing conflict.

[25] Tydeus responds in an imperative manner to Lycurgus' comminatory speech addressed to the Argive princes.

[26] This persuasive speech is tantamount to a command because Adrastus is superior in station to Tydeus.

[27] This command is also an instruction in that Adrastus is emphasising the explicit nature of an equestrian skill in his direction to Polynices.

No.	Book/Lines	Lines of Verse	Addressor(s)	Addressee(s)	Cluster: Speech No.
(19)	8.34-79[28]	45	Pluto	Underworld deities and Tisiphone	M
(20)	9.835-37	2 7/12	Mars	Diana	M
(21)	9.885-900, 901-07	22 5/12	Parthenopaeus	Dorceus	M
(22)	10.126-31	6	Iris[29]	Somnus	M
(23)	10.393	7/12	Amphion	Dymas and Hopleus	M
(24)	10.492	1	Megareus	Theban sentry	M
(25)	10.592-98	5 1/2	Tiresias	Theban oracular attendant[30]	M
(26)	11.122-33	12	Jupiter	Olympian gods	M
(27)	11.201f.	1 1/6	Megaera	Polynices	M
(28)	11.557-60	2 5/6	Polynices	Argive companions	M
(29)	11.669-72	3 7/12	Creon	Oedipus	T:1
(30)	12.590-98	8 3/4	Theseus[31]	Creon, Phegeus	M

DELIBERATIONS

No.	Book/Lines	Lines of Verse	Addressor(s)	Addressee(s)	Cluster: Speech No.
(1)	1.468-73	5 5/12	Adrastus	Polynices and Tydeus	T:5
(2)	2.102-19	18	Ghost of Laius[32]	Eteocles	M
(3)	2.152-72	21	Adrastus	Tydeus and Polynices	T:1
(4)	2.393-409	17	Tydeus[33]	Eteocles	D:1
(5)	2.649-54	5	Menoetes	Tydeus	D:1
(6)	3.269-91	22 5/12	Venus	Mars	D:1
(7)	3.367-81	13 1/2	Polynices	Eteocles, Argives, Tydeus	D:1
(8)	3.687-710	24	Argia	Adrastus	D:1
(9)	4.318-40	22 7/12	Atalanta	Parthenopaeus	M
(10)	4.610-24	14 1/4	Tiresias	Ghost of Laius	T:6

---

[28] There are interrogatory and vituperative elements in Dis' speech, but they serve to establish the basis of the underworld god's command to Tisiphone to avenge the apparent transgression to his suzerainty.

[29] This command from Jupiter is relayed by Iris to Somnus.

[30] Tiresias responds to the Thebans' persuasive speech to foretell their city's destiny, briefly apostrophises Thebes and Pietas, then commands the oracular attendant to set the altars and assist him in his interpretation of the oracle, which is the essential purpose of the prophet's speech.

[31] Theseus intromits a curt apostrophe addressed to Creon in his command to Phegeus; the command is the most important part of the speech.

[32] Disguised as Tiresias.

[33] Tydeus threatens Eteocles with the consequences of not honouring his agreement with Polynices to alternate years of rule.

No.	Book/Lines	Lines of Verse	Addressor(s)	Addressee(s)	Cluster: Speech No.
(11)	5.43-47	5	Adrastus	Hypsipyle	D:5
(12)	5.104-29, 132-42	36 5/12[34]	Polyxo[35]	Theban women	M
(13)	5.245-47	2 1/6	Hypsipyle[36]	Thoas	M
(14)	6.816f.	1 7/12	Tydeus and Hippomedon[37]	Capaneus	T:1
(15)	7.155-92	38	Bacchus	Jupiter	D:1
(16)	7.247-52	5 7/12	Antigone[38]	Phorbas	D:1
(17)	7.483-85	2	Jocasta	Argive warriors	M
(18)	7.497-527	30 1/4	Jocasta	Polynices, Argive warriors	D:1
(19)	7.539-59	20 5/12	Tydeus[39]	Argive warriors, Jocasta, Polynices	D:2
(20)	8.138-50	12 1/4	Palaemon	Adrastus	M
(21)	8.735-44	9 1/4	Tydeus[40]	Argive warriors	M
(22)	9.157-65, 166-68	9 1/3	Tisiphone[41]	Hippomedon	M
(23)	9.211-17	6 7/12	Hippomedon	Tydeus' steed	M
(24)	9.511-19	8 1/6	Juno	Jupiter	M
(25)	9.812-14	2 7/12	Diana[42]	Parthenopaeus	D:1

---

[34] This figure includes Venus' command to Polyxo recounted by Polyxo to Hypsipyle (5.136, 137f.).

[35] Hypsipyle recounts this speech of Polyxo to Adrastus and the Argive warriors in her narrative (5.49ff.).

[36] Hypsipyle relates this speech in her narrative to Adrastus (5.49ff.).

[37] The two heroes' persuasion of Capaneus to spare Alcidimas emanates from Adrastus' command to his troops to save the youth (6.809-12).

[38] Antigone addresses a direct question to Phorbas on whether the Argives can hold the Thebans and their allied armies at bay, then asks for a description of the allied armies; her request is tantamount to a simple deliberation, for Phorbas replies by cataloguing the Theban troops for Antigone.

[39] Although Tydeus' speech is a responsion to the persuasion of Jocasta (7.497-527) and is mainly an attempt to dissuade Polynices from going to Thebes, it is also intended to urge the Argive warriors to greater fury (cf. 7.559-63).

[40] Since Tydeus is in his death throes, he is in a position only to request a last wish; his comrades need heed his words only as the persuasion of a dying man.

[41] Disguised as Halys the Inachian.

[42] Disguised as Dorceus, Parthenopaeus' charge.

300

No.	Book/Lines	Lines of Verse	Addressor(s)	Addressee(s)	Cluster: Speech No.
(26)	9.815-19	5	Parthenopaeus[43]	Diana	D:2
(27)	9.825-30	5 7/12	Venus[44]	Mars	M
(28)	10.206-11	4 1/2	Amphiaraus' spirit[45]	Thiodamas	M
(29)	10.330-35	5 7/12	Actor	Thiodamas	M
(30)	10.351-59	9	Hopleus[46]	Dymas	D:1
(31)	10.423-30	7 5/12	Dymas	Theban warriors	D:1
(32)	10.431-34[47]	3 3/4	Amphion	Dymas	D:2
(33)	10.584-87	2 5/12	Thebans[48]	Thebans	D:1
(34)	10.662-71	10	Virtus[49]	Menoeceus	D:1
(35)	10.690-718	28 5/12	Creon[50]	Menoeceus	D:1
(36)	11.76-112	37	Tisiphone	Megaera	M
(37)	11.155-92	38	Polynices[51]	Adrastus	M
(38)	11.242-45[52]	4	Aegyptus	Eteocles	M
(39)	11.257f.	7/12	Companion of Eteocles (1)	Eteocles	M
(40)	11.260-62	1 5/12	Companion of Eteocles (4)	Eteocles	M
(41)	11.269-96	27 5/6	Creon[53]	Eteocles	D:1
(42)	11.329-53	25	Jocasta	Eteocles	M

---

[43] Parthenopaeus responds to the persuasion of the disguised Diana, but he in turn attempts to persuade the goddess, whom he believes to be Dorceus, that he should accept Amphion's challenge; the persuasive element and appeal to family loyalty in Parthenopaeus' address distinguishes the speech from a mere responsion.

[44] The words of the goddess are designed to provoke Mars to drive Diana from the battlefield.

[45] Thiodamas recounts this advisory speech of Amphiaraus in his cohortation (10.188-218).

[46] Hopleus' series of questions is designed to spur Dymas to assist him in recovering the corpses of Tydeus and Parthenopaeus.

[47] Although the tone of this speech is deliberative, the central purpose of Amphion's indirect question *quid fracti exanguesque parent* (10.433) in the central portion of his brief speech is to elicit from Dymas the desired information about the plans of the Argive host; the persuasory air of the speech is subsidiary to his primary purpose of obtaining valuable intelligence about the enemy's plans.

[48] The Theban crowd's tone of speech is importunate, but the *uulgus* is scarcely in a position to demand abdication by Eteocles.

[49] Disguised as Manto the prophetess.

[50] Creon only urges Menoeceus not to accept his fate; he does not command him.

[51] Polynices informs Adrastus of his resolve to challenge his brother in single combat, that he will not be hindered from his purpose, and asks that his father recover his body for burial.

[52] Also reportorial.

[53] Creon vituperates Eteocles to dissuade him from changing his resolve to meet Polynices' challenge.

No.	Book/Lines	Lines of Verse	Addressor(s)	Addressee(s)	Cluster: Speech No.
(43)	11.363-82	19 1/6	Antigone	Polynices	M
(44)	11.429-35	5 2/3	Adrastus	Polynices, Eteocles	M
(45)	11.594f.	1 1/3	Oedipus[54]	Antigone	M
(46)	11.708-39	31	Antigone	Creon	T:3
(47)	12.149-66	17 7/12	Ornytus[55]	Widows of Argive leaders	M
(48)	12.196-204	8 1/3	Argia[56]	Argive widows	M
(49)	12.299-308	10	Juno	Diana	M
(50)	12.333-35	2 3/4	Argia[57]	Polynices	M
(51)	12.406-08	3	Menoetes	Argia and Antigone	T:5
(52)	12.458	1/4	Antigone[58]	Theban soldiers	M
(53)	12.458	1/6	Argia	Theban soldiers	M
(54)	12.459	1/4	Antigone	Theban soldiers	M
(55)	12.459	1/3	Argia	Theban soldiers	M
(56)	12.546-86	41	Evadne	Theseus	M

DESCRIPTIONS

No.	Book/Lines	Lines of Verse	Addressor(s)	Addressee(s)	Cluster: Speech No.
(1)	3.502-15	14	Melampus[59]	Amphiaraus, Apollo	D:1
(2)	3.516-45	29 3/4	Amphiaraus[60]	Melampus	D:2
(3)	4.519-35	17	Manto	Tiresias	T:2
(4)	4.553-78	26	Manto[61]	Tiresias	T:4

---

[54] Although Oedipus is Antigone's father, his imperative speech is rather more a persuasion because of his subservient position now that he is blind and depends on her as a guide.

[55] Ornytus warns and advises the widows in attempting to dissuade them from burying the dead.

[56] A speech of resolution where Argia deflects in advance the widows' objections to her resolve.

[57] Argia's persuasory address is recounted by herself in her apostrophic speech (12.322-48).

[58] Judging by the lines immediately preceding this speech—*haec fratris rapuisse, haec coniugis artus / contendunt vicibusque probant* (12.457f.)—Antigone may be the first to speak in the sequence of four brief speeches spanning lines 458f. She would then issue the third speech in the sequence, while Argia would deliver the second and fourth speeches. Whether it is in fact Antigone or Argia who speaks first is difficult to ascertain; nevertheless, it is clear they each speak twice. The most obvious explanation for the confusion is that Statius wishes to portray both women as being capable of delivering any two of the speeches in the sequence, since they are clearly united in their love for Polynices.

[59] Melampus directs questions to Amphiaraus (12.502-05) and Apollo (512f.), but his speech is mainly a description of the portents he sees.

[60] Amphiaraus responds to Melampus' question (3.502-15) indirectly; his description of the celestial portents dominates the passage where he speaks.

[61] Manto responds to Tiresias' command (4.536-48) for a description of the Theban and Argive ghosts; the priestess catalogues only the Theban spirits.

No.	Book/Lines	Lines of Verse	Addressor(s)	Addressee(s)	Cluster: Speech No.
(5)	7.254-89	36	Phorbas[62]	Antigone	D:2
(6)	7.294-358, 363-73	75 7/12	Phorbas[62]	Antigone	D:4
(7)	12.246-54	9	Menoetes	Argia	M

SPEECHES OF ENCOURAGEMENT[63]

No.	Book/Lines	Lines of Verse	Addressor(s)	Addressee(s)	Cluster: Speech No.
(1)	2.620-23	3 3/4	Chromis[64]	Theban warriors	M
(2)	3.348-65	17 1/4	Tydeus	Argives and Adrastus	M
(3)	3.607-18	10 5/6	Capaneus[65]	Achaeans, Amphiaraus	D:1
(4)	4.811[66]	1/6	Argus	Argive warriors	M
(5)	4.812[67]	1/6	Argive warriors	*inter se*	I
(6)	6.618[68]	1/6	Arcadian warriors	*inter se*	I
(7)	6.726-30	4 5/6	Adrastus[69]	Phlegyas, Achaean competitors	M
(8)	7.375-90	15 5/12	Eteocles	Theban warriors	M
(9)	8.600-05	5 1/4	Menoeceus[70]	Theban warriors	M
(10)	9.12-24	11 5/6	Eteocles	Theban warriors	M
(11)	10.21-35	14 1/4	Eteocles	Theban warriors	M

---

[62] Phorbas' descriptions are in response to Antigone's deliberation (7.247-52) and question (291-93).

[63] I do not distinguish between the allocution and the cohortation, which are the two types of combat exhortations; strictly speaking, an allocution is an address by an emperor to his troops, while the cohortation is a speech by a general to his troops. The noncombat exhortation is a general speech of encouragement.

[64] Chromis taunts the Theban warriors, but the overriding purpose of his jeering is to drive them to fight.

[65] Capaneus scolds the Achaeans and taunts and threatens Amphiaraus, but the main purpose of his speech is to exhort the Achaeans to take up arms against Thebes.

[66] This cry by the warriors shows strong emotion and is a source of encouragement to the troops.

[67] Hill (1983) considers this one-word speech to be a question. I am in agreement with most editors, who punctuate it as an exclamation; for the classification see previous note.

[68] A brief hortatory *propositio* amounting to 'Let's fight!' Hill (1983) and other editors do not enclose '[*ad*] *arma*' in inverted commas.

[69] Adrastus apostrophises Phlegyas before making a brief athletic exhortation to the boxing competitors.

[70] Menoeceus taunts the Theban warriors in order to rally them.

No.	Book/Lines	Lines of Verse	Addressor(s)	Addressee(s)	Cluster: Speech No.
(12)	10.188-218[71]	31[72]	Thiodamas	Achaean leaders	M
(13)	10.236-44	8 7/12	Adrastus	Achaean warriors	M
(14)	10.266-68	1 11/12	Adrastus	Achaean warriors	M
(15)	10.269-71	2 5/12	Thiodamas	Achaean warriors	M
(16)	10.482-86	4 7/12	Capaneus	Argive warriors	M
(17)	11.478-81	3 5/12	Pietas[73]	Argive and Theban warriors	M
(18)	12.642-48	7	Theseus	Attic warriors	M

FORENSIC ORATIONS

No.	Book/Lines	Lines of Verse	Addressor(s)	Addressee(s)	Cluster: Speech No.
(1)	1.214-47	34	Jupiter	Olympian gods	D:1
(2)	1.250-82	32 7/12	Juno	Jupiter	D:2

SPEECHES OF MOURNING AND CONSOLATION

No.	Book/Lines	Lines of Verse	Addressor(s)	Addressee(s)	Cluster: Speech No.
(1)	3.151-68 (Lam)	18	Ide	Ide's sons[74]	M
(2)	3.179-213 (Con)	35	Aletes	Thebans	M
(3)	5.608-35 (Lam)	27 1/4	Hypsipyle	Opheltes	M
(4)	6.138-73, 174-76, 180-84 (Lam)	42 5/6	Eurydice (Opheltes' mother)	Opheltes	M
(5)	8.174-207 (Epi)	34	Argive troops	*inter se*	I
(6)	9.49-72, 75f. (Lam)	25 1/6	Polynices	Tydeus	M
(7)	9.376-98 (Lam)	23	Ismenis	Crenaeus, Jupiter	D:3[75]
(8)	10.793-814 (Lam)	22	Eurydice (Menoeceus' mother)	Menoeceus	M
(9)	11.605-26, 630f. (Lam)	23 5/12	Oedipus	Eteocles and Polynices	M
(10)	12.72-92, 94-102[76] (Lam)	29 1/4	Creon	Menoeceus	M

---

[71] Thiodamas recounts the deliberative speech of Amphiaraus' spirit, who appears to him in a vision, but the main purpose of his speech is to exhort the Achaean leaders to make a nocturnal attack on the Theban camp.

[72] Including the deliberation of Amphiaraus' spirit recounted by Thiodamas (10.206-11).

[73] Disguised as a male warrior.

[74] Names not mentioned.

[75] Ismenis apostrophises Crenaeus primarily, Jupiter briefly, in this speech.

[76] The second part of Creon's speech consists of a threat of death to anyone who attempts to give the final rites of burial to the Argives.

No.	Book/Lines	Lines of Verse	Addressor(s)	Addressee(s)	Cluster: Speech No.
(11)	12.322-48 (Lam)	27[77]	Argia	Polynices	M

NARRATIONS

No.	Book/Lines	Lines of Verse	Addressor(s)	Addressee(s)	Cluster: Speech No.
(1)	1.557-672	115 5/6[78]	Adrastus[79]	Tydeus and Polynices	T:6
(2)	5.49-498	449 5/6[80]	Hypsipyle	Adrastus and Argive warriors	D:6
(3)	8.622-35	13 7/12	Ismene	Antigone	M
(4)	12.392-404[81]	12 1/4	Argia	Antigone	T:4

ORACULAR AND PROPHETIC SPEECHES

No.	Book/Lines	Lines of Verse	Addressor(s)	Addressee(s)	Cluster: Speech No.
(1)	3.620-47 (Int)	26 11/12	Amphiaraus	Achaeans	D:2
(2)	4.583-602[82] (Int)	18 3/4	Tiresias	Manto	T:5
(3)	4.626-44 (Pro)	18 2/3	Ghost of Laius[83]	Tiresias, Eteocles	T:7
(4)	5.647 (Ora)	1	Priestess	Lycurgus	M
(5)	5.681-89 (Pro)	8 1/3	Lycurgus[84]	Tydeus	Te:5
(6)	5.733-52 (Ora)	20	Amphiaraus[85]	Adrastus and Argive princes	M
(7)	9.650-62[86] (Int)	12 3/4	Apollo	Diana	D:1
(8)	10.610-15 (Ora)	6	Tiresias	Thebans	M

---

[77] This figure includes Argia's deliberative speech recounted by herself to Polynices (12.333-35).

[78] Including Coroebus' speech related by Adrastus (1.643-61).

[79] Adrastus' narrative is an explanation for the rites of Apollo; he then subsequently addresses a question to Polynices concerning his identity.

[80] This figure includes the speeches recounted by Hypsipyle in her narrative made earlier by herself (5.245-47) and others (104-29, 132-36, 137, 139-42; 136, 137f.; 271-84; 491f.).

[81] Although this speech ends in a series of questions, it is primarily a brief narrative of Polynices' behaviour.

[82] Tiresias also commands Manto to cease with her description of the Argive spirits.

[83] Laius' ghost also addresses his grandsons, of whom only Eteocles is present; he also vituperates Oedipus.

[84] Lycurgus' response to Tydeus' threat is an explanation of his misconstruction of Tydeus' intent, which serves as the foundation for Lycurgus' subsequent prophetic comments in the same speech.

[85] Amphiaraus' mood is imperative and the second half of his speech is a brief *consolatio* (5.746-52), but the central purpose of his speech is to interpret the oracle that enjoins on the Argives the duty of paying honours to Archemorus.

[86] Apollo interprets his own oracles for Diana on the fate of Parthenopaeus (see 9.662).

SPEECH AND RHETORIC IN STATIUS' *THEBAID*

No.	Book/Lines	Lines of Verse	Addressor(s)	Addressee(s)	Cluster: Speech No.

PRAISE AND BLAME SPEECHES

No.	Book/Lines	Lines of Verse	Addressor(s)	Addressee(s)	Cluster: Speech No.
(1)	1.173-96 (Vit)	23 1/3	A Theban	Thebans, Jupiter[87]	M
(2)	3.59-77, 83-87 (Vit)	22 7/12	Maeon[88]	Eteocles	M
(3)	5.491f.[89] (Vit)	2	Lemnian crowd	*inter se*	I
(4)	6.906-08[90] (Vau)	2 7/12	Tydeus	Tydeus' companions	M
(5)	7.663-68[91] (Vau)	5 1/6	Eunaeus	Argive warriors	D:1
(6)	8.502-16 (Lau)	14 7/12	Hercules[92]	Minerva	M
(7)	9.544-46 (Vau)	2 1/6	Hypseus	Aonian warriors	M
(8)	11.259f.[93] (Vit)	1 2/3	Companion of Eteocles (3)	Eteocles	M
(9)	11.484-92 (Vit)	8 1/6	Tisiphone	Pietas	M
(10)	11.677-707 (Vit)	30 5/12	Oedipus[94]	Creon	T:2
(11)	12.382-85[95] (Vit)	3 1/6	Antigone	Argia	T:3

PRAYERS

No.	Book/Lines	Lines of Verse	Addressor(s)	Addressee(s)	Cluster: Speech No.
(1)	1.56-87	32	Oedipus	Underworld gods	M
(2)	1.498-510	12 7/12	Adrastus	Nox, Fortuna	M
(3)	1.643-61	19	Coroebus	Apollo	M
(4)	1.682-720	37 7/12	Adrastus	Polynices, Apollo[96]	T:8, M
(5)	2.715-42	28	Tydeus	Minerva	M
(6)	3.471-96	25 7/12	Amphiaraus	Jupiter	M

---

[87] The anonymous Theban apostrophises Jupiter briefly (1.178-80) in his vituperation of Polynices and Eteocles, but his speech appears to be directed mainly to his compatriots.

[88] The vituperative tone of Maeon's speech overshadows his account of the Thebans' encounter with Tydeus, his prophetic words, and a brief farewell to the king.

[89] A series of rhetorical questions constituting a vituperation.

[90] A rhetorical question intended as a boast.

[91] This speech begins as a command but concludes as a boast.

[92] Hercules' address commences in an interrogative manner but works its way into a laudation of Minerva.

[93] A difficult speech to classify because of its brevity and the context in which it appears. The predominant feature of the speech is its vituperative tone.

[94] Oedipus' words are in response to Creon's command to depart from Thebes, but the blind man's vituperation of Creon predominates his speech.

[95] A speech of self-deprecation.

[96] Adrastus briefly addresses Polynices before making a prayer of moderate length to Apollo.

No.	Book/Lines	Lines of Verse	Addressor(s)	Addressee(s)	Cluster: Speech No.
(7)	4.383-404	21 7/12	Bacchic priestess[97]	Bacchus	M
(8)	4.473-87	15	Tiresias	Pluto	M
(9)	4.501-18	18 1/12	Tiresias	Underworld goddesses	T:1
(10)	4.753-71	19	Adrastus	Hypsipyle[98]	D:1
(11)	4.832-50	19	Argive chieftain	Nymph of Langia	M
(12)	6.197-201[99]	4 7/12	Lycurgus	Jupiter	M
(13)	6.633-37	5	Parthenopaeus	Diana	M
(14)	7.93-103	10 1/4	Adrastus	Opheltes	M
(15)	7.730-35	5 5/6	Hypseus	Asopus	M
(16)	7.779-88	10	Amphiaraus[100]	Apollo	D:2
(17)	8.90-122	33	Amphiaraus[101]	Pluto	D:2
(18)	8.303-38	35 1/2	Thiodamas	Tellus	M
(19)	8.588-91	3 7/12	Tydeus	Minerva	M
(20)	9.506-10	4	Hippomedon	Mars	M
(21)	9.548-50	2 7/12	Capaneus	Capaneus' right arm[102]	M
(22)	9.608-35	27 5/12	Atalanta	Diana	M
(23)	10.67-69	3	Argolic mothers	Juno	M
(24)	10.337-45	9	Thiodamas	Apollo	M
(25)	10.365-70	5	Dymas	Cynthia	M
(26)	10.762-73	12	Menoeceus	Battle gods and Apollo	M
(27)	11.210-25	16	Eteocles	Jupiter	M
(28)	11.248f.	1 1/6	Eteocles	Jupiter	M
(29)	11.504-08	5	Polynices	Underworld gods	M
(30)	12.256-67	11 1/4	Argia	Thebes	M
(31)	12.771-73	1 7/12	Theseus	Argive deified souls	M

QUESTIONS

No.	Book/Lines	Lines of Verse	Addressor(s)	Addressee(s)	Cluster: Speech No.
(1)	1.438-46	8 5/12	Adrastus	Tydeus and Polynices	T:1
(2)	2.334-52	17 11/12	Argia	Polynices	D:1
(3)	2.535	5/6	Tydeus	Theban warriors	M

---

[97] The queen of the Bacchantes addresses Bacchus directly, but she also prophesies the death-struggle between Eteocles and Polynices and blames the former for Thebes' woes.

[98] Adrastus mistakens Hypsipyle for Diana, so addresses the exiled queen in prayer form.

[99] Lycurgus invokes Jupiter bitterly and tearfully with words that are lamentable in tone; hence the speech could be considered to be a brief lament.

[100] Amphiaraus responds to Apollo's advice to accept his approaching death, then prays to the divinity in what is the predominant part of the speech.

[101] Amphiaraus responds to Pluto's peremptory threat before attempting to assuage his anger.

[102] Capaneus addresses his right arm as if it were a deity.

No.	Book/Lines	Lines of Verse	Addressor(s)	Addressee(s)	Cluster: Speech No.
(4)	3.546	5/12	Melampus[103]	Amphiaraus	D:3
(5)	5.20-27	7 5/6	Adrastus	Hypsipyle	D:3
(6)	7.77-80	4	Mars	Mercury	M
(7)	7.123-26	3 1/6	Argive crowd	*inter se*	I
(8)	7.291-93	3	Antigone	Phorbas	D:3
(9)	7.490-92	2 1/4	Jocasta	Argive princes	M
(10)	11.258f.	1	Companion of Eteocles (2)	Eteocles	M
(11)	12.366f.	1 1/12	Antigone	Argia	T:1

RESPONSIONS[104]

No.	Book/Lines	Lines of Verse	Addressor(s)	Addressee(s)	Cluster: Speech No.
(1)	1.448-50 (to Que)	1 3/4	Tydeus and Polynices	Adrastus	T:2
(2)	1.452-65 (to Que)	13	Tydeus	Adrastus	T:3
(3)	1.465 (to Que)	3/4	Polynices	Adrastus	T:4
(4)	1.676-81 (to Que)	5 7/12	Polynices	Adrastus	T:7
(5)	2.176-88 (to Del)	12 1/4	Tydeus	Adrastus	T:2
(6)	2.189-97 (to Del)	8 5/12	Polynices	Adrastus	T:3
(7)	2.356-62 (to Que)	7	Polynices	Argia	D:2
(8)	2.415-51 (to Del)	36 5/12	Eteocles	Tydeus	D:2
(9)	2.655-59 (to Del)	3 1/3	Tydeus	Menoetes	D:2
(10)	3.295-316 (to Del)	21 7/12	Mars	Venus	D:2
(11)	3.388-93 (to Del)	5 5/6	Adrastus	Polynices	D:2
(12)	3.546f. (to Que)	1	Amphiaraus	Melampus	D:4
(13)	3.712-20 (to Del)	8 5/12	Adrastus	Argia	D:2
(14)	4.776-85 (to Del)	9 1/4	Hypsipyle	Adrastus	D:2

---

[103] See p. 281, n. 10.

[104] The twenty-eight speeches in this category include responses to deliberative speeches (seventeen), direct questions (eight), challenges (one), threats (one) and responses (one).

No.	Book/Lines	Lines of Verse	Addressor(s)	Addressee(s)	Cluster: Speech No.
(15)	5.29-39 (to Que)	10 7/12	Hypsipyle	Adrastus	D:4
(16)	6.819-22 (to Del)	3 1/4	Capaneus	Tydeus and and Hippomedon	T:2
(17)	7.195-221 (to Del)	26 5/12	Jupiter	Bacchus	D:2
(18)	10.360-63 (to Del)	3 1/2	Dymas	Hopleus	D:2
(19)	10.436-38, 441 (to Del)	3 5/12	Dymas	Amphion	D:3
(20)	10.588 (to Del)	5/6	Thebans	Thebans	D:2
(21)	10.680f. (to Del)	1 7/12	Menoeceus	Virtus[105]	D:2
(22)	10.722-34 (to Del)	12 5/12	Menoeceus	Creon	D:2
(23)	11.298-308 (to Del)	10 1/3	Eteocles	Creon	D:2
(24)	11.389-92 (to Cha)	3 1/3	Eteocles	Polynices	D:1[106]
(25)	11.393-95 (to Res)	2 5/6	Polynices	Eteocles	D:2
(26)	11.750-54 (to Del)	4 2/3	Creon	Antigone	T:4
(27)	12.374-80 (to Que)	6 5/12	Argia	Antigone	T:2
(28)	12.689-92 (to Thr)	3 1/4	Creon	Phegeus[107]	M

---

[105] Disguised as Manto.

[106] Eteocles responds to Polynices' challenge, which he is understood to have made, but this is the first speech in direct discourse made in the dialogue.

[107] Creon's response is to Theseus' threat of war reported to have been delivered to the Theban king by the herald (12.683-86).

No.	Book/Lines	Lines of Verse	Addressor(s)	Addressee(s)	Cluster: Speech No.

SOLILOQUIES

No.	Book/Lines	Lines of Verse	Addressor(s)	Addressee(s)	Cluster: Speech No.
(1)	3.6f., 9-18	9 5/6	Eteocles	-------	M
(2)	4.200-10[108]	10 5/6	Argia	-------[109]	M
(3)	4.669-78	8 1/4	Bacchus	-------	M
(4)	6.372-83	11 3/4	Apollo	-------	M
(5)	10.845-47[110]	2 11/12	Capaneus	-------	M
(6)	10.909f.	1 1/2	Jupiter	-------[111]	M

TAUNTS

No.	Book/Lines	Lines of Verse	Addressor(s)	Addressee(s)	Cluster: Speech No.
(1)	2.641	5/6	Brother of Periphas (*sine nomine*)[112]	Tydeus	M
(2)	2.661-68	7	Tydeus	Theban warriors	M
(3)	7.677-79	2 1/4	Capaneus	Eunaeus	D:2
(4)	8.472f.	1 7/12	Tydeus	Idas	M
(5)	8.582f.	1 1/6	Tydeus	Atys	M
(6)	9.96-103	7 7/12	Eteocles	Hippomedon	M
(7)	9.137-39	2 1/3	Hippomedon	Leonteus	M
(8)	9.294-301	7 5/6	Hippomedon	Panemus	M
(9)	9.476-80	4 7/12	Hippomedon	Ismenos	M
(10)	9.557-59	2 5/12	Capaneus	Hypseus	M
(11)	9.779-87	8 3/4	Amphion	Parthenopaeus	D:1

---

[108] On the surface this speech is difficult to classify. Although Argia makes reference to Polynices by using the personal pronoun *tu* (4.204) or *te* (202, 208), the surrounding narrative does not make it clear whether Argia is actually soliloquising, apostrophising Polynices in his absence, or addressing him directly in person. The circumstances of her speech show, however, that she is not speaking face to face with her husband, since he is already departing with the Argive army for Thebes (4.74-92). While the reflective nature of her words resemble the style of the soliloquy (and therefore is subsumed and discussed under this heading), there is the possibility that Argia is apostrophising Polynices, given the personal pronouns and the lack of explicit narrative direction.

[109] On Argia's address to her husband Polynices in this speech, see previous note.

[110] This speech is probably a soliloquy, but Capaneus could just as well be addressing his Argive comrades.

[111] Although Jupiter addresses Capaneus literally (*tune etiam feriendus*?, 10.909), he does not do so directly. Jupiter reflects on what he believes to have been the giants' blasphemous challenge to the authority of the gods in Phlegra where he struck them down with lightning and wonders how man can be so bold as to challenge that power of the gods. The speech is intended to inform the reader what is passing through Jupiter's mind; the cosmocrator does not intend for Capaneus to hear or respond to his words.

[112] The anonymous brother of Periphas taunts Tydeus while in his death throes.

STATISTICAL APPENDIX 2

No.	Book/Lines	Lines of Verse	Addressor(s)	Addressee(s)	Cluster: Speech No.
(12)	9.790-800	11	Parthenopaeus	Amphion	D:2
(13)	10.873-77	3 5/6	Capaneus	Thebans	M
(14)	10.925f.	1 5/6	Capaneus	Jupiter and Olympian gods (*oblique*)	M
(15)	11.548-51	4	Polynices	Eteocles	M
(16)	11.568-72	4 1/3	Polynices	Eteocles	M
(17)	12.779-81	2 11/12	Theseus	Creon	D:2

THREATS

No.	Book/Lines	Lines of Verse	Addressor(s)	Addressee(s)	Cluster: Speech No.
(1)	2.452-67	14 1/12	Tydeus	Eteocles	D:3
(2)	3.648-69	21	Capaneus	Amphiaraus	D:3
(3)	5.656-60	4	Lycurgus[113]	Argive princes	Te:1
(4)	5.672-79	7 5/6	Tydeus[114]	Lycurgus	Te:4
(5)	8.84f.	1 5/12	Pluto[115]	Amphiaraus	D:1
(6)	9.663-67	4 1/3	Diana	Apollo[116]	D:2
(7)	12.761-66	5 11/12	Creon	Theseus	D:1

---

[113] Although Lycurgus questions and commands in his speech, the effect is that of a threat directed at Hypsipyle.

[114] Tydeus taunts and challenges Lycurgus in his comminatory speech.

[115] Pluto phrases his threat to Amphiaraus as a question.

[116] Diana addresses Apollo, but her threat is directed against the Argive warrior who will slay Parthenopaeus (cf. 9.875f.).

STATISTICAL APPENDIX 3

SPEECHES BY CHARACTERS

Table 6. Divine and Human Speeches and Speakers: Totals by Book

Book	Speeches	Divine Speeches	Human Speeches	Divine Speakers[1]	Human Speakers
1	15	3	12	2	6
2	20	3	17	3	8
3	20	3	17	3	11
4	18	3	15	2	10
5	19	2	17	2	10
6	15	1	14	1	8
7	21	5	16	4	11
8	15	3	12	2	7
9	30	11	19	8	9
10	35	5[2]	30	5[3]	15
11	31	6	25	4	12
12	26	1	25	1	7
Total	265	46[2]	219	19[4,5]	62[6]

Table 7. Comparison Between Speeches by Central Figures

Character	No. of Speeches	Lines of Verse	Ave. Length
Tydeus	24	186 1/3	7.8
Adrastus	22	296 1/3	13.5
Capaneus	14	75 7/12	5.4
Polynices	13	119 1/6	9.2

---

[1] Including groups and spirits of the dead.

[2] Including the deliberation of Amphiaraus' spirit (10.206-11).

[3] Including Amphiaraus' spirit.

[4] This figure counts each speaker or group of speakers only once, although he/she/it may have spoken on more than one occasion in more than one book.

[5] Not including Amphiaraus' spirit.

[6] Including Amphiaraus (and his spirit).

312

Character	No. of Speeches	Lines of Verse	Ave. Length
Argia	12[7]	128 7/12	11.7[8]
Eteocles	10	126 1/6	12.6
Amphiaraus	9[9]	152 1/3	16.9
Antigone	9	73 1/2	8.2
Jupiter	7	142 1/4	20.3
Creon	7	102 11/12	14.7
Tiresias	7	90 5/12	12.9
Hippomedon	7	29 1/3	4.2

Table 8. Speeches by Divinities, Demigods and Spirits

	Addressor	Speech Type	Book/Lines	Lines of Verse	Addressee(s)
(1)	Apollo	Sol	6.372-83	11 3/4	-------
		Com	7.772-77	5 11/12	Amphiaraus
		O&P (Int)	9.650-62	12 3/4	Diana

Apollo: 3 speeches; 30 5/12 lines; ave. 10.1 lines per speech

	Addressor	Speech Type	Book/Lines	Lines of Verse	Addressee(s)
(2)	Bacchus	Sol	4.669-78	8 1/4	-------
		Com	4.684-96	12 5/6	Water nymphs
		Com	5.271-84	13 1/6	Thoas, Hypsipyle
		Del	7.155-92	38	Jupiter
		Apo	10.888f.	1 1/2	Jupiter

Bacchus: 5 speeches; 73 3/4 lines; ave. 14.8 lines

	Addressor	Speech Type	Book/Lines	Lines of Verse	Addressee(s)
(3)	Diana	Thr	9.663-67	4 1/3	Apollo
		Apo	9.713-25	12 1/12	Menoeceus
		Del	9.812-14	2 7/12	Parthenopaeus

Diana: 3 speeches; 19 lines; ave. 6.3 lines

	Addressor	Speech Type	Book/Lines	Lines of Verse	Addressee(s)
(4)	Hercules	P&B (Lau)	8.502-16	14 7/12	Minerva
(5)	Iris	Com	10.126-31	6	Somnus

---

[7] This figure includes Argia's deliberative speech recounted by herself to Polynices (12.333-35).

[8] Excluding the recounted deliberation of Argia to Polynices (12.333-35).

[9] This figure includes the deliberation of Amphiaraus' spirit reported by Thiodamas to the Achaean leaders (10.206-11).

Addressor	Speech Type	Book/Lines	Lines of Verse	Addressee(s)
(6) Ismenis	Apo	9.356	1/6	Crenaeus
	M&C (Lam)	9.376-98	23	Crenaeus

Ismenis: 2 speeches; 23 1/6 lines; ave. 11.6 lines

(7) Ismenos	Apo	9.421-45	24 5/6	Jupiter, Bacchus, Hippomedon

(8) Juno	For	1.250-82	32 7/12	Jupiter
	Del	9.511-19	8 1/6	Jupiter
	Del	12.299-308	10	Diana

Juno: 3 speeches; 50 3/4 lines; ave. 16 11/12 lines

(9) Jupiter	For	1.214-47	34	Olympian gods
	Com	1.285-302	16 3/4	Juno, Mercury
	Com	3.229-52	23 7/12	Mars, Olympian gods
	Com	7.6-33	28	Mercury
	Res (to Del)	7.195-221	26 5/12	Bacchus
	Sol	10.909f.	1 1/2	Capaneus
	Com	11.122-33	12	Olympian gods

Jupiter: 7 speeches; 142 1/4 lines; ave. 20.3 lines

(10) Laius' spirit	Del	2.102-19	18	Eteocles
	O&P (Pro)	4.626-44	18 2/3	Tiresias, Eteocles

Laius' spirit: 2 speeches; 36 2/3 lines; ave. 18.3 lines

(11) Mars	Com	3.295-316	21 7/12	Venus
	Que	7.77-80	4	Mercury
	M&C (Lam)	9.835-37	2 7/12	Diana

Mars: 3 speeches; 28 1/6 lines; ave. 9.4 lines

(12) Megaera	Com	11.201f.	1 1/6	Polynices

(13) Minerva	Com	2.686-90	4	Tydeus

(14) Pietas	Apo	11.465-70, 471	5 1/3	Natura
	Enc (Coh)	11.478-81	3 5/12	Argive and Theban warriors

Pietas: 2 speeches; 8 3/4 lines; ave. 4.4 lines

(15) Pluto	Com	8.34-79	45	Underworld deities and Tisiphone
	Thr	8.84f.	1 5/12	Amphiaraus

Pluto: 2 speeches; 46 5/12 lines; ave. 23.2 lines

Addressor	Speech Type	Book/Lines	Lines of Verse	Addressee(s)
(16) A Shade	Apo	2.19-25	6 5/6	Laius
(17) Tisiphone	Del	9.157-65, 166-68	9 1/3	Hippomedon
	Del	11.76-112	37	Megaera
	P&B (Vit)	11.484-92	8 1/6	Pietas
Tisiphone: 3 speeches; 54 1/2 lines; ave. 18.2 lines				
(18) Venus	Del	3.269-91	22 5/12	Mars
	Com	5.136, 137f.	2 1/4	Polyxo
	Del	9.825-30	5 7/12	Mars
Venus: 3 speeches; 30 1/4 lines; ave. 10.1 lines				
(19) Virtus	Del	10.662-71	10	Menoeceus

Table 9. Speeches by Humans

The following appendix records alphabetically the speeches of human characters.

Addressor	Speech Type	Book/Lines	Lines of Verse	Addressee(s)
(1) Actor	Del	10.330-35	5 7/12	Thiodamas
(2) Adrastus	Que	1.438-46	8 5/12	Tydeus and Polynices
	Del	1.468-73	5 5/12	Polynices and Tydeus
	Pra	1.498-510	12 7/12	Nox, Fortuna
	Nar	1.557-672	115 5/6[10]	Tydeus and Polynices
	Pra	1.682-720	37 7/12	Polynices, Apollo
	Del	2.152-72	21	Tydeus and Polynices
	Res (to Del)	3.388-93	5 5/6	Polynices
	Res (to Del)	3.712-20	8 5/12	Argia
	Pra	4.753-71	19	Hypsipyle
	Que	5.20-27	7 5/6	Hypsipyle
	Del	5.43-47	5	Hypsipyle
	Com	5.669-71[11]	1 7/12	Lycurgus and Tydeus
	Com	5.701-03	2 1/3	Argive warriors
	Com	6.319f.	1 1/4	Polynices

---

[10] Including Coroebus' speech recounted by Adrastus (1.643-61).

[11] A joint address with Amphiaraus.

Addressor	Speech Type	Book/Lines	Lines of Verse	Addressee(s)
	Com	6.627-30	3 5/12	Idas and other running contestants
	Enc (Exh)	6.726-30	4 5/6	Phlegyas, Achaean competitors
	Com	6.809-12	4	Achaean warriors
	Com	6.914-19	5 7/12	Agreus and Polynices
	Pra	7.93-103	10 1/4	Opheltes
	Enc (Coh)	10.236-44	8 7/12	Achaean warriors
	Enc (Coh)	10.266-68	1 11/12	Achaean warriors
	Del	11.429-35	5 2/3	Polynices and Eteocles

Adrastus: 22 speeches; 296 1/3 lines; ave. 13.5 lines per speech

(3)	Aegyptus	Del	11.242-45	4	Eteocles
(4)	Aletes	M&C (Con)	3.179-213	35	Thebans
(5)	Amphiaraus	Pra	3.471-96	25 7/12	Jupiter
		Des	3.516-45	29 3/4	Melampus
		Res (to Que)	3.546f.	1	Melampus
		O&P (Int)	3.620-47	26 11/12	Achaeans
		Com	5.669-71[12]	1 7/12	Lycurgus and Tydeus
		O&P (Ora)	5.733-52	20	Adrastus and Argive princes
		Pra	7.779-88	10	Apollo
		Pra	8.90-122	33	Pluto
		Del	10.206-11[13]	4 1/2	Thiodamas

Amphiaraus (and his spirit): 9 speeches; 152 1/3 lines; ave. 16.9 lines

(6)	Amphion	Tau	9.779-87	8 3/4	Parthenopaeus
		Com	10.393	7/12	Dymas and Hopleus
		Del	10.431-34	3 3/4	Dymas

Amphion: 3 speeches; 13 1/12 lines; ave. 4.4 lines

(7)	Antigone	Del	7.247-52	5 7/12	Phorbas
		Que	7.291-93	3	Phorbas
		Del	11.363-82	19 1/6	Polynices
		Del	11.708-39	31	Creon
		Que	12.366f.	1 1/12	Argia
		P&B (Vit)	12.382-85	3 1/6	Argia

---

[12] Spoken jointly with Adrastus.

[13] This speech is delivered by Amphiaraus' spirit.

Addressor	Speech Type	Book/Lines	Lines of Verse	Addressee(s)
	Apo	12.437-46	10	Argia, Eteocles, Polynices
	Del[14]	12.458	1/4	Theban soldiers
	Del[14]	12.459	1/4	Theban soldiers

Antigone: 9 speeches; 73 1/2 lines; ave. 8.2 lines

(8) Arcadian warriors	Enc (Coh)	6.618	1/6	*inter se*

(9) Argia	Que	2.334-52	17 11/12	Polynices
	Del	3.687-710	24	Adrastus
	Sol	4.200-10	10 5/6	-------
	Del	12.196-204	8 1/3	Argive widows
	Apo	12.209-19	10 1/12	Polynices, Ornytus
	Pra	12.256-67	11 1/4	Thebes
	M&C (Lam)	12.322-48	24 1/4[15]	Polynices
	Del	12.333-35	2 3/4	Polynices
	Res (to Que)	12.374-80	6 5/12	Antigone
	Nar	12.392-404	12 1/4	Antigone
	Del[16]	12.458	1/6	Theban soldiers
	Del[16]	12.459	1/3	Theban soldiers

Argia: 12 speeches;[17] 128 7/12 lines; ave. 11.7 lines[18]

(10) Argive chieftain	Pra	4.832-50	19	Nymph of Langia

(11) Argive crowd	Que	7.123-26	3 1/6	*inter se*

(12) Argive warriors	Enc (Exh)	4.812	1/6	*inter se*
	M&C (Epi)	8.174-207	34	*inter se*

Argive warriors: 2 speeches; 34 1/6 lines; ave. 17.1 lines

(13) Argolic mothers	Pra	10.67-69	3	Juno

(14) Argus	Enc (Exh)	4.811	1/6	Argive warriors

---

[14] See p. 302, n. 58.

[15] This figure excludes Argia's deliberative speech recounted by herself to Polynices (12.333-35).

[16] See p. 302, n. 58.

[17] This figure includes Argia's deliberative speech recounted by herself to Polynices (12.333-35).

[18] Excluding the recounted deliberation of Argia to Polynices (12.333-35).

Addressor	Speech Type	Book/Lines	Lines of Verse	Addressee(s)
(15) Atalanta	Del	4.318-40	22 7/12	Parthenopaeus
	Pra	9.608-35	27 5/12	Diana

Atalanta: 2 speeches; 50 lines; ave. 25 lines

(16) Bacchantes' queen	Pra	4.383-404	21 7/12	Bacchus
(17) Brother of Periphas	Tau	2.641	5/6	Tydeus
(18) Capaneus	Enc (Coh)	3.607-18	10 5/6	Achaeans, Amphiaraus
	Thr	3.648-69	21	Amphiaraus
	Cha	5.565-70	4 5/6	Serpent
	Cha	6.734-37	3 2/3	Achaean warriors
	Res (to Del)	6.819-22	3 1/4	Tydeus and Hippomedon
	Tau	7.677-79	2 1/4	Eunaeus
	Pra	9.548-50	2 7/12	Capaneus' right arm
	Tau	9.557-59	2 5/12	Hypseus
	Apo	9.562-65	3 5/6	Hippomedon
	Enc (Coh)	10.482-86	4 7/12	Argive warriors
	Sol	10.845-47	2 11/12	Argive warriors
	Tau	10.873-77	3 5/6	Thebans
	Cha	10.899-906	7 3/4	Jupiter and Olympian gods
	Tau	10.925f.	1 5/6	Jupiter and Olympian gods (*oblique*)

Capaneus: 14 speeches; 75 7/12 lines; ave. 5.4 lines

(19) Chromis	Enc (Coh)	2.620-23	3 3/4	Theban warriors
(20) Companion of Eteocles (1)	Del	11.257f.	7/12	Eteocles
(21) Companion of Eteocles (2)	Que	11.258f.	1	Eteocles
(22) Companion of Eteocles (3)	P&B (Vit)	11.259f.	1 2/3	Eteocles
(23) Companion of Eteocles (4)	Del	11.260-62	1 5/12	Eteocles

318

Addressor	Speech Type	Book/Lines	Lines of Verse	Addressee(s)
(24) Coroebus	Pra	1.643-61	19	Apollo
(25) Crenaeus	Cha	9.340-43	3 1/6	Hippomedon
	Apo	9.350	1/6	Ismenis

Crenaeus: 2 speeches; 3 1/3 lines; ave. 1.7 lines

Addressor	Speech Type	Book/Lines	Lines of Verse	Addressee(s)
(26) Creon	Del	10.690-718	28 5/12	Menoeceus
	Del	11.269-96	27 5/6	Eteocles
	Com	11.669-72	3 7/12	Oedipus
	Res (to Del)	11.750-54	4 2/3	Creon
	M&C (Lam)	12.72-92, 94-102	29 1/4	Menoeceus
	Res (to Thr)	12.689-92	3 1/4	Phegeus
	Thr	12.761-66	5 11/12	Theseus

Creon: 7 speeches; 102 11/12 lines; ave. 14.7 lines

Addressor	Speech Type	Book/Lines	Lines of Verse	Addressee(s)
(27) Dymas	Res (to Del)	10.360-63	3 1/2	Hopleus
	Pra	10.365-70	5	Cynthia
	Del	10.423-30	7 5/12	Theban warriors
	Res (to Del)	10.436-38, 441	3 5/12	Amphion

Dymas: 4 speeches; 19 1/3 lines; ave. 4.8 lines

Addressor	Speech Type	Book/Lines	Lines of Verse	Addressee(s)
(28) Eteocles	Res (to Del)	2.415-51	36 5/12	Tydeus
	Sol	3.6f., 9-18	9 5/6	-------
	Enc (Coh)	7.375-90	15 5/12	Theban troops
	Enc (Coh)	9.12-24	11 5/6	Theban warriors
	Tau	9.96-103	7 7/12	Hippomedon
	Enc (Coh)	10.21-35	14 1/4	Theban warriors
	Pra	11.210-25	16	Jupiter
	Pra	11.248f.	1 1/6	Jupiter
	Res (to Del)	11.298-308	10 1/3	Creon
	Res (to Cha)	11.389-92	3 1/3	Polynices

Eteocles: 10 speeches; 126 1/6 lines; ave. 12.6 lines

Addressor	Speech Type	Book/Lines	Lines of Verse	Addressee(s)
(29) Eunaeus	P&B (Vau)	7.663-78	5 1/6	Argive warriors
(30) Eurydice (Menoeceus' mother)	M&C (Lam)	10.793-814	22	Menoeceus
(31) Eurydice (Opheltes' mother)	M&C (Lam)	6.138-73, 174-76, 180-84	42 5/6	Opheltes
(32) Evadne	Del	12.546-86	41	Theseus

SPEECH AND RHETORIC IN STATIUS' *THEBAID*

Addressor	Speech Type	Book/Lines	Lines of Verse	Addressee(s)
(33) Hippomedon	Cha	6.656-59	2 5/12	Achaean warriors
	Del	6.816f.[19]	1 7/12	Capaneus
	Tau	9.137-39	2 1/3	Leonteus
	Del	9.211-17	6 7/12	Tydeus' steed
	Tau	9.294-301	7 5/6	Panemus
	Tau	9.476-80	4 7/12	Ismenos
	Pra	9.506-10	4	Mars
Hippomedon: 7 speeches; 29 1/3 lines; ave. 4.2 lines				
(34) Hopleus	Del	10.351-59	9	Dymas
(35) Hypseus	Pra	7.730-35	5 5/6	Asopus
	P&B (Vau)	9.544-46	2 1/6	Aonian warriors
Hypseus: 2 speeches; 8 lines; ave. 4 lines				
(36) Hypsipyle	Res (to Del)	4.776-85	9 1/4	Adrastus
	Res (to Que)	5.29-39	10 7/12	Adrastus
	Nar	5.49-498	447 2/3[20]	Adrastus and Argive warriors
	Del	5.245-47	2 1/6	Thoas
	M&C (Lam)	5.608-35	27 1/4	Opheltes
Hypsipyle: 5 speeches;[21] 496 11/12 lines; ave. 124.2 lines[22]				
(37) Ide	M&C (Lam)	3.151-68	18	Ide's sons
(38) Ismene	Nar	8.622-35	13 7/12	Antigone
(39) Jocasta	Del	7.483-85	2	Argive warriors
	Que	7.490-92	2 1/4	Argive princes
	Del	7.497-527	30 1/4	Polynices, Argive warriors
	Del	11.329-53	25	Eteocles
Jocasta: 4 speeches; 59 1/2 lines; ave. 14.9 lines				

---

[19] Spoken jointly with Tydeus.

[20] Including the reported speeches of Polyxo (5.104-29, 132-36, 137, 139-42), Venus (136, 137f.), Bacchus (271-84) and the Lemnian crowd (491f.), but excluding Hypsipyle's own speech that she relates to Adrastus and the Argive army (245-47).

[21] Including Hypsipyle's own recounted speech (5.245-47).

[22] Excluding Hypsipyle's own reported speech (5.245-47).

Addressor	Speech Type	Book/Lines	Lines of Verse	Addressee(s)
(40) Lemnian crowd	P&B (Vit)	5.491f.	2	*inter se*
(41) Lycurgus	Thr	5.656-60	4	Argive princes
	O&P (Pro)	5.681-89	8 1/3	Tydeus
	Pra	6.197-201	4 7/12	Jupiter

Lycurgus: 3 speeches; 16 11/12 lines; ave. 5.6 lines

(42) Maeon	P&B (Vit)	3.59-77, 83-87	22 7/12	Eteocles
(43) Manto	Des	4.519-35	17	Tiresias
	Des	4.553-78	26	Tiresias

Manto: 2 speeches; 43 lines; ave. 21.5 lines

(44) Megareus	Com	10.492	1	Theban sentry
(45) Melampus	Des	3.502-15	14	Amphiaraus, Apollo
	Que	3.546	5/12	Amphiaraus

Melampus: 2 speeches; 14 5/12 lines; ave. 7.2 lines

(46) Menoeceus	Enc (Coh)	8.600-05	5 1/4	Theban warriors
	Res (to Del)	10.680f.	1 7/12	Virtus[23]
	Res (to Del)	10.722-34	12 5/12	Creon
	Pra	10.762-73	12	Battle gods and Apollo

Menoeceus: 4 speeches; 31 1/4 lines; ave. 7.8 lines

(47) Menoetes (Theban warrior)	Del	2.649-54	5	Tydeus
(48) Menoetes (Argia's attendant)	Des	12.246-54	9	Argia
	Del	12.406-08	3	Argia and Antigone

Menoetes: 2 speeches; 12 lines; ave. 6 lines

(49) Oedipus	Pra	1.56-87	32	Underworld gods
	Del	11.594f.	1 1/3	Antigone
	M&C (Lam)	11.605-26, 630f.	23 5/12	Eteocles and Polynices
	P&B (Vit)	11.677-707	30 5/12	Creon

Oedipus: 4 speeches; 87 1/6 lines; ave. 21.8 lines

---

[23] Disguised as Manto.

Addressor	Speech Type	Book/Lines	Lines of Verse	Addressee(s)
(50) Ornytus	Del	12.149-66	17 7/12	Widows of Argive leaders
(51) Palaemon	Del	8.138-50	12 1/4	Adrastus
(52) Parthenopaeus	Pra	6.633-37	5	Diana
	Tau	9.790-800	11	Amphion
	Del	9.815-19	5	Diana[24]
	Com	9.885-900, 901-07	22 5/12	Dorceus

Parthenopaeus: 4 speeches; 43 5/12 lines; ave. 10.9 lines

(53) Phorbas	Des	7.254-89	36	Antigone
	Des	7.294-358, 363-73	75 7/12	Antigone

Phorbas: 2 speeches; 111 7/12 lines; ave. 55.8 lines

(54) Polynices	Res (to Que)	1.448-50[25]	1 3/4	Adrastus
	Res (to Que)	1.465	3/4	Adrastus
	Res (to Que)	1.676-81	5 7/12	Adrastus
	Res (to Del)	2.189-97	8 5/12	Adrastus
	Res (to Que)	2.356-62	7	Argia
	Del	3.367-81	13 1/2	Eteocles, Argives, Adrastus
	M&C (Lam)	9.49-72, 75f.	25 1/6	Tydeus
	Del	11.155-92	38	Adrastus
	Res (to Res)	11.393-95	2 5/6	Eteocles
	Pra	11.504-08	5	Underworld gods
	Tau	11.548-51	4	Eteocles
	Com	11.557-60	2 5/6	Argive companions
	Tau	11.568-72	4 1/3	Eteocles

Polynices: 13 speeches; 119 1/6 lines; ave. 9.2 lines

(55) Polyxo	Del	5.104-29, 132-42	36 5/12	Lemnian women
(56) Priestess	O&P (Ora)	5.647	1	Lycurgus
(57) A Theban	P&B (Vit)	1.173-96	23 1/3	Thebans, Jupiter

---

[24] Disguised as Phereclus.

[25] Spoken jointly with Tydeus.

STATISTICAL APPENDIX 3

Addressor	Speech Type	Book/Lines	Lines of Verse	Addressee(s)
(58) Thebans	Del	10.584-87	2 5/12	Thebans
	Res (to Del)	10.588	5/6	Thebans

Thebans: 2 speeches; 3 1/4 lines; ave. 1.6 lines

(59) Theseus	Com	12.590-98	8 3/4	Creon, Phegeus
	Enc (Coh)	12.642-48	7	Attic troops
	Pra	12.771-73	1 7/12	Argive spirits
	Tau	12.779-81	2 11/12	Creon

Theseus: 4 speeches; 20 1/4 lines; ave. 5.1 lines

(60) Thiodamas	Pra	8.303-38	35 1/2	Tellus
	Enc (Coh)	10.188-218	31[26]	Achaean leaders
	Enc (Coh)	10.269-71	2 5/12	Achaean warriors
	Pra	10.337-45	9	Apollo

Thiodamas: 4 speeches; 77 11/12 lines; ave. 19.5 lines

(61) Tiresias	Pra	4.473-87	15	Pluto
	Pra	4.501-18	18 1/12	Underworld goddesses
	Com	4.536-48	12 5/6	Manto
	O&P (Int)	4.583-602	18 3/4	Manto
	Del	4.610-24	14 1/4	Ghost of Laius
	Com	10.592-98	5 1/2	Thebans
	O&P (Ora)	10.610-15	6	Thebans

Tiresias: 7 speeches; 90 5/12 lines; ave. 12.9 lines

(62) Tydeus	Res (to Que)	1.448-50[27]	1 3/4	Adrastus
	Res (to Que)	1.452-65	13	Adrastus
	Res (to Del)	2.176-88	12 1/4	Adrastus
	Del	2.393-409	17	Eteocles
	Thr	2.452-67	14 1/12	Eteocles
	Que	2.535	5/6	Theban warriors
	Cha	2.547-49	2 5/12	Theban warriors
	Res (to Del)	2.655-59	3 1/3	Menoetes
	Tau	2.661-68	7	Theban warriors
	Com	2.697-703	7	Maeon
	Pra	2.715-42	28	Minerva
	Enc (Coh)	3.348-65	17 1/4	Argives and Adrastus
	Com	5.663f.	3/4	Lycurgus
	Thr	5.672-79	7 5/6	Lycurgus

---

[26] Including the recounted speech of Amphiaraus' spirit (10.206-11).

[27] Spoken jointly with Polynices.

Addressor	Speech Type	Book/Lines	Lines of Verse	Addressee(s)
	Del	6.816f.[28]	1 7/12	Capaneus
	P&B (Vau)	6.906-08	2 7/12	Tydeus' companions
	Del	7.539-59	20 5/12	Argive warriors, Jocasta, Polynices
	Com	7.612-14	2 5/12	Jocasta, Antigone and Ismene
	Tau	8.472f.	1 7/12	Idas
	Tau	8.582f.	1 1/6	Atys
	Pra	8.588-91	3 7/12	Minerva
	Cha	8.664-72	8 5/12	Theban warriors
	Cha	8.677-79	2 5/6	Eteocles
	Del	8.735-44	9 1/4	Argive warriors

Tydeus: 24 speeches; 186 1/3 lines; ave. 7.8 lines

---

[28] Spoken jointly with Hippomedon.

STATISTICAL APPENDIX 4

DISGUISED CHARACTERS' SPEECHES

Table 10. List of Disguised Characters' Speeches

Book/Lines	Lines of Verse	Speaker	Disguised Figure
(1) 2.102-19	18	Ghost of Laius	Tiresias
(2) 9.157-65, 166-68	9 1/3	Tisiphone	Halys
(3) 9.812-14	2 7/12	Diana	Dorceus
(4) 10.662-71	10	Virtus	Manto
(5) 11.201f.	1 1/6	Megaera	Phereclus
(6) 11.478-81	3 5/12	Pietas	A male warrior

STATISTICAL APPENDIX 5

COLLECTIVE AND TANDEM SPEECHES

Table 11. Collective Speeches

	Book/Lines	Speech Type	Addressors
(1)	4.812	Enc (Exh)	Argive warriors
(2)	5.491f.[1]	P&B (Vit)	Lemnian crowd
(3)	6.618[1]	Enc (Coh)	Arcadian warriors
(4)	7.123-26	Que	Argive crowd
(5)	8.174-207	M&C (Epi)	Argive troops
(6)	10.67-69	Pra	Argolic mothers
(7)	10.584-87[2]	Del	Thebans
(8)	10.588[2]	Res (to Del)	Thebans

Table 12. Tandem Speeches

	Book/Lines	Speech Type	Addressors
(1)	1.448-50	Res (to Que)	Tydeus and Polynices
(2)	5.669-71	Com	Adrastus and Amphiaraus
(3)	6.816f.	Del	Tydeus and Hippomedon

---

[1] Lipscomb (1909: 45) omits this speech from his list of collective speeches.

[2] See p. 289 n. 17.

GODS, HUMANS AND OBJECTS OF ADDRESS

*Table 13. Number of Occasions Figures Addressed
and Number of Speeches by Central Figures*

Character	No. of Times Addressee/Speaker	No. of Occasions Addressed[1]	No. of Speeches
Tydeus	38	14	24
Adrastus	35	13	22
Polynices	33[2]	20[2]	13
Eteocles	30	20	10
Argive warriors[3]	20	17	3
Jupiter	19	12	7
Argia	19[2]	7	12[2]
Antigone	18	9	9
Capaneus	16	2	14
Theban warriors[4]	15	15	0
Amphiaraus	15	6	9
Creon	13	6	7
Hippomedon	13	6	7
Apollo	10	7	3
Tiresias	10	3	7

---

[1] Not including speeches addressed indirectly to an individual, as in the soliloquy where Jupiter addresses Capaneus literally (*tune etiam feriendus*, 10.910) but actually does not intend that Capaneus hear or respond to his verbal reflexion. These figures also do not include general conversations (*inter se*) where individuals in a group speak informally to one another (5.491f., 6.618, 7.123-26, 8.174-207).

[2] This figure includes Argia's deliberative speech recounted by herself to Polynices (12.333-35).

[3] Including allied Achaean and Arcadian troops; not including Attic warriors and groups of Argive and Achaean citizenry, princes and athletic competitors.

[4] Not including groups of Theban citizenry.

Table 14. Nonhuman and Nondivine Objects of Address

Book/Lines	Addressed Object	Speaker
5.565-70	Serpent	Capaneus
9.211-17	Tydeus' steed	Hopleus
9.548-50	Capaneus' right arm	Capaneus

Table 15. Personified Objects and Abstracts Addressed

Book/Lines	Addressed Object	Speaker
1.498-510	Nox, Fortuna	Adrastus
11.465-70, 471	Natura	Pietas
11.484-492	Pietas	Tisiphone

INSERTED SPEECHES

Table 16. List of Inserted Speeches[1]

	Book/Lines	Lines of Verse	Speech Type	Speaker	Reporter(s) of Speech
(1)	1.643-61	19	Pra	Coroebus	Adrastus
(2)	5.104-29, 132-42	36 5/12[2]	Del	Polyxo	Hypsipyle
(3)	5.136, 137f.[3]	2 1/4	Com	Venus	Polyxo, Hypsipyle[4]
(4)	5.245-47	2 1/6	Del	Hypsipyle	Hypsipyle
(5)	5.271-84	13 1/6	Com	Bacchus	Hypsipyle
(6)	5.491f.	2	P&B (Vit)	Lemnian crowd	Hypsipyle
(7)	10.206-11	4 1/2	Del	Amphiaraus' spirit	Hypsipyle
(8)	12.333-35	2 3/4	Del	Argia	Polynices

---

[1] An inserted speech is also referred in this book as a reported, recounted, related or speech within a speech.

[2] Including Venus' command recounted by Polyxo and Hypsipyle (5.136, 137f.).

[3] A reported speech within a reported speech within a speech.

[4] Recounted by Polyxo to Hypsipyle, who in her narrative relates it to Adrastus.

MONOLOGUES AND SPEECH CLUSTERS

Table 17. Totals by Book for Monologues and Speech Clusters

Book	Speeches	Monologues	Dialogues	Trialogues	Tetralogues	General Interlocutions
1	15	6	1	1	0	0
2	20	10	3	1	0	0
3	20	7	5	0	0	0
4	18	8	1	1	0	1
5	19	9	0[1]	0	1	1
6	15	12	0	1	0	1
7	21	7	5	0	0	1
8	15	12	1	0	0	1
9	30	21	4	0	0	0
10	35	24	5	0	0	0
11	31	23	2	1	0	0
12	26	19	1	1	0	0
Total	265	158	28	6	1	5

Table 18. Monologues

No.	Book/Lines	Lines of Verse	Speaker(s)	No.	Book/Lines	Lines of Verse	Speaker(s)
			MONOLOGUES: SOLILOQUIES				
(1)	3.6-7, 9-18	9 5/6	Eteocles	(2)	4.200-10	10 5/6	Argia
(3)	4.669-78	8 1/4	Bacchus	(4)	6.372-83	11 3/4	Apollo
(5)	10.845-47	2 11/12	Capaneus	(6)	10.909f.	1 1/2	Jupiter

---

[1] There is one dialogue between Adrastus and Hypsipyle that continues from book 4.

STATISTICAL APPENDIX 8

No.	Book/Lines	Lines of Verse	Speaker(s)	No.	Book/Lines	Lines of Verse	Speaker(s)
			MONOLOGUES: NO REPLY				
(1)	1.56-87	32	Oedipus	(2)	1.173-96	23 1/3	A Theban
(3)	1.292-302[2]	10 5/12	Jupiter	(4)	1.498-510	12 7/12	Adrastus
(5)	1.643-61[3]	19	Coroebus	(6)	1.696-720[4]	25	Adrastus
(7)	2.19-25	6 5/6	A Shade	(8)	2.102-19	18	Ghost of Laius
(9)	2.535	5/6	Tydeus	(10)	2.547-49	2 5/12	Tydeus
(11)	2.620-23	3 3/4	Chromis	(12)	2.641	5/6	Brother of Periphas
(13)	2.661-68	7	Tydeus	(14)	2.686-90	4	Minerva
(15)	2.697-703	7	Tydeus	(16)	2.715-42	28	Tydeus
(17)	3.59-77, 83-87	22 7/12	Maeon	(18)	3.151-68	18	Ide
(19)	3.179-213	35	Aletes	(20)	3.229-52	23 7/12	Jupiter
(21)	3.348-65	17 1/4	Tydeus	(22)	3.471-96	25 7/12	Amphiaraus
(23)	4.318-40	22 7/12	Atalanta	(24)	4.383-404	21 7/12	Queen of the Bacchantes
(25)	4.473-87	15	Tiresias	(26)	4.684-96	12 5/6	Bacchus
(27)	4.811	1/6	Argus	(28)	4.832-50	19	Argive chieftain
(29)	5.104-29, 132-42[5]	36 5/12	Polyxo	(30)	5.136, 137f.[6]	2 1/4	Venus
(31)	5.245-47[5]	2 1/6	Hypsipyle	(32)	5.271-84[5]	13 1/6	Bacchus
(33)	5.565-70	4 5/6	Capaneus	(34)	5.608-35	27 1/4	Hypsipyle
(35)	5.647	1	Priestess	(36)	5.701-03	2 1/3	Adrastus
(37)	5.733-52	20	Amphiaraus	(38)	6.138-73, 174-76, 180-84	42 5/6	Eurydice
(39)	6.197-201	4 7/12	Lycurgus	(40)	6.319f.	1 1/4	Adrastus
(41)	6.627-30	3 5/12	Adrastus	(42)	6.633-37	5	Parthenopaeus
(43)	6.656-59	2 5/12	Hippomedon	(44)	6.726-30	4 5/6	Adrastus
(45)	6.734-37	3 2/3	Capaneus	(46)	6.809-12	4	Adrastus
(47)	6.906-08	2 7/12	Tydeus	(48)	6.914-19	5 7/12	Adrastus
(49)	7.6-33	28	Jupiter	(50)	7.77-80	4	Mars
(51)	7.93-103	10 1/4	Adrastus	(52)	7.375-90	15 5/12	Eteocles

---

[2] Part of a speech where Jupiter addresses Mercury after conversing with Juno.

[3] Related by Adrastus in his narrative (1.557-672).

[4] Portion of an address where Adrastus converses with Tydeus and Polynices.

[5] A speech recounted by Hypsipyle in her narrative (5.49-498).

[6] A speech within a speech recounted by Hypsipyle (5.49-498).

No.	Book/Lines	Lines of Verse	Speaker(s)	No.	Book/Lines	Lines of Verse	Speaker(s)
(53)	7.483-85	2	Jocasta	(54)	7.490-92	2 1/4	Jocasta
(55)	7.730-35	5 5/6	Hypseus	(56)	8.34-79	45	Pluto
(57)	8.138-50	12 1/4	Palaemon	(58)	8.303-38	35 1/2	Thiodamas
(59)	8.472f.	1 7/12	Tydeus	(60)	8.502-16	14 7/12	Hercules
(61)	8.582f.	1 1/6	Tydeus	(62)	8.588-91	3 7/12	Tydeus
(63)	8.600-05	5 1/4	Menoeceus	(64)	8.622-35	13 7/12	Ismene
(65)	8.664-72	8 5/12	Tydeus	(66)	8.677-79	2 5/6	Tydeus
(67)	8.735-44	9 1/4	Tydeus	(68)	9.12-24	11 5/6	Tydeus
(69)	9.49-72, 75f.	25 1/6	Polynices	(70)	9.96-103	7 7/12	Eteocles
(71)	9.137-39	2 1/3	Hippomedon	(72)	9.157-65, 166-68	9 1/3	Tisiphone
(73)	9.211-17	6 7/12	Hippomedon	(74)	9.294-301	7 5/6	Hippomedon
(75)	9.340-43	3 1/6	Crenaeus	(76)	9.421-45	24 5/6	Ismenos
(77)	9.476-80	4 7/12	Hippomedon	(78)	9.506-10	4	Hippomedon
(79)	9.511-19	8 1/6	Juno	(80)	9.544-46	2 1/6	Hypseus
(81)	9.548-50	2 7/12	Capaneus	(82)	9.557-59	2 5/12	Capaneus
(83)	9.562-65	3 5/6	Capaneus	(84)	9.608-35	27 5/12	Atalanta
(85)	9.713-25	12 1/12	Diana	(86)	9.825-30	5 7/12	Venus
(87)	9.835-37	2 7/12	Mars	(88)	9.885-900, 901-07	22 5/12	Parthenopaeus
(89)	10.21-35	14 1/4	Eteocles	(90)	10.67-69	3	Argolic mothers
(91)	10.126-31	6	Iris	(92)	10.188-218	26 1/2	Thiodamas
(93)	10.206-11[7]	4 1/2	Amphiaraus' spirit	(94)	10.236-44	8 7/12	Adrastus
(95)	10.266-68	1 11/12	Adrastus	(96)	10.269-71	2 5/12	Thiodamas
(97)	10.330-35	5 7/12	Actor	(98)	10.337-45	9	Thiodamas
(99)	10.365-70	5	Dymas	(100)	10.393	7/12	Amphion
(101)	10.482-86	4 7/12	Capaneus	(102)	10.492	1	Megareus
(103)	10.592-98	5 1/2	Tiresias	(104)	10.610-15	6	Tiresias
(105)	10.762-73	12	Menoeceus	(106)	10.793-814	22	Menoeceus' mother
(107)	10.873-77	3 5/6	Capaneus	(108)	10.888f.	1 1/2	Bacchus
(109)	10.899-906	7 3/4	Capaneus	(110)	10.925f.	1 5/6	Capaneus
(111)	11.76-112	37	Tisiphone	(112)	11.122-33	12	Jupiter
(113)	11.155-92	38	Polynices	(114)	11.201f.	1 1/6	Megaera
(115)	11.210-25	16	Eteocles	(116)	11.242-45	4	Aegyptus
(117)	11.248f.	1 1/6	Eteocles	(118)	11.257f.	7/12	Companion of Eteocles (1)

---

[7] Related by Thiodamas in his speech (10.188-218).

No.	Book/Lines	Lines of Verse	Speaker(s)	No.	Book/Lines	Lines of Verse	Speaker(s)
(119)	11.258f.	1	Companion of Eteocles (2)	(120)	11.259f.	1 2/3	Companion of Eteocles (3)
(121)	11.260-62	1 5/12	Companion of Eteocles (4)	(122)	11.329-53	25	Jocasta
(123)	11.363-82	19 1/6	Antigone	(124)	11.429-35	5 2/3	Adrastus
(125)	11.465-70, 471	5 1/3	Pietas	(126)	11.478-81	3 5/12	Pietas
(127)	11.484-92	8 1/6	Tisiphone	(128)	11.504-08	5	Polynices
(129)	11.548-51	4	Polynices	(130)	11.557-60	2 5/6	Polynices
(131)	11.568-72	4 1/3	Polynices	(132)	11.594f.	1 1/3	Oedipus
(133)	11.605-26, 630f.	23 5/12	Oedipus	(134)	12.72-92, 94-102	29 1/4	Creon
(135)	12.149-66	17 7/12	Ornytus	(136)	12.196-204	8 1/3	Argia
(137)	12.209-19	10 1/12	Argia	(138)	12.246-54	9	Menoetes
(139)	12.256-67	11 1/4	Argia	(140)	12.299-308	10	Juno
(141)	12.322-48	27	Argia	(142)	12.333-35[8]	2 3/4	Argia
(143)	12.437-46	10	Antigone	(144)	12.458	1/4	Antigone
(145)	12.458	1/6	Argia	(146)	12.459	1/4	Antigone
(147)	12.459	1/3	Argia	(148)	12.546-86	41	Evadne
(149)	12.590-98	8 3/4	Theseus	(150)	12.642-48	7	Theseus
(151)	12.689-92	3 1/4	Creon	(152)	12.771-73	1 7/12	Theseus

Table 19. Speech Clusters

No.	Book/Lines	Lines of Verse[9]	Speaker(s)	No.	Book/Lines	Lines of Verse[9]	Speaker(s)
			DIALOGUES: TWO SPEECHES				
(1)	2.334-62	24 11/12	Argia, Polynices	(2)	2.649-59	8 1/3	Menoetes, Tydeus
(3)	3.269-316	44	Venus, Mars	(4)	3.367-93	18 11/12	Polynices,[10] Adrastus
(5)	3.687-720	32 5/12	Argia, Adrastus	(6)	7.155-221	64 5/12	Bacchus, Jupiter

---

[8] A speech of Argia recounted by herself.

[9] Not including narrative between speeches.

[10] Polynices addresses his comments to the Argives, including Adrastus.

SPEECH AND RHETORIC IN STATIUS' *THEBAID*

No.	Book/Lines	Lines of Verse	Speaker(s)	No.	Book/Lines	Lines of Verse	Speaker(s)
(7)	7.663-79	7 5/12	Eunaeus,[11] Capaneus	(8)	7.772-88	15 11/12	Apollo, Amphiaraus
(9)	8.84-122	34 5/12	Pluto, Amphiaraus	(10)	9.650-67	17 1/12	Apollo, Diana
(11)	9.779-800	19 3/4	Amphion, Parthenopaeus	(12)	9.812-19	7 7/12	Diana,[12] Parthenopaeus
(13)	10.351-63	12 1/2	Hopleus, Dymas	(14)	10.584-88	3 1/4	Thebans (two groups)
(15)	10.662-81	11 7/12	Virtus,[13] Menoeceus	(16)	10.690-734	40 5/6	Creon, Menoeceus
(17)	11.269-308	38 1/6	Creon, Eteocles	(18)	11.389-95	6 1/6	Eteocles, Polynices
(19)	12.761-81	8 5/6	Creon, Theseus				

DIALOGUES: THREE SPEECHES

No.	Book/Lines	Lines of Verse	Speaker(s)	No.	Book/Lines	Lines of Verse	Speaker(s)
(1)	1.214-92	72 11/12	Jupiter,[14] Juno	(2)	2.393-467	67 1/2	Tydeus, Eteocles
(3)	3.607-69	58 3/4	Capaneus,[15] Amphiaraus	(4)	7.497-614	53 1/12	Jocasta, Tydeus[16]
(5)	9.350-98	23 1/3	Crenaeus, Ismenis	(6)	10.423-41	14 7/12	Dymas,[17] Amphion

DIALOGUES: FOUR SPEECHES

No.	Book/Lines	Lines of Verse	Speaker(s)	No.	Book/Lines	Lines of Verse	Speaker(s)
(1)	3.502-47	45 1/6	Amphiaraus, Melampus	(2)	7.247-373	120 1/6	Antigone, Phorbas

---

[11] Eunaeus speaks to the Argive warriors; Capaneus replies.

[12] Disguised as Dorceus.

[13] Disguised as Manto.

[14] Jupiter replies to Juno before addressing Mercury in the final part of his speech (1.292-302).

[15] Capaneus speaks to Amphiaraus and the Achaeans, while Amphiaraus replies to the Achaeans.

[16] Jocasta addresses Polynices and the Argive warriors; Tydeus attempts to dissuade them from heeding the persuasion of Jocasta, but his statement is intended for her indirectly as a rebuttal of her argument. In his speech Tydeus commands Antigone to depart from the camp.

[17] Dymas addresses the Theban warriors; Amphion responds.

No.	Book/Lines	Lines of Verse	Speaker(s)	No.	Book/Lines	Lines of Verse	Speaker(s)

DIALOGUE: SIX SPEECHES

| 4.753-85, 5.20-498 | 501 1/2 | Adrastus, Hypsipyle[18] |

TRIALOGUE: TWO SPEECHES

| 6.816-22 | 4 5/6 | Tydeus and Hippomedon, Capaneus |

TRIALOGUE: THREE SPEECHES

| 2.152-97 | 41 2/3 | Adrastus, Tydeus, Polynices |

TRIALOGUE: FOUR SPEECHES

| 11.669-754 | 69 2/3 | Creon, Oedipus, Antigone |

TRIALOGUE: FIVE SPEECHES

| 12.366-408 | 25 11/12 | Antigone, Argia, Menoetes |

TRIALOGUE: SEVEN SPEECHES

| 4.501-644 | 125 7/12 | Tiresias,[19] Manto, Ghost of Laius |

TRIALOGUE: EIGHT SPEECHES

| 1.438-695[20] | 163 1/3 | Adrastus, Tydeus, Polynices |

---

[18] Hypsipyle addresses Adrastus and the Argive warriors in her long narrative (5.49-498).

[19] Tiresias addresses the underworld goddesses in the first speech of the trialogue.

[20] After making a final address to Polynices, Adrastus prays to Apollo (1.696-720).

SPEECH AND RHETORIC IN STATIUS' *THEBAID*

No.	Book/Lines	Lines of Verse	Speaker(s)	No.	Book/Lines	Lines of Verse	Speaker(s)

TETRALOGUE: FIVE SPEECHES

| | 5.656-89 | 22 1/2 | Tydeus, Adrastus and Amphiaraus, Lycurgus | | | | |

GENERAL INTERLOCUTIONS

(1)	4.812	1/6	Argive warriors	(2)	5.491f.[21]	2	Lemnian crowd
(3)	6.618	1/6	Arcadian warriors	(4)	7.123-26	3 1/6	Argive crowd
(5)	8.174-207	34	Argive troops				

---

[21] Recounted by Hypsipyle in her narrative (5.49-498).

SPEECHES COMMENCING, CONCLUDING OR INTERRUPTED IN MIDVERSE BY NARRATIVE

Table 20. Totals by Book for Speeches Commencing, Concluding or Interrupted in Midline by Narrative

Book	No. of Speeches	No. Beg. Within the Verse	Pct. Beg. Within the Verse	No. Concl. Within the Verse	Pct. Concl. Within the Verse	No. Beg. or Concl. Within the Verse	Pct. Beg. or Concl. Within the Verse	No. Int. Within the Verse by Narr.	Pct. Int. Within the Verse by Narr.	No. Beg., Concl. or Int. Within Verse by Narr.	Pct. Beg., Concl. or Int. Within Verse by Narr.
1	15	8	53.3	6	40.0	12	80.0	2	13.3	12	80.0
2	20	9	45.0	9	45.0	11	55.0	5	25.0	13	65.0
3	20	9	45.0	13	65.0	16	80.0	2	10.0	16	80.0
4	18	7	38.9	9	50.0	11	61.1	4	22.2	13	72.2
5	19	12	63.2	8	53.3	13	68.4	5	26.3	15	78.9
6	15	10	66.7	4	26.7	11	73.3	4	26.7	13	86.7
7	21	10	47.6	8	38.1	14	66.7	4	19.0	16	76.2
8	15	8	53.3	7	46.7	12	80.0	5	33.3	12	80.0
9	30	17	56.7	13	43.3	25	80.0	7	23.3	26	86.7
10	35	16	45.7	13	37.1	21	60.0	7	20.0	25	71.4
11	31	16	51.6	16	51.6	19	61.3	8	25.8	22	70.1
12	26	6	23.1	14	53.8	16	61.5	7	26.9	19	73.1
Total	265	128	48.3	120	45.3	181	**68.3**	60	22.6	202	**76.2**

Table 21. Totals by Type for Speeches Commencing, Concluding or Interrupted in Midline by Narrative

Speech Type	No. of Speeches	No. Beg. Within the Verse	Pct. Beg. Within the Verse	No. Concl. Within the Verse	Pct. Concl. Within the Verse	No. Beg. or Concl. Within the Verse	Pct. Beg. or Concl. Within the Verse	No. Int. Within the Verse by Narr.	Pct. Int. Within the Verse by Narr.	No. Beg., Concl. or Int. Within Verse by Narr.	Pct. Beg., Concl. or Int. Within Verse by Narr.
Apo	10	3	30.0	5	50.0	7	70.0	5	50.0	9	90.0
Cha	8	6	75.0	5	62.5	7	87.5	3	37.5	8	100.0
Com	30	20	66.7	10	33.3	20	66.7	7	23.3	22	73.3
Del	56	22	39.3	27	48.2	35	62.5	10	17.9	38	67.9
Des	7	2	28.6	0	0.0	2	28.6	1	14.3	2	28.6
Enc	18	12	66.7	10	55.6	15	83.3	3	16.7	16	88.9
For	2	1	50.0	0	0.0	1	50.0	0	0.0	1	50.0
M&C	11	0	0.0	2	18.2	2	18.2	3	27.3	4	36.4
Nar	4	2	50.0	1	25.0	3	75.0	0	0.0	3	75.0
O&P	8	4	50.0	4	50.0	5	62.5	1	12.5	5	62.5
P&B	11	5	45.5	8	72.7	10	90.9	2	18.2	10	90.9
Pra	31	11	35.5	12	38.7	18	58.0	3	9.7	18	58.0
Que	11	6	54.5	5	45.5	9	81.8	3	27.3	10	90.9
Res	28	17	60.7	18	64.3	26	92.3	6	21.4	27	96.4
Sol	6	3	50.0	3	50.0	4	66.7	3	50.0	6	100.0
Tau	17	10	58.8	6	35.3	12	70.6	6	35.3	16	94.1
Thr	7	4	57.1	4	57.1	5	71.4	4	57.1	7	100.0
Total	265	128	48.3	120	45.3	181	**68.3**	60	22.6	202	**76.2**

Table 22. Statistical Evidence for Tables 20 and 21

The following table provides the statistical evidence for the totals shown in tables 20 and 21. The number (in brackets) and lines of each speech by book are shown, then are followed by information in parentheses that indicates the speech type (preceding the colon), whether the speech commences and concludes within the verse, as well as showing the number of interruptions by narrative and parenthetic elements within the verse. 'B' indicates that the speech commences at the start of the verse; 'E' shows that it closes at the end of the metrical line; and 'M' denotes that the speech commences or concludes in the middle of the verse. The number indicates the numbers of interruptions within the verse. For example, 5.701-03 (Com: M, E, 1) indicates that the speech contained within the lines cited is a command, commences in the middle of line 701, concludes at the end of verse 703, and is interrupted once by narrative or parenthetic expression.

BOOK ONE

[1] 56-87 (Pra: B, E, 0), [2] 173-96 (P&B: M, E, 1), [3] 214-47 (For: B, E, 0), [4] 250-82 (For: M, E, 0), [5] 285-302 (Com: M, E, 0), [6] 438-46 (Que: M, E, 0), [7] 448-50 (Res: M, M, 0), [8] 452-65 (Res: M, M, 0), [9] 465 (Res: M, E, 0), [10] 468-73 (Del: B, M, 0), [11] 498-510 (Pra: B, M, 0), [12] 557-672 (Nar: B, E, 0), [13] 643-61 (Pra: B, M, 0), [14] 676-81 (Res: B, M, 0), [15] 682-720 (Pra: M, E, 1).

BOOK TWO

[1] 19-25 (Apo: B, E, 1), [2] 102-19 (Del: B, E, 0), [3] 152-72 (Del: B, E, 0), [4] 176-88 (Res: M, M, 0), [5] 189-97 (Res: M, M, 0), [6] 334-52 (Que: M, M, 1), [7] 356-62 (Res: B, E, 0), [8] 393-409 (Del: B, E, 0), [9] 415-51 (Res: B, M, 0), [10] 452-67 (Thr: M, M, 1), [11] 535 (Que: M, E, 0), [12] 547-49 (Cha: B, M, 0), [13] 620-23 (Enc: M, E, 0), [14] 641 (Tau: B, E, 1), [15] 649-54 (Com: B, E, 0), [16] 655-59 (Res: M, M, 1), [17] 661-68 (Tau: M, M, 0), [18] 686-90 (Com: M, M, 0), [19] 697-703 (Com: B, E, 0), [20] 715-42 (Pra: B, E, 0).

BOOK THREE

[1] 6-7, 9-18 (Sol: M, M, 2), [2] 59-77, 83-87 (P&B: B, M, 1), [3] 151-68 (M&C: B, E, 0), [4] 179-213 (M&C: B, E, 0), [5] 229-52 (Com: M, E, 0), [6] 269-91 (Del: B, M, 0), [7] 295-316 (Res: B, M, 0), [8] 348-65 (Enc: M, M, 0), [9] 367-81 (Del: M, M, 0), [10] 388-93 (Res: M, E, 0), [11] 471-96 (Pra: B, M, 0), [12] 502-15 (Des: B, E, 0), [13] 516-45 (Des: M, E, 0), [14] 546 (Que: B, M, 0), [15] 546f. (Res: M, M, 0), [16] 607-18 (Enc: B, M, 0), [17] 620-47 (O&P: M, M, 0), [18] 648-69 (Thr: (M, M, 0), [19] 687-710 (Del: B, E, 0), [20] 712-20 (Res: B, M, 0).

BOOK FOUR

[1] 200-10 (Sol: B, E, 1), [2] 318-40 (Del: M, E, 0), [3] 383-404 (Pra: B, M, 0), [4] 473-87 (Pra: B, E, 0), [5] 501-18 (Pra: B, M, 1), [6] 519-35 (Des: B, E, 0), [7] 536-48 (Com: B, E, 1), [8] 553-78 (Des: B, E, 0), [9] 583-602 (O&P: M, M, 1), [10] 610-24 (Del: M, M, 0), [11] 626-44 (O&P: B, M, 0), [12] 669-78 (Sol: M, M, 0), [13] 684-96 (Com: M, E, 0), [14] 753-71 (Pra: B, E, 0), [15] 776-85 (Res: B, M, 0), [16] 811 (Enc: M, M, 0), [17] 812 (Enc: M, M, 0), [18] 832-50 (Pra: B, E, 0).

BOOK FIVE

[1] 20-27 (Que: B, E, 1), [2] 29-39 (Res: M, E, 0), [3] 43-47 (Del: B, E, 0), [4] 49-498 (Nar: M, E, 0), [5] 104-29, 132-42 (Del: B, E, 1), [6] 136, 137f. (Com: M, E, 1), [7] 245-47 (Del: M, M, 0), [8] 271-84 (Com: M, M, 0), [9] 491f. (P&B: B, E, 0), [10] 565-70

(Cha: M, M, 1), [11] 608-35 (M&C: B, M, 0), [12] 647 (O&P: B, E, 0), [13] 656-60 (Thr: M, M, 0), [14] 663f. (Com: M, M, 0), [15] 669-71 (Com: M, M, 0), [16] 672-79 (Thr: M, E, 0), [17] 681-89 (O&P: M, M, 0), [18] 701-03 (Com: M, E, 1), [19] 733-52 (O&P: B, E, 0).

BOOK SIX

[1] 138-73, 174-76, 180-84 (M&C: B, E, 2), [2] 197-201 (Pra: M, E, 0), [3] 319f. (Com: M, M, 1), [4] 372-83 (Sol: M, E, 0), [5] 618 (Enc: M, M, 0), [6] 627-30 (Com: M, E, 0), [7] 633-37 (Pra: B, E, 0), [8] 656-59 (Cha: M, M, 0), [9] 726-30 (Enc: B, E, 1), [10] 734-37 (Cha: M, E, 1), [11] 809-12 (Com: B, E, 0), [12] 816f. (Del: B, M, 0), [13] 819-22 (Res: M, E, 0), [14] 906-08 (P&B: M, E, 0), [15] 914-19 (Com: M, E, 0).

BOOK SEVEN

[1] 6-33 (Com: B, E, 0), [2] 77-80 (Que: B, E, 1), [3] 93-103 (Pra: M, E, 0), [4] 123-26 (Que: M, E, 0), [5] 155-92 (Del: B, E, 0), [6] 195-221 (Res: M, E, 0), [7] 247-52 (Que: M, E, 0), [8] 254-89 (Des: B, E, 0), [9] 291-93 (Que: B, E, 0), [10] 294-358, 363-73 (Des: M, E, 1), [11] 375-90 (Enc: B, M, 0), [12] 483-85 (Del: M, M, 0), [13] 490-92 (Que: B, M, 0), [14] 497-527 (Del: B, M, 0), [15] 539-59 (Del: B, M, 0), [16] 612-14 (Com: M, M, 0), [17] 663-68 (P&B: M, M, 0), [18] 677-79 (Tau: M, M, 1), [19] 730-35 (Pra: M, E, 0), [20] 772-77 (Com: B, E, 1), [21] 779-88 (Pra: B, E, 0).

BOOK EIGHT

[1] 34-79 (Com: B, E, 0), [2] 84f. (Thr: B, M, 1), [3] 90-122 (Pra: B, E, 0), [4] 138-50 (Del: B, M, 1), [5] 174-207 (M&C: B, E, 0), [6] 303-38 (Pra: M, M, 0), [7] 472f. (Tau: M, E, 0), [8] 502-16 (P&B: B, M, 0), [9] 582f. (Tau: B, M, 0), [10] 588-91 (Pra: M, E, 1), [11] 600-05 (Enc: M, M, 1), [12] 622-35 (Nar: M, E, 0), [13] 664-72 (Cha: M, M, 0), [14] 677-79 (Cha: M, E, 0), [15] 735-44 (Del: M, E, 1).

BOOK NINE

[1] 12-24 (Enc: M, M, 0), [2] 49-72, 75f. (M&C: B, M, 1), [3] 96-103 (Tau: B, M, 0), [4] 137-39 (Tau: M, E, 0), [5] 157-65, 166-68 (Del: M, M, 1), [6] 211-17 (Del: M, E, 0), [7] 294-301 (Tau: B, E, 1), [8] 340-43 (Cha: M, M, 0), [9] 350 (Apo: B, M, 0), [10] 356 (Apo: M, M, 0), [11] 376-98 (M&C: B, E, 0), [12] 421-45 (Apo: M, E, 0), [13] 476-80 (Tau: M, E, 0), [14] 506-10 (Pra: M, M, 0), [15] 511-19 (Del: M, M, 0), [16] 544-46 (P&B: B, M, 0), [17] 548-50 (Pra: M, E, 0), [18] 557-59 (Tau: M, E, 1), [19] 562-65 (Apo: B, M, 1), [20] 608-35 (Pra: B, M, 0), [21] 650-62 (O&P: M, E, 0), [22] 663-67 (Thr: B, E, 1), [23] 713-25 (Apo: M, E, 1), [24] 779-87 (Tau: M, E, 0), [25] 790-800 (Tau: M, E, 0), [26] 812-14 (Del: B, M, 0), [27] 815-19 (Del: B, E, 0), [28] 825-30 (Del: M, E, 0), [29] 835-37 (Com: M, E, 0), [30] 885-900, 901-07 (Com: B, E, 0).

BOOK TEN

[1] 21-35 (Enc: B, M, 0), [2] 67-69 (Pra: B, E, 0), [3] 126-31 (Com: B, E, 0), [4] 188-218 (Enc: B, E, 0), [5] 206-11 (Del: M, M, 1), [6] 236-44 (Enc: M, E, 0), [7] 266-68 (Enc: M, M, 0), [8] 269-71 (Enc: M, E, 0), [9] 330-35 (Del: M, E, 0), [10] 337-45 (Pra: B, E, 0), [11] 351-59 (Del: B, E, 0), [12] 360-63 (Res: M, M, 0), [13] 365-70 (Pra: M, M, 0), [14] 393 (Com: M, M, 0), [15] 423-30 (Del: M, E, 0), [16] 431-34 (Del: B, E, 1), [17] 436-38, 441 (Res: M, E, 2), [18] 482-86 (Enc: M, E, 0), [19] 492 (Com: B, E, 0), [20] 584-87 (Del: M, E, 0), [21] 588 (Res: M, E, 0), [22] 592-98 (Com: M, M, 1), [23] 610-15 (O&P: B, E, 0), [24] 662-71 (Del: B, E, 0), [25] 680f. (Res: M, M, 0), [26] 690-718 (Del: B, M, 0), [27] 722-34 (Res: B, M, 0), [28] 762-73 (Pra: B, E, 0), [29] 793-814 (M&C: B, E, 0), [30] 845-47 (Sol: B, E, 1), [31] 873-77 (Tau: M, M, 0), [32] 888f. (Apo: B, M, 0), [33] 899-906 (Cha: B, E, 1), [34] 909f. (Sol: B, M, 0), [35] 925f. (Tau: B, E, 1).

BOOK ELEVEN

[1] 76-112 (Del: B, E, 0), [2] 122-33 (Com: B, E, 0), [3] 155-92 (Del: B, E, 0), [4] 201f. (Com: M, M, 0), [5] 210-225 (Pra: B, E, 0), [6] 248f. (Pra: M, M, 0), [7] 242-45 (Del: B, E, 0), [8] 257f. (Del: M, M, 0), [9] 258f. (Que: M, M, 0), [10] 259f. (P&B: M, M, 0), [11] 260-262 (Del: M, M, 0), [12] 269-296 (Del: B, E, 1), [13] 298-308 (Res: M, M, 1), [14] 329-53 (Del: B, E, 0), [15] 363-82 (Del: B, M, 0), [16] 389-92 (Res: M, M, 0), [17] 393-95 (Res: B, E, 1), [18] 429-35 (Del: M, M, 0), [19] 465-70, 471 (Apo: B, E, 3), [20] 478-81 (Enc: M, E, 1), [21] 484-92 (P&B: M, M, 0), [22] 504-08 (Pra: B, E, 0), [23] 548-51 (Tau: B, E, 0), [24] 557-60 (Com: M, M, 0), [25] 568-72 (Tau: M, M, 0), [26] 594f. (Del: B, M, 1), [27] 605-26, 630f. (M&C: B, E, 0), [28] 669-72 (Com: M, E, 1), [29] 677-707 (P&B: B, M, 0), [30] 708-39 (Del: M, M, 0), [31] 750-54 (Res: M, E, 1).

BOOK TWELVE

[1] 72-92, 94-102 (M&C: B, E, 1), [2] 149-66 (Del: B, M, 0), [3] 196-204 (Del: B, M, 1), [4] 209-19 (Apo: B, M, 1), [5] 246-54 (Des: B, E, 0), [6] 256-67 (Pra: B, M, 0), [7] 299-308 (Del: B, E, 0), [8] 322-48 (M&C: B, E, 0), [9] 333-35 (Del: M, E, 0), [10] 366f. (Que: B, M, 1), [11] 374-80 (Res: B, M, 0), [12] 382-85 (P&B: B, M, 0), [13] 392-404 (Nar: B, M, 0), [14] 406-08 (Del: B, E, 0), [15] 437-46 (Apo: B, E, 0), [16] 458 (Del: M, M, 0), [17] 458 (Del: M, M, 0), [18] 459 (Del: B, M, 0), [19] 459 (Del: M, M, 0), [20] 546-86 (Del: B, E, 0), [21] 590-98 (Com: M, E, 0), [22] 642-48 (Enc: B, E, 0), [23] 689-92 (Res: B, M, 1), [24] 761-66 (Thr: B, E, 1), [25] 771-73 (Pra: M, M, 0), [26] 779-81 (Tau: B, E, 1).

OPENING, INTERPOSING AND
CLOSING FORMULAS TO SPEECHES

Table 23.   Totals for Opening, Interposing and Closing Formulas to Speeches

Formula	Total Number	Opening	Interposing	Closing
ait	39	3	31	5
sic ait	15	1	0	14
dixerat	13	0	0	13
dixit	13	0	0	13
inquit	13	0	13	0
dicens, -tem, -ti	9	1	0	8
incipit, -iunt	9	9	0	0
refert	9	6	1	2
sic fatus	9	0	0	9
profatur	8	8	0	0
clamat	7	0	6	1
tunc [profatur, etc.]	7	7	0	0
uociferans	7	4	0	3
dicit	4	0	0	4
exclamat	4	4	0	0
hortatur	4	4	0	0
increpat	4	4	0	0
iterat	4	3	0	1
sic orsus, -a	4	2	0	2
uix ea [fatus, etc.]	4	0	0	4
audierat, -ant	3	0	0	3
increpitans	3	3	0	0
nec plura [uerba, etc.]	3	0	0	3
precatur	3	3	0	0
reddit, -didit	3	3	0	0
rogat	3	2	0	1
adfatur	2	2	0	0
adfatus, -a	2	2	0	0
conclamat	2	2	0	0
incohat	2	2	0	0
interfatus, -a	2	1	0	1
uocat	2	2	0	0

Table 24. Catalogue by Book of Opening, Interposing and Closing Formulas to Speeches

The following table provides the evidence for the totals in table 23 by listing the book, line numbers and type of formula of each speech for the most common speech formulas. 'O' indicates that Statius introduces the indicated speech with an introductory verb or verbal phrase; 'I' denotes that he intromits the formulaic word or phrase after the commencement of the speech; and 'C' indicates that the specified word or phrase signifies the termination of the speech.

ait

[1] 1.173-96 (I), [2] 1.557-672 (I), [3] 1.682-720 (I), [4] 2.19-25 (I), [5] 2.334-52 (I), [6] 2.641 (I), [7] 2.655-59 (I), [8] 2.697-703 [C], [9] 4.501-18 (I), [10] 4.536-48 (I), [11] 4.583-602 (I), [12] 5.20-27 (I), [13] 5.669-71 (O), [14] 6.726-30 (I), [15] 6.734-37 (I), [16] 7.772-77 (I), [17] 8.138-50 (I), [18] 8.582f. (C), [19] 8.588-91 (I), [20] 9.157-65 (I), [21] 9.294-301 (I), [22] 9.557-59 (I), [23] 9.562-65 (I), [24] 10.431-34 (I), [25] 10.680f. (C), [26] 10.845-47 (I), [27] 10.888f. (C), [28] 10.909f. (C), [29] 10.925f. (I), [30] 11.269-96 (I), [31] 11.298-308 (O), [32] 11.465-70 (I), [33] 11.471 (I), [34] 11.594f. (I), [35] 12.196-204 (I), [36] 12.209-19 (I), [37] 12.366f. (O), [38] 12.761-66 (I), [39] 12.779-81 (I).

sic ait

[1] 2.356-62 (C), [2] 6.185b (C), [3] 6.914-19 (C), [4] 8.588-91 (C), [5] 9.49-72 (C), [6] 9.421-45 (C), [7] 9.548-50 (C), [8] 10.365-70 (O), [9] 10.436-38 (C), [10] 10.482-86 (C), [11] 10.662-71 (C), [12] 10.762-73 (C), [13] 11.750-54 (C), [14] 12.590-98 (C), [15] 12.761-66 (C).

dixerat

[1] 2.393-409 (C), [2] 2.649-54 (C), [3] 2.715-42 (C), [4] 4.473-87 (C), [5] 4.684-96 (C), [6] 5.672-79 (C), [7] 7.6-33 (C), [8] 7.254-89 (C), [9] 8.34-79 (C), [10] 9.476-80 (C), [11] 10.337-45 (C), [12] 11.210-25 (C), [13] 12.546-86 (C).

dixit

[1] 2.102-19 (C), [2] 3.229-52 (C), [3] 4.753-71 (C), [4] 5.136, 137f. (C), [5] 6.180-84 (C), [6] 6.372-83 (C), [7] 9.608-35 (C), [8] 10.126-31 (C), [9] 10.206-11 (C), [10] 11.465-70 (C), [11] 12.94-102 (C), [12] 12.256-67 (C), [13] 12.642-48 (C).

inquit

[1] 4.200-10 (I), [2] 5.136, 137f. (I), [3] 6.319f. (I), [4] 7.677-79 (I), [5] 8.84f. (I), [6] 8.600-05 (I), [7] 9.713-25 (I), [8] 10.206-11 (I), [9] 10.436-38 (I), [10] 11.393-95 (I), [11] 11.699-72 (I), [12] 11.750-54 (I), [13] 12.689-92 (I).

dicens, -tem, -ti

[1] 1.56-87 (C), [2] 3.712-20 (C), [3] 7.294-358 (C), [4] 10.925f. (C), [5] 11.557-60 (C), [6] 11.630f. (C), [7] 12.72-92 (C), [8] 12.209-19 (C), [9] 12.382-85 (O).

incipit, -iunt

[1] 1.448-50 (O), [2] 2.176-88 (O), [3] 2.715-42 (O), [4] 3.269-91 (O), [5] 4.684-96 (O), [6] 5.49-498 (O), [7] 8.303-38 (O), [8] 9.421-45 (O), [9] 12.246-54 (O).

refert

[1] 1.250-82 (O), [2] 1.465 (C), [3] 5.29-39 (O), [4] 5.681-89 (O), [5] 6.627-30 (O), [6] 7.77-80 (C), [7] 7.195-221 (O), [8] 7.779-88 (O), [9] 9.663-67 (I).

sic fatus

[1] 1.498-510 (C), [2] 3.471-96 (C), [3] 4.383-404 (C), [4] 5.681-89 (C), [5] 7.375-90 (C), [6] 7.612-14 (C), [7] 9.12-24 (C), [8] 10.269-71 (C), [9] 12.149-66 (C).

profatur

[1] 7.155-92 (O), [2] 7.363-73 (O), [3] 8.34-79 (O), [4] 9.812-14 (O), [5] 9.885-900 (O), [6] 11.76-112 (O), [7] 11.363-82 (O), [8] 12.374-80 (O).

clamat

[1] 2.620-23 (C), [2] 3.6f. (I), [3] 3.607-18 (I), [4] 5.565-70 (I), [5] 5.701-03 (I), [6] 8.735-44 (I), [7] 11.478-81 (I).

tunc [profatur, etc.]

[1] 1.468-73 (O), [2] 1.498-510 (O), [3] 3.502-15 (O), [4] 4.753-71 (O), [5] 6.372-83 (O), [6] 8.677-79 (O), [7] 9.96-103 (O).

uociferans

[1] 2.452-67 (C), [2] 3.348-65 (O), [3] 5.656-60 (O), [4] 6.174-76 (C), [5] 6.819-22 (O), [6] 7.663-68 (O), [7] 10.188-218 (C).

dicit

[1] 4.583-602 (C), [2] 6.819-22 (C), [3] 10.845-47 (C), [4] 12.689-92 (C).

exclamat

[1] 4.473-87 (O), [2] 9.506-10 (O), [3] 10.393 (O), [4] 12.590-98 (O).

hortatur

[1] 5.43-47 (O), [2] 9.548-50 (O), [3] 10.269-71 (O), [4] 10.482-86 (O).

increpat

[1] 9.137-39 (O), [2] 9.835-37 (O), [3] 10.873-77 (O), [4] 11.548-51 (O).

iterat

[1] 5.49-498 (C), [2] 5.132-37 (O), [3] 6.174-76 (O), [4] 12.94-102 (O).

sic orsus, -a

[1] 3.295-316 (C), [2] 7.247-52 (O), [3] 8.502-16 (C), [4] 10.126-31 (O).

uix ea [fatus, etc.]

[1] 1.438-46 (C), [2] 7.363-73 (C), [3] 12.299-308 (C), [4] 12.437-46 (C).

audierat, -ant

[1] 2.152-72 (C), [2] 6.627-30 (C), [3] 7.730-35 (C).

increpitans

[1] 2.620-23 (O), [2] 11.484-92 (O), [3] 11.669-72 (O).

nec plura [uerba, etc.]

[1] 2.189-97 (C), [2] 9.96-103 (C) [3] 11.568-72 (C).

precatur

[1] 1.56-87 (O), [2] 9.608-35 (O), [3] 11.504-08 (O).

reddit, -didit

[1] 1.285-302 (O), [2] 4.626-44 (O), [3] 4.776-85 (O).

rogat

[1] 2.535 (C), [2] 10.423-30 (O), [3] 11.429-35 (O).

adfatur

[1] 9.211-17 (O), [2] 11.155-92 (O).

adfatus, -a

[1] 4.553-78 (O), [2] 7.6-33 (O).

conclamat

[1] 4.811 (O), [2] 12.437-46 (O).

incohat

[1] 8.622-35 (O), [2] 11.122-33 (O).

interfatus, -a

[1] 2.176-88 (C), [2] 7.291-93 (O).

uocat

[1] 10.330-35 (O), [2] 11.248f. (O).

POTENTIAL SPEECHES IN
TRUE AND VIRTUAL *ORATIO OBLIQUA*

Table 25. Catalogue of Potential Speeches in
True and Virtual Oratio Obliqua *by Book*

No.	Lines	Type of Oratio Obliqua	Probable Speech Type[1]	Speaker(s)	Context
			BOOK ONE		
(1)	43f.	V	Com	Hippomedon	Call for a commemorative song
(2)	168f.	V	P&B	Thebans	Dissatisfaction with Eteocles
(3)	314f.	V	Sol	Polynices	Depression of Polynices
(4)	315f.	T	Sol	Polynices	Complaint over delaying year
(5)	317-19	T	Sol	Polynices	Desire for Theban kingship
(6)	320	T	Sol	Polynices	Idleness of exile
(7)	396f.	T	O&P	Apollo	Prophecy
(8)	491f.	V	Sol	Adrastus	Oracular pronouncements
(9)	514f.	T	Com	Adrastus	Renewal of banquet
(10)	552-54	V	Pra	Adrastus	Invocation to Apollo and Olympians
			BOOK TWO		
(1)	48-50	T	Nar	Rumor	Entrance to underworld
(2)	51-54	T	Nar	Arcadian husbandmen	Underworld clamour
(3)	146f.	V	Sol	Adrastus	Reflexion on fate
(4)	147f.	T	Sol	Adrastus	Reflexion on fate and new arrivals
(5)	198f.	V	Del	Adrastus	Verbal reinforcement of promises
(6)	199f.	T	Del	Adrastus	Vowing of assistance to Tydeus and Polynices
(7)	201-13	T	Nar	Rumor	Marriage of Argia and Deipyle
(8)	309-21	T	Sol	Oedipus	Oedipus' brooding over fate
(9)	363f.	V	Gre	Polynices	Greeting of Tydeus
(10)	364-70	V	Del	Polynices and Tydeus	Discussion on future action

---

[1] An additional speech type of 'Greeting' (G) is made here.

No.	Lines	Type of *Oratio Obliqua*	Probable Speech Type	Speaker(s)	Context
(11)	370	V	Del	Tydeus	Volunteering for embassy to Eteocles
(12)	388	V	P&B	Polynices	Complaints over loss of rule
(13)	390f.	V	Res	Tydeus	Declaration of name and purpose of embassy
(14)	601	T	P&B	Briareus	Complaints over idle hands in combat against Olympians

BOOK THREE

No.	Lines	Type of *Oratio Obliqua*	Probable Speech Type	Speaker(s)	Context
(1)	19-21	T	P&B	Eteocles	Eteocles' self-reproach over ambush of Tydeus
(2)	21	V	P&B	Eteocles	Eteocles' self-reproach over ambush of Tydeus
(3)	31f.	V	P&B	Agenorean prince	Lucifer and the sun
(4)	50-52	V	M&C	Herdsman	Loss of cattle
(5)	91f.	V	M&C	Theban councillors	Maeon's speech to Eteocles
(6)	145f.	V	P&B	Shades	Witches' disturbance of shades
(7)	169-73	V	M&C	Thebans	Lamentation
(8)	214-16	T	P&B	Aletes	Eteocles' transgressions
(9)	219f.	T	Com	Jupiter	Summoning of Mars
(10)	338-42	T	Nar	Tydeus	Ambush of embassy to Eteocles
(11)	400-05	V	Nar	Tydeus	Ambush of embassy
(12)	429f.	T	Enc	Bellona	Urging of Rumor to spread truth or falsehood
(13)	443-51	T	Sol	Adrastus	Reflexion on future actions
(14)	462-65	T	Nar	Argives	Tales of Perseus
(15)	497f.	V	Pra	Amphiaraus	Request of Jupiter for foreknowledge
(16)	592f.	V	Del	Hellenes	Urging for war

BOOK FOUR

No.	Lines	Type of *Oratio Obliqua*	Probable Speech Type	Speaker(s)	Context
(1)	10	V	Coh	Bellona	Incitation of troops
(2)	30	T	M&C	Sailors	Grieving over strong winds
(3)	53f.	T	Nar	*dicitur*	Legend concerning Elisson River
(4)	59[2]	V	M&C	Ephyre	Consolation of Ino
(5)	146f.	V	Enc	Hercules	Call to arms
(6)	157f.	V	Pra	Tyrinthian troops	Hercules' deeds
(7)	231f.	V	Enc	Hellenic parents	Parents' encouragement of youths

---

[2] A recounted indirect speech.

No.	Lines	Type of *Oratio Obliqua*	Probable Speech Type	Speaker(s)	Context
(8)	256-59	T	Nar	*dicitur*	Diana's presentation of arms to Parthenopaeus
(9)	276-78	T	Nar	*dicitur*	Birth of Arcadians
(10)	282-84	T	Nar	*dicitur*	Arcadians' despair over darkness
(11)	310f.	T	Nar	[Rumor]	Parthenopaeus
(12)	347	T	Nar	[Rumor]	Argive descent on Thebes
(13)	353-55	V	M&C	Thebans	Lamentation over prospect of war
(14)	409-14	T	Res	Tiresias	Rites of Lethe
(15)	668-70	V	Com	Bacchus	Silencing of musical instruments

BOOK FIVE

No.	Lines	Type of *Oratio Obliqua*	Probable Speech Type	Speaker(s)	Context
(1)	556	V	Nar	Parthenopaeus	Hypsipyle's mourning
(2)	637	V	P&B	Hypsipyle	Blaming of princes for Opheltes' death
(3)	638f.	V	Nar	[Fama]	News of Opheltes' death
(4)	693f.	T	P&B	Argives	Rumor of Hypsipyle's death
(5)	696f.	V	P&B	Argives	Rebellion against Lycurgus and Jupiter
(6)	697f.	V	M&C	Argive women	Grief of Argive women
(7)	719f.	V	Gre	Hypsipyle	Meeting of sons Euneus and Thoas

BOOK SIX

No.	Lines	Type of *Oratio Obliqua*	Probable Speech Type	Speaker(s)	Context
(1)	2-4	T	Nar	Fama	Preparation for Nemean games
(2)	34-36	V	M&C	Hypsipyle	Lamentation over Opheltes' death
(3)	44f.	V	M&C	Pelasgians	Lamentation over Opheltes
(4)	46-50	V	M&C	Adrastus	Consolation
(5)	52f.	V	Pra	Sailors	Prayers to gods
(6)	94-96	T	Nar	*dicitur*	Nemean wood
(7)	122-25	T	Nar	*dicitur*	Funeral rites
(8)	221-23	T	Com	Prophet	Funeral rites
(9)	249-51	V	Enc	Rumor	Summoning of crowd to view unarmed battles
(10)	302-05	T	Nar	*dicitur*	Tale of Arion
(11)	322-24	V	Com	Sun	Sun's advice to Phaethon
(12)	322-34	T	Nar	*dicitur*	Rumour about Admetus and his mares
(13)	358-64	V	Nar	Apollo	Tales of gods and nature
(14)	412f.	V	Que, Res	Pelasgians	Pelasgians' shouts
(15)	428-30	V	Thr	Arion	Arion's threat to charioteer

No.	Lines	Type of *Oratio Obliqua*	Probable Speech Type	Speaker(s)	Context
(16)	461-66	V	Enc	Various Greeks	Chariot race
(17)	548f.	V	Com, M&C	Adrastus	Presentation of athletic prizes
(18)	561f.	V	Del	Greeks	Calling of Parthenopaeus
(19)	566-68	T	Nar	*dicitur*	Tales of Parthenopaeus
(20)	609-10	T	Pra	Parthenopaeus	Vow
(21)	641f.	V	P&B	Parthenopaeus	Footrace and victory
(22)	646f.	V	Que	Adrastus	Announcement of discus event
(23)	660f.	V	Res	Greek warriors	Response to Hippomedon's challenge
(24)	689	V	P&B	Argives	Phlegyas' discus throw
(25)	698f.	V	Pra	Menestheus	Prayer to Hermes
(26)	747f.	V	P&B, Com	Capaneus	Scorning of athletic opposition
(27)	893-96	T	Nar	Fama	Tale of Hercules and Antaeus
(28)	921-23	T	Com	Adrastus	Praising of Polynices
(29)	924-28	T	Del	Greek chieftains	Urging of Adrastus for athletic exploit
(30)	942-44	T	Nar	Greek chieftains	Explanations of fateful potent

BOOK SEVEN

No.	Lines	Type of *Oratio Obliqua*	Probable Speech Type	Speaker(s)	Context
(1)	4	T	P&B	Atlas	Quaking of the sky
(2)	81	V	Com	Mercury	Jupiter's admonitory message to Mars
(3)	108f.	T	Com	Mars	Incitation of Pavor
(4)	114f.	T	Nar	Pavor	Terrorising of Argive troops
(5)	135	T	Enc	Argive warriors	Argive call to arms
(6)	146f.	V	Sol	Bacchus	Lament over fate of Thebes
(7)	227-29	T	Nar	Theban messenger	Argive advance on Thebes
(8)	232f.	V	Com	Eteocles	Catalogue of Argive troops
(9)	390-92	V	Com	Eteocles	Drawing up of Theban troops
(10)	407	V	O&P	Priestesses	Portents of impending warfare
(11)	414f.	T	Nar	Arcadians	Tale of Lycaon
(12)	415f.[3]	T	Nar	Pisa	Account of Oenomaus
(13)	419f.	V	Nar	Country dwellers	Account of River Inachus' rage
(14)	420f.	V	Nar	A rustic	Story of Palaemon's lament
(15)	457f.	V	Nar	Rumor and Timor	Cataloguing of Argive troops
(16)	460	V	Pra	Thebans	Argive advance on Thebes
(17)	460f.	V	Enc	Thebans	Argive descent upon Thebes

---

[3] An indirect speech within an indirect speech.

350

No.	Lines	Type of *Oratio Obliqua*	Probable Speech Type	Speaker(s)	Context
(18)	462f.	V	M&C	Thebans	Argive march on Thebes
(19)	465	V	Pra	Thebans	Argive advance on Thebes
(20)	468f.	V	Pra	Oedipus	Argive march on Thebes
(21)	535f.	V	Del	Ismene and Antigone	Appeal to Polynices
(22)	615	V	Enc	Tydeus	Rejection of Jocasta's entreaty
(23)	615	V	P&B	Argive troops	Rejection of Jocasta's entreaty

BOOK EIGHT

No.	Lines	Type of *Oratio Obliqua*	Probable Speech Type	Speaker(s)	Context
(1)	18-20	T	Apo	Styx	Descent of Amphiaraus into lower world
(2)	22	V	Com	Pluto	Judgement of shades' former lives
(3)	27-29	V	Del	Minos	Judgement of souls
(4)	30f.	V	P&B	Styx	Judgement of souls
(5)	170-72	V	P&B	Argives	Death of Amphiaraus
(6)	172f.	T	Apo	Argives	Amphiaraus' death
(7)	225f.	V	P&B, Nar	Thebans	Celebration of Amphiaraus' death
(8)	240-54	T	Nar	*dicitur*	Oedipus' delight in the war
(9)	247[4]	V	Res	Oedipus	Conversation at social dinner
(10)	251[4]	V	Enc	Oedipus	Theban social banquet
(11)	275	V	Com	Adrastus	Summoning of Argive council
(12)	276f.	T	Que	Argive councillors	Nomination of successor to Amphiaraus
(13)	277-79	V	Del	Argive councillors	Election of Thiodamas
(14)	283-85	T	Del	Thiodamas	Appointment as successor to Amphiaraus
(15)	298-300	T	Com	Thiodamas	Invocation of Tellus
(16)	452	V	P&B	Inachian twins	Spoiling of corpses
(17)	454f.	V	P&B	Jupiter	Ion's defeat of Daphneus
(18)	579f.	V	Tau	Atys	Mini-*aristeia* of Atys
(19)	607-13	V	M&C	Ismene and Antigone	Contemplation of fate
(20)	641f.	T	Com	Jocasta	Death of Atys
(21)	642-44	T	Com	Atys	Atys' dying words
(22)	722	V	Apo	Aonians and Pelasgians	Mortal wounding of Tydeus
(23)	729	V	Com	Tydeus	Tydeus' dying moment

---

[4] A recounted indirect speech.

SPEECH AND RHETORIC IN STATIUS' *THEBAID*

No.	Lines	Type of *Oratio Obliqua*	Probable Speech Type	Speaker(s)	Context

BOOK NINE

No.	Lines	Type of *Oratio Obliqua*	Probable Speech Type	Speaker(s)	Context
(1)	3f.	T	P&B	Argives	Report of Tydeus' death
(2)	32-35	V	Nar	Fama	Reaction to Tydeus' death
(3)	77-80	V	P&B	Adrastus	Polynices' lament over Tydeus
(4)	192	V	P&B	Husbandmen	Shepherd's killing of lion
(5)	302	V	Tau	Hippomedon	*Aristeia* of Hippomedon
(6)	400-03	T	Nar	*dicitur*	Tale of Leucothea
(7)	416f.	V	Nar	Nymphs	Death of Crenaeus
(8)	597f.	V	Nar	Nymphs	Tale of Arcadian oak
(9)	603f.	V	M&C	Atalanta	Atalanta's fear for Parthenopaeus
(10)	709f.	V	P&B	Sidonian nymphs	*Aristeia* of Parthenopaeus
(11)	733-35	V	Pra	Atalanta	Fear of Atalanta for her son

BOOK TEN

No.	Lines	Type of *Oratio Obliqua*	Probable Speech Type	Speaker(s)	Context
(1)	1f.	V	Com	Jupiter	Approach of night
(2)	36	V	Nar	Thebans	Assembling of Theban warriors
(3)	49-53	V	Pra	Argive matrons	Appeal against Thebes
(4)	80-82	V	Com	Juno	Juno's imposition of sleep upon the Thebans
(5)	222f.	V	Com	Thiodamas	Selection of warriors for nocturnal sortie
(6)	223-26	V	P&B, Del	Theban troops	Thiodamas' choice of troops
(7)	346	V	Com	Thiodamas	Triumph of Argives
(8)	451f.	V	Tau	Amphion	Argive triumph
(9)	456f.	V	P&B	Greek crowd	Argive triumph
(10)	566	V	Pra	Theban elders	Panic in Thebes
(11)	571f.	V	Enc	Theban matrons	Marshalling of Theban troops
(12)	580f.	V	Apo	Thebans	Despair over ensuing warfare
(13)	581f.	T	Del	Thebans	Despair over imminent conflict
(14)	589-91	V	Del	Thebans	Entreaty to Tiresias for prognostication
(15)	682-84	T	P&B	Theban crowd	Menoeceus' acceptance of his fate
(16)	786-88	V	P&B	Thebans	Celebration of Menoeceus' death
(17)	911	V	Del	Olympians	Arrogance of Capaneus

352

No.	Lines	Type of *Oratio Obliqua*	Probable Speech Type	Speaker(s)	Context
				BOOK ELEVEN	
(1)	7	V	Gre	Olympians	Death of Capaneus
(2)	144f.	T	Que	Polynices	Polynices' challenge
(3)	196f.	V	Del	Adrastus	Polynices' challenge
(4)	231	V	M&C	Theban soothsayer	Sacrifice to Jupiter
(5)	232f.	T	Com	Eteocles	Sacrifice to Jupiter
(6)	418	T	M&C	Theban elders	Duel between Eteocles and Polynices
(7)	418f.	V	Com	Theban matrons	The duel
(8)	420f.	T	Com	Pluto	The duel
(9)	461-64	T	P&B, Thr	Pietas	The duel
(10)	637f.	V	M&C	Jocasta	Deaths of Polynices and Eteocles
(11)	662f.	T	Com	Creon	Cruelty of Creon
				BOOK TWELVE	
(1)	26-28	V	M&C	Thebans	Funeral rites
(2)	173-76	V	Del	Theban widows	Encounter with Ornytus
(3)	276	T	Apo	Woods, rivers, seas, clouds	Ceres' search for Persephone
(4)	290	T	Pra	Argia	Argia's search for Polynices
(5)	389f.	V	M&C, Nar	Argia and Antigone	Meeting of Argia and Antigone
(6)	427f.	T	Pra	Argia and Antigone	Cremation of Polynices
(7)	452-55	V	Nar	Argia and Antigone	Arrest of Argia and Antigone
(8)	469f.	V	Com	Juno	Argive widows' descent upon Athens
(9)	476-78	V	P&B	Athenians	Public protestation against Creon
(10)	600	V	Enc	Theseus	Assembling of Greek troops
(11)	674-76	V	Sol	Theseus	Greek army's departure for Thebes
(12)	684-86	T	Thr	Phegeus	Theseus' message to Creon
(13)	752f.	V	Cha	Theseus	Duel between Creon and Theseus
(14)	754-56	V	Enc, Thr	Creon	The duel
(15)	758	V	Com	Creon	The duel
(16)	784f.	T	Del	Thebans	Theseus' victory
(17)	805	V	Nar	Argia	Tale of cruel watchmen

STATISTICAL APPENDIX 12

RHETORICAL AND SIMPLE (DIRECT)
QUESTIONS IN SPEECH AND NARRATIVE

*Table 26. Totals by Book for Rhetorical
and Simple (Direct) Questions*

Book	Rhetorical Questions in Speeches	Rhetorical Questions in Narrative	Simple Questions in Speeches[1]
1	25	9	2
2	17	5	1
3	36	4	2
4	22	4	0
5	32	4	2
6	13	6	0
7	42	5	2
8	47	3	1
9	50	8	0
10	41	6	0
11	70	5	1
12	47	5	1
Total	442	65	12

Table 27. Rhetorical Questions in Speeches

This table provides the evidence on which the totals in the second column of table 26 is based. There are a number of variations in interrogation marks from the text of Hill (1983).

BOOK ONE

[1] 79, [2] 79f. (Oedipus); [3] 173-75, [4] 177f., [5] 178-80, [6] 180-85, [7] 189, [8] 191 (Theban); [9] 215f., [10] 227-31 (Jupiter); [11] 250f., [12] 259, [13] 263f., [14] 266-70, [15] 280 (Juno); [16] 440f., [17] 442f. (Adrastus); [18] 448f. (Tydeus and Polynices); [19] 455f., [20] 456f., [21] 461 (Tydeus); [22] 651, [23] 654f., [24] 655f. (Coroebus); [25] 682 (Adrastus).

---

[1] There are no simple questions in the narrative (as opposed to the speeches) of the *Thebaid*.

354

STATISTICAL APPENDIX 12

BOOK TWO

[1] 178f., [2] 179-81 (Tydeus); [3] 189f. (Polynices); [4] 334f., [5] 337-39, [6] 343f., [7] 344f., [8] 351 (Argia); [9] 431f., [10] 438f., [11] 448 (Eteocles); [12] 548 (Tydeus); [13] 620f., [14] 622, [15] 623 (Chromis); [16] 658, [17] 664-66 (Tydeus).

BOOK THREE

[1] 7, [2] 9, [3] 9f., [4] 10f., [5] 11f. (Eteocles); [6] 151f., [7] 152f., [8] 153f., [9] 154-56 (Ide); [10] 269f., [11] 271f., [12] 273, [13] 273f., [14] 282f., [15] 288-90 (Venus); [16] 306-10 (Mars); [17] 369 (Polynices); [18] 502-05, [19] 513 (Melampus); [20] 537, [21] 537f. (Amphiaraus); [22] 608, [23] 609-11 (Capaneus); [24] 629f., [25] 630f., [26] 631, [27] 631f., [28] 632, [29] 632, [30] 633-35, [31] 644f., [32] 646 (Amphiaraus); [33] 651, [34] 652-55, [35] 657-59 (Capaneus); [36] 703f. (Argia).

BOOK FOUR

[1] 203-05 (Argia); [2] 318f., [3] 319, [4] 320f., [5] 325f., [6] 339f. (Atalanta); [7] 503f., [8] 504f., [9] 505f., [10] 507-11 (Tiresias); [11] 533-35 (Manto); [12] 537-40, [13] 586f., [14] 592-96, [15] 596f., [16] 612-14, [17] 618f. (Tiresias); [18] 626-28, [19] 629f. (Ghost of Laius); [20] 673-75 (Bacchus); [21] 776f., [22] 781 (Hypsipyle).

BOOK FIVE

[1] 36 (Hypsipyle); [2] 112f., [3] 113f., [4] 114-16, [5] 117-19, [6] 120, [7] 129, [8] 132f., [9] 136 (Polyxo); [10] 241f., [11] 242-44 (Hypsipyle); [12] 282f. (Bacchus); [13] 322, [14] 350, [15] 379 (Hypsipyle); [16] 491, [17] 492, [18] 492 (Lemnian crowd); [19] 609-12, [20] 613, [21] 613-15, [22] 622, [23] 623, [24] 624, [25] 625, [26] 633f., [27] 634f. (Hypsipyle); [28] 656f., [29] 657 (Lycurgus); [30] 672-76, [31] 676-78 (Tydeus); [32] 685 (Lycurgus).

BOOK SIX

[1] 141f., [2] 143f., [3] 144, [4] 149, [5] 152, [6] 156f., [7] 168f., [8] 182f., [9] 184 (Eurydice); [10] 372f. (Apollo); [11] 658f. (Hippomedon); [12] 819-22 (Capaneus); [13] 906-08 (Tydeus).

BOOK SEVEN

[1] 20 (Jupiter); [2] 123, [3] 123f., [4] 126, [5] 155 (Argive crowd); [6] 156, [7] 157, [8] 161, [9] 161f., [10] 162-65, [11] 171-73, [12] 173f., [13] 175, [14] 180, [15] 180, [16] 181, [17] 188 (Bacchus); [18] 199f., [19] 214 (Jupiter); [20] 247f. (Antigone); [21] 342-44 (Phorbas); [22] 490f., [23] 491f., [24] 497f., [25] 498f., [26] 500, [27] 501, [28] 503f., [29] 508, [30] 511f., [31] 523f. (Jocasta); [32] 542-44, [33] 544, [34] 546f., [35] 548f., [36] 550f., [37] 556, [38] 559, [39] 613f. (Tydeus); [40] 677f. (Capaneus); [41] 780; [42] 781 (Amphiaraus).

SPEECH AND RHETORIC IN STATIUS' *THEBAID*

BOOK EIGHT

[1] 34f., [2] 35f., [3] 36, [4] 36, [5] 38, [6] 44-46, [7] 48f., [8] 50f., [9] 51, [10] 52f., [11] 65, [12] 84f. (Pluto); [13] 95, [14] 100, [15] 109f., [16] 118f. (Amphiaraus); [17] 140f. (Palaemon); [18] 174f., [19] 175f., [20] 176, [21] 177-80, [22] 180f., [23] 189, [24] 189f., [25] 191f., [26] 193f. (Argive troops); [27] 317, [28] 317, [29] 318, [30] 318f. (Thiodamas); [31] 502f., [32] 503f., [33] 514f. (Hercules); [34] 602, [35] 602f., [36] 604f. (Menoeceus); [37] 622, [38] 623, [39] 623f., [40] 627f., [41] 633 (Ismene); [42] 664, [43] 668f., [44] 669, [45] 671, [46] 671, [47] 677-79.

BOOK NINE

[1] 12f., [2] 15f., [3] 23f. (Eteocles); [4] 49-52, [5] 55f., [6] 59, [7] 60, [8] 69, [9] 70f., [10] 71, [11] 75f. (Polynices); [12] 96f. (Eteocles); [13] 159, [14] 166, [15] 167, [16] 167f. (Tisiphone); [17] 211f. (Hippomedon); [18] 376f., [19] 377, [20] 381, [21] 381, [22] 382, [23] 385f., [24] 388f., [25] 389f., [26] 390-92 (Ismenis); [27] 421-26, [28] 426f., [29] 439-41, [30] 441 (Ismenos); [31] 476f., [32] 477-80, [33] 506-09, [34] 509f. (Hippomedon); [35] 511f., [36] 516, [37] 516f., [38] 518, [39] 519 (Juno); [40] 622, [41] 627f., [42] 630 (Atalanta); [43] 714f., [44] 715f. (Diana); [45] 779f. (Amphion); [46] 791f., [47] 799 (Parthenopaeus); [48] 825-27, [49] 827f., [50] 829f. (Venus).

BOOK TEN

[1] 206-09, [2] 209f. (Amphiaraus' spirit); [3] 236f., [4] 237, [5] 238, [6] 238f. (Adrastus); [7] 269, [8] 270f. (Thiodamas); [9] 351-53, [10] 353f., [11] 355 (Hopleus [for Tydeus' mother]);[2] [12] 436f. (Dymas); [13] 586f. (Thebans); [14] 592f. (Tiresias); [15] 690, [16] 691, [17] 691f., [18] 692f., [18] 696-99, [19] 699-701, [20] 708-10 (Creon); [21] 793f., [22] 795, [23] 795, [24] 798, [25] 799-801, [26] 800, [27] 802, [28] 804, [29] 804, [30] 805f., [31] 813 (Eurydice [Menoeceus' mother]); [32] 874f., [33] 876f. (Capaneus); [34] 888, [35] 889 (Bacchus); [36] 899f., [37] 900f., [38] 902f., [39] 905f. (Capaneus); [40] 909, [41] 910 (Jupiter).

BOOK ELEVEN

[1] 83f., [2] 101 (Tisiphone); [3] 168, [4] 174, [5] 182, [6] 185 (Polynices); [7] 258f. (Companion of Eteocles [2]); [8] 273-75, [9] 280f., [10] 281f., [11] 286-88, [12] 288-90, [13] 290, [14] 292f., [15] 295f. (Creon); [16] 329f., [17] 330f., [18] 331f., [19] 332f., [20] 334f., [21] 335f., [22] 336f., [23] 343, [24] 348f., [25] 352f. (Jocasta); [26] 365, [27] 365f., [28] 366f., [29] 377, [30] 377-79, [31] 379f. (Antigone); [32] 393 (Polynices); [33] 430, [34] 430, [35] 431 (Adrastus); [36] 465f., [37] 480 (Pietas); [38] 484f., [39] 487f., [40] 489-92 (Tisiphone); [41] 548, [42] 568f. (Polynices); [43] 605f., [44] 606, [45] 612f., [46] 613f., [47] 617-19, [48] 630, [49] 631 (Oedipus); [50] 672 (Creon); [51] 677, [52] 679, [53] 680, [54] 682f., [55] 683, [56] 685, [57] 688f., [58] 690, [59] 691, [60] 692, [61] 694f.,

---

[2] On this rhetorical question see p. 16.

356

[62] 696f., [63] 697f., [64] 706 (Oedipus); [65] 723f., [66] 724f., [67] 725f., [68] 730f., [69] 733f., [70] 735 (Antigone).

BOOK TWELVE

[1] 80f., [2] 84f., [3] 86f. (Creon); [4] 149, [5] 149f., [6] 154f., [7] 160-62, [8] 163-65 (Ornytus); [9] 209-11, [10] 211f., [11] 212f., [12] 217, [13] 218 (Argia); [14] 251f. (Menoetes); [15] 256-60 (Argia); [16] 302-04 (Juno); [17] 322-24, [18] 328, [19] 329, [20] 330f., [21] 331f., [22] 333, [23] 333f., [24] 336, [25] 341, [26] 341f., [27] 343, [28] 379 (Argia); [29] 382f. (Antigone); [30] 402, [31] 403, [32] 403f. (Argia); [33] 438f., [34] 440f., [35] 443, [36] 444 (Antigone); [37] 550f., [38] 561f., [39] 562, [40] 568, [41] 573 (Evadne); [42] 590f., [43] 591-93, [44] 593f. (Theseus); [45] 689f., [46] 765f., [47] 766 (Creon).

Table 28. Rhetorical Questions in the Narrative

The following list furnishes the evidence on which totals in the third column of table 26 are based.

[1] 1.3f., [2] 5f., [3] 41, [4] 41f., [5] 42, [6] 155f., [7] 156-61, [8] 161f., [9] 165-68; [10] 2.212f., [11] 304f., [12] 488, [13] 488f., [14] 629f.; [15] 3.102-04, [16] 214-16, [17] 551-53, [18] 556f.; [19] 4.145f., [20] 184, [21] 254f., [22] 374-77; [23] 5.534f., [24] 535f., [25] 536f., [26] 710-12; [27] 6.79-81, [28] 405f., [29] 513f., [30] 563-65, [31] 692f., [32] 934; [33] 7.452, [34] 572, [35] 651, [36] 652, [37] 704f.; [38] 8.162f., [39] 163, [40] 390; [41] 9.309, [42] 490, [43] 495, [44] 526, [45] 744, [46] 752f., [47] 772f., [48] 838; [49] 10.70, [50] 215f., [51] 260f., [52] 273f., [53] 285f., [54] 858; [55] 11.40, [56] 147f., [57] 428f., [58] 656f., [59] 659; [60] 12.239f., [61] 472f., [62] 698, [63] 698f., [64] 718-20, [65] 810-12.

Table 29. Simple (Direct) Questions in Speeches

This table furnishes the evidence for the totals in the fourth column of table 26; there are no direct questions in the narrative.

[1] 1.443f. (Adrastus), [2] 1.668f. (Coroebus), [3] 2.535 (Tydeus), [4] 3.512, [5] 3.546 (Melampus), [6] 5.24, [7] 5.25 (Adrastus), [8] 7.77 (Mars), [9] 7.291 (Antigone), [10] 8.671f. (Tydeus), [11] 10.433 (Amphion), [12] 12.366f. (Antigone).

STATISTICAL APPENDIX 13

THE SPEECHES IN THE *ACHILLEID*

There are thirty-two speeches in the *Achilleid* totalling 438 1/3 verses out of 1127 lines of text.[1] The percentage of direct speech in the text is 33.9; the average length of the speeches is 13.7 lines; and the frequency of occurrence is one speech for every 35.2 lines of text.[2] These figures are comparable to those of the *Thebaid* (see stat. app. 1, table 1). The longest speech is Achilles' narrative of seventy-two lines (2.96-167), while the shortest speech of 1 1/4 lines is made by Lycomedes (1.738f.).

Eight speeches are made by Thetis, while six are spoken by her son. Fourteen speeches are deliberative in classification.[3] Almost one-third of the speeches are addressed wholly or partly to the protagonist Achilles.

Table 30. Conspectus of the Achilleid *by Speeches*[4]

No.	Line Nos.	Lines of Verse	Speech Type[5]	Cluster: Speech No.	Addressor(s)	Addressee(s)
				BOOK ONE		

1-94: Introduction and dedication. Thetis anticipates the danger to Achilles and implores Neptune to sink the fleet of Paris returning to Troy.

No.	Line Nos.	Lines of Verse	Speech Type	Cluster: Speech No.	Addressor(s)	Addressee(s)
(1)	31-51	20 1/12	Sol	M	Thetis	-------
(2)	61-76	15 5/6	Del	D:1	Thetis	Neptune
(3)	80-94	15	Res (to Del)	D:2	Neptune	Thetis

---

[1] The breakdown is 306 1/3 lines in the first book, 101 in book 2. Lipscomb (1909: 15) mentions thirty-two speeches, but his figure of 455 lines of speech is greatly inflated.

[2] Lipscomb's (1909: 15) figures are forty per cent, 14.22 lines, and one speech in thirty-five lines, respectively. One of the reasons for the excessive figures is that Lipscomb counts part lines as complete verses.

[3] Over one-half (seventeen) of the speeches are deliberative in intent, including two prayers and one speech of encouragement.

[4] For an explanation of the abbreviations, see pp. 275f.

[5] Additional speech types of 'Greeting' (Gre) and 'Responsion to Greeting' (Res [to Gre]) are made here; these categories are not used in classifying the direct speeches in the *Thebaid* and *Silvae*.

No.	Line Nos.	Lines of Verse	Speech Type	Cluster: Speech No.	Addressor(s)	Addressee(s)

95-197: Thetis prevails upon Chiron to release Achilles into her care.

(4)	127-41	13 2/3	Que	D:1	Thetis	Chiron
(5)	143-58	14 2/3	O&P (Pro)	D:2	Chiron	Thetis

198-282: Thetis hides Achilles at the court of Lycomedes in Scyros and persuades him to wear feminine clothing.

(6)	252-74	22 5/12	Del	M	Thetis	Achilles

283-396: Achilles falls in love with Deidamia. Thetis instructs Achilles how to impersonate a maiden and entrusts him to Lycomedes.

(7)	319-22	3	Del	M	Thetis	Achilles
(8)	339-42	3 1/3	Del	M	Thetis	Achilles
(9)	350-62	12 5/6	Com	M	Thetis	Lycomedes
(10)	384-96	13	Del	M	Thetis	Scyros

397-559: The Greeks make preparations for the Trojan War. After Calchas divulges where Thetis has concealed Achilles, Ulysses and Diomedes depart for Scyros to find him.

(11)	496-513	18	Del	M	Protesilaus	Calchas
(12)	526-35	10	Del	M	Calchas	Thetis, Achilles
(13)	539-45	6 5/12	Del	D:1	Diomedes	Ulysses
(14)	546-52	7	Res (to Del)	D:2	Ulysses	Diomedes

560-674: Achilles forces himself upon Deidamia.

(15)	624-39	15 3/4	Sol	M	Achilles	-------
(16)	650-60	11	Del	M	Achilles	Deidamia

675-818: Lycomedes provides hospitality for Ulysses and Diomedes after their arrival in Scyros.

(17)	712-17	5 3/4	Que	D:1	Diomedes	Ulysses
(18)	719-25	7	Res (to Que)	D:2	Ulysses	Diomedes
(19)	728-37	9 1/4	Gre	D:1	Ulysses	Lycomedes
(20)	738f.	1 1/4	Res (to Gre)	D:2	Lycomedes	Ulysses
(21)	775-83	9[6]	Enc (Coh)	D:1	Lycomedes	Achaeans

---

[6] Including the spurious line after 780 reading: *possem, plena forent mihi gaudia; namque iuuarem.*

No.	Line Nos.	Lines of Verse	Speech Type	Cluster: Speech No.	Addressor(s)	Addressee(s)
(22)	785-93, 796-802, 807-11	19 1/2	Del	D:2	Ulysses	Lycomedes,[7] Achilles (*oblique*)
(23)	812-14	2 7/12	Res	D:3	Lycomedes	Ulysses

819-926: Achilles is discovered when he selects armour from an array of gifts offered by Ulysses and Diomedes to the maidens of the court.

(24)	867-74	6 1/2	Del	M	Ulysses	Achilles
(25)	892-908, 909f.	18 1/2	Del	M	Achilles	Lycomedes

927-60: Deidamia bemoans the approaching departure of Achilles.

(26)	931-55	25	Del	M	Deidamia	Achilles

BOOK TWO

1-22: Ulysses, Diomedes and Achilles depart from Scyros.

(1)	17-19	2 7/12	Pra[8]	M	Achilles	Thetis

323-85: Ulysses diverts Achilles' thoughts from Deidamia and recites the origins of the Trojan War.

(2)	32-42	10 1/12	Del	D:1	Ulysses	Achilles
(3)	43-48	5 3/4	Del	D:2	Achilles	Ulysses
(4)	50-83	34	Nar	D:3	Ulysses	Achilles

86-167: Achilles relates the story of his youth.

(5)	86-93	7 7/12	Del	D:1	Diomedes	Achilles
(6)	96-167	72	Nar	D:2	Achilles	Diomedes

---

[7] Although Ulysses replies to Lycomedes' exhortation, the central purpose of the wily Ithacan's speech is to induce Achilles to come out of hiding and join the Achaean expedition to Troy.

[8] This prayer goes uncited by Appel, who cites (1909: 51) two prayers in the *Achilleid* (1.1ff., 384ff.); the former is the poet's prayer to the goddess of the Muses and Apollo, while the latter is in fact a deliberation rather than a prayer.

STATISTICAL APPENDIX 14

THE SPEECHES IN THE *SILVAE*

There are twenty-five speeches in the *Silvae*[1] totalling 567 verses[2] out of 3893 lines of text.[3] The percentage of direct speech is 14.6;[4] the average length of the speeches is 22.7 lines; and the frequency of occurrence is one speech for every 155.7 lines of text. These figures indicate that the demand for speech in the *Silvae* occurs far less frequently than in the *Thebaid* or *Achilleid*.[5] The longest speech is Statius' deliberation of sixty-six lines (*Silv.* 4.4.12-77); the shortest speech is 1 3/4 lines (*Silv.* 5.5.47f.).[6]

Divinities deliver over one-half of the speeches (fourteen) in the *Silvae*, compared with one-sixth in the *Thebaid*[7] and over one-fourth in the *Achilleid*.[8] In the *Silvae* Venus delivers three speeches; Hercules makes two. Domitian is the addressee on two occasions; Pollius, Earinus and Crispinus are addressed twice each.

Five of the speeches are commands; there are four laudations, three deliberations, three prayers, and three speeches of mourning and consolation.

---

[1] Van Dam (1984: 507) lists twenty-two speeches, excluding from consideration *Silv.* 2.4.24-37 (which he refers to erroneously as 'II 4, 22 ff.'), 3.2.5-49, and 3.4.100-05 (which he fails to note). Like Van Dam, I do not consider 3.4.1ff. to be a speech.

[2] Van Dam (1984: 507), citing three fewer speeches, maintains that there are '*ca.* 515 1/2' lines of speech; he rounds off part-lines to the nearest half-line.

[3] Van Dam (1984: 507) counts 3793 verses, although he uses the same text I do (ed. Marastoni [1970]).

[4] Compare the figure of thirteen per cent mentioned by Van Dam (1984: 507).

[5] See stat. apps. 1 and 13.

[6] Van Dam (1984: 508) rounds this off to two lines in length.

[7] See pp. 13f., stat. app. 3, tables 6 and 8.

[8] See stat. app. 13, table 30.

Table 31. List of the Speeches in the Silvae[9]

No.	Line Nos.	Lines of Verse	Speech Type[10]	Cluster: Speech No.	Addressor(s)	Addressee(s)
			BOOK ONE			
(1)	1.74-83	10	P&B (Lau)	M	Curtius	Domitian
(2)	2.65-102	37 5/6	Del	D:1	Amor	Venus
(3)	2.106-40	35	Res (to Del)	D:2	Venus	Amor
(4)	2.162-93	32	Com	M	Venus	Violentilla
(5)	4.61-105	44 1/2	Com	M	Apollo	Aesculapius
			BOOK TWO			
(1)	3.24-26	2 1/3	Que	M	Diana	Companions of Diana
(2)	3.43-52	10	Pra	M	Pan	A tree
(3)	4.24-37	14	M&C (Epi)	M	*aliquis*	Parrots
(4)	7.41-104[11]	53 1/3	O&P (Pro)	M	Calliope	Lucan
			BOOK THREE			
(1)	1.91-116	25 1/4	Com	M	Hercules	Pollius
(2)	1.166-83	18	O&P (Pro)	M	Hercules	Pollius
(3)	2.5-49	45	Pra	M	Statius	Neptune
(4)	3.182-204	22 7/12	M&C (Epi)	M	Etruscus *iunior*	Etruscus *senior*
(5)	4.32-45	13	Com	M	Venus	Earinus
(6)	4.95-97	2 5/6	Com	M	A Cupid[12]	Earinus
(7)	4.100-05	5	Pra	M	A Cupid	Aesculapius
			BOOK FOUR			
(1)	1.17-43	27	P&B (Lau)	M	Janus	Augustus
(2)	3.72-94	23	Tha	M	Vulturnus	Domitian
(3)	3.124-63	40	P&B (Lau)	M	The Sibyl of Cumae	Domitian
(4)	4.12-77	66	Del	M	Statius	Marcellus

---

[9] See pp. 275f. for an explanation of the abbreviations.

[10] An additional speech type of 'Thanksgiving' (Tha) is made here; this category is not used in classifying the speeches in the *Thebaid* and *Achilleid*.

[11] This figure is rounded due to the hendecasyllabic part-line of speech (line 41).

[12] Not Venus, as Van Dam (1984: 507) claims.

STATISTICAL APPENDIX 14

No.	Line Nos.	Lines of Verse	Speech Type	Cluster: Speech No.	Addressor(s)	Addressee(s)
				BOOK FIVE		
(1)	1.177-93	17	M&C (Con)	M	Priscilla	Abascantus
(2)	1.239-41	2 7/12	P&B (Lau)	M	*aliquis*	*aliquis*
(3)	2.84-96	13	Del	M	Statius[13]	Crispinus
(4)	2.144-49	6	Nar	M	Inhabitant of Caledonia	Crispinus
(5)	5.47f.	1 3/4	Del	M	*aliquis*	Statius

---

[13] The speaker is not Crispinus, as Van Dam (1984: 507) asserts.

WORKS CITED AND ABBREVIATIONS USED

Reference is made to the works of ancient Latin and Greek writers by the standard abbreviations. The text used of the *Thebaid* is edited by Hill (1983). References to the *Achilleid* and *Silvae* are from the editions by Marastoni (1970 and 1974, respectively). References to the treatises of the Greek rhetoricians are from the edition by Hammer (1854-56) of Spengel's *Rhetores Graeci* and are accompanied by the abbreviation 'Sp.' preceding the volume, page and line numbers; the references to Aphthonius are either from Hammer or to pages and lines in Rabe's (1928) edition. References to the treatise of pseudo-Dionysius come from the reprinted edition by Usener and Radermacher (1965); the abbreviation 'Rad.' precedes the page and line numbers of the text. All of the references to the works of the minor Latin rhetoricians are from the edition by Halm (1863), as indicated by the name of 'Halm' accompanying these references (e.g., Beda *De Trop*. Halm 615.27-30). All other references to classical writers mentioned are from the editions in the Oxford Classical Series. The spelling and punctuation of the texts have been retained generally for citatory purposes, except that I have changed the lower-case consonants *v* and *j* where necessary to the consonantal *u* and *i*, respectively.

Modern works appearing in the following list are cited in the notes by the authors' names and dates of publication.

MODERN WORKS CITED

Ahl, F. M. (1974) Review of Vessey (1973), *Philological Quarterly* 53: 141-44.
_____. (1986) 'The *Thebaid*: A Reconsideration', *Aufstieg und Niedergang der römischen Welt* 2.32.5: 2803-2912.
Appel, G. (1909) *De Romanorum Precationibus*. Giessen.
Aricò, G. (1960) 'Sul mito di Lino e Corebo in Stat. *Theb*. I 557-668', *Rivista di Filologia e di Istruzione Classica* 88: 277-85. =*Ricerche Staziane* (Palermo 1972): 75-85.
_____. (1972) *Ricerche Staziane*. Palermo.
Bakhtin, M. M. (1986) 'The Problem of Speech Genres', in C. Emerson and M. Holquist (edd.; tr. V. W. McGee), *Speech Genres and Other Late Essays*: 60-102. Austin.
Barth, C. (ed.) (1664) *P. Papinius Statius, Quae Exstant, Caspar Barthius Recensuit et Animadversionibus Locupletissimis Illustravit*. Zwickau.

Bateson, F. W. (1966) *English Poetry: A Critical Introduction*². London.

Brass, H. (1923) *Questiones Statianae Metricae et Prosodicae*. Diss. Rostock.

Burck, E. (1979) 'Die *Thebais* des Statius', in E. Burck (ed.), *Das römische Epos*: 300-351. Darmstadt.

Burgess, J. F. (1978) *Man and the Supernatural in Statius' Thebaid: A Study in Consistency of Theme and Mood*. Diss. Reading.

Burgess, T. C. (1902) *Epideictic Literature*. Chicago.

Butler, H. E. (1909) *Post-Augustan Poetry from Seneca to Juvenal*. Oxford.

Cairns, F. J. (1972) *Generic Composition in Greek and Roman Poetry*. Edinburgh.

Clarke, M. L. (1949) 'Rhetorical Influences in the *Aeneid*', *Greece and Rome* 18: 14-27.

Cumont, F. V. M. (tr. T. J. McCormack) (1956) *The Mysteries of Mithra*. Repr. New York.

Curtius, E. C. (tr. W. R. Trask) (1953) *European Literature and the Latin Middle Ages*. New York.

Dam, H.-J. van (1984) *P. Papinius Statius. Silvae Book II: A Commentary*. Leiden.

Daniels, E. D. (1905) *A Study of P. Papinius Statius' Thebais and His Imitation of Virgil's Aeneid*. Baltimore.

Dimsdale, M. S. (1915) *A History of Latin Literature*. Repr. Freeport 1971.

Dominik, W. J. (1990) 'Monarchal Power and Imperial Politics in Statius' *Thebaid*', in A. J. Boyle (ed.), *The Imperial Muse: Flavian Epicist to Claudian*: 74-97. Bendigo. =*Ramus* 18 (1989): 74-97.

———. (forthcoming) *The Mythic Voice of Statius: Power and Politics in the Thebaid*.

Duff, J. W. (1927) *A Literary History of Rome in the Silver Age from Tiberius to Hadrian*. London.

Eissfeldt, E. (1904) 'Zu den Vorbildern des Statius', *Philologus* 63: 378-424.

Elderkin, G. W. (1906) *Aspects of the Speech in the Later Greek Epic*. Baltimore.

Endt, J. (1903) 'Botenberichte bei Vergil und Ovid', *Wiener Studien* 25: 293-307.

Farron, S. G. (1979-80) 'The Roman Invention of Evil', *Studies in Antiquity* 1: 12-46.

Fenik, B. (1968) *Typical Battle Scenes in the Iliad: Studies in the Narrative Techniques of Homeric Battle Description*. Wiesbaden.

Fingerle, A. (1939) *Typik der homerischen Reden*. Diss. Munich.

Fontanier, P. (1968) *Les Figures du discours*. Paris.

Fortgens, H. W. (1934) *P. Papinii Statii de Opheltis Funere Carmen Epicum, Theb. Lib. VI, 1-295: Versione Batava Commentarioque Exegetico Instructus*. Zutphen.

Frank, E. (1965) 'La composizione della *Tebaide* di Stazio', *Rendiconti dell'Istituto Lombardo, Classe de Lettere, Scienze morali e storiche* 99: 309-18.

Garrod, H. W. (1906) *P. Papini Stati Thebaid et Achilleis.* Oxford.

Gjerløw, J. (1956) 'Bemerkungen über einige Einleitungen zur direkten Rede in Vergils *Aeneis*', *Symbolae Osloenses* 32: 44-68.

Glaesener, H. (1899) 'Les Caractères dans la *Thébaïde* de Stace', *Musée Belge* 3: 97-117.

Gluck, J. J. (1964) 'Reviling and Monomachy as Battle Preludes in Ancient Warfare', *Acta Classica* 7: 25-31.

Gossage, A. J. (1969) 'Virgil and the Flavian Epic', in D. Dudley (ed.), *Virgil*: 67-93. London.

_____. (1972) 'Statius', in D. R. Dudley (ed.), *Neronians and Flavians: Silver Latin* 1: 184-235. London/Boston.

Götting, M. (1969) *Hypsipyle in der Thebais des Statius.* Wiesbaden.

Halm, C. (ed.) (1863) *Rhetores Latini Minores.* Leipzig.

Hammer, C. (ed.) (1854) *Rhetores Graeci ex Recognitione Leonardi Spengel* 2. Leipzig.

_____. (1856) *Rhetores Graeci ex Recognitione Leonardi Spengel* 3. Leipzig.

Hampel, E. (1908) *De Apostrophe apud Romanorum Poetas Usu.* Diss. Jena.

Heinze, R. (1908). *Vergils epische Technik.* Leipzig and Berlin. Repr. Stuttgart, 1957.

Helm, R. (1892) *De Papinii Statii Thebaide.* Berlin.

Herescu, N. (1960) *La Poésie latine: Étude des structures phonique.* Paris.

Heslop, T. (1962) *The Speeches in Lucan.* Thesis Manchester.

Highet, G. (1972) *The Speeches in Vergil's Aeneid.* Princeton.

_____. (1974) 'Speech and Narrative in the *Aeneid*', *Harvard Studies in Classical Philology* 78: 189-229.

Hill, D. E. (ed.) (1983) *P. Papini Stati Thebaidos Libri XII.* Leiden.

Hinnels, J. R. (1975) 'Reflections on the Bull-slaying Scene', in J. R. Hinnels (ed.), *Mithraic Studies* 2: 290-312. Manchester.

Holland, J. E. (1976) *Studies on the Heroic Tradition in the Thebaid of Statius.* Diss. Missouri, Columbia.

Jahnke, R. (1898) *Lactantii Placidi Qui Dicitur Commentarios in Statii Thebaida et Commentarium in Achilleida.* Leipzig.

Kabsch, E. (1968) *Funktion und Stellung des zwölften Buches der Thebais des P. Papinius Statius.* Diss. Kiel.

Kate, R. ten (1955) *Quomodo Heroes in Statii Thebaide Describantur Quaeritur.* Diss. Groningen.

Kenney, E. (1966) Review of Cancik (1965), *Classical Review* 16: 331-33.

Klinnert, T. C. (1970) *Capaneus-Hippomedon: Interpretationem zur Heldendarstellung in der Thebais des P. Papinius Statius.* Berlin.

———. (ed.) (1973) *P. Papini Stati Thebais.* Leipzig.

Klotz, A. (ed.) (1908) *P. Papini Stati Thebais.* Leipzig.

Knight, J. (1966). *Roman Vergil².* London.

Krumbholz, G. (1955) 'Der Erzählungsstil in der *Thebais* des Statius', *Glotta* 34: 93-138, 231-60.

Kvíčala, J. (1881) *Neue Beitrage zur Erklarung der Aeneis.* Prague.

Kytzler, B. (1955) *Statius-Studien: Beitrage zum Verstandnis der Thebais.* Diss. Berlin.

———. (1986) 'Zum Aufbau der statianischen Thebais. Pius Coroebus, *Theb.* I 557-692', *Aufstieg und Niedergang der römischen Welt* 2.32.5: 2913-2924.

Laidlaw, W. A. (1951) *Latin Literature.* London.

Leaf, W. (ed.) (1902) *Iliad 2².* London.

Legras, L. (1905) *Étude sur la Thébaïde de Stace. Les Légendes thébaines en Grèce et à Rome.* Paris.

Leo, F. (ed.) (1892-93) *De Statii Silvis.* Göttingen.

Lewis, C. S. (1936) *The Allegory of Love: A Study in Medieval Tradition.* Oxford.

Lipscomb, H. S. (1909) *Aspects of the Speech in the Later Roman Epic.* Baltimore.

Loesch, W. K. (1927) *Die Einfürung der direkten Rede bei den epischen Dichtern der Römer bis zur domitianischen zeit.* Diss. Erlangen.

Lohrisch, H. (1905) *De Publii Papinii Statii Silvarum Poetae Studiis Rhetoricis.* Diss. Halle.

Lunderstedt, R. (1913) *De Synechdochae Apud P. Papinium Statium Usu.* Diss. Jena.

Mackay, L. A. (1965) 'Statius in Purgatory', *Classica et Mediaevalia* 26: 293-305.

Mackie, C. J. (1988) *The Characterisation of Aeneas.* Edinburgh.

Maher, A. G. (ed.) (1950) *An Edition of Book Eleven of Statius' Thebaid.* Diss. London.

Manning, C. E. (1978) 'Grief in Statius' Epicedia', *Journal of the Australasian Universities Language and Literature Association* 50: 251-60.

Marastoni, A. (ed.) (1970) *P. Papini Stati Silvae².* Leipzig.

———. (ed.) (1974) *P. Papini Stati Achilleis.* Leipzig.

Marouzeau, J. (1954) *Traité de stylistique latine³.* Paris.

Mendell, C. W. (1967) *Latin Poetry: The Age of Rhetoric and Satire.* Hamden.

Moerner, F. (1890) *De P. Papinii Statii Thebaide Quaestiones Criticae Grammaticae Metricae.* Diss. Königsberg.

Moore, C. H. (1921) 'Prophecy in Ancient Epic', *Harvard Studies in Classical Philology* 32: 99-175.

Mozley, J. H. (ed. and tr.) (1928) *Statius, with an English Translation* 1. London/Cambridge, Massachusetts.

Mulder, H. M. (ed.) (1954) *P. Papinii Statii Thebaidos Liber II Commentario Exegetico Aestheticoque Instructus.* Diss. Groningen.

Müller, O. (1861) *Quaestiones Statianae.* Berlin.

Newmyer, S. T. (1979) *The Silvae of Statius: Structure and Theme.* Leiden.

Norden, E. (1898) *Die antike Kunstprosa vom VI. Jahrhundert v. Chr. bis in die Zeit der Renaissance.* Leipzig.

_____. (1913) *Agnostos Theos: Untersuchungen zur Formengeschichte religiöser Rede.* Leipzig/Berlin.

Obrycki, K. (1975). 'Rola Parównan Kompozycyjnych w *Tebaidzie* Stacjusza', *Meander* 30: 353-63.

Ogilvie, R. M. (1980) *Roman Literature and Society.* Sussex/Totowa.

Rabe, H. (ed.) (1928) *Ioannis Sardiani Commentarium in Aphthonii Progymnasmata.* Leipzig.

Ribbeck, O. (1892) *Geschichte der römischen Dichtung: Dichtung der Kaiserherrschaft* 3. Stuttgart/Berlin.

Schanz, M. (1913) *Geschichte der römischen Literatur bis zum Gesetzgebungswerk des Kaisers Justinian* 2.2. Munich.

Schetter, W. (1960) *Untersuchungen zur epischen Kunst des Statius.* Wiesbaden.

Schneidewin, M. (1884) 'Statistisches zu Homeros und Vergilius', *Neue Jahrbücher für Philologie* 1: 129ff.

Schubert, W. (1984) *Jupiter in den Epen der Flavierzeit.* Frankfurt.

Schwabe, L. (tr. G. C. W. Warr) (1892) *Teuffel's History of Roman Literature* 2: *The Imperial Period.* London.

Snijder, H. (ed.) (1968) *P. Papinius Statius, Thebaid: A Commentary on Book III with Text and Introduction.* Amsterdam.

Steele, R. B. (1918) 'The Similes in Latin Epic Poetry', *Transactions of the American Philological Association* 49: 83-100.

Summers, W. C. (1920) *The Silver Age of Latin Literature.* London.

Turolla, E. (1956) 'La poesia epica di P. Papinio Stazio', *Orpheus* 3: 134-51.

Usener, H., and L. Radermacher (edd.) (1965) *Dionysius Halicarnaseus Quae Extant* 6. Repr. Leipzig.

Venini, P. (1961a) 'Studi sulla *Tebaide* di Stazio. La composizione', *Rendiconti dell'Istituto Lombardo, Classe de Lettere, Scienze morali e storiche* 95: 55-88.

_____. (1961b) 'Studi sulla *Tebaide* di Stazio. L'imitazione', *Rendiconti dell'Istituto Lombardo, Classe de Lettere, Scienze morali e storiche* 95: 371-400.

_____. (1968) 'A proposito di alcuni recenti studi sulla composizione della *Tebaide* staziana', *Athenaeum* 56: 131-38.

WORKS CITED AND ABBREVIATIONS USED

Vermaseren, M. J. (1963) *Mithras, the Secret God.* London.

Vessey, D. W. T. (1971) '*Exitiale Genus*: Some Notes on Statius, *Thebaid* I', *Latomus* 30: 375-82.

_____. (1973) *Statius and the Thebaid.* Cambridge.

_____. (1982) 'Flavian Epic', in E. Kenney (ed.), *Cambridge History of Classical Literature* 2: 558-80.

Volkmann, R. (1885). *Die Rhetorik der Griechen und Römer in systematischer Übersicht*[2]. Leipzig.

Watkiss, L. (1966) *The Thebaid of Statius: A Reappraisal.* Diss. London.

Wilkinson, L. (1963) *Golden Latin Artistry.* Cambridge.

Williams, G. (1978) *Change and Decline: Roman Literature in the Early Empire.* Berkeley.

Williams, R. D. (ed.) (1972) *P. Papini Stati Thebaidos Liber X.* Leiden.

Wilson, W. H. (1898) *The Metaphor in the Epic Poems of P. Papinius Statius.* Baltimore.

INDEX OF MAIN PASSAGES DISCUSSED

This index lists the main passages discussed from the *Thebaid*. (Page numbers appear in parentheses.) Passages cited as additional illustration are not included in this list.

INDEX OF SPEECH AND RHETORICAL SUBJECTS

This index covers the 'Introduction', chapters 1-6 and the 'Afterword'.